OUT of
OBSCURITY
The LDS Church in the
Twentieth Century

Sidney B. Sperry

OUT of
OBSCURITY
The LDS Church in the
Twentieth Century

DESERET BOOK COMPANY

SALT LAKE CITY, UTAH

Visit us at www.deseretbook.com

Library of Congress Cataloging-in-Publication Data
  Sperry Symposium (29th : 2000)
    Out of obscurity : the 29th annual Sperry Symposium.
      p.   cm.
    Includes bibliographical references.
    ISBN 1-57345-842-2
    1. Church of Jesus Christ of Latter-day Saints—History—20th century—
  Congresses.   I. Title
  BX8611.S78   2000
  289.3'32'0904—dc21
                                                        00-034631

Printed in the United States of America   72082-6727
  10   9   8   7   6   5   4   3   2   1

CONTENTS

PREFACE

At the dedication of the Kirtland Temple, the Prophet Joseph Smith pleaded, "Remember all thy church, O Lord, . . . that thy church may come forth out of the wilderness of darkness, and shine forth fair as the moon, clear as the sun" (D&C 109:72–73). In the twentieth century, members of The Church of Jesus Christ of Latter-day Saints witnessed an answer to the prophetic pleading.

From the beginning of the century to the end of the era, a dramatic coming "forth out of the wilderness of darkness" was seen on every hand (D&C 109:73). For example, in 1901 five out of every six Latter-day Saints lived in the western United States, predominantly in the intermountain area, and only 250,000 claimed membership. By the end of the century, Church membership was growing at the rate of a million members every three and a half years. Approximately 375 buildings were constructed annually to provide houses of worship for the mushrooming membership. And by February 1996, more Latter-day Saints were living outside of the United States than residing within.

By the end of the twentieth century, "there [was] not a city in the United States or Canada of any consequence which [did] not have a Latter-day Saint congregation," remarked President Gordon B. Hinckley. "It is the same in Mexico. It is the same in Central and South America. Likewise in New Zealand and Australia, in the islands of the sea, and in Japan, Korea, Taiwan, the Philippines. In Europe our congregations are everywhere" (*Ensign*, November 1997, 68).

The coming forth out of obscurity and out of darkness in the twentieth century was prophesied millennia before in Daniel's vision as a stone rolling forth to fill the whole earth (see Daniel 2:45). As members rededicated their time, talents, and lives to the work of the Master, the stone in the twentieth century moved forward at an accelerated pace. Setting the pace for members to follow were prophets, seers, and revelators. For example, President Hinckley in 1996 addressed 315,649 Latter-day Saints, most of them living beyond the borders of the United

States. In his outreach effort to be with the Saints, he logged 85,442 miles and spoke in twenty-two nations abroad and in thirteen states within the United States. His outreach to the membership in South and Central America was particularly poignant. "We have now been in all the nations of South America and Central America, and we have seen miracles, with the great gatherings of 30,000, 40,000, and 50,000 in football stadiums," said President Hinckley. "These are all Latter-day Saints. In each case as we left there was a great waving of handkerchiefs, with tears in their eyes and tears in ours" (*Ensign*, November 1997, 67).

The message of each prophet in the twentieth century was keep the commandments and move forward with an eye single to the glory of God. Members of the Church answered the prophetic call by inviting all to "come unto Christ" and enjoy the restoration of the gospel. They spoke of the importance of family, priesthood, and temple building. Through sophisticated satellite networks, advanced technology, the Internet, and a myriad of other resources they carried the gospel message to more people than ever before.

As the century ended, millions had access to sessions of general conference and Tabernacle Choir broadcasts. A new Church logo that prominently features the words *Jesus Christ* was well received. Although an estimated 83 million copies of the Book of Mormon were in circulation, news reporters clamored for more information about the Church. Members took to heart President Hinckley's statement: "None of us ever need hesitate to speak up for this Church, for its doctrine, for its people, for its divine organization and divinely given responsibility. It is true. It is the work of God" (*Ensign*, November 1996, 51).

Elder David B. Haight observed: "The world is prepared for us to move forward, and we are entering a period of tremendous growth and opportunity. Barriers are coming down" (as cited in Sheri L. Dew, *Go Forward with Faith: The Biography of Gordon B. Hinckley* [Salt Lake City: Deseret Book, 1996], 534). The century saw the Iron Curtain fall and communism arrested, wars and rumors of wars, blatant societal ills, and a world in commotion. Yet the century was filled with a rich outpouring of the Holy Spirit, with revelations, gifts, and miracles abounding. It was a century in which changes in quorums, programs, correlation, humanitarian service, and more has blessed Latter-day Saints in their individual lives. And with that blessing, members stepped forward with assurance and spoke of Jesus Christ and the

Restoration, for they knew that "no unhallowed hand can stop the work from progressing; persecutions may rage, mobs may combine, armies may assemble, calumny may defame, but the truth of God will go forth boldly, nobly, and independent, till it has penetrated every continent, visited every climb; swept every country, and sounded in every ear, till the purposes of God shall be accomplished, and the Great Jehovah shall say the work is done" (Joseph Smith, *History of the Church of Jesus Christ of Latter-day Saints,* ed. B. H. Roberts, 2d ed. rev., 7 vols. [Salt Lake City: The Church of Jesus Christ of Latter-day Saints, 1932–51], 4:540).

This unique compilation is a commemorative volume in remembrance of the century past and joins other volumes published in memory of the meritorious service of Dr. Sidney B. Sperry. We trust that this collection of perceptive and inspirational essays on the twentieth century will enlighten and bless each reader. We recognize that the selected papers do not adequately detail each significant event of the past century. Yet we hope readers will discover much that is of worth. Some papers highlight traditional studies of doctrine and prophecy, while others feature the men and women who made a difference. Each has been written by a faithful Latter-day Saint, who professes a testimony of the Savior and the Restoration. The views presented in the papers are those of the respective authors, and we thank them for their contribution.

Of special mention is colleague Richard O. Cowan, former chair of the department of Church history and doctrine at Brigham Young University. His wise counsel and lifelong study of the Church in the twentieth century has proven invaluable to the committee. Likewise, we acknowledge Patty Smith from the Religious Education Faculty Support Center at BYU for her assistance in the organization of the Sperry Symposium and in helping prepare this volume. Special thanks is extended to Suzanne Brady and her colleagues at Deseret Book Company for editing and coordinating the publication of *Out of Obscurity: The Church in the Twentieth Century.*

> Susan Easton Black
> Randy L. Bott
> Dee R. Darling
> Fred E. Woods
>
> SIDNEY B. SPERRY SYMPOSIUM COMMITTEE

Come Sound the Trump

(Sperry Symposium – BYU – 2000)

Text by
John V. Pearson

Music by
Janice Kapp Perry

Jubilantly ♩ = 69

1. Come sound the trump. Send forth the word. Let ev - 'ry na - tion hear That
2. On ev - er - last - ing hills once stood Few tem - ples of our Lord. But
3. The prom - is - es of A - bra - ham For which some had to wait Are
4. Who are these might - y peo - ple found Where none be - fore have been? They

Je - sus Christ, the Son of God, In glo - ry now ap - pears. Let
now they shine from ev - 'ry hill And rise from dis - tant shores. From
giv - en now to ev - 'ry soul Who comes through Je - sus' gate. And
are the saints of Je - sus Christ Who serve and fol - low Him. Now,

ev - 'ry peo - ple come and see, Let ev - er - y - one draw near. Come
Brit - ish Isles to Af - ri - ca, From Chi - na to Pe - ru, The
king - doms, pow'rs, e - ter - nal lives, And glo - ry ev - er - more Are
led by proph - ets of our Lord, The gos - pel has rolled forth To

hear His voice and shout for joy, For Christ, the Lord, is here.
ev - er - last - ing bless - ings flow And are re - stored a - new.
giv - en to the faith - ful who Are saved by Christ, the Lord.
bring the king - dom of our God To ev - 'ry soul on earth.

D&C 65:2, 5-6. D&C 132:19
Official Declaration 2

CHAPTER ONE

"MAY THE KINGDOM OF GOD GO FORTH"

MARLIN K. JENSEN

Capturing the essence of the history of The Church of Jesus Christ of Latter-day Saints during the twentieth century is a rather formidable task. To begin with, there is so much of it, and it is so multifaceted. The Lord's command on the day the Church was organized that "there shall be a record kept among you" (D&C 21:1) has always been taken very seriously by the institutional Church and by many individual members. Thus, perhaps no other religion from its earliest beginnings has enjoyed a greater abundance of both primary and secondary sources from which to analyze and reconstruct its past. If, as some of our critics allege, the Prophet Joseph Smith committed a fraud on the world, he certainly made no effort personally, and left no instructions to his followers, to conceal the evidence!

Another challenge in identifying the true spirit of the Church's history in the twentieth century is in striking an editorial balance between the significance of the headline events of that time period and the reservoir of goodness resulting from the quiet but rich lives lived by individual Latter-day Saints. President Joseph F. Smith once stated the principle this way: "Those things which we call extraordinary, remarkable, or unusual may make history, but they do not make real life."[1] Thus, the real story of the Church in the twentieth century, or in any period of time for that matter, is the real-life story of the struggles, trials, and triumphs of ordinary followers of Christ doing their best as individuals and as a community of believers to

Elder Marlin K. Jensen, a member of the First Quorum of the Seventy since April 1989, serves as one of the seven presidents of the Seventy.

1

walk in his prescribed paths. The best record of much of that aspect of Church history is appropriately being kept, as one of our hymns reminds us, by angels above who silent notes take.[2]

A third and perhaps most significant consideration I have had in mind as I have thought about the Church's history in the twentieth century is that by the Lord's own words this Church's history is the history of "the only true and living church upon the face of the whole earth" (D&C 1:30). I firmly believe that declaration, and thus the exclusive use of the usual secular methods of historical research and analysis are in my opinion quite inadequate in capturing the essence of any part of the Church's remarkable spiritual past. I believe, as Isaiah wrote, that the Lord's thoughts are not our thoughts nor are his ways our ways (Isaiah 55:8). I am convinced that the history of the Lord's Church cannot fully be understood nor appreciated without acknowledging the hand of the Lord in all that has occurred and then examining its historical record in that light. A 1904 statement by the prophet Joseph F. Smith confirms this view and is pertinent today:

"It has not been by the wisdom of man that this people have been directed in their course until the present; it has been by the wisdom of Him who is above man and whose knowledge is greater than that of man, and whose power is above the power of man; for it is unto God, our Father, we are indebted for the mercies we have enjoyed and for the present prosperous condition of the people of God . . . throughout the world. The hand of the Lord may not be visible to all. There may be many who can not discern the workings of God's will in the progress and development of this great latter-day work, but there are those who see in every hour and in every moment of the existence of the Church, from its beginning until now, the overruling, almighty hand of Him who sent His Only Begotten Son to the world."[3]

Discerning the "overruling, almighty hand" of God in Church history is not always easy. Only he knows the end from the beginning and has all things present before him. If he can make provision for a needed second set of plates hundreds of years before Martin Harris's misfortune, who but the most spiritual knows at any given moment where he may be taking us? My own feeling is that it might be well for us to remember that although God's children are very important to the accomplishment of his purposes, we often are not unlike the young children at an amusement park who drive those little centrally controlled race cars that travel a circular course on a metal rail with their wheels several inches off the ground. The young, excited drivers furiously pump the gas pedals and spin the steering wheels, fully believing they are having some influence, but the cars go at a speed and in a direction that are largely determined by park management!

Having explained the nature of my historiographic concerns, I proceed now—as a nonhistorian—to share some observations about the Church's history in the twentieth century. I do so from the vantage point of having lived during nearly sixty of those one hundred years and of having served as a priesthood leader during nearly forty of them. It has truly been a remarkable and wonderful time to be alive.

THE CENTURY'S BEGINNING AND END IN CONTRAST

The first thing that I want to point out about the twentieth century is the interesting contrast between its beginning and end. In fact, the contrast may be symbolic of one of the most positive things that has happened to the Church in the twentieth century.

Coming on the heels of the Manifesto and the granting of Utah's statehood, the century began on quite an optimistic note. President Lorenzo Snow was already well along with his signature emphasis on the observance of the law of tithing and the reduction of Church debt. He had also initiated a revitalized effort to carry the gospel to all the world. Public opinion seemed to have shifted from opposition to at least neutrality. This proved to be but a brief respite, however, as early in the new century negative attitudes toward the Church were revived and then heightened by political and journalistic jousting between Utah's LDS and non-LDS populations. These were picked up and amplified by the national and European presses so that the Church and its beliefs and practices were again scrutinized and vilified in many parts of the world.

It is perhaps not coincidental that during this renewed period of suspicion and ill will, in the ninth year of the administration of President Joseph F. Smith, a baby boy named Gordon Bitner Hinckley was born on 23 June 1910 in Salt Lake City, the first child of Bryant S. and Ada Bitner Hinckley. With the life expectancy of U.S. males at that time being fifty years, no one would have expected the baby boy to exceed that norm by at least forty years and be instrumental in leading the Church at the end of the twentieth century into its most sustained period of public understanding and acceptance. But President Gordon B. Hinckley has certainly done that and much, much more.

CHURCH GROWTH

I think all of us are aware and justifiably pleased that the Church has experienced tremendous growth in the past century. There were only about 268,000 members in 1900 and nearly 11 million by the century's end. It remained for a nonmember sociologist, however, Dr. Rodney Stark of the University of Washington, to tell the world just how phenomenal LDS growth patterns have been. He shocked the world of religious sociologists in 1984 by characterizing Mormonism as "the rise of a new world faith" and by projecting future membership to be 60 million by the year 2080 if a growth rate of 30 percent per decade persists. Based on historical rates of growth, that is a very reasonable expectation.

By way of follow-up and perhaps to refute critics of his 1984 projections, Dr. Stark published a second essay in 1996 entitled "So Far, So Good: A Brief Assessment of Mormon Membership Projections." He noted with satisfaction that in 1995 Church membership exceeded his 1984 estimates by almost a million members.

While such growth is something for which we should be very grateful and it reflects the vitality and appeal of the LDS way of life, President Hinckley constantly reminds us that management of worldwide growth is our biggest challenge. With more members now living outside the United States than within it and with Spanish on a course to become the predominant language spoken by Church members in the next twenty-five years, we have our work cut out for us, but the prospects are exciting.

BY THEIR FRUITS YE SHALL KNOW THEM

Something else that has impressed me as I have reflected on the significance of the twentieth century is that with an additional one hundred years the Church has now existed long enough to have a rather extensive track record. Although 170 years is a comparatively short period of time for a religious movement to grow and mature and for the benefits of its ideology to be reflected in the lives of its adherents, substantial evidence now exists that obedience to the covenants and ordinances of the restored gospel contributes significantly to a happy, healthy, and productive way of life. This fact comports with the test announced by the Savior for distinguishing true prophets from false ones—we are to know them by their fruits (Matthew 7:15–20).

A very tangible fruit of the restored gospel which has become especially apparent during the twentieth century is the care provided by the Church to the poor and needy. Beginning formally with the institution of the welfare program in 1936, the Church has encouraged self-reliance on the part of its members and has taught and followed basic welfare principles for providing the necessities of life for needy members. No one can visit the central bishops' storehouse in Salt Lake City and see the variety of foodstuffs and other household and clothing goods produced at welfare projects throughout the United States and Canada and not stand in awe of the generosity of the Latter-day Saints and the genius of a program which permits us to help one another in the Lord's own way.

In the last fifteen years, Church resources have also permitted an outreach to people of all faiths and nations in extending humanitarian aid. This service has touched 146 nations through thousands of projects involving the teaching of skills and other forms of self-help as well as the delivery of tons of clothing, food, medical equipment and supplies, educational materials, and millions in cash. The Church has assisted those in distress from war, earthquake, flood, drought, and other disasters.

The Church's commitment to the education of the intellect as well as the spirit has produced other notable gospel fruits. Gospel doctrines encourage Church members to educate their total beings toward greater temporal and spiritual independence, character values, and social conscience. An interesting evidence of this commitment is a study that shows a high degree of religiosity among educated Latter-day Saints. This positive trend runs counter to society in general.

The health code embodied in the Word of Wisdom has also resulted in measurable benefits to those who obey its principles. Latter-day Saints live appreciably longer lives and have significantly

lower levels of cancer, heart disease, and other serious medical conditions. Spiritual blessings also accrue, including an increase in
knowledge, capacity, and peace of mind. (In this connection, I can't
help parenthetically quoting one of our critics who, in reference to
the self-discipline required by the Word of Wisdom, once quipped
that Mormons don't really live longer, it just seems like it!)

Latter-day Saints also have an exemplary record of family life, and
Latter-day Saint homes face a lower incidence of problems plaguing
society generally: divorce rates among Latter-day Saints married in
the temple are very low, a stark contrast to broader statistics; the rate
of teen pregnancies, abortions, and children born out of wedlock is
low as well. There are fewer single-parent homes and less juvenile
delinquency associated with fatherless families; crime and substance
abuse among Latter-day Saints fall below the norm.

A fruit or by-product of gospel living I particularly appreciate is
the opportunity for personal involvement provided by a Church
organization that "hath need of every member" (D&C 84:110). There
is something wonderful about the personal growth and fulfillment
experienced by Church members who labor without pay in providing the leadership, teaching, and concern for the welfare of others
which are hallmarks of this Church. The spirit of this unique system
is epitomized for me each time I read the *Church News* and note the
dozens of accomplished men and women who are called each year
to preside over missions and temples and when I consider the hundreds of stake presidents and thousands of bishops who likewise
respond each year to calls to serve. This constant turnover in lay leaders from all walks of life certainly proves that in the kingdom of God
there is no aristocracy.

In enumerating some of the fruits of the restored gospel which
become more and more apparent the longer the Church exists, I
don't mean to appear boastful. I fully realize that some of the most
desirable outcomes of gospel living can't be quantified or measured.
There are certainly many areas in which we continue to struggle and
fall short, depending on our individual application of gospel principles. Nevertheless, I think it's safe to say that in the past century
the collective goodness and accomplishment of Church members is
something of which the rest of the world has begun to take notice.

A conversation I had on a plane flight from Detroit to Toronto

several years ago with an Arizona businessman captures the perception I think is out there in the minds of many not of our faith and
helps explain the goodwill toward the Church and its members
which now generally exists across the world. As I entered the plane
that day, I introduced myself to my seatmate and after a little small
talk asked him to tell me about his family. He affectionately described
his wife and children and then politely asked me about mine. I
showed him a small family photo I carry and did my best to share
my feelings about the most important people in my life. The spirit at
that point was so good I decided to share briefly the truths contained
in the first missionary discussion. I talked of our belief in a loving
Heavenly Father, of his plan of happiness, and of its restoration
through the Prophet Joseph Smith. I shared my testimony of the
Book of Mormon and the role of the Holy Ghost in finding the truth.
The man seemed genuinely interested, and so I courageously
inquired if I might have two missionaries call on him at his home in
Phoenix. Without hesitation he replied with a resounding "No, I
don't want that!" I recoiled with some surprise, and our conversation
at that point went dead. I felt embarrassed and was worried I had
been too aggressive. I retreated to my newspaper, and he began working on his laptop computer.

As the plane landed in Toronto, I wondered what I might say in
parting to smooth the situation over. Before I could gather my wits,
this fine gentleman said, "Mr. Jensen, before you go, I have something I want to say to you."

I thought to myself, *Here it comes,* but gave him my full attention.
"You are the third Mormon man I have sat next to on an airplane in
the last 18 months," he said, "and you are all alike!"

"How is that?" I gently inquired.

"You all talk about your families," he said, "and you all believe
deeply in your religion."

Then he said something that I will never forget: "There must be
something right about Mormonism!"

There is much that is right about Mormonism, and one of the
unmistakable lessons of the twentieth century for which we need to
be very grateful is that the world is beginning to realize just that.

THE FAMILY: CONSTANCY AMID CHANGE

In a world of shifting values and in some cases no values at all, the eternal truths upon which the gospel is based have positioned the Church in the last century to be an anchor in a sea of change. Nowhere is this more apparent than in the Church's efforts throughout the twentieth century to safeguard the institution of the family as the basic unit of the Church and of society. Continuing concern for serious challenges to marriage and family led the First Presidency and Quorum of the Twelve Apostles in 1995 to take the unusual step of issuing to the entire world a proclamation on the subject of the family. In nine powerful paragraphs the Lord's standard and will concerning marriage relationships and family life were unequivocally set forth. I feel this inspired and boldly worded document will stand for generations to come as a prophetic and definitive statement on the family and its place in God's plan.

THE PROPHETIC MANTLE

In prospecting through one hundred years of the Church's history, one forms the distinct impression that in a sense the history of the Church in any era is the history of its prophet-president. Holding and exercising all the keys of the priesthood, the prophet rightfully enjoys a position of great respect and influence. When the Church was organized, the Saints were admonished by the Lord concerning the prophet to "give heed unto all his words and commandments" (D&C 21:4). History records that by and large (the repeal of prohibition in 1933 being a notable exception) the Saints have obediently heeded their prophets' counsel. This has resulted in great blessings for individual members and for the institutional Church.

Another impressive manifestation of the prophetic mantle has been the ability of the prophets as seers to peek around the corners of the future. This dimension of a prophet's powers was aptly described by Nephi as he explained to his brothers that "by the Spirit are all things made known unto the prophets, which shall come upon the children of men according to the flesh" (1 Nephi 22:2). Through the years, the inspired declarations and teachings of the prophets have provided guidance to the Saints for the avoidance of worldly pitfalls and have often positioned the Church and its membership to prepare proactively for conditions that at the time were yet unforeseen.

I hope you won't mind my sharing a personal experience in this regard.

In 1997 Elder W. Eugene Hansen and I were asked to host the Honorable Michael Moore, attorney general of Mississippi, during a brief visit he made to Utah and Church headquarters. In a wide-ranging conversation with Mr. Moore, Elder Hansen and I raised questions about the lawsuit he had filed against the large American tobacco companies on behalf of the state of Mississippi. We knew Mississippi had recovered a sizable judgment and that other states, including Utah, were then undertaking similar action. We asked him specifically upon what legal theory the state of Mississippi's claim had been based.

Much to our surprise, Mr. Moore informed us that the state's cause of action had been based on a theory of "conspiracy," which the evidence eventually conclusively showed existed among the tobacco companies and even among their lawyers. As Mr. Moore talked of his conspiracy theory and the efforts made by the tobacco companies to hide from the public the addictive and harmful effects of tobacco, my mind almost instinctively turned to section 89 of the Doctrine and Covenants. A copy of that book of scripture was quickly located, and after briefly explaining the background and import of section 89, I asked Mr. Moore to read verse 4.

We listened attentively as he slowly and deliberately read that verse out loud in his appealing southern accent: "Behold, verily, thus saith the Lord unto you: In consequence of evils and designs which do and will exist in the hearts of *conspiring* men in the last days, I have warned you, and forewarn you, by giving unto you this word of wisdom by revelation" (italics added).

The scriptural reference to "conspiring men" was not lost on Mr. Moore. As he finished reading verse 4, a broad smile came across his face, and with a twinkle in his eyes he said, "I never dreamed in visiting Utah I might find 10 million people who would agree with my conspiracy theories!"

My heart burned within me that day and has many times since as I have thought about Joseph Smith's gifts as a prophet and seer. There is really no other explanation for the origin of that 1833 revelation. It waited until nearly the end of the twentieth century for an almost literal public verification of one of its key passages. In the hearts of the faithful Saints who have heeded its message for nearly 170 years, however, there has never been any doubt about its authenticity or relevance.

The truth of the principle this anecdote illustrates—that prophets know beforehand through the Spirit what is going to befall mankind—was borne out again and again during the course of the Church's development in the twentieth century. President Lorenzo Snow's revelation regarding tithing, for example, not only brought the Church out of the fiscal bondage it was in at the start of the century but it also helped lay the firm financial foundation on which the rapidly growing Church would eventually keep up with the demand for the construction of new meetinghouses, provide for an expanding educational system, support a worldwide missionary effort, and finance the building of temples and family history work at an unprecedented rate. Anyone who doubts the inspired financial course on which President Snow set the Church need only to talk today with the leaders of other denominations whose constant concern and focus are the raising of money. Tithing truly is the Lord's law of finance, and we need to acknowledge gratefully its blessings in our personal lives as well as in the Church as an institution.

Emphasizing the importance of the home and the responsibility of parents to teach their children the gospel is another area where prophetic foresight is traceable throughout the past century. In 1915 President Joseph F. Smith and his counselors urged the inauguration of a weekly home evening throughout the Church, during which time fathers and mothers were to gather their families and teach them the gospel. I am certain no social scientist of that early time could have foreseen the tremendous decline in the institutions of marriage and family that would occur in the second half of the twentieth century, but through revelation a prophet could and did. Other prophets who followed, particularly President David O. McKay, had similar insights and shared their own unique encouragement and warnings regarding home and family. Those who have heeded their inspired counsel have been blessed in accordance with the original promise of President Smith and his counselors: "Love at home and obedience to parents will increase. Faith will be developed in the hearts of the youth of Israel, and they will gain power to combat the evil influence and temptations which beset them."[4]

What I have pointed out about the prophetic perspective on the future concerning the Word of Wisdom, tithing, and family home evening could be said with equal force of the Book of Mormon, the temple, and the retention of new converts, all themes on which our three most recent prophets have dwelt. Each of these prophetic points of emphasis in its own way is undoubtedly as important a message for the Latter-day Saints as was Noah's five-day forecast regarding a certain impending storm for the Saints of his day. Based on the course of the Church's history in the twentieth century, we ought to sing "We Thank Thee, O God, for a Prophet" with even greater fervor.[5]

THE PRIESTHOOD

Any commentary on the Church's history in the twentieth century must include mention of the momentous 1978 revelation which extended priesthood and temple blessings to all worthy male members of the Church without regard to race or color. For all of us old enough to remember the June 9 announcement that year, it will always remain a joyous moment frozen in time. From then on for the first time it could truly be said that "every man might speak in the name of God the Lord" (D&C 1:20).

Also important to the Church and its future are the organizational changes which have been made to the Quorums of the Seventy since 1975. Beginning modestly with the organization of the First Quorum of the Seventy in that year, a gradual unfolding of priesthood government has taken place, including the assimilation of assistants to the Twelve into the First Quorum of the Seventy in 1976, the implementation of area presidencies in 1984, the dissolution of stake seventies quorums in 1986, the creation of the Second Quorum of the Seventy in 1989, and the creation of the office of area authority seventy and three additional quorums of the Seventy in 1997. Today there are 276 members of the Seventy who help supervise the work of the Church under the direction of the Quorum of the Twelve Apostles in 28 areas scattered across the earth. The organization is now in place to govern the Church in the exciting and challenging years of growth and expansion that lie ahead.

THE SCRIPTURES

An experience I had as a newly called Seventy will illustrate a point I would like to make about the role of the scriptures in the Church during the past century. I, along with eleven other men, was called as a Seventy in April 1989. The first orientation session we all attended was conducted by Elder Marion D. Hanks, then one of the seven presidents of Seventy. As the meeting began, I noticed I had forgotten to bring my scriptures but hoped my oversight would go unnoticed. This was a blessing I was denied, however, as early in the meeting Elder Hanks called on me to read a passage from the Doctrine and Covenants. When he saw that I was groping for my neighbor's scriptures, Elder Hanks said, "Brother Jensen, do you own a set of scriptures?"

"I do," I replied. "They are unfortunately in my office."

"Why don't you go get them?" Elder Hanks asked.

In the most self-conscious moment of my life, I dashed to my office, retrieved my scriptures, and returned to the meeting room.

As I tried inconspicuously to take my seat, Elder Hanks, in his best Brooklyn accent said, "Brother Jensen, when ya come tuh Church, ya bedder bring da books!" I have done that unfailingly ever since. And I am not alone in observing that practice. In the past twenty years particularly, there has been a tremendous surge of interest in personal scripture study and in the use of the scriptures in teaching and speaking about the gospel. The publication of the Latter-day Saint edition of the scriptures beginning in 1979 undoubtedly gave impetus to this very healthy trend. It has been enhanced by President Benson's encouragement regarding the Book of Mormon and by the correlation in a four-year cycle of the youth and adult Sunday curriculum using the scriptures as the foundation. A thrilling sight each Sunday everywhere in the world is the great number of Latter-day Saints of all ages carrying their scriptures to and from Church. The resultant increase in gospel scholarship and faith has made this development one of the crowning achievements of the past century.

A CHRIST-CENTERED CHURCH

Any student of Christianity in the closing decades of the twentieth century knows there has been a crisis in Christology, the doctrine of Christ's work and person. Relativism and historical skepticism have led many to doubt the truth regarding Christ's person and mission. The work of Robert Funk's so-called Jesus Seminar in recent years is one example of this very regrettable trend. He and his scholarly associates have classified all the sayings and deeds attributed to Jesus into categories: certainly inauthentic, probably inauthentic, probably authentic, and certainly authentic. Decisions regarding classification were made by majority vote of seminar members.

In contrast to this lamentable state of affairs stand the strong testimonies of our Savior which have been borne unfailingly by God's chosen prophets and apostles throughout the past century. This consistent witness is at the very heart and soul of this Church. On 1 January 2000, the First Presidency and Quorum of the Twelve Apostles commemorated the birth of Jesus Christ two millennia ago by issuing to the world their collective testimony of the living Christ. Among other inspiring assertions in a beautifully worded document, these fifteen committed men testified that Christ's "life, which is central to all human history, neither began in Bethlehem nor concluded on Calvary. He was the Firstborn of the Father, the Only Begotten Son in the flesh, the Redeemer of the world." It is a fact of history in this Church in the twentieth century that such a ringing conviction of the reality of our Savior's birth, death, and atoning sacrifice has been carried in the hearts of literally millions of Latter-day Saints. With the current prophets and apostles we join in saying, "God be thanked for the matchless gift of His divine Son."[6]

PROPHECY FULFILLED

I conclude my remarks concerning the Church in the twentieth century by humbly admitting my inability to do justice to the task at hand. The kingdom of God on earth in any age defies total comprehension and analysis by man. It is God's work, and he alone knows its heights and depths. Only with the help of the Holy Ghost, who gives life and meaning to all that we do, can we ever hope to fully understand and appreciate all that God has provided for us. Only with the help of the Spirit can we come to know not just *what* has happened in our remarkable history but more importantly *why* it happened and what God's intentions and designs for us are. Nevertheless, he has said he reveals his secrets unto his servants, the prophets (Amos 3:7), and they in turn have often shared these secrets in the form of prophecies. The Church's course over the last one hundred years unquestionably fulfills prophecy. For example—

- Israel is in the process of being gathered (D&C 110:11). Sixty thousand incredible young missionaries are evidence of this as they preach the gospel "in all the world, for a witness unto all nations" (Joseph Smith–Matthew 1:31). A significant part of this gathering involves bringing God's elect to the temple and the covenants and ordinances to be found there. Thus, the importance of President Gordon B. Hinckley's small-temple initiative in bringing the temple to the people cannot be overstated. His name will rightfully be enshrined in the history of the final years of the twentieth century and the beginning years of the twenty-first century as the temple-building president.

- "Jacob shall flourish in the wilderness" (D&C 49:24). Who can doubt that the descendants of Jacob who settled this Great Basin kingdom have flourished?

- "The Lamanites shall blossom as the rose" (D&C 49:24). Father Lehi's descendants from North, Central, and South America and the isles of the sea are joining the Church in large numbers and are making progress in other important ways.

- The hearts of the children are being turned to their fathers and the hearts of fathers to their children (Malachi 4:5, 6; D&C 2). From Elijah in the Kirtland Temple to *www.familysearch.org,* progress in genealogical and temple work has been remarkable.

- The name of Joseph Smith shall "be had for good and evil among all nations, kindreds, and tongues" (Joseph Smith–History 1:33). This prophecy would be nothing but a presumptuous assertion from a young farm boy were it not for the fact that it has been literally fulfilled.

- "The God of heaven [shall] set up a kingdom, which shall never be destroyed" (Daniel 2:44–45; D&C 65). This prophecy is being fulfilled at the present time as the Church continues to grow and spread across the earth. President Gordon B. Hinckley has referred to Daniel's interpretation of Nebuchadnezzar's dream many times since his ordination as prophet in 1995.

"THE SUMMIT OF THE AGES"

Where do we now stand as we leave the twentieth century and begin the twenty-first? In his magnificent October 1999 general conference address, President Gordon B. Hinckley said, "We stand on the summit of the ages."[7] What can one see from that summit as a new millennium dawns?

To be sure, one sees great possibilities as well as great challenges. There will be unbelievable advancements in technology, bioengineering, medicine, and pharmacology. There will be a continuing decline of values and morals, and the family will be under determined attack. Secularization will increase as faith in God wanes and the idea of absolute truth surrenders to notions of tolerance and relativism. In the midst of it all, The Church of Jesus Christ of Latter-day Saints will continue its onward march. The Prophet Joseph eloquently declared in the Wentworth Letter that "no unhallowed hand [could] stop the work from progressing"—and it hasn't; that "the truth of God [would] go forth boldly, nobly, and independent"—it has and it will.[8]

I testify that God lives, that Jesus is his living Son, that through the Prophet Joseph Smith the kingdom of God has been restored to earth. I pray that we will help God's kingdom to go forth, that the kingdom of heaven may come (D&C 65:5).

NOTES

1. Joseph F. Smith, "Common-place Things," *Juvenile Instructor* 40 (15 December 1905): 752.

2. *Hymns of The Church of Jesus Christ of Latter-day Saints* (Salt Lake City: The Church of Jesus Christ of Latter-day Saints, 1985), no. 237.

3. Joseph F. Smith, Conference Report, April 1904, 2.

4. James R. Clark, comp., *Messages of the First Presidency of The Church of Jesus Christ of Latter-day Saints*, 6 vols. (Salt Lake City: Bookcraft, 1965–75), 4:339.

5. *Hymns*, no. 19.

6. "The Living Christ: The Testimony of the Apostles," *Ensign*, April 2000, 2.

7. Gordon B. Hinckley, Conference Report, October 1999, 94.

8. Joseph Smith, *History of The Church of Jesus Christ of Latter-day Saints*, ed. B. H. Roberts, 2d ed. rev., 7 vols. (Salt Lake City: The Church of Jesus Christ of Latter-day Saints, 1932–51), 4:540.

CHAPTER TWO

THE LATTER-DAY SAINT CENTURY

RICHARD O. COWAN

Events during the 1800s laid important foundations for the twentieth-century Church. Joseph Smith presided over the exciting era of restoration during which essential gospel doctrines were revealed and key elements of Church organization were set into place. As a counterpoint to these glorious developments, however, the Saints were repeatedly driven from their homes. These difficult times culminated in the shocking murder of the Prophet himself.

Under the leadership of Brigham Young, the Mormon pioneers made their epic trek across the plains and founded hundreds of new communities in the Rocky Mountains. The Saints' relative isolation enabled them to gain the strength needed for the Church to survive. When a new wave of persecution erupted during the 1880s, the Church was capably led by John Taylor who earlier had edited newspapers defending the Saints. As feelings toward the Mormons improved during the following decade, President Wilford Woodruff, one of the greatest missionaries the Church has ever known, directed the opening or reopening of several mission fields and helped advance other aspects of the Church's work during this time of growing goodwill.

As important as the nineteenth century had been in establishing the Church on a firm foundation, the twentieth century would carry it to significantly greater heights. When the new century dawned,

Richard O. Cowan is a professor of Church history and doctrine at Brigham Young University.

the Church was led by Lorenzo Snow, the last president of the same generation as the founding Prophet.

The circumstances of the Saints at the beginning of the century were a far cry from the status the Church would enjoy a hundred years later. Horse-drawn buggies dominated the streets of Salt Lake City; automobiles were still rare and generally unaffordable novelties. Steam-powered railroad trains were the prime mode of long-distance transportation, the Wright brothers being two or three years away from opening the air age with their history-making flight. Some people had telephones, but their use was not yet widespread.

In 1900 the Church had just over a quarter of a million members, most of whom lived in the traditional area of pioneer settlement in the Rocky Mountains. Were it not for the notoriety arising from the former practice of plural marriage, the Mormons would likely have been considered a relatively obscure religious sect. The Church had only nineteen missions, with most located in North America and Western Europe and a few in the Pacific. There were forty stakes, all in the Intermountain West. The four operating temples were all in Utah. There were no weekly priesthood meetings nor auxiliary classes for adults.

The story of how the Church progressed during the twentieth century from those small dimensions is an interesting one. As had been the case in the nineteenth century, each prophet was well suited to the needs of his time and made a significant contribution to the Church's development. Church programs and activities unfolded significantly during President Joseph F. Smith's administration. The Relief Society launched its Mothers' Class in 1902. Four years later, the Sunday School added its first class for adults; it eventually came to be known as the Gospel Doctrine class and would play a key part in the Saints' study of their faith. The first seminary for high school students was opened in 1912, and the following year the Young Men's Mutual Improvement Association officially adopted the Boy Scout program.

Before this time the various priesthood quorums conducted business meetings at different times from each other, typically only monthly and sometimes not at all during the summer. By 1909 Elder David O. McKay, a relatively new member of the Twelve, had become chairman of the General Priesthood Committee, which instructed all

wards to hold weekly priesthood meetings under the bishop's direction. At first these gatherings were on Monday evenings, but soon
they were shifted to Sunday mornings to avoid conflicts with farm
or other weekday chores.

During the opening decades of the twentieth century, the flourishing auxiliary organizations became the publishers of the magazines serving the Latter-day Saints. In 1901 the Sunday School took
over the *Juvenile Instructor,* and the following year the Primary
launched its *Children's Friend.* The Relief Society gave its name to a
new magazine in 1915, and the Young Men's and Young Women's
MIA sponsored the *Improvement Era,* which rapidly became the
Church's basic magazine for adults.

During the years following the close of World War I, the Saints
increasingly turned their attention outward. Near the end of 1920,
President Heber J. Grant assigned Elder David O. McKay to make an
inspection tour of the Church's missions worldwide. This year-long
assignment gave Elder McKay and his general authority associates an
international perspective that they did not have before. On
Christmas day in 1925, Elder Melvin J. Ballard, another member of
the Twelve, dedicated South America for the preaching of the gospel.
During this same decade many Latter-day Saints left Utah in search
of improved economic opportunities. Most of them went to Southern
California, where the local Latter-day Saint ward or branch became
their extended family or home away from home. Howard W. Hunter,
a young man who had come there from Idaho, later affirmed that in
Los Angeles he had his "first real awakening to the gospel."[1] Nearly
three-quarters of a century later he would become president of the
Church. The first modern stake outside the intermountain area was
organized in Los Angeles in 1923; another followed in San Francisco
four years later.

As the Saints increasingly came in contact with people not of their
faith, the Church gave added attention to sharing the gospel. In 1925
the Church opened the Missionary Home and Preparatory Training
School in some old homes just north of the Beehive House on State
Street in Salt Lake City. The new medium of radio was also used. In
1922 President Grant participated in the first broadcast over Salt Lake
radio station KZN; soon afterward the Church bought the station and
changed its call letters to KSL. In 1929 the Mormon Tabernacle Choir

launched its weekly broadcasts, which have become the longest running continuous program in the history of United States network radio.

The Great Depression of the 1930s hit Utah and surrounding areas particularly hard. President Heber J. Grant, who had learned the virtues of industry and thrift from his widowed mother, was able to teach these qualities to the Saints during this time of economic distress. Only a small number of members, including a future Church president Gordon B. Hinckley, who served in England, were able to fill missions during the Depression. While the nationwide unemployment rate peaked at 25 percent, the jobless rate in Salt Lake City's west side reached twice that level. Harold B. Lee, a thirty-year-old stake president in this disadvantaged area, created food production projects and set up a stake cannery and storehouse to aid those in need. Impressed with his inspired initiative, the First Presidency in 1935 invited him to implement similar programs throughout the Church. The resulting introduction of the welfare plan helped the Saints better live the principles of hard work, cooperation, and stewardship, which had been introduced a century earlier. The Depression accelerated the Saints' exodus to other parts of the country; and growth in these areas was reflected in the organization of stakes in such centers as New York, Chicago, Denver, Portland, Seattle, and Washington, D.C.

Perhaps few external events influenced the direction of Church growth more than did World War II. Missionary work was almost completely shut down as war spread across Europe and the Pacific, and thousands of Latter-day Saint young men responded to calls for military service. Church activities in North America were severely restricted. Hundreds of Saints in Europe lost their homes or even their lives. There was, however, a silver lining to the dark cloud of war. Latter-day Saint servicemen were able to introduce the gospel where missionaries had not been able to serve. One such serviceman, Boyd K. Packer, a young airman assigned to occupation duty in postwar Japan, helped teach and baptize the family of Tatsui Sato; Brother Packer would eventually be called to the Twelve, and Brother Sato would become a Church leader and translator as the gospel once again was introduced to Japan.

George Albert Smith became president of the Church just as World

War II was ending. Noted for his Christlike love, he was the ideal leader to help the Saints and the world overcome the feelings of hatred engendered by the war. In 1946 he sent Elder Ezra Taft Benson, who had been called to the Twelve just three years earlier, to Europe. Elder Benson enjoyed remarkable spiritual experiences as he visited the war-devastated Saints, supervised the distribution of welfare supplies, and directed the reopening of missionary work. President Smith, who also had long shown a concern for the Lamanites, organized the Indian Committee with another new apostle, Spencer W. Kimball, at its head. For years, President Smith had spearheaded the erection of markers to commemorate pioneer trails and accomplishments. It was fitting, therefore, that he should be serving as president of the Church during the 1947 Pioneer Centennial and have the privilege of unveiling the imposing *This Is the Place* monument.

Unprecedented international growth characterized the 1950s and 1960s when David O. McKay presided over the Church. The first Church president to have graduated from college, President McKay had the broadened background that enabled him to relate well with leaders around the world. Using the inspired slogan "every member a missionary," he challenged the Saints to become more involved in sharing the gospel. Steps to enhance the work of full-time missionaries at this time included outlining effective gospel discussions and organizing what became a series of Missionary Training Centers around the world.

Unlike many organizations whose rate of growth declines as they become larger, the Church's growth rate during the second half of the twentieth century was almost double that of the first. Membership grew most rapidly in Latin America, resulting in an increasingly diverse Church membership. In 1955 the Church's first "overseas" temple was dedicated near Bern, Switzerland, and the first stake outside North America and Hawaii was organized three years later at Aukland, New Zealand. Within the United States, The Church of Jesus Christ of Latter-day Saints became one of the half dozen largest faiths in the nation.

In the midst of this era of growth, the general authorities worked to ensure that the Church was fulfilling its divine mission as effectively as possible. Under the leadership of Elder Harold B. Lee and the general priesthood committee, moves were made to eliminate unwanted duplication among Church programs and to place all activities more squarely under the direction of the priesthood. As part of this priesthood correlation emphasis, the Church in 1965 published a family home evening manual and soon afterward designated Monday nights for this activity. In 1971 existing Church magazines in English were consolidated into the *Ensign* for adults, the *New Era* for youth, and the *Friend* for children.

Joseph Fielding Smith served as the Church's president from 1970 until 1972. Throughout his sixty-year ministry in the Quorum of the Twelve Apostles, he had taught the truths of the gospel clearly and forcefully through his sermons and writings. Under his leadership, the curriculum in the Sunday School's Gospel Doctrine class was changed to emphasize a study of the standard works rather than of books written about the scriptures.

Because both President McKay and President Smith had lived into their mid-nineties, when Harold B. Lee became president of the Church at age seventy-three, most Latter-day Saints expected to enjoy his leadership for many years. Just a year and a half later, however, they were shocked to hear of his unexpected death. As had been the case with Joseph Fielding Smith, Harold B. Lee's brief presidency represented the capstone of many decades of significant leadership. During his presidency he emphasized the importance of meeting the needs of Church members in diverse circumstances. The Church gave more attention to single adults, members of ethnic minorities, and the disabled. While the earlier Welfare Plan had given attention to the "poor and the needy," new social and health programs provided aid to the "sick and the afflicted" (D&C 52:40).

Spencer W. Kimball, who became the next prophet in 1973, had experienced poor health for a number of years. Some members, therefore, expected that his administration might be even shorter than those of his two predecessors. Much to their surprise, however, President Kimball served for over a decade, and many remarkable developments blessed the Church during that time. In 1976 the First Quorum of the Seventy was organized as a quorum of general authorities to help administer the growing Church. In 1978 President Kimball received a revelation extending priesthood blessings to worthy men of all races (see Official Declaration 2). This led to the opening of new mission fields in such areas as Africa and the Caribbean. Beginning in 1980, Church meetings formerly held at various times throughout the week were consolidated into a single three-hour block on Sundays. This move not only conserved energy but freed time for families to enjoy more activities on their own and to increase community service.

At this time, new editions of the standard works were published. Cross-references in the Bible linked doctrinal teachings in all four standard works, truly making them, as Ezekiel had prophesied, "one in thine hand" (Ezekiel 37:17). The Doctrine and Covenants now included sections 137–38, the first numbered sections to be added in a century. Both contained insights which would provide a doctrinal foundation for the unprecedented emphasis on temple activity that was about to unfold. Also added was Official Declaration 2, the announcement of the 1978 revelation on the priesthood. The five-hundred-page Topical Guide, the Bible Dictionary, improved chapter headings, maps, and other helps were all designed to support and enhance the Saints' personal study of the scriptures. Referring to the publication of these new editions of the scriptures, Elder Boyd K. Packer remarked, "As the generations roll on, this will be regarded, in the perspective of history, as the crowning achievement in the administration of President Spencer W. Kimball."[2]

A series of remarkable events in Eastern Europe during the 1980s had a direct connection to Latter-day Saint developments. In the late 1970s, President Kimball had visited Warsaw and "dedicated the land of Poland and blessed its people that the work of the Lord might go forth."[3] In 1980 the Solidarity labor movement in Poland defeated the Communist government in a democratic election. This unprecedented development was a catalyst in the process that brought down other Communist regimes during the coming decade.

Then, in 1989, the Berlin Wall was opened for the first time in decades, and soon the formerly separate East and West Germany were reunited. Just four years before, the Freiberg Germany Temple had been dedicated in the German Democratic Republic. At the cornerstone ceremony for the Jordan River Temple in 1981, President Ezra Taft Benson had affirmed that even the area surrounding a temple is blessed because God's power is manifested in His holy house.[4] Perhaps this was one factor contributing to the remarkable changes that opened doors to the gospel in this region. It seems appropriate that President Benson, who had over the years repeatedly decried the evils of "godless communism," was serving as the prophet when communism collapsed. At a time when religious faith seemed to be declining around the world, President Benson also frequently admonished the Saints to study the Book of Mormon, in order to strengthen their conviction that Jesus is the Christ.

As the twentieth century entered its concluding decades, the fruits of faithful tithe paying became apparent. Internally, by 1990 the total cost of erecting chapels and operating local programs was covered from the general Church funds. Externally, during the 1980s and 1990s the Church increasingly reached out to the world, contributing millions of dollars in relief during famines, floods, earthquakes, and other disasters. This humanitarian aid was given to those in need regardless of their religion.

Temple activity directs attention to eternal spiritual values. President Howard W. Hunter, who led the Church for only nine months in 1994 and 1995, riveted the Saints' focus on temple service. He invited "the members of the Church to establish the temple of the Lord as the great symbol of their membership and the supernal setting for their most sacred covenants. It would be the deepest desire of my heart to have every member of the Church temple worthy."[5] This same emphasis was continued by President Hunter's successor, Gordon B. Hinckley, who had dedicated more temples than anyone else in Church history even before becoming president of the Church. While there were forty-seven temples in service when he assumed this office in 1995, he announced the goal of having more than one hundred of these sacred structures dedicated by the end of the year 2000. This objective was achieved with the dedication of the Boston Massachusetts Temple on 1 October of that year. These new temples included the first to be part of a larger building (Hong Kong), the first to be an older building reconstructed (Vernal, Utah), and dozens of much smaller temples that would make the blessings of the house of the Lord available even to remote and isolated groups of Saints.

While the number of temples was exploding, there also came incredible strides in family history. Computers enabled the Saints to gather huge quantities of vital information and then make it readily available at nearly three thousand family history centers around the world. A new website, *www.familysearch.org*, quickly became one of the most popular addresses on the Internet.

The Lord has declared that his Church needed to be brought forth "out of obscurity" (D&C 1:30). This became a theme of President Hinckley's administration. The Church adopted a logo heralding the words "Jesus Christ" in its name. The First Presidency and the Twelve issued a proclamation to the world declaring the sanctity and central role of the family. President Hinckley was interviewed more than once on prime-time television and at numerous press conferences. Having a private jet at his disposal, he traveled more widely than any previous president of the Church. During the first five years of his administration, he covered nearly a quarter of a million miles (more than the distance to the moon), visited fifty-eight countries and spoke to more than 2.2 million people, thus blessing a multitude of Latter-day Saints and others worldwide.[6]

Meanwhile, the Church continued to grow. It had reached the million member milestone during the pioneer centennial year of 1947 and passed the 10 million mark in the pioneer sesquicentennial year of 1997. Within a few months of that sesquicentennial year, there were more members outside of the United States than within it. Near the end of 1998, the Church organized its 2,500th stake. Area authorities were appointed in 1995 to help train and supervise local leaders and became members of the Third, Fourth, and Fifth Quorums of the Seventy two years later.

As remarkable as the achievements of the Latter-day Saint century have been, the future suggests an even more remarkable destiny for the Church. In Old Testament times the prophet Daniel looked forward to the time when God's kingdom would roll forth to fill the whole earth (Daniel 2:26–45). In a latter-day revelation the Lord referred to Daniel's prophecy as he taught the Church's ultimate mission. He encouraged us to work and pray "that his kingdom may go forth upon the earth, that the inhabitants thereof may receive it, and be prepared for the days to come, in the which the Son of Man shall come down in heaven, clothed in the brightness of his glory" (D&C 65:5).

Elder Bruce R. McConkie of the Quorum of the Twelve Apostles likened a review of the Church's past accomplishments to standing on a mountain peak from which "the view is glorious." But, he continued, "Our joy and rejoicing is not in what lies below, not in our past—great and glorious as that is—but in our present and in our future. . . . From the top of the peak . . . we can look forward, crest upon crest, to the Zion of God which one day will be ours if we walk in the course charted by those who have gone before."[7] He later suggested that "the Church is like a great caravan—organized, prepared, following an appointed course." Although there may be opposition and other challenges along the way, "ahead is the celestial city, the eternal Zion of our God, where all who maintain their position in the caravan shall find food and drink and rest."[8]

NOTES

1. Eleanor Knowles, *Howard W. Hunter* (Salt Lake City: Deseret Book, 1994), 71.

2. Boyd K. Packer, in Conference Report, October 1982, 75.

3. "Poland Dedicated by Pres. Kimball," *Church News,* 17 September 1977, 3.

4. "New Temple a Landmark of Beauty," *Church News,* 22 August 1981, 8.

5. "President Hunter Pledges Life, Strength, Full Measure of Soul to the Service of Jesus Christ," *Church News,* 11 June 1994, 14.

6. "Looking into the Faces of Faithful Latter-day Saints," *Church News,* 4 March 2000, 8.

7. Bruce R. McConkie, in Conference Report, April 1980, 97–98.

8. Bruce R. McConkie, in Conference Report, October 1984, 105.

CHAPTER THREE

A LENGTHENING STRIDE, 1951 THROUGH 1999

BRENT L. TOP

"For I will work a work in your days," the Old Testament prophet Habakkuk declared, "which ye will not believe, though it be told you" (Habakkuk 1:5). Although this prophecy dealt directly with events surrounding Habakkuk's day, his words are, nonetheless, a remarkable reflection of the work of the Lord in the latter half of the twentieth century. The recent growth of the Church, perhaps unequaled in any previous period of history, has been such as to, in the words of President Boyd K. Packer, "astound even those who watch it closely."[1] It is not just the numerical growth that is so astounding, although that is dramatic and visible. Even more, it is how the Lord has opened the windows of heaven and poured out upon the Church, its leaders, and members inspiration and blessings that have opened doors to the Church throughout the world, have strengthened Church programs and units, and have transformed souls of young and old alike.

In the April 1981 general conference, President Spencer W. Kimball outlined the mission of the Church, which is to help all mankind to come unto Christ through proclaiming the gospel, redeeming the dead, and perfecting the Saints.[2] These three fundamental missions, revealed by the Lord in holy writ and reiterated by latter-day prophets, guide the Church in all that it does. The last fifty years have been filled with marvels and miracles in the work of the Church in these

Brent L. Top is a professor of Church history and doctrine and associate dean of Religious Education at Brigham Young University.

26

three areas, causing both members and outside observers to be "astonished beyond measure" (Helaman 3:25).

PROCLAIMING THE GOSPEL

From the very outset of his administration President David O. McKay admonished the Saints to greater involvement in taking the gospel to the world. Not only did President McKay call for increased numbers of full-time missionaries, but he also pleaded for more significant efforts by each member of the Church in sharing the gospel with others. In June 1961 the Church held its first official training seminar for new mission presidents. In that setting, President McKay outlined his vision for taking the gospel to the world. In his talk he coined a phrase that became a watchword to the Saints: "Every member a missionary."[3] In the decades that followed that historic event, monumental strides were made in three specific areas of this mission of the Church—the expansion of the full-time missionary corps, the extension of member-missionary efforts, and the use of modern technologies for spreading the gospel around the world.

Increased Numbers of Full-Time Missionaries

"Now is the moment in the timetable of the Lord," declared President Spencer W. Kimball, "to carry the gospel farther than it has ever been carried before—farther geographically, and farther in density of coverage."[4] The missionary force of the Church increased dramatically during the past five decades. The numbers of full-time missionaries increased significantly, as did the expanding reach of the gospel message evidenced by the increased numbers of missions, many of which were in nations never before open to the Church. Yet there were still challenges to be faced and obstacles to be overcome.

Perhaps the greatest challenge to the unprecedented expansion of the Church's missionary efforts came during the Vietnam War. As the conflict escalated, the government's need for young men to serve in the military put an enormous squeeze on the Church's ability to have these young men serving in the mission field. In a letter dated 22 September 1965, the First Presidency announced a new missionary quota. The arrangement with the Selective Service allowed for one full-time missionary per ward each six months. Even though the quotas were transferrable within stakes, many young men who had long counted on and prepared for missionary service were now faced with the real possibility of not being able to serve.

"This is a matter that greatly worries me. My phone rings constantly both day and night asking for some liberalization of quotas so that more young men may go on missions," Elder Gordon B. Hinckley recorded in his journal. As a member of the Quorum of the Twelve Apostles, Elder Hinckley served as the managing director of the Priesthood Missionary Committee. "At the same time I am under pressure from the military incident to the war in Vietnam," he continued. "I pray night and morning that somehow our Father in His power will bring to pass a cessation of hostilities there so that our young men may go without restriction into the world and teach the gospel of peace."[5] Despite the temporary reduction of the missionary force imposed by this quota, the hand of the Lord was manifest in other ways. The LDS servicemen in Vietnam were missionaries in their own right, sharing the gospel with fellow soldiers and planting seeds of goodwill that would someday be harvested in southeast Asia. Even amidst the horrors of war, countless conversions and miraculous missionary experiences resulted.

With the conclusion of the war, the numbers of full-time missionaries steadily increased. This impressive growth, particularly during the decades of the 1970s and 80s, can be largely attributed to President Spencer W. Kimball's charge that "every [worthy] young man should fill a mission."[6] At the Paris, France, area conference in 1976, he further called on the young men of foreign countries to serve missions in their own lands "because they know the people and they know the customs, and above all they know the language well." Referring to the difficulty of obtaining visas for American missionaries to serve in some countries, President Kimball further urged young men in all nations to be missionaries. "We hope we will have enough well-trained, worthy local young men to carry on the work if, by chance, the doors be closed against the Americans. And, anyway, the responsibility is yours."[7] With the prophet's urgent appeal to the Church to "lengthen your stride," not only did the numbers of young men serving full-time missions skyrocket, but the expansion also included many young women, as well as numerous older couples who sacrificed the comforts of home and the leisure of retirement to respond to the Lord's call.

"When I ask for more missionaries," President Spencer W. Kimball declared, "I am not asking for more testimony-barren or unworthy missionaries. I am asking that we start earlier and train our missionaries better in every branch and every ward in the world."[8] The resulting improvement of missionary preparation was both individual and institutional. The prophet urged prospective missionaries, as well as their parents, to begin serious mission preparation early in life. He identified three specific areas of preparation: moral worthiness, doctrinal knowledge and personal testimony, and finances.[9]

To further assist with individual missionary preparation, the Church greatly expanded its own preparation efforts. As early as 1925 there had been a Church Missionary Home and Preparatory Training School in Salt Lake City. It expanded to accommodate the increased numbers of missionaries. In this mission home missionaries received instruction in doctrine, Church programs, and missionary skills and were inspired by messages from general authorities. In 1961 a special language training program was developed for missionaries who were experiencing lengthy delays in obtaining visas to enter such countries as Mexico and Argentina.

Due to its great success, the Language Training Mission (LTM) was formally organized in 1963. All missionaries going to Portuguese- or Spanish-speaking nations were first sent to BYU for several weeks of language training. In 1964 German was added to the LTM. French and Italian soon followed. Scandinavian languages and Dutch were added to the expanded Language Training Mission established at Ricks College in 1969. Training in the Asian and Pacific languages was done at the Church College of Hawaii. In 1973 the Church announced that all of these missionary training facilities, including the mission home in Salt Lake City, would be consolidated and housed in a new $15 million Missionary Training Center near the BYU campus.[10]

With the hundreds of full-time missionaries from foreign countries responding to the prophet's admonition, in 1977 the Church announced the formation of Missionary Training Centers (MTCs) in various nations outside the United States. The first of these foreign MTCs was located in Sao Pãulo, Brazil. These would provide spiritual, doctrinal, and practical instruction for missionaries who would have otherwise been unable to receive such training. In the years since, additional MTCs have been built on virtually every continent and on several islands of the Pacific.

Elder Robert L. Simpson, a member of the First Quorum of the Seventy and managing director of the Missionary Department, reported a direct correlation between increased baptisms in the areas of these satellite MTCs and the increased training the missionaries received there. Similarly, leaders of the Church reported that much of the missionary success in those areas came from the improved confidence of the local missionaries trained in these MTCs. The benefits of this major missionary preparation effort also yielded significant spiritual dividends to the Church even after these missionaries returned to their home wards and branches. "The additional spirituality and confidence and the increase in number of temple recommend holders will greatly benefit the Church in the future—as well as now."[11]

Member-Missionary Endeavors

From the earliest days of the Restoration, the Lord, through direct revelation and through the teachings of modern prophets, taught that "it becometh every man who hath been warned to warn his neighbor" (D&C 88:81). While each of the presidents of the Church since the time of the Prophet Joseph Smith have stressed this covenant obligation of members, the latter half of the twentieth century saw perhaps the most extensive and successful member-missionary efforts in the history of the Church. "Every member a missionary," declared President David O. McKay. This slogan served as a constant reminder of our individual covenant to "stand as witnesses of God at all times and in all things, and in all places" (Mosiah 18:9).

During this time Church members not only were reminded from the pulpit of the need for member involvement in missionary work but were also given formal programs and training to assist in sharing the gospel with friends, neighbors, and relatives. In 1977 President Spencer W. Kimball stressed the need for members of the Church of all ages to share referrals with the full-time and stake missionaries and to invite their friends to participate in the programs and organizations of the Church. "We cannot stress too strongly the need to do missionary work in the framework of priesthood correlation," he declared, "so that investigators are fellowshipped and tied into the programs of the Church in such a way that they promptly become active and faithful members."[12]

Formal training in how to be successful member-missionaries followed the prophet's charge. The entire October 1977 issue of the *Ensign* was devoted to helping members become more actively involved in missionary endeavors. The articles gave very specific and practical suggestions for sharing gospel messages as well as information that would inspire and motivate Church members.

In 1982 each member of the Church participated in a member-missionary class. Six lessons were taught during Sunday School time to guide members in recognizing the blessings of missionary service. They were taught to identify friends and acquaintances who might want to hear the gospel, to be good examples, to make their homes "gospel-oriented," to engage others in gospel conversation, and to friendship and fellowship. The full-time missionaries worked closely with stake missionaries and local priesthood leaders in following up on these lessons and the opportunities that came from them. Missionaries and members became more "equally yoked" in the work of proclaiming the gospel to the world. There began to be a greater realization of President Kimball's goal "that the members do the finding and the full-time missionaries do the teaching."[13]

Other formal programs for member-missionary work followed. Elder M. Russell Ballard introduced the Set-a-Date Program in the October 1984 general conference. "Write down a *date* in the near future on which you will have someone ready to be taught the gospel," he urged the Saints. "Do not worry that you do not have someone already in mind. Let the Lord help you as you pray diligently for guidance." He further promised a "great increase in building the kingdom of God" if members would prayerfully "set a date" and work to have someone ready to receive the gospel in the coming year.[14] Untold thousands were baptized into the Church through diligent member-missionary efforts like these.

With President Ezra Taft Benson's renewed emphasis on the Book of Mormon, another very successful member-missionary program was reinvigorated: the Family-to-Family Book of Mormon Program. Begun on a limited scale nearly twenty years earlier, this program allowed members of the Church—families, couples, or individuals— to purchase copies of the Book of Mormon and place a picture and testimony on the inside cover. The books were then given to acquaintances or distributed by stake and full-time missionaries. Additional testimony- and picture-laden copies were sent to missions throughout the world so that full-time missionaries could give them to people they encountered.

Church leaders reported that these "testimony-bearing copies of the Book of Mormon" were very effective in opening doors and hearts to the message of the Book of Mormon and the restored gospel and also in strengthening the personal testimonies of the members who donated the books.[15] This program was just one of the many ways that the Church, through institutional programs and individual efforts, sought to fulfill President Benson's vision of "flooding the earth with the Book of Mormon."[16]

Spreading the Gospel through Modern Technology

"We must more effectively proclaim the gospel of Jesus Christ through the media," declared President Ezra Taft Benson. "We must see to it that we more effectively utilize technology to help bring the gospel message to our people and the people of the world."[17] The "information age" of the latter half of the twentieth century brought with it many innovative technological advances that enabled the Church to proclaim the gospel to millions more of God's children than had been possible in earlier generations. Although the Church had used radio to broadcast general conference, Tabernacle Choir weekly programs, and other special events, it was the popularity of television that provided new opportunities for the Church and its members to be seen in new light.

Not only did the Church move naturally into television broadcasts of Music and the Spoken Word and general conference sessions, but it also entered into what might be characterized as "mainstream media markets." This was done in a variety of ways. Missionary efforts found their way into the print media in 1978 when the Church sponsored special feature inserts in the *Reader's Digest* explaining many of the Church's beliefs and views on the family. These inserts were seen by millions of people around the globe and did much to enhance greater understanding and tolerance of the Church. They created a more positive environment for missionary work.

For the electronic media, the Church's Public Communications department produced award-winning television (and radio) advertisements known as the *Homefront* series. These ads focused on marriage and family relationships and provided practical helps in humorous, yet thought-provoking ways. Numerous inquiries regarding the Church and its beliefs resulted from these popular ads that are still produced. Other television ads were more direct in promoting the Book of Mormon and its further witness of the resurrected Lord. As a result of this campaign, thousands of requests for copies of the Book of Mormon flooded Church headquarters, and numerous referrals were sent to full-time missionaries in many parts of the world.

The missionary reach of the Church through the medium of television also included professionally produced programs such as "Mr. Krueger's Christmas," which starred Hollywood actor Jimmy Stewart, and a film adaptation of O. Henry's "The Last Leaf." The former was shown on network television during the Christmas season and the latter on Easter weekend. Each of these excellent productions ended with an inspirational message regarding the Savior and an invitation to learn more about the Church. The quality as well as the messages of these fine programs piqued great interest in the Church and opened many doors to missionaries.

The 1960s saw the Church becoming involved in what President David O. McKay characterized as "one of the most unique and effective missionary efforts in [the Church's] history."[18] Although the Church had had limited participation or small exhibits in previous world fairs and international expositions, the Mormon Pavilion at the 1964–65 New York City World's Fair was monumental—monumental in its size and beauty, in its immediate missionary success, and especially in its impact on the Church's future use of audiovisual technology and in the development of exhibits and displays for visitors' centers around the world.

"The Pavilion has given us a new vision of missionary work," President Wilburn C. West of the Eastern States Mission reported.[19] Thousands joined the Church as a direct result of visiting this pavilion and numerous other visitors to the pavilion who did not join the Church shared their positive views of Mormonism with friends and neighbors, who in turn opened their doors to missionaries. Missionary referrals obtained at the pavilion were still being used by missionaries around the world a generation later.

Two of the highlights of this pavilion were the film produced by the BYU Motion Picture Studio, *Man's Search for Happiness,* and a replica of the *Christus* statue by Danish sculptor Bertel Thorvaldsen. These, along with other displays and exhibits first used at the New York World's Fair, were subsequently used in new visitors' centers on Temple Square and in other locations, including exhibits and pavilions at other world fairs. Six million visitors to the Mormon Pavilion in New York were introduced to the Church's beliefs and practices, and millions more obtained similar instruction through visitors' centers and other world fair pavilions. In 1970 nearly seven million people from all around the globe visited the Church's pavilion at the Osaka, Japan, World Exposition.[20]

The latter half of the twentieth century will be known not only as the information age for the world in general but also as an important technological information age in taking the gospel to all nations via radio, television, computers, satellites, and publications using means that would have seemed virtually impossible only a generation or two earlier.

In the 1980s the Church also became involved in programming for a new cable television network—VISN (later called the Faith and Values Network). The Tabernacle Choir broadcasts, special programs dealing with improving marriage and family relationships, and Church produced films, such as the dramatic portrayal of the Savior's last days, "Behold the Lamb of God," were all part of that programming. On this network something else was done that had never before been broadcast over mass media. A shortened version of an LDS sacrament meeting—complete with a ward and presiding officers, speakers, and a choir—was broadcast. This was an effective public relations tool, providing an opportunity for those not of our faith to see what a Latter-day Saint worship service is really like and to hear gospel messages taught. These sacrament meeting broadcasts were seen by thousands of people throughout the country.

Among the various lengthened strides in missionary efforts of the Church, there were two remarkable events in recent decades that dwarfed all others in opening doors of nations and touching individual lives. Most members of the Church during this period readily admitted they never would have dreamed that such things would occur in their lifetimes. President Kimball, in general conference and in his travels throughout the world, repeatedly urged "every family, every night and every morning, in family prayer and in secret prayers, too, pray to the Lord to open the doors of other nations so that their people, too, may have the gospel of Jesus Christ."[21] These prayers were answered in a miraculous manner.

In 1978 the Lord revealed that the time had come for all worthy males to hold the priesthood. This opened the doors for proclaiming the gospel in many nations in Africa and made the fulness of gospel blessings available to millions more of God's children throughout the world. This revelation profoundly affected the missionary efforts of the Church and the mission of perfecting the Saints and redeeming the dead. The second event—the 1989 fall of the Iron Curtain, which miraculously opened the doors of many nations in eastern Europe— likewise furthered the three-fold mission of the Church.

Results of the Revelation on the Priesthood

With the internationalization of the Church and the complexities of administering such a dynamic and fast-growing worldwide organization, the challenges resulting from the priesthood restrictions drew the attention of the leaders of the Church. For many years the issue had been discussed at the highest levels and studied intensely. In the early 1960s, President David O. McKay received numerous letters from people in Nigeria and Ghana pleading that missionaries be sent to them and that units of the Church be established in the nations of West Africa. President McKay wrote to these good men and women of Africa urging them to be prayerful and patient but declaring that the time was not yet for the taking of the gospel to Africa. The Church literature that was sent in response to those inquiries became treasured and much used "handbooks" for these faithful people. Although there was no priesthood or official link to the Church, these believing Africans even went so far as to establish their own churches—patterned after what they had read in the Church materials in their possession—often even naming their organizations The Church of Jesus Christ of Latter-day Saints.

Sympathetic to the prayers, faith, and righteousness of black men and women around the globe, many of whom were already members of the Church, President McKay felt the importance and growing urgency of the issue. Yet no change in the policy was immediately forthcoming. In his journal, the prophet noted that this issue was much like the one that faced the early apostles—whether to take the gospel to the gentiles. In like manner, President McKay stated that the issue would only be resolved in the same way—through divine revelation.[22] Indeed, the revelation did come, but not for nearly two decades.

Experiences with the Church leaders and members in South America brought the issue once again to the mind of President Spencer W. Kimball. With the announcement of a temple to be built in São Paulo, Brazil, he recognized the administrative difficulties that local leaders would face in determining who could hold the priesthood and receive temple blessings, considering the almost impossible task of ascertaining ethnicity. This, along with many other concerns, prompted President Kimball to once again have the issue studied and discussed by the Brethren.

The heavens were opened and the revelation came in the Salt Lake Temple to the members of the First Presidency and the Twelve who were there assembled in prayer on 1 June 1978. "There was a hallowed and sanctified atmosphere," President Gordon B. Hinckley recounted. "For me, it felt as if a conduit opened between the heavenly throne and the kneeling, pleading prophet of God who was joined by his Brethren. The Spirit of God was there. And by the power of the Holy Ghost there came to that prophet an assurance that the thing for which he prayed was right, that the time had come, and that now the wondrous blessings of the priesthood should be extended to worthy men everywhere regardless of lineage. Every man in that circle, by the power of the Holy Ghost, knew the same thing."[23]

This historic event brought profound blessings to individuals as well as the entire Church. Perhaps nowhere, however, did this revelation have such dramatic effects—both immediate and long-term— than on the continent of Africa. Soon, missionaries were called to preach the gospel and establish branches in nations long denied that blessing. A decade later there were nearly twenty thousand black members of the Church in Africa.

Not only did this revelation immediately affect the mission of the Church in proclaiming the gospel to the world, but it also aided in the perfecting of the Saints by making temple blessings available to thousands of others who had previously not had the privilege. As important as each of these results of the revelation was, more expansive was the effect even beyond the veil. The blessings of the gospel were made available to millions upon millions of God's children through the latter-day work of redemption of the dead. Prior to that momentous June day in 1978, vicarious temple ordinances could not be performed for a major portion of Heavenly Father's children. The "long awaited day" not only changed the Church but also affected the entire family of God—both in time and eternity.

The Iron Curtain Came Down

At the end of World War II, the largest concentration of Latter-day Saints outside of North America found itself behind the Iron Curtain. Efforts were made to help those Latter-day Saints feel connected to the Church, but it became increasingly difficult as the years of Communist rule rolled on. Not only were the members of the Church in those lands adversely affected by the partition, but missionary efforts were brought to a halt by Communist governments. The Iron Curtain stifled political freedom and religious liberty. Through the 1950s and 60s, only small inroads were made, but efforts by the Church continued. On a rare visit of Church leaders to Saints in eastern bloc countries, Elder Thomas S. Monson of the Quorum of the Twelve Apostles in 1968 promised the East German members: "If you will remain true and faithful to the commandments of God, every blessing any member of the Church enjoys in any other country will be yours."[24] It must have seemed impossible at the time, but little by little, what seemed to be insurmountable roadblocks were miraculously removed by the Lord—each step preparing the way for the next.

Church leaders met with government officials and explained how laws against freedom of travel to the West made it impossible for entire families to go to the temple in Switzerland. The discussions led to a surprising governmental decision: "build a temple here!" At the October 1982 general conference, it was announced that a temple "behind the Iron Curtain" would be built in Freiberg, East Germany.[25] The next miracle occurred in 1988 when President Monson and Elder Russell M. Nelson once again met with government officials and obtained permission for missionaries from the German Democratic Republic to serve as full-time missionaries abroad, as well as for full-time missionaries from outside East Germany to come to that land to spread the gospel. In other Communist countries, similar efforts by various leaders and Church representatives were also proving fruitful as the groundwork was slowly, but surely, being laid for a dramatic new era of missionary work.

Then, to the amazement of millions of television viewers around the world, the Berlin Wall was opened on 9 November 1989, heralding the dismantling of the Iron Curtain and announcing a new age of freedom. "We have witnessed in the past few weeks, and particularly in recent days, miracles undreamed of only a short time ago," President Gordon B. Hinckley declared at the 1989 First Presidency Christmas Fireside. "The shackles of enslavement are falling. The ruthless atheism that in some areas has hung as a cloud of darkness for decades is now being dissipated."[26]

Within months the Church was preparing missionaries and establishing missions in countries that had earlier been part of or under the control of the former Soviet Union. In 1990 the Church received official recognition in the Russian Republic. By the mid-1990s full-time missionaries were serving in fifteen newly created missions in countries reaching from central Europe to Siberia. Thousands joined the Church, and scores of branches were established. As Daniel prophesied, the small stone cut out of the mountain without hands was, indeed, beginning to fill the earth.

REDEEMING THE DEAD

The latter half of the twentieth century is often characterized as the "information age" due to the many technological advances and modern inventions that are blessing humanity with greater access to information and knowledge than ever before. The mission of the Church has also benefitted from this age of technology. Speaking of how satellites, computers, and other advanced technologies are furthering the work of the Church, Elder M. Russell Ballard declared: "I happen to believe these things have been inspired and created for the building of the kingdom of God. If others use them, that's fine, but their basic purpose is to help spread the gospel."[27] Perhaps nowhere have these modern technological innovations aided the mission of the Church more than in the area of family history.

Temples to Dot the Earth

"One of our greatest responsibilities," President David O. McKay declared in the April 1954 general conference, "is to make accessible to faithful members of the Church in foreign lands suitable Houses of the Lord. Tens of thousands of them are not able to come where temples are. . . . Ours is the duty to carry the temple to them."[28] Thus began the greatest era of temple building in the history of the Church to that time. And it was not just the number of temples that were to be built that blessed the Saints but also the use of technology within the walls of the temples.

In late 1953 President David O. McKay gave Gordon B. Hinckley an assignment that would transform the way temple work was done in the Church. "As you know, we are building a temple in Switzerland," President McKay stated, "and it will be different from our other temples in that it must serve members who speak many languages. I want you to find a way to present the temple instruction in the various languages of Europe while using a minimum number of temple workers."[29] Brother Hinckley's response to this challenge resulted in an innovative method of presenting the temple ceremony through the use of film with simultaneous translations into several languages. This inspired innovation, which is now used in all the temples except Salt Lake and Manti, expedited the work and made the blessings of temple worship available to many more faithful Saints.

President McKay's vision of taking temples to the members around the world began to be fulfilled in the late 1950s with the dedication of the first "overseas" temples in England, Switzerland, and New Zealand. The pace of temple building quickened in the 1960s and 70s with the building of temples in Oakland, California; Ogden and Provo, Utah; and Washington, D.C. As prophets had long promised, temples were truly beginning to "dot the earth."[30]

Even as these temples were being built, the leaders of the Church were seriously pondering how more temples could be built in many more places in order to bless many more members. As the new Washington D.C. Temple was being built, Elder Gordon B. Hinckley, who was serving as the chairman of the Temple Committee, mused about what more could be done. He wrote in his journal: "Are not the saints in South America . . . as worthy of the blessings of the temple as the people in Washington?" His journal later records an idea that he was wrestling with. "The Church could build [many smaller] temples for the cost of the Washington Temple [then under construction]. It would take the temples to the people instead of having the people travel great distances to get to them."[31]

This idea became reality beginning in the late 1970s and into the 1990s. Between 1974 and 1995 the number of temples dramatically increased from sixteen to forty-seven. In 1974 there were only three overseas temples—in England, Switzerland, and New Zealand. By 1995, however, there were an additional twenty temples "dotting" the earth—spanning the globe from Polynesia to Asia, South Africa, Australia, and Europe, as well as Mexico and Central and South America. This era of temple building throughout the world was but a prelude to even more dramatic expansion.

After President Gordon B. Hinckley, who had years earlier pondered the possibility of many small temples, became the president of the Church, he announced an almost immediate doubling of the number of temples, even smaller temples in more outlying areas of the Church. This development came as a result of revelation that had come through a prophet's earnest pleadings with the Lord and the faith of Saints around the world. "I believe that no member of the Church has received the ultimate which this Church has to give until he or she has received his or her temple blessings in the house of the Lord." President Hinckley declared:

"Accordingly, we are doing all that we know how to do to expedite the construction of these sacred buildings and make the blessings received therein more generally available.

"But there are many areas of the Church that are remote, where the membership is small and not likely to grow very much in the near future. Are those who live in these places to be denied forever the blessings of the temple ordinances? While visiting such an area a few months ago, we prayerfully pondered this question. The answer, we believe, came bright and clear."[32]

He then proceeded to announce where these many temples would be built and how they would be operated and maintained by the local leaders and members. This announcement was greeted with both joy and amazement by Saints throughout the world. Only a decade or two earlier, the membership of the Church could scarcely have imagined a hundred temples in operation around the globe by the end of this century.[33]

Technological Advances Aid Genealogical Research

In 1894 the Genealogical Society was founded "to establish and maintain a Genealogical Library . . . ; to teach members how to compile acceptable family records and to trace their pedigrees; and to foster temple ordinances."[34] Perhaps no one at the time could have imagined the means by which family history would be conducted or how expansive such work would be a century later. At the end of World War II, after months of negotiations with government and religious leaders, the Genealogical Society obtained permission to microfilm records in many countries in Europe. In the 1960s and 1970s, the work of microfilming was expanded significantly into many more countries of Europe, as well as into Asia, Latin America, and the South Pacific. Microfilm technology allowed the Church to open branch genealogical libraries where local Saints could access many of the same resources that were housed in Salt Lake City.[35] Temples were being brought to the Saints around the world, along with the means whereby members of the Church could engage more productively in family history work.

From the microfilmed records, names of deceased people were identified through the Church's extraction program. Millions of names of people, extracted from records unavailable only decades earlier, were gleaned and prepared to receive vicarious temple ordinances. Nearly 90 percent of all the names submitted for temple work in the 1980s came from the extraction program. In time, computer technology revolutionized the entire field of genealogical research. In 1994 Elder Russell M. Nelson of the Quorum of the Twelve Apostles reported that "2,150 busy and productive family history centers have been established throughout the world.

"For example, the FamilySearch Center in the Joseph Smith Memorial Building has served hundreds of thousands of visitors, at least two-thirds of whom have found something in the computer file about their ancestors.

"More than 300,000 copies of the Church's computer program Personal Ancestral File™ are used in libraries and homes by many hundreds of thousands of people. Our FamilySearch program is used by millions of genealogical researchers throughout the world, most of whom are not members of our church. TempleReady™ allows convenient and almost immediate clearance by personal computer of names for temple ordinances that formerly required much time and labor."[36]

The information age of the last half of the twentieth century provided the Church with means whereby millions of God's children were able to receive the ordinances of the temple. In 1988 the one hundred millionth vicarious endowment for the dead was performed. Approximately 90 percent of all of the temple ordinances for the dead performed in all the temples of the Church have been done since 1951.[37] To make these family history resources available to an even wider audience—both in and out of the Church—an official family history website was launched in May 1999; *www.family-search.org* became one of the most popular sites on the Internet, receiving one hundred million hits from all over the world on its second official day of service.[38]

Accentuating the urgency of this mission of the Church to redeem the dead, two previously received revelations—Joseph Smith's vision of the celestial kingdom and Joseph F. Smith's vision of the redemption of the dead"—were canonized in 1976 and subsequently included in the Doctrine and Covenants as sections 137 and 138 in the 1981 edition. New revelations had not been added to the standard works for nearly a century. This monumental event profoundly testified of the merciful plan of salvation that makes the gospel available to all on both sides of the veil. The messages of these two great visions reminded the entire Church that, as the Prophet Joseph Smith declared, "Their salvation is necessary and essential to our salvation," and our deceased loved ones cannot be made perfect without our labors in their behalf (see D&C 128:15). From an eternal perspective, the information age will be hailed as much more than an era of technology. It has been and will continue to be an unprecedented era of salvation of the souls of men.

PERFECTING THE SAINTS

The Church has experienced remarkable growth in numbers during the last several decades, but perhaps even more important has been the spiritual growth in the lives of its members. This increased spirituality of the Church and the strength of its various units throughout the world was due in large part to important organizational changes, renewed doctrinal emphases, and inspired program enhancements revealed during this time period. These combined efforts to assist in the mission of perfecting the Saints blessed individual members of the Church with strengthened testimonies of the gospel, increased knowledge of the scriptures, and fortified homes with a renewed emphasis on the home as "the place to save society."[39]

Family Home Evening

President Joseph F. Smith in 1915 had urged all families in the Church to hold home evening so that "fathers and mothers may gather their boys and girls about them in the home and teach them the word of the Lord."[40] Although Church leaders on several occasions referred to President Smith's admonition and advised families to adopt some form of family home evening, there was no formal churchwide program as such until 1965 when President McKay announced a formalized family home evening that was to be an integral part of the "priesthood program of teaching and living the gospel in the home." The family home evening manual was a major resource in this program and was complemented by lessons in Relief Society and the Melchizedek Priesthood Quorums.

"The home is the basis of a righteous life, and no other instrumentality can take its place nor fulfill its essential functions," President McKay wrote in the preface of the Church's first official family home evening manual. "The problems of these difficult times cannot better be solved in any other place, by any other agency, by any other means, than by love and righteousness, and precept and example, and devotion to duty in the home."[41] The family home evening program became institutionalized with subsequent manuals published and distributed each year. Many years later when the Church stopped producing a yearly manual, the *Family Home Evening Resource Book* was prepared, along with an accompanying video that supplemented the lessons and ideas included in the manual. Family home evening became even more entrenched as an official program of the Church in 1971 when the First Presidency designated Monday evenings as the time for these family gatherings and advised that no other Church activities were to be scheduled on that night.[42]

Consolidated Meeting Schedule

In February 1980 the First Presidency announced another major modification to existing Church programs in an effort to strengthen the family and increase personal spirituality. The Sunday meeting schedule of the Church was consolidated into a three-hour block. In a letter to stake presidencies and bishoprics the First Presidency declared: "The purpose of the consolidated meeting is (1) to reemphasize personal and family responsibility for learning, living, and teaching the gospel and (2) to allow Church members more time for personal gospel study, for service to others, and for meaningful activities."[43]

At the very core of this important change was the family. The flexibility of meeting schedules and freeing of time was intended to increase home-centered Sabbath activities that would strengthen personal testimonies and bring families closer to each other—to "help every Latter-day Saint home become a place where family members love to be."[44]

A decade later another major policy change had far-reaching effects on the Church, but none more important than its effect on the home. The change in the budget policies allowed the activities and operating expenses of local units to be paid out of the general tithes and offerings of the Church rather than locally raised budget funds. While it seemed on the surface to be merely a financial or temporal matter, "The effect of it will be spiritual," Elder Boyd K. Packer prophesied.

"This change in budgeting will have the effect of returning much of the responsibility for teaching and counseling and activity to the family where it belongs. While there will still be many activities, they will be scaled down in cost of both time and money. There will be fewer intrusions into family schedules and in the family purses.

"Church activities must be replaced by family activities. Just as we have been taught with temporal affairs, the spirit of independence, thrift, and self-reliance will be reenthroned as guiding principles in the homes of Latter-day Saints."[45]

With all of the emphasis on the home, both in program and policies as well as teachings from the pulpit, the Church ensured that the parents were not left alone in their sacred responsibilities. Many other resources came from the Church in the latter half of the century to complement the family and to spiritually strengthen the individual.

Priesthood Correlation

One of the most significant developments in the history of the Church, although one that is not well known or understood, was the priesthood correlation work of the 1960s. President Harold B. Lee was probably the most influential figure in this development. His efforts, along with those of other brethren, began shortly after World War II, but were not fully brought to fruition until the mid-1960s. The three specific areas of priesthood correlation—priesthood home teaching, a coordinated curriculum for the classes and quorums of the Church, and the simplification of Church programs to focus on what would best further the mission of the Church—were designed to strengthen homes and increase the spirituality of the Saints. "Priesthood correlation is that system of church administration in which we take all the programs of the Church," taught Elder Bruce R. McConkie, and "wrap them in one package, operate them as one program, involve all members of the Church in the operation—and do it all under priesthood direction." He further explained: "The basic principles of priesthood correlation grow out of this statement: The family is the most important organization in time or in eternity. The Church and all its organizations are service agencies to help families and individuals. Home teachers represent the Lord, the bishop, and the priesthood leader in making available to the family and the individual the help of the Church and all its organizations."[46]

The Priesthood home teaching program, which came out of the developments in Correlation of the 1960s, replaced earlier programs such as "block teaching" and "ward teaching." Similarly, in earlier years the various organizations and auxiliaries of the Church had had their own magazines and courses of study. Correlation brought all of these independent efforts under one united head, all working together to meet the spiritual aims of the Church. In 1971 three new Church magazines were published under the supervision of the general authorities—*Ensign* for adults, *New Era* for youth, and *Friend* for children.

Also during this time a coordinated Sunday School curriculum was developed that made each volume of scripture a course of study for the year. Similarly, there came greater correlation between the

Melchizedek Priesthood study guides and the Relief Society study manuals—eventually culminating in the 1990s with even more coordinated lesson materials for children, youth, and adults. All of this was to complement and unify the family in worship and gospel study.

New Edition of the Scriptures

In 1979 the Church published a new English edition of the King James Version of the Holy Bible. This monumental undertaking yielded a volume that contained not only the Bible, but also a five-hundred-page Topical Guide, a uniquely LDS Bible Dictionary, and an enhanced system of footnotes and cross-references that linked the Bible with all the other standard works. In 1981 the new edition of the triple combination—Book of Mormon, Doctrine and Covenants, and Pearl of Great Price—was published with similar helps and reference guides.

This significant project was first approved by President Harold B. Lee and subsequently directed by President Spencer W. Kimball, who assigned three members of the Quorum of the Twelve Apostles to serve as the Scripture Publication Committee—Elders Thomas S. Monson, Boyd K. Packer, and Bruce R. McConkie. Numerous other scholars and experts both from within the Church and without assisted in this inspired task.

"During the last twenty years I have had a variety of assignments," Elder Packer stated at the completion of the project. "I have regarded all of them with respect. Some very few I have regarded with deep reverence. One of these has been the assignment to have something to do with the publication of the scriptures." Elder Packer further stated the value of these new scriptures went far beyond just convenience or even increased scholarship: "This exertion is a monumental protection and preservation for the Church and kingdom of God upon the earth. I bear my humble witness that the inspiration of the Almighty has attended this—that we have not been alone."[47]

Growing out of the publication of the new editions of the scriptures came many other developments to bless the Church and make all the curricula more scripture based. These included the restructuring of all the lesson materials in the Church and the translation and publication of scriptures and other materials in the languages of the world. The effect of these new scriptures went far beyond just classrooms and quorum discussion. They would assist in raising up a new generation who would love and use the scriptures more than ever before and in turn be blessed with greater spiritual power and protection. "As the generations roll on," Elder Packer declared, "this will be regarded, in the perspective of history, as the crowning achievement in the administration of President Spencer W. Kimball."[48]

The Old Testament prophet Ezekiel prophesied of two sticks, or records—a stick of Judah and a stick of Joseph—that would someday come together and become "one stick; and they shall become one in thine hand" (Ezekiel 37:17). Latter-day Saints have long seen that prophecy as concerning the coming forth of the Book of Mormon. With the new edition of the scriptures, however, the stick of Judah and the stick of Joseph are, as Elder Packer testified, "now woven together in such a way that as you read one, you are drawn to the other; as you learn from one, you are enlightened by the other. They are indeed one in our hands. Ezekiel's prophecy now stands fulfilled."[49]

The Power of the Book of Mormon

With the publication of the new editions of the standard works and the renewed emphasis on scripture study, the Church was on the verge of yet another great blessing and another lengthening of our collective and individual strides. In March 1986 in a meeting of the general authorities, President Ezra Taft Benson told them that he had felt moved upon by the Holy Spirit in a manner similar to the way President Lorenzo Snow had felt when he declared to the Church the need to be more faithful in paying tithing. President Benson declared the Lord was inspiring him to preach the need to return to the Book of Mormon as "the keystone of our religion." At the solemn assembly where he was sustained as the newly ordained president of the Church, President Benson prophetically declared:

"Unless we read the Book of Mormon and give heed to its teachings, the Lord has stated in section 84 of the Doctrine and Covenants that the whole Church is under condemnation: 'And this condemnation resteth upon the children of Zion, even all.' (V. 56.) The Lord continues: 'And they shall remain under this condemnation until they repent and remember the new covenant, even the Book of Mormon and the former commandments which I have given them,

not only to say, but to do according to that which I have written.'
(V. 57.)

"Now we not only need to *say* more about the Book of Mormon,
but we need to *do* more with it. Why? The Lord answers, 'That
they may bring forth fruit meet for their Father's kingdom; otherwise there remaineth a scourge and judgment to be poured out upon
the children of Zion.' (V. 58.) We have felt that scourge and judgment! . . .

"The Book of Mormon has not been, nor is it yet, the center of our
personal study, family teaching, preaching, and missionary work. Of
this we must repent."[50]

Throughout his entire administration, President Benson emphasized the need to study from the Book of Mormon, to teach and
counsel our families from the Book of Mormon, and to use it more
in our Church callings and assignments. Only by doing this, he
taught, could the spiritual scourge and condemnation be lifted. As
the members of the Church responded to his prophetic pleadings,
blessings were realized—both institutionally and individually.
Increased spirituality resulted. Vital principles of the plan of salvation were understood through a more intense examination of the
Book of Mormon. Homes and families, as well as classes and quorums, were blessed by the renewed emphasis on the Book of
Mormon.

"It is not just that the Book of Mormon teaches us truth, though it
indeed does that," President Benson declared. "It is not just that the
Book of Mormon bears testimony of Christ, though it indeed does
that too. But there is something more. There is a power in the book
which will begin to flow into your lives the moment you begin a serious study of the book. You will find greater power to resist tempta-
tion. You will find the power to avoid deception."[51]

Everywhere President Benson spoke, he emphasized the power of
the Book of Mormon. His administration, with all of its many accomplishments, will be forever remembered, not only for his teachings
and testimony of the Book of Mormon, but also for the outpouring
of blessings that the Church enjoyed during this period. At the conclusion of the April 1986 general conference, President Benson pro-
nounced an apostolic blessing, a prophetic promise, upon the
Church:

"Now, in the authority of the sacred priesthood in me vested, I invoke my blessing upon the Latter-day Saints and upon good people everywhere.

"I bless you with increased discernment to judge between Christ and anti-Christ. I bless you with increased power to do good and to resist evil. I bless you with increased *understanding* of the Book of Mormon. I promise you that from this moment forward, if we will daily sup from its pages and abide by its precepts, God will pour out upon each child of Zion and the Church a blessing hitherto unknown—and we will plead to the Lord that He will begin to lift the condemnation—the scourge and judgment."[52]

Perhaps millions of members could testify, in their own personal way, how President Benson's blessing was realized in their own lives. Speaking in October 1986 general conference, Elder Henry B. Eyring reflected the feelings of the Saints, when he declared: "I bear my testimony that I have been blessed as [President Benson] promised, and I have seen new blessings come to people I love. I am grateful that God honors the promises he makes through his prophet."[53]

Whether it be structural changes, program innovations, the new editions of the scriptures, or any number of developments that characterize the latter half of the twentieth century, we have witnessed the opening of the windows of heaven in remarkable ways. We live in a day of almost continual fulfillment of what the Prophet Joseph Smith simply, yet profoundly, declared in the ninth article of faith: "We believe all that God has revealed, all that He does now reveal, and we believe that He will yet reveal many great and important things pertaining to the Kingdom of God."

When one looks back on the history of the Church since 1951, it is easy to be amazed at what has occurred—the unparalleled growth, the international expansion, the increased numbers of missionaries and temples, program and organizational enhancements, and new revelations and new scriptures. Each of these is miraculous in its own way. But, singly or collectively, they cannot fully explain the strength of the Church in these decades. They are but outward manifestations of something far greater—the real miracle of the latter-day restoration.

"The remarkable progress of this church is not so much the result of the requirements of the Church upon its members," President

Gordon B. Hinckley testified, "as it is the result of the conviction in the hearts of those members that this is in very deed the work of God, and that happiness and peace and satisfaction are found in righteous service." Truly, the strength of the Church is found in individual testimonies, personal spirituality, and faithful obedience to the commandments of God. This is a latter-day miracle that has resulted in growth that, as President Hinckley described, "is truly astounding . . . and what we have seen is but a foretaste of greater things yet to come."[54]

NOTES

1. Boyd K. Packer, in Conference Report, October 1989, 19.

2. Spencer W. Kimball, in Conference Report, April 1981, 3.

3. Conference Report, April 1959, 122.

4. Spencer W. Kimball, "Always a Convert Church," *Ensign,* September 1975, 3.

5. Sheri L. Dew, *Go Forward with Faith: The Biography of Gordon B. Hinckley* (Salt Lake City: Deseret Book, 1996), 267.

6. Spencer W. Kimball, "When the World Will Be Converted," *Ensign,* October 1974, 8.

7. Spencer W. Kimball, *The Teachings of Spencer W. Kimball,* ed. Edward L. Kimball (Salt Lake City: Bookcraft, 1982), 550.

8. Kimball, "When the World Will Be Converted," 7.

9. Spencer W. Kimball, "Advice to a Young Man: Now Is the Time to Prepare," *New Era,* June 1973, 8–9.

10. Richard O. Cowan, *The Church in the Twentieth Century* (Salt Lake City: Bookcraft, 1985), 283–86.

11. "Satellite MTCs," *Ensign,* December 1979, 63.

12. Spencer W. Kimball, "It Becometh Every Man," *Ensign,* October 1977, 7.

13. Ibid., 6.

14. M. Russell Ballard, "Write Down a Date," *Ensign,* November 1984, 15–17.

15. "The Family-to-Family Book of Mormon Program," *Ensign,* May 1987, 101–2.

16. Ezra Taft Benson, "Flooding the Earth with the Book of Mormon," *Ensign,* November 1988, 4–6.

17. Ezra Taft Benson, *The Teachings of Ezra Taft Benson* (Salt Lake City: Bookcraft, 1988), 72.

18. Richard J. Marshall, "The New York World's Fair—A Final Report," *Improvement Era*, December 1965, 1170.

19. Ibid.

20. Gerald Joseph Peterson, "History of Mormon Exhibits in World Expositions," Master's thesis, Brigham Young University, 1974.

21. Kimball, *Teachings of Spencer W. Kimball*, 586.

22. Francis M. Gibbons, *Spencer W. Kimball: Resolute Disciple, Prophet of God* (Salt Lake City: Deseret Book, 1995), 292–93.

23. Gordon B. Hinckley, "Priesthood Restoration," *Ensign*, October 1988, 70.

24. Thomas S. Monson, in Conference Report, April 1989, 65–69.

25. "Temple Approved, First Stake Created in German Democratic Republic," *Ensign*, November 1982, 102–3; Thomas S. Monson, "Thanks Be to God," *Ensign*, May 1989, 51.

26. "European Reform Called Gift to World," *Deseret News*, 4 December1989; "A Season of Love That Is Felt Anew," *Church News*, 9 December 1989, 3.

27. "Elder Ballard Is Busy, Always Well-Organized," *Church News*, 8 March 1980, 4.

28. "President McKay's Conference Address," *Church News*, 10 April 1954, 3.

29. Dew, *Go Forward with Faith*, 176.

30. President Brigham Young declared in 1856: "To accomplish this work there will have to be not only one temple, but thousands of them" (*Journal of Discourses*, 26 vols. [London: Latter-day Saints' Book Depot, 1854–56], 3:394). In 1906 President Joseph F. Smith prophesied that not only would there be a temple in Europe someday, but the time would come when temples would be built "in diverse countries of the earth" (translated from *Der Stern*, 19 August 1906, 332). Elder Bruce R. McConkie stated, "We expect to see the day when temples will dot the earth" (*The Millennial Messiah* [Salt Lake City: Deseret Book, 1982], 277).

31. Dew, *Go Forward with Faith*, 325.

32. Gordon B. Hinckley, in Conference Report, October 1997, 68.

33. By the end of 1999 there were 115 temples in operation, under construction, or announced.

34. Archibald F. Bennett, "The Genealogical Society of Utah," *Improvement Era*, April 1935, 225.

35. Richard O. Cowan, *Temples to Dot the Earth* (Salt Lake City: Bookcraft, 1989), 211–17.

36. Russell M. Nelson, in Conference Report, October 1994, 114.

37. Cowan, *Temples to Dot the Earth*, 218–19.

38. "Today We Are Taking a Historic Step," *Church News*, 29 May

1999, 3; "Wide Publicity Given to New Family History Website," *Church News*, 5 June 1999, 6.

39. Spencer W. Kimball, "Home: The Place to Save Society," *Ensign*, January 1975, 2–10.

40. James R. Clark, comp., *Messages of the First Presidency*, 6 vols. (Salt Lake City: Bookcraft, 1965–75), 4:338–39.

41. David O. McKay, cited in *Family Home Evening Manual* (Salt Lake City: Corporation of the President of The Church of Jesus Christ of Latter-day Saints, 1965), iii.

42. "Mondays Slated for Family Home Evenings," *Church News*, 10 October 1970, 3.

43. Spencer W. Kimball, Nathan Eldon Tanner, and Marion G. Romney.

44. "Church Consolidates Meeting Schedules," *Ensign*, March 1980, 73.

45. Boyd K. Packer, "Teach Them Correct Principles," *Ensign*, May 1990, 89–90.

46. Bruce R. McConkie, "Let Every Man Learn His Duty—The Ten Commandments of Priesthood Correlation and the Home Teaching Constitution" (Salt Lake City: Deseret Book, 1976), 2.

47. Lucille C. Tate, *Boyd K. Packer: A Watchman on the Tower* (Salt Lake City: Bookcraft, 1995), 213–15.

48. Boyd K. Packer, in Conference Report, October 1982, 75.

49. Ibid.; see also Boyd K. Packer, "Using the New Scriptures," *Ensign*, December 1985, 53.

50. Ezra Taft Benson, "Cleansing the Inner Vessel," *Ensign*, May 1986, 5–6.

51. Benson, *Teachings of Ezra Taft Benson*, 54.

52. Ezra Taft Benson, in Conference Report, April 1986, 100.

53. Henry B. Eyring, in Conference Report, October 1986, 94.

54. Gordon B. Hinckley, *Teachings of Gordon B. Hinckley* (Salt Lake City: Deseret Book, 1997), 98–99.

CHAPTER FOUR

EZRA TAFT BENSON: THE EISENHOWER YEARS

REED A. BENSON

The service of Elder Ezra Taft Benson of the Quorum of the Twelve Apostles in the Cabinet of the president of the United States brought more favorable and widespread publicity to the Church than it had received in any previous eight-year period in its history. This Cabinet position was the highest government office ever held by a member of the Church up to that time. Near the end of 1952, when president-elect Dwight D. Eisenhower invited Elder Ezra Taft Benson of the Council of the Twelve to serve as secretary of agriculture, President David O. McKay encouraged Elder Benson to accept the offer if it was made "in the proper spirit."[1] He did accept, and he became one of only two Cabinet members who served the full two terms of the Eisenhower administration.

Elder Benson was heralded across the nation in the news media as the first clergyman in a century to serve in the Cabinet. President David O. McKay said, "The appointment is a distinct honor to him and one he will fill with credit to himself and to the nation. We are happy that a prominent member of the Church has received this position."[2]

Secretary Benson testified before congressional committees repeatedly, was interviewed extensively, held press conferences frequently, traveled widely, and spoke often. His books *Farmers at the Crossroads*, *Freedom to Farm*, and *Crossfire: My Eight Years with Eisenhower*, published by Doubleday, tell where he stood and what he did about it.

Reed A. Benson is a professor of ancient scripture at Brigham Young University.

Near the close of his tenure, a selection of his addresses covering home, Church, and country as well as agriculture was published under the title *So Shall Ye Reap*. Former United States president Herbert Hoover wrote the foreword and Elder Harold B. Lee of the Council of the Twelve Apostles wrote the introduction.

Ezra Taft Benson's broad visibility as a world leader of The Church of Jesus Christ of Latter-day Saints in combination with his fine example and principled stand in a very controversial political role resulted in widespread favorable media coverage. That coverage blessed the Church as well as the nation and had worldwide ramifications for good. His influence touched the lives of many he met, including heads of state, and prepared the way for missionary work on a broad scale.

TOUGH TASK

His selection as secretary of agriculture was greeted with approbation. There was universal agreement on one thing—Benson knew agriculture. The position would be the "hot seat" in Washington.[3] Immediately after Secretary Benson's swearing in, President Eisenhower remarked, "Welcome to a tough assignment."[4] Farm prices were going down; surpluses were building up. One Cabinet member commented, "Every night when I go to bed I thank God I'm not the Secretary of Agriculture."[5] Times were so difficult that it was predicted Secretary Benson would be the first cabinet officer to resign. "Elder Benson's Going to Catch It" was the caption of a *Saturday Evening Post* article on 28 March 1953. The subtitle said, in part, "Ez is a pious man, a high priest of the Mormons."[6]

Eisenhower was right—this was indeed going to be a tough task.

IN GOD WE TRUST

Elder Benson believed that "except the Lord build the house, they labour in vain that build it" (Psalm 127:1). Therefore, at the first preinaugural Cabinet meeting, he felt impressed to ask Eisenhower if it might not be fitting to begin Cabinet meetings with prayer. Eisenhower called on Elder Benson for that first prayer. When there was no prayer at the next cabinet meeting, Secretary Benson wrote the president, pleading for prayer. Eisenhower considered the matter, and prayer was offered in every one of the more than two hundred

Cabinet meetings held during the ensuing eight years.[7] Staff members took their turns offering prayer in Secretary Benson's staff meetings.

When a lengthy drought hit the Southwest, Secretary Benson suggested to the governor of Texas a day of fasting and prayer for rain. Within three days a two-inch rainfall came, prompting a local paper to say that Secretary Benson "has contacts that are literally out of this world."[8] The *New York Times Magazine* ran a long article entitled "Benson: Prayer, Persuasion and Parity."[9] The *Reader's Digest* issue of November 1954 carried an article on prayer by Secretary Benson, entitled "The Best Advice I Ever Had."

TELLING THE TRUTH

Secretary Benson believed that to sit by in silence when the truth should be told makes cowards of men. To that end, he held hundreds of press conferences—more than any other cabinet member—issuing statements and submitting himself to questions. At his first press conference he distributed his "General Statement on Agricultural Policy." The opening line read, "The supreme test of any government policy, agricultural or other, should be 'How will it affect the character, morale, and well-being of our people?'" It went on to talk about God-given freedom and then stated, "A completely planned and subsidized economy weakens initiative, discourages industry, destroys character, and demoralizes the people."[10]

He faced the continual grillings of congressional committees, some of which were fierce. Always he maintained composure and dignity. At least three times he addressed the National Press Club. He delivered thousands of speeches—some to only a handful of farmers, others to as many as sixty-five thousand.[11] He appeared on numerous radio and television shows, such as *Meet the Press*.

He believed that truth, if given sufficient time and coverage, fares well. He spoke from knowledge and with courage.

CHARACTER COUNTS

At the beginning of his administration, the *Farm Journal* reported, "Ezra Benson is going to shock Washington. He's in the habit of deciding everything on principle."[12]

It didn't take long for Washington to learn that Secretary Benson

was a man of convictions who was willing to fight for them. Friend
and foe alike admired his stand for principle. He was like a breath of
fresh air among the politically expedient. He said, "I refuse to believe
that what is right is *not* good politics."[13] A *Life* Magazine editorial put
it this way: "The politicians have been complaining . . . Benson is no
politician, which may mean he is qualifying for higher honors."[14]

The *New York Times Magazine,* in an article entitled, "The Benson
Formula for Serenity," explained the Secretary's inner calm: "One reason is his religion. . . . He acts like a man whose conscience is always
clear."[15]

During one of Secretary Benson's several battles with the White
House staff, the chief of staff told Secretary Benson's team to get off
their "puritanical white horse." Later, the same man wrote that Ezra
was "rugged and right."[16]

"Farmers Like a Man Who Stands by His Convictions" was the
caption of a 2 June 1958 *Life* Magazine article quoting Secretary
Benson. "Don't Let Unpopularity Scare You" was the title of an article
he wrote for *This Week* magazine, dated 17 August 1958. Broadcaster
Paul Harvey wrote, "Ezra Benson is a rare man in politics, thoroughly
sincere, uncompromising, and above all, a good man."[17]

Secretary Benson's actions did not go unnoticed in the Church.
President David O. McKay declared to the Council of the Twelve:
"Only the present responsibilities of the President himself exceed
those which Brother Benson is carrying. . . . Out of it all stands before
the American people Brother Benson's integrity and honesty of purpose . . . and in that declaration and radiant manifestation of character he has brought great credit to himself, the Council, and the
Church."[18]

SPREADING THE WORD

A Mormon apostle dealing with farming issues in terms of individual responsibility, integrity, and freedom soon caught the attention of the national news media. On *Time* magazine's 13 April 1953
front cover was a picture of Secretary Benson along with his statement: "No real American wants to be subsidized." Only once before
had a Mormon leader been on *Time's* cover—President George Albert
Smith in 1947. Secretary Benson was also on the front covers of
U.S. News & World Report, Newsweek, New York Times Magazine, and

numerous other magazines. He also appeared later on another front cover of *Time*.

The news media picked up on the principled and consistent fight he was waging and gave him increased recognition and support. "Bravo, Cousin Ezra! He Promises a Sane New Day for Agriculture," declared the front page of *Barron's* 16 February 1953 issue. "Respect Comes the Hard Way" was *Life* magazine's caption of the same date. "Hold On, Ezra, Help's Coming," cried the *Richmond News Leader* of 21 February 1953. A *Time* magazine article was entitled "Apostle at Work."[19] And *Collier's* editorial, with a sketch of Secretary Benson weathering the waves, was entitled "Benson Turns a Tide."[20]

FAMILY FOCUS

Ed Murrow had a very popular nationally televised weekly program called *Person to Person*. The television cameras visited celebrities, who conducted the viewers on a tour of their homes. Murrow approached Secretary Benson to be on the show, but in place of the tour, Murrow agreed to let the family put on a Mormon family home evening. Family members displayed talents, sang "Love at Home," and answered questions. They made comments on missionary work, individual and family prayer, chores, and family fun.

Several million viewers watched, and the mail poured in. United Press International reported that the show featuring the Benson family brought Murrow "more fan mail than any other in history."[21]

Secretary Benson's wife, Flora, hosted at her home a luncheon for the wives of the president, vice-president, and the members of the Cabinet. She and her daughters prepared the meal themselves. There were no cocktails, tea, coffee, or playing cards. "We'll try to make it up to you in our way," she said. And she did. The family provided entertainment along with the BYU Madrigal Singers, a group in which daughter Barbara was a soloist. Afterwards, Mamie Eisenhower wrote of "the atmosphere of peace and love abiding" in the home that "made all of us come away with a deep feeling of joy."[22]

Mrs. Benson was honored by the National Home Fashions League as Homemaker of the Year. Mamie Eisenhower, from her hospital bed, expressed her pleasure at the honor Mrs. Benson received.

The following are typical headlines dealing with the Benson family during the Eisenhower years:

"Christian Science Monitor Praises Wife of Secretary" (*Church News,* 21 February 1953).

"The Benson Family Shows Why a Nation Is As Strong As Its Home" (*NEA News Page,* New York, 9 and 11 July, 1954).

"The Benson Formula: Give Each Child a Vote" (*Parade Magazine,* 2 January 1955).

"Busy Ezra Benson Sets Aside One Night a Week for His Six Children" (*Boston Sunday Globe,* 17 June 1956).

DUTY, HONOR, COUNTRY

Like a good scout, Secretary Benson did his duty to God and his country. The Boy Scouts of America honored him with their highest awards: the Silver Beaver, Antelope, and Buffalo. Later he received world scouting's highest award—the Bronze Wolf.

Universities across the country from Maine to Hawaii bestowed upon him honorary doctoral degrees. The Italian government gave him Italy's highest decoration, the High Cross of the Order of Merit of the Italian Republic.

During the Hungarian Revolution of 1956, Secretary Benson expressed his anguish over the lack of support from the United States for the Hungarian fighters for freedom. He drafted a blistering statement responding to "Russia's brutality," and President Eisenhower used the statement with only minor changes.[23]

From his agricultural attachés in Cuba, Secretary Benson learned of Fidel Castro's communistic connections. He alerted the State Department to this fact at the very same time Castro was being glamorized in the media as a "Cuban patriot" and "decidedly anti-communist."[24]

MEETING WORLD LEADERS

Secretary Benson traveled the world extensively, visiting more than forty countries to promote American agriculture exports and good will.[25] In his first three years, he logged more than three hundred thousand miles—more than any other Cabinet member except the secretary of state.[26]

His national stature put him in contact with premiers, presidents, kings, and rulers, along with ministers of agriculture, ambassadors, and the news media. His position and respectability gained him access to government leaders at the highest level, opening doors for future missionary work and providing opportunities for gospel discussions and the distribution of the Book of Mormon to many, including heads of state.

He met with numerous leaders of Central and South America. Among the many other world leaders he met with were Premier Khrushchev of the Soviet Union, King Hussein of Jordan, President Tito of Yugoslavia, Prime Minister Nehru of India, Prime Minister U Nu of Burma, President Chiang Kai-shek of Nationalist China, and Prime Minister Ben-Gurion of Israel.

Secretary Benson talked with Ben-Gurion about Orson Hyde's dedication of Palestine for the return of the descendants of Judah and even suggested a commemorative garden honoring the event. His suggestion later became a reality.[27] In a letter to President Howard W. Hunter dated 2 June 1994, Teddy Kollek, the former mayor of Jerusalem, spoke of his acquaintance with Secretary Benson during the Eisenhower years. He wrote, "It was under Ezra Taft Benson's leadership that so many ties between your community and Jerusalem were formed and it was through his perseverance and understanding that the Jerusalem Center for Near Eastern Studies of Brigham Young University was made possible."[28]

BUILDING THE KINGDOM

In addition to opening doors for God's kingdom with his contacts around the world, Secretary Benson shared the word at home. He sent Eisenhower lengthy excerpts from the Book of Mormon prophesying about the destiny of America.

Hundreds of news reports included in-depth discussions of the Church. Magazines with circulation totals of hundreds of millions also carried similar stories. His favorable actions were often linked with the Church.

He spoke before audiences of other faiths. One such occasion drew wide attention. While visiting Russia in 1959, decades before the Berlin Wall came down, Secretary Benson made an unscheduled appearance at the Central Baptist Church in Moscow and delivered extemporaneous remarks before the congregation of at least a thousand people. He counseled them to keep the commandments and to pray, "to reach out and tap that Unseen Power which gives us strength." He bore his witness of the Savior and promised "that the truth will endure." The congregation spontaneously broke into singing "God Be with You Till We Meet Again," waved their hand-kerchiefs, and eagerly grasped the visitors' hands as they moved down the aisle.[29]

In a lengthy article in the *U.S. News & World Report* of 26 October 1959, Grant Salisbury wrote, "It turned out to be one of the most moving experiences in the lifetime of many of us." Tom Anderson, editor of *Farm and Ranch* magazine, wrote: "Imagine getting your greatest spiritual experience in atheistic Russia! . . . It was the most heart-rending and most inspiring scene I've ever witnessed."[30]

When Secretary Benson left office, he delivered some nine thou-sand names of prominent people he knew to the missionary depart-ment for follow-up visits by the missionaries. One non-Mormon on his staff, Kenneth Scott, attributed Secretary Benson's example as a prime motivator for his joining the Church. Kenneth Scott's son is now a member of the Quorum of the Twelve Apostles—Elder Richard G. Scott.[31]

ON TO THE VICTORY

In 1953, as controversy surrounding Secretary Benson raged, Elder Harold B. Lee prophesied to the Saints attending stake conference in Washington, D.C.: "There will be many who will belittle [Brother Benson] and will try to destroy him and destroy his reputation and destroy his influence in his high place. . . . But the glory and majesty attached to the name of Ezra Taft Benson will never die so long as Brother Benson continues to live the gospel of Jesus Christ. . . . And you and I who are in this congregation will live one day to see what I have said verified."[32]

After Secretary Benson's first major victory with the Congress, *Scripps-Howard* columnist Howard Lucey wrote, "They . . . called him stupid and denounced him as the worst Secretary of Agriculture in history and demanded that President Eisenhower fire him. But Ezra Taft Benson stood his ground and took the pounding. Today he has emerged as hero of the biggest legislative victory the Eisenhower administration has had."[33] "Ezra," Eisenhower said, "is the shining star in the firmament of my administration."[34]

The *Wall Street Journal* declared that the biggest victory in the election of 1954 belonged to "Ezra Taft Benson and his farm program."[35] Lloyd Burlingame, a commentator at NBC, wrote, "Hundreds of politicians won victories for themselves . . . but Secretary Benson won a victory for the United States of America."[36] On President Benson's ninetieth birthday, the president of the United States honored him with the Presidential Citizens Medal, citing him as "one of the most distinguished Americans of his time" because of his "lifetime of dedicated service to country, community, church and family."[37]

At the close of his eight years as secretary of agriculture, commendations were published in papers from coast to coast. He was called "the greatest agricultural statesman of all time." The *Dallas Morning News* of 20 February 1961 reported, "What a man that old Mormon secretary of agriculture turned out to be. . . . Where Benson had a free hand, he showed intelligence, fidelity and results."[38] But the finest tribute, as far as Elder Benson was concerned, came from President David O. McKay, who told him that his work in Washington would "stand for all time as a credit to the Church and the nation," as well as to his family and to himself.[39] Clearly, Secretary Ezra Taft Benson helped bring the Church out of obscurity on a positive and broad scale never before realized.

NOTES

1. Sheri L. Dew, *Ezra Taft Benson: A Biography* (Salt Lake City: Deseret Book, 1987), 254.

2. Ibid., 258.

3. Ibid., 254.

4. Ibid., 265.

5. Ibid., 293.

6. *Saturday Evening Post*, 28 March 1953, 22.

7. Dew, *Ezra Taft Benson*, 269.

8. Ibid., 280–81.

9. Ibid., 527.

10. Ezra Taft Benson, *Crossfire: The Eight Years with Eisenhower* (New York: Doubleday, 1962), 602.

11. Dew, *Ezra Taft Benson*, 280.

12. Ibid., 259.

13. Ibid., 288.

14. Ibid., 273.

15. Ibid., 295–96, 528.

16. Ibid., 291.

17. Ibid., 322.

18. Ibid., 296–97.

19. Ibid., 527.

20. Ibid., 528.

21. Ibid., 297–98.

22. Ibid., 300–302.

23. Ibid., 320.

24. Ibid., 364.

25. Ibid., 303.

26. Ibid., 319.

27. Ibid., 325, 433.

28. "Tributes and Messages of Appreciation," *Ensign,* July 1994, 21.

29. Dew, *Ezra Taft Benson,* 342–44.

30. Ibid., 344.

31. Ibid., 352.

32. Ibid., 276–77.

33. Ibid., 289–90.

34. Ibid., 291.

35. Ibid., 291.

36. Ibid., 291.

37. Citation presented with the Presidential Citizens Medal.

38. Dew, *Ezra Taft Benson,* 358–59.

39. Benson, *Crossfire,* 519.

CHAPTER FIVE

Russia and the Restoration

GARY BROWNING

Within the LDS community, we would agree that one very important benefit of the societal restructuring in Eastern Europe and Russia after Mikhail Gorbachev's rise to power has been a dramatic increase in freedom of conscience. This is especially true as it has facilitated the search for and espousal of religious belief.

For most of the twentieth century and long before, freedom of conscience had been restricted in Russia. Russians have considered unity of thought and loyalty to a single state authority the best guarantors of security for those living in an immense space with few natural barriers to hinder aggressive neighbors. In prehistoric times the Russians sought protection from their prince and from pagan gods such as Perun, god of thunder and lightning; Svarog, the sun god; and Dazhbog, giver of fertility and life.

According to Russian chronicles, in 988 Prince Vladimir of Kiev accepted Christianity, having invited Orthodox missionaries from the Byzantine Empire to teach and baptize his subjects. In 1453 with the fall of Byzantium to the Turks, a Russian nationalist consciousness and messianic vision arose, according to which Russia had become the eminent protector of Christianity and the "third Rome," which would stand forever, chosen and dauntless. As in Byzantium, the ideal of "one faith and one empire" spread throughout Russia.

For more than a millennium, since 988, Russian Orthodox traditions developed and solidified. They are seen today in a heritage of

Gary Browning is a professor of Russian language and literature at Brigham Young University.

strikingly beautiful cathedrals and village churches with glistening gilded cupolas and spiritually moving icons, liturgy, choral music, sacraments, church holy day celebrations, and a literature of saints' lives. Russian Orthodoxy incorporates a very old Russian preference for what some call "communitarianism," or *sobornost*—the preeminence of group over individual priorities, unity of beliefs and mores, general economic equality, and political and military solidarity.

Of course the Russian Orthodox Church faced challenges to her authority and hegemony. But it remained immensely influential, regardless of a seventeenth-century schism by those opposed to correcting errors that had crept into the Russian Orthodox liturgy, Peter the Great's eighteenth-century reforms in church administration, and Nicholas II's early twentieth-century proclamations on relative religious liberty.

Then, for more than seventy years (1917 to 1988), Communists, who adapted and incorporated into their ideology many of Orthodoxy's secular values and symbols, severely restricted religion. Although successive Soviet constitutions of 1918, 1929, 1936, and 1977 all claimed to guarantee freedom of religious worship, in reality believers paid a heavy price for their faith, at times losing their liberty or their lives.

All of this changed, slowly at first, with Gorbachev's ascent to power in March 1985. While Gorbachev frequently spoke of *glasnost'*, *perestroika, demokratizatsiia,* and *"novoe myshlenie"* or *new thinking* in foreign policy, most Soviets adjusted slowly. It was not until 1988, at the time of the commemoration of one thousand years of Orthodoxy in Russia, that church *and* secular officials finally realized Gorbachev was serious and sincere about allowing freedom of thought and expression in religion.

In October 1990 a new law, "On Freedom of Conscience and Religious Organizations," was passed. It was among the most liberal legislation on freedom of thought and worship ever passed in Russia or abroad and was supported by the December 1993 Russian federal constitution which declares in section 1, article 14, that "religious associations [churches] shall be . . . equal before the law."[1]

Unfortunately, the liberal 1990 law almost immediately gave rise to abuses, including those by several pseudoreligious groups promoting bizarre, offensive, and even destructive behavior. In addition, inherently secular organizations sprang up, bereft of spiritual content and seeking a church's tax-exempt status to more profitably engage in business. This and a disdain for many insensitive and often irresponsible foreign religious groups led to demands for revision of the 1990 law. A new law was passed but was not signed by Russian president Yeltsin in 1993. It was subsequently revised, passed, signed, and implemented in October 1997. Although language in the 1997 law is clearly threatening to such religious associations as the LDS Church, in practice the subsequent normative acts and interpretations from the Russian Ministry of Justice responsible for implementation of the law have been, thus far, of no serious harm to the LDS Church, which was fully reregistered and again legally recognized in 1998.

Before continuing with the subject of this chapter, the LDS Church in Russia, I will outline the broader East European context[2] in which the Church maintained a presence. Prior to World War II, approximately eight thousand LDS members resided in what, after the war, would become the German Democratic Republic (GDR) or, colloquially, East Germany. By 1969 when the Dresden Mission was established to support GDR members (although without full-time missionaries) about thirty-seven hundred members remained of the prewar eight thousand. Immigration to the Federal Republic of Germany and harsh ideological constraints imposed on the Saints in the GDR had taken their toll. In 1982 stakes were created in Freiberg and Leipzig, and in 1985 the Freiberg Germany Temple was dedicated. In 1988 the Dresden Mission was renewed, German missionaries were allowed to go abroad, and foreign missionaries were permitted to serve in the GDR. Late in 1989 the Berlin Wall was torn down, and in 1990 the two Germanies were reunited.

In 1929 Elder John A. Widtsoe dedicated Czechoslovakia for preaching the gospel, but when Hitler invaded the country a decade later, the Church faced severe trials. The fewer than two hundred members of the Church struggled to maintain themselves with little contact from Church headquarters, until the period from 1946 to 1950 when a mission again operated in the country. The years from 1950 to 1989 once more were times of trial. In 1990 the Church was legally recognized and the mission reorganized.

Poland granted the Church recognition in 1977, the same year President Spencer W. Kimball dedicated Poland for missionary work.

Permission to have missionaries serve in Poland was granted in 1986, a mission established in 1990, and the beautiful new Warsaw chapel dedicated in June 1991.

Hungary's approximately one hundred LDS members converted between the end of the nineteenth century and 1914 remained without regular Church support from the time of World War I until the Church was recognized in June 1988. As in Czechoslovakia and Poland, a mission began operating in 1990.

It was also July 1990 when the first LDS mission in Russia, originally named Finland Helsinki *East,* was established, but much had occurred relative to the LDS Church in Russia prior to that time. In 1903 apostle Francis M. Lyman visited Russia to gauge the spirit of the people and land and to seek inspiration regarding whether missionary work should commence there. His impressions regarding the Church's prospects were quite positive, and in St. Petersburg and Moscow, he "dedicated the land and turned the key for the preaching of the Gospel in the empire of Russia."[3] Circumstances, including concern for the safety of missionaries and new members, however, persuaded the First Presidency to wait for further improvements before assigning missionaries.

While in St. Petersburg, Elder Lyman met with the Lindelof family, who were baptized in St. Petersburg in 1895. Brother Lindelof's mother had been converted in Finland, then a semiautonomous Russian Grand Duchy, before her goldsmith son moved to the wealthy Russian capital. After living sixteen years in St. Petersburg, Johan Lindelof asked the mission president in Sweden to send a missionary to teach and baptize him and his wife. This was accomplished, and the Lindelofs became possibly the only Russian citizens to receive the gospel and baptism in Russia until the time of Gorbachev.[4]

Under Communist rule from 1917 to 1991, religion in Russia was disparaged and at times virtually prohibited. During this period André Anastasion, a Russian emigré who joined the Church in England in 1917 (the year the Bolsheviks seized power in Russia), prepared for the day missionary work would begin in his native land. Urged initially by Elder John A. Widtsoe, Brother Anastasion worked diligently on his translation of the Book of Mormon into Russian for fifty-five years, from 1925 until his death in 1980. In 1980 the first twenty-five hundred copies of the Book of Mormon in Russian were published.

Prior to the 1988 watershed year, Church leaders, most prominently Elder Russell M. Nelson of the Quorum of the Twelve Apostles and Hans B. Ringger of the Seventy, met with the Soviet Council on Religious Affairs officers to build bridges of understanding and clarify procedures for establishing the Church in Russia. At that time, a principal requirement was for twenty Soviet citizens in a locality to sign an application requesting registration of their religious community. But missionaries were not allowed to proselyte to convert these twenty new members.

Soon, however, unanticipated events led to the conversion of many more than twenty members. A few Russian citizens were baptized while visiting abroad in Hungary, the United States, Italy, and Finland. Elder Ringger authorized Finnish mission president Steven R. Mecham to provide Russian-speaking Finnish home and visiting teachers to strengthen these newly baptized members. The Russian members, especially the Leningrad Terebenin family, arranged for guests to meet with the Finns and become more familiar with Church teachings.

During the October 1989 European mission presidents' training seminar held in Hungary, Elder Nelson informed President Mecham of Finland and President Dennis B. Neuenschwander, then of the Austria Vienna East Mission and now of the Seventy, that the First Presidency and Quorum of the Twelve Apostles had decided the time had come to begin official missionary work among citizens of the Soviet Union. Initial emphasis was to be in Leningrad and Vyborg, Russia, the latter town midway between Helsinki and Leningrad, and in Tallinn, Estonia, across the bay from Finland. President Neuenschwander is fluent in Russian and had recently visited Leningrad and Moscow on Church assignment. He reported to Elder Ringger that Finnish members and missionaries, who lived closest to these areas, and many of whom spoke Russian, were well positioned to teach and fellowship in that part of the Soviet Union.

Elder Ringger, the two Finnish stake presidents, and President Mecham called six Finnish couples, all the wives being familiar with Russian, to serve in Russia and Estonia on weekends in a fellowshipping and leadership training capacity. When the first full-time missionaries began visiting the three Soviet Union cities early in 1990, the Finnish couples continued their essential fellowshipping and training work and provided referrals for missionaries. As long as baptizing new converts in Leningrad seemed potentially dangerous, converts were invited on short trips to Finland for baptism there.

Initially, Finland Helsinki missionaries entered Russia and Estonia on tourist visas and remained only a few days, then a week or two, or even a month. Later, with considerable effort, Russian and Estonian LDS members arranged for personal guest visas for missionaries that lasted for up to three months. With the registration of the LDS Russian Religious Association in May 1991, the Church received legal authority to issue invitations resulting in visas for missionaries to serve for up to two full years.

Working diligently under President Mecham, the missionary force gradually grew to sixteen and accomplished much by the time of the July 1990 organization of the Finland Helsinki East Mission. Between January and July, LDS Church membership grew to 156 Soviets: 80 in Leningrad, 43 in Tallinn, 26 in Vyborg, and 7 in Moscow. In Moscow, full-time missionaries had not yet begun serving, but American embassy personnel and businessmen had undertaken effective member missionary and fellowshipping programs.

A great facilitator of early missionary success among the Soviets was a pent-up hunger to learn more of life's spiritual meaning. This, coupled with an initial inclination to regard beliefs from the West as generally superior to those obligatory under Communism, created an environment of receptive minds and hearts.

Problems remained, however. It may be that the Russian members enduring and often overcoming their challenges as they struggled to establish a Russian Zion compare to our forebears' efforts in such places as Kirtland, Far West, Nauvoo, Winter Quarters, and Salt Lake City, in quest of an American Zion.

In the beginning, the limited range of LDS materials in Russian was troubling for Russians, who are voracious readers. The Bible, Book of Mormon, and the *Joseph Smith Testimony* pamphlet were available from 1990. But initially the other standard works, hymns, periodicals, missionary discussions, lesson manuals, administrative handbooks, and auxiliary materials were not yet translated. Today these inadequacies have been overcome.

Though it was difficult, apartments for missionaries were located with the generous help of Soviet members, although facilities for Sunday meetings and a mission office and home posed greater problems. With effort, arrangements could be made to hold Sunday meetings in music or elementary schools, libraries, and theaters or "houses of culture" operated by city departments and other enterprises. Difficulties arose when, after a few weeks or months, local managers unexpectedly demanded much more money or simply informed branch leaders that they must find new facilities by the following Sunday in order for the manager to accommodate a better paying client.

Acquiring more permanent meetinghouse facilities has proven especially difficult. Local government officials are hesitant to make building lots available for new meetinghouses unless the dominant church and local citizens approve. Obtaining that approval is not easy. Similar problems arise in purchasing existing facilities, although even greater barriers result from the exorbitant prices. Currently, the only newly constructed LDS facility in Russia is located in Vyborg. Rental facilities, typically a floor in a multistory building, a few secured with long-term leases, have been somewhat easier to acquire, however.

The Word of Wisdom, law of chastity, and tithing present challenges to Russian members, as they do in other countries. Russians tend to be heavy tea drinkers and smokers. During Renaissance times, traveling merchants introduced vodka, for which Russian men in particular have developed a strong attachment. Members who stoically refrain from vodka are severely tested during important holidays and especially at family celebrations when eating and drinking abundantly is considered socially mandatory. At times like these, peer pressure can feel crushing.

Russia's ongoing, severe economic upheaval, characterized by high inflation relative to the West and low, often deferred, wages or unemployment, exacts a heavy toll on our members. It is hard to focus on spiritual things when even modest material needs remain unfilled. Pressures are great to seek a second job in order to cover essential expenses. Summers present a particular challenge, as many members feel they must spend weekends working at their garden plots in order to survive—literally survive—the winter. The plots are usually located considerable distances from their city apartments. Time constraints and public transportation costs may complicate members' efforts to return to the city for Sunday worship.

For all of these reasons and more, maintaining and increasing priesthood leadership pools presents a serious challenge. In addition, it is difficult for many men to "endure to the end," to continue functioning in a leadership capacity over a long period of time. Fatigue becomes a factor. Another difficulty is the fact that some of our finest leaders have emigrated to the West. One might have hoped they would remain and build up the Russian Zion, but few missionaries who have experienced the harsh living conditions in Russia would feel inclined to judge them. Most in their place, given the opportunity, would do the same.

Three additional challenges are particularly troubling. First, seventy years of antireligious propaganda have had a profound effect on Russian thinking. Of course some Russians preserved their beliefs and even imbued children and grandchildren with faith. Others, while knowing little about religion, rebelled against the Soviet line when it became possible and eagerly sought spiritual meaning and fulfillment. But most Russians were affected, drop by drop, by the propaganda poison to which they were subjected all their lives.

Generations of Soviets grew up believing, as Marx claimed, that religion is only superstition, an "opiate of the people," that there is no God, no afterlife, no eternal meaning to human existence. Life is material, period. Only what one can see, hear, feel, smell, and taste is true. Science provides or will eventually provide all the answers. Although Soviet antireligion teaching in schools, through the media, and at work may have been crude and excessive, over time it appears to have succeeded in millions of lives.

I recall an exemplary member of the Church who had qualified to receive the Melchizedek Priesthood. During our interview he expressed concern that his now deceased parents, whom he loved dearly and who had sincerely accepted atheism and taught him to be like them, may now be disappointed in him for being baptized into a church and on the verge of holding its higher priesthood. We talked about how his parents must feel in an afterlife that they formerly believed did not exist, how they may be among those who had heard and even accepted the teachings of Jesus Christ, how it is possible they could now or at some point depend on their son to provide for them saving ordinances, and how it would be important to pray for inspiration to know what steps he should take. This he did, and as a result he chose to be ordained an elder.

The second serious challenge to the growth of The Church of Jesus Christ of Latter-day Saints in Russia is the pervasive influence of the Russian Orthodox Church. Even for Russians who profess no faith, Orthodoxy feels deeply Russian. It is an ethnic marker, much like Catholicism in Italy or Lutheranism in Scandinavia. For centuries Russian soldiers went to battle with a priest's blessing. Wonder-working icons inspired rich and poor alike. Even today Orthodox prelates attend all important state functions, implicitly sanctioning them through their presence.

From Orthodoxy, Russians have come to adore the Virgin Mary, or as she is called in Russian, the Mother of God. It is she who intercedes for the sinner, consoles the disconsolate, and preserves the highest ideal of purity, compassion, and tenderness. Russia's most holy icon is the Virgin of Vladimir, Vladimir for a time, after Kiev, being the capital of Russia. The icon is from the early twelfth century and depicts the Mother of God inclining her head to her right in order to touch her cheek to that of the child. Jesus' left arm encircles his mother's neck and rests gently on her chin. This portrayal of deep affection and tenderness was uncommon in icons of the time and helped establish the standard for all subsequent Russian schools of iconography.

In many cases, far more than tea and vodka, Russian LDS members miss in their worship the adoration of the Mother of God. A fervent love for her is deep in their spiritual genes, as is their reverence for the inspiring hagiographies or saints' lives. An early example of the saints' lives is the story of the first two Russian Orthodox saints, Boris and Gleb. Boris and Gleb were younger sons of Prince Vladimir, the christianizer of ancient Rus'. Upon Vladimir's death, their older brother, power hungry and treacherous, conspired to murder his brothers. The latter, though aware of their older brother's intentions, meekly submitted to him, and died rather than oppose him with armed force, which surely would have resulted in the deaths of many others.

With this hagiography begins the Russian emphasis on the saints imitating the Savior's meek sacrifice and martyrdom, rather than the perception of Christ as a powerful and vengeful ruler common in both Roman and Byzantine traditions of the time. Even today, with all Russia's cruelty, the images of the tender Mother of God and the courageous and meek Boris and Gleb provide a revered ideal and counterpoint to violence when there may be little else of holiness to which Russians can cling.

The final challenge I would mention relates mainly to Protestant Christianity. In addition to the broad atheistic and Russian Orthodox layers in society, there is another thinner but precious social stratum composed of those prepared by the Spirit to open their minds and hearts to Christianity. The problem occurs when other faiths, including those already established in Russia in the nineteenth and early twentieth centuries, such as the Baptists, Seventh-Day Adventists, Methodists, Jehovah's Witnesses, and others reach those prepared before LDS missionaries can. Then our task becomes far more difficult. If these Russians ready to accept the truth hear the appealing messages of our Protestant brothers and sisters, they may join their churches, become emotionally and spiritually integrated with fellow believers, and be less likely to respond to our message of restored Christianity. Our urgent task is to reap the harvest of souls, not merely glean after the vigorous efforts of others.

With all these and other challenges, it is a tribute to our committed Russian members, inspired Church leaders in Salt Lake and Frankfurt, and devoted missionaries whom they assign to Russia that so much Church growth and development has occurred there.

As of the year 2000, there are thirteen LDS missions in the former Soviet Union: eight in Russia alone, two in the very productive Ukraine, one in the Baltics (Lithuania Vilnius), one in Mongolia, and one in Armenia. The eight Russian missions in the order they were established are Moscow and St. Petersburg (1992), Samara (1993), Rostov-on-the-Don and Novosibirsk (1994), Yekaterinburg (1995), Moscow South (1997), and Vladivostok (1999). Church membership in these eight missions is approximately ten thousand, with about seven hundred missionaries serving there at any given time. As of late 2000, no stakes exist in Russia, but some areas are approaching the level of strength when creation of a stake could occur. Plans to build a temple in Kiev, Ukraine, were announced in 1998, although construction has not yet begun.

Finally, I quote from the conversion account of Nina Bazarskaia, a stalwart sister from Voronezh who was baptized in December 1992. As a child she wondered why her mother's family was often mentioned, but no one ever spoke of her father's relatives.

"Only when I grew older did I understand the reason. My father's parents came from a family of Orthodox clergy. My great-grandfather was a deacon, and Grandpa was a priest in the Orthodox Church. . . . My great-grandfather (who was ninety), my uncles, and my grandfather were arrested and sent to a concentration camp in the north where they perished. . . . This entire family history was shrouded in secrecy because it was dangerous to talk about such things out loud right up until 1989. . . .

"I grew up with God, but never went to church, and I didn't read the Bible until I was forty. Once I became an adult, I tried to attend church in other cities when I went on professional trips. Prayers before the icons of Jesus Christ and the Virgin Mary, and repentant tears always brought my soul a quiet peace and comfort."[5]

Sister Bazarskaia first heard about the Church from Brigham Young University professor Robert Blair at an international professional conference. Then BYU students arrived in Voronezh to teach English to nursery school children. Sister Bazarskaia became acquainted with them and began attending their Sunday worship services.

"At first I wasn't going to change anything in my life. 'Would it really be impossible to be a member of the Orthodox Church and at the same time follow the principles of the Mormons?' I would ask myself. But soon after that I felt it would not be possible to continue that way for long. Sooner or later I would have to decide for myself which side I would be on: with the Orthodox Church or with these new, unfamiliar people, whom I wanted to be like.

"This choice tortured me and would not allow me a moment's peace. All the while it seemed to me that by choosing the Mormons, I would betray the faith of my fathers and that God would not forgive me for this apostasy. I prayed and asked God for an answer, and it came. One day during the summer while I was sitting on the bank of a river gazing into the water and persistently thinking about the choice I had to make, I heard a distinct voice, which said: 'You will not betray anyone, you'll simply progress farther and believe more deeply. And Christ will remain the same.'"

Soon after, Sister Bazarskaia studied the gospel with missionaries and was baptized; she was followed by her teenage son two months later and her husband in a year. Their son served a mission in the Baltic States. Brother Bazarskii served as Voronezh branch president. In time Brother and Sister Bazarskii were sealed for time and all eternity in the Salt Lake Temple. Sister Bazarskaia concludes her account, "This Church gives people hope, and with hope it is easier to overcome those trials which are sent to us. I know I am not alone. My family, friends, and brothers and sisters are with me, as is our Heavenly Father, who wants me to be happy."

In 1843 the Prophet Joseph Smith appointed two missionaries to serve as vanguard to Russia—Orson Hyde of the Quorum of the Twelve Apostles and George J. Adams, a prolific baptizer during his years as a missionary in England. The Prophet declared that with the vast Russian empire are connected "some of the most important things concerning the advancement and building up of the Kingdom of God in the last days, which cannot be explained at this time."[6] While for several reasons, including Joseph's martyrdom, the Hyde-Adams mission did not take place, now missionaries and Russian members are helping to fulfill the Prophet's vision for Russia, as is occurring in missions around the world. This is among the twentieth century's great miracles we gratefully celebrate today.

NOTES

1. *Http://www.departments.bucknell.edu/russian.const/ch1.html.*

2. Material for this section on the German Democratic Republic, Czechoslovakia, Poland, and Hungary came from Bruce A. Van Orden, *Building Zion: The Latter-day Saints in Europe* (Salt Lake City: Deseret Book, 1996), 193–212, 267–83.

3. Joseph J. Cannon, "President Lyman's Travels and Ministry," *Millennial Star,* 27 August 1903, 548.

4. A. J. Höglund, "Introduction of the Gospel into Russia," *Millennial Star,* 27 June 1895, 414. Persistent rumors of nineteenth-century "Mormony" living along the Volga River call for additional attention.

5. Gary Browning, *Russia and the Restored Gospel* (Salt Lake City: Deseret Book, 1997), 291–94. All quotations from Nina Bazarskaia's account are from this work. *Bazarskaia* is the feminine form of Nina's surname; *Bazarskii* is the masculine form.

6. Joseph Smith, *History of The Church of Jesus Christ of Latter-day Saints,* ed. B. H. Roberts, 2d ed. rev., 7 vols. (Salt Lake City: The Church of Jesus Christ of Latter-day Saints, 1932–51), 6:41.

CHAPTER SIX

INTERNATIONAL TOURS OF THE TABERNACLE CHOIR

CYNTHIA DOXEY

The Tabernacle Choir's international tours have been important in the acceptance and progress of The Church of Jesus Christ of Latter-day Saints in many countries. Jerold Ottley, the choir's recently retired music director, has stated that "the Tabernacle Choir is the flag-bearer that leads the parade."[1] In other words, while the choir is not the "parade," or the actual good news of the gospel, it can often prepare individuals and countries to receive the preaching of the gospel. The choir has been able to open doors for the Church and touch people's lives in ways that other Church emissaries could not. At the end of the most recent concert tour to Europe in 1998, Elder Gene R. Cook told the choir in Lisbon, Portugal:

"I don't know when we have had more news coverage for The Church of Jesus Christ of Latter-day Saints than we've had in the past three weeks. . . . The impact in the press was great. . . . I don't know of anything that has brought the Church out of obscurity in the time that I've been here any more than what has happened these last few weeks. It has been phenomenal."[2]

The Tabernacle Choir has helped bring the Church out of obscurity during their major international tours, through the publicity and media associated with the tours, the effect of the concerts themselves, the relationships built between Church and community leaders, and the missionary experiences of choir and Church members.[3]

Cynthia Doxey is an assistant professor of Church history and doctrine at Brigham Young University.

INTERNATIONAL CONCERT TOURS

Throughout the last century, the Salt Lake Mormon Tabernacle Choir has played an important role in The Church of Jesus Christ of Latter-day Saints because of its high visibility as one of the Church's most well-known entities. In fact, President Ronald Reagan described the choir as "America's most renowned musical ensemble."[4] Until the late 1890s, the Tabernacle Choir's role was to provide music for Church meetings at the Salt Lake Tabernacle. In the twentieth century, however, the choir gained a national and international reputation that has helped to bring the Church wider recognition.

The choir's first tour was to the Columbian Exposition in Chicago in 1893. Since that time, the choir has been on numerous tours, made many recordings, and received a number of musical and recording awards. Since the first European tour in 1955, the Tabernacle Choir has made tours to several foreign countries, including Brazil, Japan, Korea, Australia, New Zealand, Israel, and many European countries (see list of concert locations at the end of this chapter). The choir itself has become more well-known in the twentieth century and has prompted many people to inquire after its sponsoring organization, The Church of Jesus Christ of Latter-day Saints.

The first Tabernacle Choir tour outside the United States was a seven-week tour to Europe in 1955. In addition to their concerts, President David O. McKay invited the choir to participate in the groundbreaking of the London Temple and the dedication of the Swiss Temple. This tour was significant because it was the first international tour and because people around the world were introduced to the Tabernacle Choir. Almost all the concerts were performed to capacity crowds, and all received favorable reviews in the media.[5]

As the Tabernacle Choir's reputation has grown, they have received more and more invitations to tour and perform throughout the world.[6] When choir leaders begin to plan a tour, they evaluate the invitations the choir has received. The possibilities are presented to the First Presidency of the Church who make the decision based on where they think the choir could do the most good for the Church.[7] Each of the international tours has had a purpose beyond just performing music to appreciative audiences. For example, the choir was appointed to represent the United States in Brisbane's world's fair celebrating Australia's bicentennial in 1988, which resulted in a tour of the South Pacific sponsored in part by the Australian Broadcasting Corporation and the Broadcasting Corporation of New Zealand.[8] Another example is the 1973 European tour, when the choir was invited by President Harold B. Lee to perform for a Church area conference in Munich. The choir combined that assignment with several other important projects, including the recording of choruses from Handel's *Messiah* with the London Philharmonic, the taping of a documentary program about the Church and the choir for Lutz Wellnitz, a German television producer, and the filming of two British Broadcasting Corporation (BBC) productions.[9]

Tabernacle Choir concert tours are both "exhilarating and exhausting."[10] International tours are perhaps even more exhilarating and exhausting than travel within the United States. The tours are generally longer and more rigorous because they entail much more travel time. The countries visited also provide new and exciting experiences for choir members. Members of the choir have little leisure time on a tour, however, because of the number of concerts, rehearsals, firesides, and receptions that are scheduled. The Spirit of the Lord has strengthened the choir to perform excellently in spite of exhaustion from a difficult tour schedule.[11] As Elder Russell M. Nelson stated, when referring to the choir, "Strength comes to an ordinary soul when given an extraordinary calling."[12]

For the international tours the choir has usually chartered the aircraft, cruise ships, trains, and buses they use because of the size of the group traveling. The first European tour in 1955 required travel by sea, air, train, and bus in crossing the Atlantic and getting around the European continent. Other tours have used similar modes of transportation, although ships have only been used in 1955, 1982, and 1998. Arranging for the travel is a colossal task because choir members often bring guests with them, meaning that five hundred to seven hundred individuals travel together on international tours.[13] One small example shows the effect of such a large group on the people who come in contact with the choir: A group of choir members asked a porter in the choir's Lisbon hotel in 1998 if he had ever heard of the Tabernacle Choir. He nodded his head and replied, "Twelve hundred suitcases," referring to the difficult task he had of sorting all the luggage and taking it to each room.[14]

Another interesting effect of tour travel comes not only from the sheer numbers involved, but the fact that the entire group embraces the same beliefs and lifestyle. Individuals keeping the Word of Wisdom often impress the attendants who serve the choir on airplanes, ships, buses, and in the hotels. The stewards on board ship in the Mediterranean in 1998 often asked about the beliefs of the Church because "other people on cruises have dull eyes and glazed expressions. But people on this cruise have eyes that look into their souls."[15] There may be no way of knowing whether the individuals serving on the ships or aircraft became members of the Church because of their contact with choir members, yet they obviously learned something more about the Church and the lifestyle of its members after being with the Tabernacle Choir.

PUBLICITY AND MEDIA INVOLVEMENT

When the choir traveled to Europe in 1955, the Church was not well-known, nor was the choir. While there was publicity and media activity for that first tour, in recent years the publicity for tours has been much greater. Over the years media attention has increased for the concert tours.[16] When the Tabernacle Choir goes on a concert tour today, there is usually a great amount of publicity about the choir and the Church in the communities visited.

Japanese television stations invited and sponsored the choir on its tours to Japan in 1979 and 1985. Udell Poulsen, the choir's manager, stated that due to the publicity received during the first tour to Japan, many more people knew of the choir, and there was a marked increase in the country's interest in the choir on its second trip. Because of the involvement of the television stations, the choir received great publicity, and the stations broadcast the concerts in Japan. This use of the media to broadcast the choir's concerts meant that the effect of the tour was increased exponentially as millions of people who did not attend the concerts were able to see them on television. Jerold Ottley was told by Elder Yoshihiko Kikuchi that the baptism rate in Japan increased after the choir's tour in 1985.[17]

Perhaps no tour has received more publicity and media involvement than the 1998 Southern European tour. Iain McKay, director of international media for Bonneville Communications, stated that European media are "very sophisticated. . . . Yet in city after city, country after country, the Choir's concerts were given major treatment."[18] Wherever the choir appeared, there were numerous interviews of choir personnel, news stories on television, radio and newspaper, and documentaries filmed about the choir's concerts. Many choir members involved in the interviews said they were blessed in being able to communicate in other languages. Kathleen Lee, who had been a missionary in France almost twenty years before the 1998 tour, stated that during interviews in Geneva and Marseilles, she thought she had perhaps been given the gift of tongues because she felt the Spirit strongly while words and phrases that she had not used for years came to her without difficulty.[19] In addition to interviews, the concerts were broadcast live or taped by national and international television stations, meaning that the choir's music could be heard by literally millions of people throughout the continent. "Talk about coming out of obscurity! Undeniably it was the Spirit of Heavenly Father that did it all."[20]

THE SPIRIT OF THE CONCERT

Of course, the major emphasis of Tabernacle Choir tours is on the preparation and execution of the music for the concerts. The choir is unique not only because of its longevity but also because of its large size and the volunteer status of its members. It is also unique because all the people involved in the choir share a common philosophy and focus in their lives, which enables the Lord's Spirit to communicate through them to the audience.[21] Therefore, the choice of music sung in concerts often reflects the beliefs as well as the talents of the musicians in the choir.

Jerold Ottley stated that in programming a concert tour, he chooses music that shows the choir's abilities to perform music of various styles. The concerts include selections from the classical choral repertoire (including both sacred and secular music), culturally specific songs associated with the countries visited, and also pieces that allow the choir members to be themselves. This music includes typical American folk tunes, African-American spirituals, and hymns or songs that express the Church's beliefs, such as "Come, Come, Ye Saints" or "I am a Child of God."[22] Audiences appreciate it when the choir learns songs in the language of their country and performs music that is significant to them. In Prague during the 1991 tour, the first encore was a Czech folk song that had been banned by the communist government for many years. When the choir began to sing this song, many in the audience stood and wept.[23]

One interesting situation in concert programming arose when the choir went to Israel in 1992. The choir leaders had to be careful in choosing music that was acceptable to people who did not believe in Christ. The sacred music was drawn from the Old Testament, and the choir had to be sensitive to other traditions in a non-Christian country. For example, in "God Be with You Till We Meet Again," the line that says, "Till we meet at Jesus' feet" was changed to "Till we meet at our Redeemer's feet."[24]

Most of the individuals in the concert audiences probably had not known much about the Church, or about the choir. As Dr. Ottley and choir members can testify, the audiences have to warm up to the music and the choir.[25] Many people come into the concert with skeptical looks on their faces, but by the end of the concert the choir usually receives a standing ovation, showing the audience's enthusiasm for the experience of the previous two hours. Most of the concerts do not end until several encores have been performed, often including the "Battle Hymn of the Republic" and "God Be with You Till We Meet Again." These concerts become an opportunity for individuals to be touched by the Spirit and, in spite of language barriers, to communicate through music the expressions of love for each other and for God.

There are many examples of experiences that show the hand of God in providing opportunities for the choir concerts to touch people's lives. One example is from the most recent European tour. Just ten days before the choir was to perform in Marseilles, France, only 150 concert tickets had been sold. Choir and Church leaders talked of canceling the concert, but then decided to continue as planned. The area's missionaries focused their energies on publicizing the concert with thousands of handbills and posters and by encouraging Church members to bring their friends. In spite of the earlier concerns, nearly two thousand people attended the concert, including many nonmembers. The concert has since been called the "miracle of Marseilles" because it revitalized the missionary work and members there.[26]

Another important concert took place when the choir sang in El Escorial, Spain, at a four-hundred-year-old royal palace. In order to perform in the basilica, a special invitation must be received from the king's organization, Patrimonio. Musical groups not associated with the Roman Catholic Church are rarely invited because of the religious significance of the basilica. However, due to several years of preparatory work by Ron Horton, a Church member living in Spain who knew members of Patrimonio, the choir was invited to sing in the basilica at El Escorial. The concert helped improve the Church's image in Spain because it was filmed by Spanish television before a private VIP audience consisting of important people from the community and the Catholic Church.[27]

BRIDGES BUILT BETWEEN THE CHURCH AND COMMUNITY

Three tours in particular exemplify the manner in which the choir's tours have built bridges between the Church and community or government leaders: the 1982 Northern European tour, the 1991 Eastern European tour, and the 1992–93 tour to Israel. Each of these tours had unique challenges and opportunities to help the Church become more well-known and accepted in the countries visited.

Northern Europe

The 1982 Northern European tour was unique because the United States' ambassadors to Norway, Finland, and Sweden at that time were members of the Church. With their support and hosting of concert receptions, choir personnel, Church, government, and civic leaders all forged lasting ties of friendship. The mayor of Copenhagen, who was not a member of the Church, gave a luncheon for the choir and guests, showing gratitude for the choir's presence in Copenhagen.[28] As Udell Poulsen remarked, the Church had come full circle in Northern Europe from the mid-nineteenth century when it was viewed as a sect and its members were persecuted, to the time when the Church's Tabernacle Choir was honored by the leaders of cities and nations.[29]

Eastern Europe

The 1991 tour to Eastern Europe was perhaps one of the most significant choir tours because of the historical events that surrounded the tour. Herold Gregory and Udell Poulsen stated that when they first began planning the tour to the Eastern Bloc countries, those countries were still under Communist rule. The Church and Choir leaders worked through the countries' governments to gain sponsorship and permission for the choir to perform in each country. Many plans had been set, but the fall of the Berlin Wall in 1989, coupled with the fall of the Communist party in many countries, meant that new sponsors and government contacts had to be found.

Adding to this somewhat precarious situation, the Gulf War broke out in early 1991, causing concern about the safety of international travel. As Wendell M. Smoot described, however, when the choir leaders were wondering whether to cancel the tour, he contacted President Gordon B. Hinckley of the First Presidency. President Hinckley desired time to make a decision, and when he next saw Brother Smoot, he stated, "The Choir will go to Europe this coming summer. The war will be over."[30] The choir members and leaders knew that the Lord wanted them to go on the tour.

The tour to Eastern Europe was also significant because the Church was just beginning in many of these countries. In some countries, the Church had only recently received official recognition and permission for proselyting missionaries. One role of this tour was to bring the Church out of obscurity. One way the choir accomplished this objective was through the VIP receptions and dinners given for government officials and civic leaders. Individuals who would not normally be contacted by missionaries because of their high standing in the community were able to gain favorable impressions of the Church through these events. Elder Russell M. Nelson of the Quorum of the Twelve Apostles accompanied the choir throughout the tour and was instrumental in creating bridges of understanding between these community leaders and the Church.[31]

Israel

In February 1992 Jerusalem mayor Teddy Kollek met with President Howard W. Hunter and Elder James E. Faust at the Brigham Young University Jerusalem Center to invite the Tabernacle Choir to perform the following December and January with the Jerusalem Symphony Orchestra.[32] Even though this tour would take choir members away from their families during the Christmas holiday, the choir willingly accepted the task and began to learn the music. Interestingly, the music they were asked to perform with the Jerusalem Symphony was the "Berlioz Requiem," which the choir was already planning to sing later in 1993 for a concert with Robert Shaw.[33]

This tour was different from others because it was the first time the choir had performed in the Middle East before both Israeli Jews and Palestinians—in separate concerts. The BYU Jerusalem Center was relatively new at the time, and the Church had received opposition from some groups in the Jewish community. The choir's concerts with the Jerusalem Symphony, along with those given for invited guests at the Jerusalem Center, were a major step in establishing good relationships for the center and the Church with both the Palestinian and Jewish communities.[34] Ann Madsen, the wife of Truman Madsen, the center's director at the time, stated that after the choir performed, the media reviews were more positive than she had ever seen, and there was also a greater sense of acceptance of the Church and the Jerusalem Center.[35] While traveling with the choir in Israel, Elder James E. Faust stated, "The end of the good you've done will never come."[36]

Missionary Experiences

Each Tabernacle Choir member is set apart as a musical missionary and is required to demonstrate worthiness for a temple recommend each year in order to remain in the choir. In effect, choir members are in the service of the Lord when they open their mouths to sing. Their lifestyles and actions while on tour should reflect their testimonies of the restored gospel and their callings as missionaries. For this reason, choir members are asked to dress appropriately throughout the tour: women in skirts or dresses, men in slacks and shirts.

The choir's 1991 tour of Eastern Europe was an opportunity to share the testimony of Christ through music in lands where the people had not been allowed to worship God for decades. This concert tour was definitely an important one for choir members and for the Church members in the countries they visited. While the numbers of baptisms due to the visit of the choir cannot be easily traced, potentially millions of individuals heard the choir's message through media coverage and concert attendance.[37]

Choir members take their commission to be musical missionaries very seriously. Choir leaders establish a missionary committee for each tour. The committee designs Articles of Faith cards in different languages, which choir members can purchase to share. In addition, choir members purchase many Tabernacle Choir recordings to give to people after concerts or at other times on tour. In 1998 the choir members carried approximately ten thousand choir CDs and tapes on tour. Sharing recordings with others is one way to communicate even when we speak different languages. This one-on-one contact with the audience allows choir members to show friendship and love, and often results in referrals for the local missionaries.[38]

Another important dimension of a tour's missionary focus is to strengthen the members of the Church in each area visited. Church members in foreign countries may never be able to see or hear the choir except during a concert tour in their area. Elder Gene R. Cook told the choir in 1998, "We greet you . . . with the greatest appreciation for the impact that you have had on the members of the Church whom I think stand a little taller because you were here."[39] The choir often provides firesides or other events free of charge in addition to the regular concerts so that Church members can attend. By seeing the choir perform, Church members may feel a greater connection with members of The Church of Jesus Christ of Latter-day Saints throughout the world.

An interesting example of the strength the choir can bring to the members was told by Herold Gregory, who is currently administrative assistant to the choir president. At the time of the 1955 tour, he was the president of the Church's East German Mission, headquartered in Berlin. The city of Berlin was the only link between the western world and Eastern Europe. President Gregory asked the choir to travel to Berlin, knowing that many of the five thousand East German Saints could come to Berlin to hear the concert, while they might never have another opportunity to come in contact with the larger Church.[40]

The Lord's hand could be seen in making the arrangements for the choir to perform in Berlin. President Gregory worked in Berlin to receive permission from the Russian authorities to allow the choir passage to Berlin, while others worked with the United States government to provide transportation for the choir on a military train. A miracle occurred as visas were obtained, and the choir was permitted to travel by military train across East Germany.[41] President Gregory said the most memorable event was the choir's arrival at the train station in Berlin:

"As they descended the stairway into the hallway, the Berlin District Choir . . . burst into a lusty rendition of 'Let the Mountains Shout for Joy.' During the second half of the anthem, the members of the Tabernacle Choir joined in, and the old station literally quaked. . . . The singing was in two languages, yet there can be no doubt that the music was in one language, the language of the heart. . . . To me, those few minutes at the station were as important and glorious as the concerts themselves."[42]

While President Gregory did not know if baptisms would result from the visit of the choir, he said that the testimonies of the members of the Church in East Germany were strengthened. Although they were isolated from the rest of the world, they felt that they were connected to the Church.

As one of the entities of The Church of Jesus Christ of Latter-day Saints, the Tabernacle Choir has provided a means whereby the Church could become more well-known and respected in other nations and could prepare the way for the preaching of the gospel. Through its international tours, the choir has brought the Church recognition in countries where it had not previously been prominent or well accepted. The benefits of the choir's international tours, including the publicity, musical concerts, connections between Church and community, and missionary efforts demonstrate the power of the Tabernacle Choir in building bridges and strengthening faith throughout the world.

SALT LAKE MORMON TABERNACLE CHOIR: MAJOR INTERNATIONAL TOURS

Grand European Tour, 1955

Glasgow, Manchester, London, Cardiff, United Kingdom; Copenhagen, Denmark; Berlin and Weisbaden, Germany; Amsterdam and Scheveningen, The Netherlands; Bern and Zurich, Switzerland; Paris, France

European Tour, 1973

Munich and Oberammergau, Germany; Paris, France; London, England

Japan and Korea Tour, 1979

Tokyo, Yokohama, Nagoya, Osaka, and Kyoto, Japan; Seoul, Korea

Brazil Tour, 1981

Sao Paulo, Brazil

Northern European Tour, 1982

Bergen and Oslo, Norway; Stockholm, Sweden; Helsinki, Finland; Copenhagen and Aalborg, Denmark; Rotterdam, The Netherlands; London, England

Japan Tour, 1985

Osaka, Nagoya, and Tokyo, Japan; Tsukuba Science Expo '85

South Pacific Tour, 1988

Honolulu, Hawaii; Auckland, Wellington, and Christchurch, New Zealand; Melbourne, Perth, Adelaide, Sydney, and Brisbane, Australia

Eastern European Tour, 1991

Frankfurt, Dresden, and Berlin, Germany; Strasbourg, France; Zurich, Switzerland; Budapest, Hungary; Vienna, Austria; Prague, Czechoslovakia; Warsaw, Poland; Moscow and Leningrad (now St. Petersburg), Russia

Israel Tour, 1992 to 1993

Jerusalem, Haifa, Tel Aviv, Israel

Southern European Tour, 1998

London, England; Brussels, Belgium; Geneva, Switzerland; Turin and Rome, Italy; Marseille, France; Barcelona, Madrid, and El Escorial, Spain; Lisbon, Portugal

NOTES

1. Author's interview of Jerold D. Ottley, Salt Lake City, Utah, 15 October 1999. Much of the information for this paper has been kindly provided by the Tabernacle Choir office or comes from the author's personal interviews with choir leaders: Wendell M. Smoot, president; Udell E. Poulsen, business manager; Herold L. Gregory, administrative assistant; and Jerold D. Ottley, former music director. In addition, some personal experiences of the author are given because of her participation as a choir member in the most recent European tour in 1998.

2. Gene R. Cook's comments to Tabernacle Choir in Lisbon,

Portugal, 1 July 1998. Transcript of talk in the Tabernacle Choir office, Salt Lake City, Utah.

3. Four similar dimensions have been previously noted by Jay M. Todd in his reports of the choir's 1991 and 1998 European tours: "An Encore of the Spirit," *Ensign,* October 1991, 32–53; "A Company of Angels," *Ensign,* October 1998, 30–37.

4. Michael Otterson, "Tabernacle Choir Tours Pacific," *Ensign,* September 1988, 77.

5. Warren John Jack Thomas, *Salt Lake Mormon Tabernacle Choir Goes to Europe* (Salt Lake City: Deseret News Press, 1957).

6. Ottley interview.

7. Author's interview of Wendell M. Smoot, Salt Lake City, Utah, 8 October 1999.

8. Otterson, "Tabernacle Choir Tours Pacific," 76–77.

9. Doyle L. Green, "The Tabernacle Choir: 106 Years of Missionary Singing," *Ensign,* November 1973, 84–88.

10. Otterson, "Tabernacle Choir Tours Pacific," 77.

11. Jerold D. Ottley, "They Came Back with Fire in Their Eyes!" *Ensign,* October 1998, 33.

12. Nelson, "These . . . Were Our Examples," *Ensign,* November 1991, 59.

13. Wendell M. Smoot, "It's Like Moving a Medium-Sized Town," *Ensign,* October 1998, 37.

14. Author's personal experience in Lisbon, Portugal, 1 July 1998.

15. Todd, "A Company of Angels," 34.

16. Iain B. McKay, "Media Challenges," *Ensign,* October 1991, 47; Iain B. McKay, "I've Never Seen Anything Like It in 20 Years!" *Ensign,* October 1998, 35.

17. Smoot interview; Ottley interview; author's interview of Udell E. Poulsen, Salt Lake City, Utah, 29 January 2000.

18. McKay, "I've Never Seen Anything Like It in 20 Years!" 35.

19. Kathleen Lee, letter to author, 10 November 1999.

20. McKay, "I've Never Seen Anything Like It in 20 Years!" 35.

21. Ottley interview.

22. Ottley interview; see also Todd, "An Encore of the Spirit," 48–52.

23. Todd, "An Encore of the Spirit."

24. LaRene Gaunt, "One Voice," *Ensign,* April 1993, 45.

25. Ottley interview.

26. Todd, "A Company of Angels," 37.

27. Ottley interview; Poulsen interview.

28. Dorothy Stowe, "Mormon Tabernacle Choir Tours Northern Europe," *Ensign*, September 1982, 78–80.

29. Poulsen interview.

30. Todd, "An Encore of the Spirit," 43.

31. Ibid., 36.

32. Author's interview of Ann N. Madsen, Provo, Utah, 27 January 2000; see also Gerry Avant, "Choir Leaves for 12-Day Tour to Holy Land," *Church News*, 26 December 1992, 3, 11.

33. Poulsen interview.

34. Madsen interview.

35. Ibid.

36. Gerry Avant, "Good Done by Choir's Visit Will Never End," *Church News*, 16 January 1993, 7.

37. McKay, "Media Challenges," 47.

38. Todd, "A Company of Angels."

39. Cook transcript.

40. Author's interview of Herold L. Gregory, Salt Lake City, Utah, 28 January 2000; see also Thomas, *Tabernacle Choir Goes to Europe*, 202–5.

41. Gregory interview; see also Thomas, *Tabernacle Choir Goes to Europe*, 202–5.

42. Herold L. Gregory, Testimonial, in Thomas, *Tabernacle Choir Goes to Europe*, 203–4.

CHAPTER SEVEN

"IN THAT DAY SHALL THE DEAF HEAR"

MARK D. ELLISON

"Faith cometh by hearing," wrote the apostle Paul, "and hearing by the word of God" (Romans 10:17). But what of those who cannot hear? For much of human history, deaf people have been assumed to be incapable of learning and therefore unable to acquire knowledge of God or develop faith in him. As absurd as that view seems at the dawn of the twenty-first century, since people with disabilities now enjoy unprecedented participation in society, it prevailed until relatively recent times. Only in the past few centuries, as the reformation era prepared the way for the Restoration, did the world change for deaf people.

With the latter-day outpouring of divine intelligence and gifts has come knowledge to facilitate the spread of the gospel and to bless all the inhabitants of the earth, including those who have never heard the gospel: "For verily the voice of the Lord is unto all men . . . and there is no eye that shall not see, neither ear that shall not hear" (D&C 1:2). The story of deaf Latter-day Saints bids reflection on how we all learn, think, and communicate about our faith, and how we interact as Saints. It is the story of a figurative "lost tribe," which in the twentieth century came out of obscurity to become fellow citizens with the Saints. As such, it bears witness of God's work in the continually unfolding restoration.

Mark D. Ellison is a Church Educational System coordinator in Tampa, Florida.

ANCIENT VIEWS OF MINISTERING TO DEAF PEOPLE

Anciently, many cultures denied deaf people the opportunities of education, marriage, inheritance, and even salvation.[1] Aristotle (c. 384–322 B.C.) is said to have declared that "those who are born deaf all become senseless and incapable of reason."[2] The Roman poet-philosopher Lucretius (c. 96–55 B.C.) expressed the prevailing opinion of his day: "To instruct the deaf, no art can ever reach / No care improve them, and no wisdom teach."[3] Among the Jews, Talmudic law forbade deaf people who could not speak from assuming full citizenship in the community. Its restrictions "were not meant to be cruel but were seen as the means of protecting such individuals from exploitation by others, while recognizing that they could not contribute fully to the religious life of the community."[4]

The Qumran community (of the Dead Sea Scrolls) did not admit people who were deaf, believing that they and those with other disabilities were in the care of the angels. By contrast, the early Christians, following the example of Jesus, tried to ease the sufferings of people with physical and mental impairments. There eventually developed, however, a Christian tradition that those who were deaf did not need to be converted. This tradition apparently dates to Augustine (A.D. 354–430), some of whose writings convey an assumption that deaf people could not be educated, and that since their deafness was caused by God, their fate was in his hands.[5]

DEAF EDUCATION

The comparatively recent idea of deaf education has Christian origins. It was a Benedictine monk, Pablo Ponce de Leon, who in 1545 began teaching the deaf children of Spanish nobles. His was the first school for the deaf. Part of the way he taught his students was with signs and a manual alphabet used by monks who took a vow of silence. A generation later, a Spanish priest named Juan Pablo Bonet wrote a book about teaching deaf people. The one-handed alphabet he described was probably that used by Ponce de Leon, and basically the same manual alphabet is used today in the United States. Deaf education in Spain eventually reached France, where in the eighteenth century a Catholic monk, Abbé Charles Michel de l'Epée, started teaching the deaf children of his parishioners. Epée and his successors enjoyed great success, news of which spread throughout Europe.

Early in the nineteenth century, Episcopal minister Thomas Hopkins Gallaudet visited the French school, where he met deaf teacher Laurent Clerc. Together, Clerc and Gallaudet established the first American school for the deaf in Hartford, Connecticut, in 1817. Over the next fifty years, the leadership of ministers and religious people led to the founding of many American schools for the deaf.[6]

THE RESTORED CHURCH AND DEAF PEOPLE

With the opening of the Hartford school in 1817, the growing movement to educate deaf children came to America just before the Prophet Joseph's first vision. During his remarkable ministry, Joseph Smith declared that "all the minds and spirits that God ever sent into the world are susceptible of enlargement,"[7] and he repeatedly taught that the gospel was to be preached "to all nations, kindreds, and tongues, in their own languages."[8] Looking back, we can see that from its beginnings, the Restoration was suited to reach out, in due time, to deaf people. In the newly restored Church, some of the early missionaries met deaf people but did not try to teach them.

In 1835 two Mormon missionaries baptized several residents of a Kentucky town, among them John and Caroline Butler. Caroline had three deaf sisters, and her family evidently knew some sign language. When one of the deaf sisters, Charity Skeen, inquired about the religious persecution arising in the area, Caroline taught her and shared her testimony as well as she could by signs. Charity then determined that she too would be baptized.[9] Probably most deaf members of the newly restored Church learned what they did of the gospel as Charity Skeen did—from relatives who had developed some means of communicating with them.

After the Church moved west, more formal efforts were undertaken to meet the needs of deaf Saints. In 1884 a school for the deaf was established on the campus of Deseret University in Salt Lake City, and in 1891 a Sunday School class for deaf members was organized there. The class served about twenty members. When the Utah School for the Deaf and Blind was moved to Ogden in 1896, a Sunday School class was set up there. These classes for deaf members

were similar to efforts being made at that time by other denominations.[10]

The latter half of the nineteenth century was a time when
American churches in general were beginning to reach out to their
deaf members. In a few metropolitan areas, ministers who knew sign
language had started conducting services for their parishioners who
were deaf. As in Utah, signed worship and religious instruction had
also begun to be offered in connection with some residential schools
for the deaf.[11]

Around 1900, LDS missionaries in England met a deaf man named
Joseph Benfell, the minister of a congregation serving about thirty
deaf people in the small town of Barnsley. He became very interested
in the elders' message, though he struggled to understand them by
lipreading, while they in turn struggled to learn sign language. After
becoming personally convinced that the missionaries taught the
truth, Joseph Benfell was baptized and relinquished his position as
minister. Nonetheless, he taught the deaf members of his former congregation, and they all became members of the Barnsley Branch.[12]

When news of these dramatic events reached the Saints in Utah, a
newspaper editorial enthusiastically called for the "elders abroad" to
"apply themselves to the study of the deaf and dumb signs, so as to
become proficient in the art of teaching them, and . . . accomplish
as good a work in some other places as that which was done
at Barnsley." It concluded, "Let the Gospel be preached also to the
deaf . . . !"[13] That turn-of-the-century call heralded the beginning of a
remarkable work.

Congregations among Deaf Latter-day Saints

In the early years of the new century, the Sunday School class for
deaf members of the Church in Ogden enjoyed steady growth. Dr.
Max W. Woodbury, a hearing man who was a teacher, principal, and
basketball coach at the school for the deaf, saw the need for the LDS
students to meet together, and he gave encouragement to the
group.[14] In 1917 the group was organized into the first deaf branch
in the Church. Dr. Woodbury was called to be the branch president,
and a building for the sole use of the branch was dedicated by
President Joseph F. Smith.[15] President Woodbury recalled that on the
day of the dedication that the prophet "was overcome on seeing so

many deaf people assembled that for a moment he said nothing, [being] greatly touched. [Then] he gave a wonderful sermon and dedicatory prayer."[16] President Woodbury served as branch president for over 50 years, and is remembered as "the beloved 'father' of the Utah deaf people."[17]

In 1948 a second deaf branch was established in Salt Lake City, an event that was reported in the *Church News* by a young Church employee named Gordon B. Hinckley.[18] His article related how the branch president, Willard E. Barlow, had first become involved with serving deaf members when he noticed that several members of his Bountiful ward were deaf. He suggested that a Sunday School class be organized for them and was promptly called to teach it, which required him to learn sign language. The class grew in size until, under the direction of President George Albert Smith, preparations were made for it to become a branch.[19]

Among Christian denominations, all-deaf congregations like these have been rare, as have deaf members of the clergy. Predominantly, most churches that have sought to serve deaf people have done so by providing sign language interpreters at their services. Religious interpreter Elaine Costello observes that while this has been "an efficient way to reach both deaf and hearing members simultaneously, deaf people tend not to participate in other functions outside the regularly scheduled services since they cannot communicate freely with the other members. Some problems may also arise from issues of confidentiality in counseling sessions where an interpreter is used to assist the exchange between the clergyman and the deaf person."[20] For deaf Latter-day Saints, therefore, deaf branches with priesthood leaders who knew sign language were (and still are) of tremendous importance.

LEADERSHIP AMONG DEAF LATTER-DAY SAINTS

Even more significant in the eyes of many deaf members was having leaders who were deaf themselves. Joe F. Brandenburg was one of the first deaf members to preside in an ecclesiastical position. Deaf since the age of three, Joe graduated from the Ogden school in 1936. He then moved to Salt Lake City, where he participated in the deaf Sunday School class and served as a stake missionary with two other men trying to "bring back the deaf who had become inactive because of their lack of understanding." The work of these stake missionaries helped the Salt Lake City deaf group grow from twenty to fifty members over the next three years. Then in 1941 Joe moved to California, one of the many deaf men who, due to draft ineligibility and ability to tolerate a noisy workplace, were encouraged to work in the wartime industries of Los Angeles. There, he and his wife, Fern, began meeting in the Vermont Ward with a newly established Sunday School class for deaf members, which became known as the Silent Class. It was taught by Joseph F. Evans, whose daughter Rhoda was deaf. The Brandenburgs, the Evanses, and other class members were called to serve as stake missionaries to the deaf community. Though wartime gas rationing and the widely dispersed deaf population made missionary work difficult, the Silent Class grew to twenty-five members by November of 1942 and over one hundred by 1946. In January 1952 a deaf branch was created, with Joseph Evans as branch president and Joe Brandenburg as his first counselor. Three and a half years later, Joe was called as branch president, the first deaf man in the Church to hold that position. "There was no one to teach me to be branch president," he recalled, "and I had to fight hard to learn how."[21] Elder John Carmack wrote that in the 1950s the beloved deaf members were the only clear minority group in the Los Angeles Stake and were "the delight of the stake," contributing actively to it.[22]

Continued missionary work made the branch grow to over three hundred members by 1970. At that time, Elder Gordon B. Hinckley visited California and spoke with President Brandenburg about the possibility of making the branch a ward, with him as bishop. President Brandenburg requested that the branch first be divided so that a congregation could meet further south in Fullerton. Consequently, the Fullerton Deaf Branch was created in 1971, but that did not long delay the formation of a deaf ward in Los Angeles. In June of 1972, Elder Howard W. Hunter met with President Brandenburg and told him that his name was well known by the First Presidency and the Twelve. Mentioning the recent reorganization of the Salt Lake City branch into a ward, with a deaf man, Lloyd Perkins, as the bishop, Elder Hunter expressed to President Brandenburg the confidence the Church leaders had in the deaf Saints.[23]

The next day Elder Hunter stood in a special conference and announced that the deaf branch was being dissolved. For a few moments the members were shocked and confused, wondering if they had done something wrong. Elder Hunter then smiled and asked for a sustaining vote for organizing the Los Angeles Deaf *Ward,* with Joe Brandenburg as its bishop. The members' hands shot up! One of the deaf members, Wayne Bennett, wrote:

"The joy of the faces of the members is something that will remain with me for life. It defies description to explain. Why do I dwell on this point so much? A very simple reason. . . . The deaf have always been a sort of second-class citizen and maybe even a third-class citizen in the world. . . . With the organization of a ward, the Church was in effect telling them that they were on an equal par with other members of the Church. No longer were they an 'orphan' organization. Now they were to be expected to do the same thing as other wards throughout the Church. The deaf members were now good enough to be bishops."[24]

After serving for five years as bishop—after his seventeen years as branch president—Joe Brandenburg was called in October 1978 to be a high councilor. This new calling required him to work with an interpreter as he sat in council with other leaders. "All these men with their college degrees, and business men," he remarked, "and I've just got a high school diploma." Brother Brandenburg even took frequent speaking assignments in hearing wards. "I can [participate in] the hearing world very well," he said. "Whether hearing or deaf, we're all equal. One of my interpreters . . . was so proud that a deaf person could preach to the hearing. [The interpreter] said that for so many years the hearing have been preaching to the deaf, and . . . now the deaf is preaching to the hearing. I'd never even really thought about that." To Joe, it was not a matter of hearing versus deaf. As he put it, "I [just] do what the Lord wants me to do." Joe Brandenburg passed away in February of 1996, by which time it was no longer unusual for deaf people to serve in such positions of responsibility as bishop, Relief Society president, high councilor, or temple ordinance worker.[25]

MISSIONARY WORK IN THE DEAF COMMUNITY

The beginnings of full-time missionary work to the deaf community include another twentieth-century pioneer, Samuel H. Judd. A giant of a man, Sam Judd is remembered for his prowess at boxing, his overpowering "bear hug" greetings, his service as a bishop, and most of all, his great talent and love for missionary work. Like Bishop Joe F. Brandenburg, he graduated from the Utah School for the Deaf before moving to Los Angeles to work in the wartime industries. For a year he didn't attend an LDS church, but visited other denominations, often feeling disappointed by what he experienced. At one church, the preacher called Sam to come forward during the service. She put her hands on Sam, spoke, and then asked Sam if he could hear now. When Sam replied that his hearing hadn't changed, she had the pianist make more noise, the congregation all fell to the floor, and Sam's friend who had invited him to church cried and accused him of not having enough faith to be healed. Not surprisingly, Sam didn't return to that church.

Some time in 1945 Sam ran into Joe Brandenburg at a deaf club. Joe, who knew Sam from their days in Utah, invited him to attend the Silent Class. Sam went the next Sunday. There, Joe's teaching about premortal life deeply affected Sam. He was not familiar with the doctrine, though he had been reared in the Church and attended the Ogden Deaf Branch. "I grew up not knowing the gospel," he explained. "I asked Joe where he learned such a thing. He said, 'From the Bible.' I wanted to see the scriptures and was surprised to learn about it." This was a profound spiritual experience, which Sam marked as the moment of his conversion—a spiritual transformation rather than a physical healing.

Sam was called upon to teach the Silent Class and later to serve as a stake missionary with his wife, Rebecca. Though these opportunities worried him, he accepted them with great determination. He received some stake missionary training with the help of an interpreter, but most of his development as a teacher came through prayer and rigorous personal study. Often, he and Rebecca would stay up until one o'clock in the morning, poring over and practicing the missionary lessons. As a result he became a powerful teacher and an effective missionary and began to see many of the people he taught join the Church.[26]

By 1980 it was estimated that Samuel Judd had "been instrumental in the conversion of some 150 deaf persons" over the sixteen years of his stake missionary service, but Sam admitted that he himself had "lost track." He was so successful a missionary that ministers of deaf congregations "warned their members not to listen to him." Sam shrugged it off, explaining, "I just teach the truth from the scriptures, and they join the Church." He succeeded Joe Brandenburg as bishop shortly before the ward was divided into two Los Angeles area deaf wards. After his service as bishop, he taught institute of religion and helped train the newly called full-time missionaries to the deaf until formal training was established at the Missionary Training Center in Provo, Utah. Years later, he and his wife returned once again to their much-loved missionary work, serving a full-time mission in Atlanta, Georgia.[27]

Prior to 1968 deaf people were generally not called on full-time missions, although a few hearing-impaired individuals with good lipreading and speech abilities had served. In 1961 two full-time missionaries, hearing sons of deaf parents, were assigned to work with the deaf branch in southern California. Late in 1968 permanent full-time missionary work in the deaf community began with the efforts of eight elders in the California Mission, four of them hearing and four deaf—Clarke Zemp, Wayne Kitchen, Wayne Bennett, and Juan A. Martinez. Several of the deaf elders had received spiritual assurances, including promises in patriarchal blessings, that they would be called on full-time missions in spite of their deafness. The newly formed district quickly felt humbled by the task before it. The deaf elders did not know the scriptures well, the hearing elders did not know sign language at all, and none of the eight had received any training in teaching deaf people. Reflecting on their first day together, Wayne Bennett recalls asking about training and teaching materials, and how the missionaries were to get around, and most of all, "Where are the deaf people?" "Go and find them," replied mission president Don H. Rasmussen, who counseled the elders to be creative and assured them that the Lord would help.[28]

The missionaries soon sought out Sam Judd and asked for the benefit of his years of missionary experience. He didn't quite know how to teach the elders other than by demonstrating how he signed as he taught the gospel. His gift for communicating enthralled the missionaries, and they went out to practice what they called the "Judd method."[29] Today we would call it American Sign Language (ASL). The natural language of perhaps half a million deaf Americans, ASL was just beginning to be studied from a linguistic perspective in the 1960s, when full-time missionary work to the deaf community was beginning. Linguists found ASL to be neither a manual code for English nor a "shorthand" signed English, but a complete and sophisticated visual language with its own vocabulary and grammar. It had developed naturally within the deaf community and had linguistic roots in the French sign language brought to America by Laurent Clerc.[30]

Since about 90 percent of deaf people have hearing parents, who do not readily know how to sign, deaf children usually acquire ASL through interaction with peers, school associates, and deaf adults.[31] This was the case with the early missionaries and with Sam Judd; though the deaf elders knew how to sign, they refined their ability to communicate with native-like competence in ASL, while also learning how to teach gospel principles. The hearing elders also benefited greatly from having Brother Judd or other deaf stake missionaries team up with them for teaching appointments.

One of these early hearing elders, Jack Rose, recalled that after he would explain a gospel principle, Sam Judd would often intervene in the teaching, and with his amazing clarity, help the confused investigator to finally understand. The missionary work flourished, leading in time to the calling of more missionaries and the establishment of more deaf wards and branches.

At one point early in their labors, Bishop Brandenburg was asked to offer a dedicatory prayer at a groundbreaking ceremony for the Wilshire Ward. While giving the prayer, he felt moved upon to declare: "From this very area where we break this ground, the Gospel of Jesus Christ shall spread across the world and all the deaf people may have the ear to hear the word of Jesus Christ." His words proved to be prophetic, for along with the establishment of more wards and branches in California, missionaries began to be sent to cities throughout the United States to labor in the deaf community, leading to the organization of more branches around the country. Those branches were further built up by returning deaf missionaries, who as a direct result of their missions enjoyed the blessings of the temple, furthered their education, and served more effectively in leadership positions. Returned missionaries also strengthened deaf members by organizing workshops and conferences and assisting in Church translation projects.[32]

In 1979 a Deaf Missionary Training Center was established in the California Ventura Mission, and for a time all deaf missionary work around the country was administered from California. Jack Rose, an institute teacher, directed the training with assistance from Sam Judd, Joe Brandenburg, and others. In 1982 training was moved to the Missionary Training Center in Provo, Utah. Since that time, missionaries to the deaf have been called to serve throughout the United States and in some foreign countries such as England, Korea, Guatemala, and Panama, where the sign languages of those countries are used. Deaf missionaries continue to serve in major metropolitan areas where sizable deaf communities exist and have generally enjoyed the same baptism and retention rates as other proselyting missionaries.[33]

Resources for Strengthening the Deaf Saints

The late 1960s and early 1970s was an era of expanding civil rights, increasing awareness of minority groups, and growing ethnic pride. It was a time when the deaf community began to more assertively define itself as a group united by its shared language and culture rather than by disability. That understanding was reflected at Church headquarters. In 1971 Elder Marvin J. Ashton assigned a full-time Church employee to work on behalf of minority cultural groups, including deaf members; the following year the First Presidency instructed local priesthood leaders to see that the needs of linguistic minority groups living within their boundaries were adequately met. The result was that along with the increasing missionary effort grew an effort to develop resources to meet the unique needs of deaf members. This work received particular encouragement in southern California.[34]

Among the growing number of Church leaders there who worked with the deaf community was Dr. Ray L. Jones, director of the National Center on Deafness at San Fernando Valley State College (now California State University–Northridge). Known for his "why not?" philosophy, Dr. Jones was especially enthusiastic about projects that could bring full gospel blessings to deaf members. In 1972 leaders from Salt Lake and southern California came together in a special conference to consider such projects, and since that time, hearing and deaf Latter-day Saints have worked together to produce many materials and resources for deaf members.[35] The developing video and computer technologies have been greatly utilized in these productions, which include the following:

A dictionary of sign language terms, produced in book and video format, which helped establish and standardize signs for gospel and ecclesiastical vocabulary.[36]

A film explaining how to perform priesthood ordinances in sign language.[37]

Church films with closed captions, interpreter inserts, or all-deaf casts.[38]

The interpreting and closed captioning of general conference.[39]

The translation of the missionary discussions into ASL.[40]

The translation of the temple endowment into ASL.[41]

A multivolume videotaped translation of the Book of Mormon in ASL, now nearing completion.[42]

The ASL Book of Mormon is a landmark work of translation. It differs from ASL translations of the Bible in how it seeks to preserve linguistic ambiguities, the styles of individual writers, and Hebraic elements in the text. Though the scriptures are available in English, the ASL translation will allow many deaf members their first real access to the Book of Mormon. Hearing loss can make English language acquisition very difficult for many deaf people; consequently, many of them struggle with reading and writing English, though they may be highly articulate in ASL. One deaf member of exceptional English literacy wrote, "Even though I am able to read and study the Book of Mormon in English, I am anxiously awaiting the ASL translation so I can study in my own language with less effort."[43]

The translation is also being done to fulfill the word of the Lord: "For it shall come to pass in that day, that every man shall hear the fulness of the gospel in his own tongue, and in his own language" (D&C 90:11); "For the Lord God giveth light unto the understanding; for he speaketh unto men according to their language, unto their understanding" (2 Nephi 31:3).[44]

The head translator of the project, Minnie Mae Wilding-Diaz, is the eldest child in an all-deaf family and holds a master's degree in teaching English as a second language. She has expressed the hope that as deaf people from all over the country view the videotapes, they will be enabled to "read" the Book of Mormon—to "understand,

enjoy, analyze, [and] learn" from it—and in this way realize King
Benjamin's plea that "the mysteries of God may be unfolded to [our]
view" (Mosiah 2:9).[45]

The ASL Book of Mormon may also fulfill another prophecy. In
the same chapter of Isaiah where we read of the book that speaks
"out of the dust," we read: "And in that day shall the deaf hear the
words of the book, and eyes of the blind shall see out of obscurity,
and out of darkness" (Isaiah 29:18). Elder LeGrand Richards once suggested that when the Book of Mormon became available in Braille, it
fulfilled Isaiah's statement, "the eyes of the blind shall see out of
obscurity, and out of darkness."[46] In that light, the ASL translation of
the Book of Mormon takes on unusual significance as a literal realization of Isaiah's promise that "the deaf," too, would "hear the
words of the book."

Deaf Latter-day Saints today remain a small but strong linguistic
minority within the Church. Just how many deaf Saints there are is
uncertain. The Church's membership department currently lists
eighty-four Church units as deaf units or units supporting a deaf
group—seven of them outside of the United States.[47] There are developing groups of deaf members in Japan, Korea, England, Italy, the
Canary Islands, and elsewhere—wherever deaf members meet
together in the Church.[48] Deaf members often seek out opportunities
to gather in large numbers at workshops and conferences.

Hearing members of the Church, encouraged by Church leaders,
often make efforts to reach out to deaf members and involve them
as much as possible in Church activities. For example, hundreds of
deaf and hearing members in the San Diego North Stake have participated in sign language classes taught by volunteers, and similar
classes have been established across the country.[49] In 1994 deaf members from Japan, accompanied by a group of hearing interpreters, visited Salt Lake City during the April general conference; they enjoyed
opportunities to interact with both hearing and deaf members from
the Salt Lake area during their visit.[50] Church publications have also
proposed ways hearing members may respond with sensitivity to
deaf members around them. All these efforts are tremendously
important. Over time, other linguistic minorities can often learn the
majority language around them and comfortably interact, but for all
that deaf people can do, they "cannot learn to hear."[51]

CONCLUSION

Deaf people today have remarkable advantages over those of previous centuries—among them the blessings of technology, education, communication, and legal protection. As we consider the historical developments that have blessed their lives, we see that many of these advances parallel the grand events of the Restoration. As the mighty religious awakening of the sixteenth century rolled through Europe, humble Christians made the first quiet efforts to teach deaf children. As American independence and religious freedom were being dramatically secured in the New World, deaf education was flourishing in parts of the Old World. As a boy prophet received revelations from God, two devoted men not far from him opened the doors of a school and the minds of their students. As deaf missionaries went forth in full-time service, greater understanding of the language of deaf Americans became available.

At each important step, the Lord seems to have supplied what was needed: people whose talents were required, technology that had to be in place. Surely we may see in these events evidence of God's hand and assurance that in the dispensation of the fulness of times, the Lord has planned for his gospel to be available to all people, both deaf and hearing. A people once believed to be uneducable have now built a heritage of faith, dedication, and service in the restored Church and enjoy the blessings of the fulness of the gospel never enjoyed by the deaf people of any previous dispensation. The call of 1900, "Let the Gospel be preached also to the deaf!"[52] is, in 2000, being answered and surpassed: Now the good news is being preached *by* deaf people. And in that very telling lies an especially impressive testimony of God's loving concern for all of his children and his consummating work in this final dispensation.

NOTES

The author expresses gratitude to the many people who assisted in his research, both hearing and deaf, LDS and non-LDS. Particular indebtedness is owed to Keith Gamache Jr., Minnie Mae Wilding-Diaz, Jack Rose, Wayne Bennett, Dan V. Mathis, Rodney and Patsy Walker, and Reverend Peggy A. Johnson. Since "the body hath need of every member," both hearing and deaf are called upon to work collectively, "that all may be edified together" (D&C 84:110).

1. Elaine Costello, *Religious Signing* (New York: Bantam, 1986), ix.

2. As cited in Jack Gannon, *Deaf Heritage: A Narrative History of Deaf America* (Silver Spring, Md.: National Association of the Deaf, 1981), xix.

3. As cited in F. A. Moeller, "Education of the Deaf and Dumb," *The Catholic Encyclopedia, Volume V* (New York: Robert Appleton Co., 1909), 316.

4. Jerome D. Schein and Lester J. Waldman, eds., *The Deaf Jew in the Modern World* (New York: Ktav Publishing House, 1986), 1.

5. S. Kent Brown, "The Dead Sea Scrolls: A Mormon Perspective," *BYU Studies* 23, 1; Jon K. Ashby, "Alexander Campbell on Evangelizing the Deaf," *Restoration Quarterly*, vol. 24, no. 1 (1981), 12–13; Augustine, "Against Julian," in R. J. Defarrari, ed., *The Fathers of the Church, vol. 35* (New York: Fathers of the Church, 1957), 115: "But, since you also deny that any infant is subject to original sin, you must answer why such great innocence is sometimes born blind; sometimes deaf. Deafness is a hindrance to faith itself, as the apostle says: 'Faith is from hearing.'" T. Arnold in *Education of Deaf-Mutes: A Manual for Teachers* cites another translation of this passage: "But this very defect [deafness] hinders faith, for one who is deaf from birth cannot learn the letters by whose knowledge he would attain to faith" (London: Werthheimer, Lea, and Co., 1888, 8); cf. Ashby, "Alexander Campbell on Evangelizing the Deaf," 12–13; Moeller, "Education of the Deaf and Dumb," 315–21. Note that all these perspectives on deaf people are views "from the outside." Mervin J. Garretson, past president of the National Association of the Deaf, points out: "It was not until the last 100 years or so that accounts written by a number of deaf persons appeared in print. These were shaped by actual experience and perception rather than by theory, assumption, and observation" (in Gannon, *Deaf Heritage*, xix).

6. Costello, *Religious Signing*, x; Moeller, "Education of the Deaf and Dumb"; Harlan Lane, *When the Mind Hears: A History of the Deaf* (New York: Random House, 1984).

7. *History of the Church*, 6:311, as cited in Larry E. Dahl and Donald Q. Cannon, eds., *The Teachings of Joseph Smith* (Salt Lake City: Bookcraft, 1997), 206.

8. Instructions to the Twelve in Kirtland, 12 November 1835, as cited in Dahl and Cannon, *Teachings of Joseph Smith*, 380; cf. D&C 90:11.

9. John Butler, Autobiography, BYU Special Collections, 1–9, as cited in Milton V. Backman Jr. and Keith W. Perkins, eds., *Writings of Early Latter-day Saints and Their Contemporaries, a Database Collection*, 2d ed., rev. and enl. (Provo, Utah: Religious Studies Center, 1996).

10. Gannon, *Deaf Heritage*, 48, 189–91; Andrew Jenson, *Encyclopedic History of The Church of Jesus Christ of Latter-day Saints* (Salt Lake City: Deseret News Publishing Co., 1941), 190–91; Dan V. Mathis, "The Deaf Latter-day Saints (Mormon) Community: Its Formation and Expansion," senior thesis, Gallaudet University, 1998, 16. The Utah State Legislature

estimated that there were forty-two "deaf-mutes" residing in the terri- tory ("Education of Deaf Mutes," *Deseret Evening News,* 23 February 1884, 2). The school began with one student and added three others within a month (see Gannon, *Deaf Heritage,* 48).

11. Costello, *Religious Signing,* xi–xiv; Gannon, *Deaf Heritage,* 181–95, which are both helpful though undocumented summaries of deaf min- istry in America. Some denominations have published more detailed histories of their deaf membership: Walter D. Uhlig, "Origins of Lutheran Deaf Work: A Chronological Sketch," *Concordia Historical Institute Quarterly* (Winter 1994): 151–57; E. Theo. DeLaney, "Ephphatha Conference: A Historical Overview," *Concordia Historical Institute Quarterly* (Summer 1977): 71–83; Peggy A. Johnson with Ruth Foxwell Farris, *The History of Christ United Methodist Church of the Deaf,* March 1995, n.p.; Otto B. Berg, *A Missionary Chronicle: Being a History of the Ministry to the Deaf in the Episcopal Church (1850–1980)* (Hollywood, Md.: St. Mary's Press, 1984); Jerome D. Schein and Lester J. Waldman, *Deaf Jew in the Modern World.*

12. Gladys Nichol, "Joseph and Annie Benfell," 6–7, manuscript in the author's possession. For a twentieth century parallel, cf. Steven A. Wolfe, "The Discussions in Sign Language," *Ensign,* August 1978, 66.

13. "The Gospel for Deaf-Mutes," *Deseret Evening News,* 18 December 1901, 102.

14. Interview of Douglas L. Hind, Manager of Special Curriculum, The Church of Jesus Christ of Latter-day Saints, 16 January 1998.

15. Gannon, *Deaf Heritage,* 189–91.

16. *LDS Deaf News,* January 1988, 1.

17. Mathis, "The Deaf Latter-day Saints," 17; plaque honoring Max William Woodbury at the Ogden Utah Branch for the Deaf.

18. Hinckley, "Years of Interest Bring Their Reward," *Church News,* 20 June 1948, 12-C.

19. Mathis, "The Deaf Latter-day Saints," 19–20.

20. Costello, *Religious Signing,* xi.

21. Brandenburg autobiography prepared for the Ventura Mission deaf training program, April 1979, in the author's possession; Brandenburg transcript of 1976 untitled talk to a group of missionaries at the institute of religion at California State University Northridge, in the author's possession, 1; Chad M. Orton, *More Faith Than Fear: The Los Angeles Stake Story* (Salt Lake City: Bookcraft, 1987), 204–5, 248.

22. John Carmack, "Unity in Diversity," *Ensign,* March 1991, 8.

23. Brandenburg untitled talk, 2; Orton, *More Faith Than Fear,* 248.

24. Bennett letter to Ray L. Jones, 26 September 1986, in "Projects to Bring Full Blessings of Church Membership to Deaf Persons," 1972–78, in the possession of Douglas L. Hind, Manager of Special Curriculum,

The Church of Jesus Christ of Latter-day Saints, 9–10. David Woodhouse of the Provo Utah Deaf Ward wrote: "The most important events or advances for deaf Latter-day Saints in the twentieth century" have been "the opportunity of having our own wards or branches run by deaf leaders, . . . the temple ordinances provided for the deaf, and missionaries for the deaf in their own language. [These comprise] the three missions of the Church" (correspondence of 7 January 2000, in the author's possession).

25. Brandenburg untitled talk, 5–6. In 1998, when Rodney Walker was called to be a sealer in the Salt Lake Temple, he was "believed to be the first non-hearing sealer in the Church" ("Deaf Sealer Serving in Salt Lake Temple: His Calling Is a 'Coming of Age' for Deaf LDS," *Church News*, 8 August 1998, 5, 7).

26. Videotaped interview with Sam and Becky Judd, 1997, transcribed by Keith Gamache Jr., 2; Samuel H. Judd, *Los Angeles Ward for the Deaf Newsletter*, April 1977, 4; Judd autobiography prepared for the Ventura Mission deaf training program, April 1979, in the author's possession, 3.

27. "Northridge—Where the Deaf Join the Mainstream," *Ensign*, October 1980, 78; Judd autobiography, 3; "Let Your Fingers Do the Talking," *Church News*, 19 August 1972, 11; Judd autobiography, 4 (the two wards were located in Torrance and San Fernando Valley); "Much Growth in the Atlanta Area," *LDS Deaf News*, January–February 1989, 1.

28. Hind interview (some of those called before the organization of the deaf missionary district in December 1968 included Tom and Virl Osmond, who served in Canada, and Paul Chamberlain, who initially served in England and was later transferred to join the work in Los Angeles); Wayne Bennett, "A Brief Chronology of the Development of the Church of Jesus Christ in Southern California among the Deaf," 22 June 1996, n.p., 1; Bennett letter to Jones, 1–3, 5–6. "For at least two, their calls came in fulfillment of patriarchal blessings which stated that they would serve missions in spite of their handicaps" (Orton, *More Faith Than Fear*, 247). Clarke Zemp had long believed he would have the opportunity to serve a full-time proselyting mission (see "And the Deaf Shall Hear," *Ensign*, January 1971, 11).

29. Bennett letter to Jones, 7.

30. Charlotte Baker-Shenk and Dennis Cokely, *American Sign Language: A Teacher's Resource Text on Grammar and Culture* (Washington, D.C.: Gallaudet University Press, 1991), 47; William C. Stokoe Jr., Dorothy C. Casterline, and Carl G. Croneberg, *A Dictionary of American Sign Language on Linguistic Principles*, Washington, D.C.: Gallaudet Press, 1965; Oliver Sacks, *Seeing Voices: A Journey into the World of the Deaf* (Los Angeles: University of California Press, 1989), 20.

31. Baker-Shenk and Cokely, *American Sign Language*, 47–61.

32. Keith Gamache Jr., senior thesis, Brigham Young University, n.d., 9; Carmack, "Unity in Diversity," 8; Brandenburg untitled talk, 4; Bennett letter to Jones, 15. Many of these branches have kept or are now assembling their own histories, and some historically-inclined deaf Saints are enthusiastic about producing a comprehensive history of deaf Latter-day Saints.

33. Bennett, "A Brief Chronology," 2; Hyrum Smith, "The Beginning of the Explosion in Missionary Work with the Deaf," *LDS Deaf News,* February 1988, 4–5; Douglas L. Hind, "The Lord's Church Is Growing," *LDS Deaf Connection,* Summer 1991, 3; Interview of Lloyd Owen, Missionary Department, The Church of Jesus Christ of Latter-day Saints, 11 January 2000.

34. Richard O. Cowan, *The Church in the Twentieth Century* (Salt Lake City: Bookcraft, 1985), 355–56; Baker-Shenk and Cokely, *American Sign Language,* 54–58; Stewart A. Durrant, "History of My Involvement in the Church Deaf Program," in "Projects to Bring Full Blessings," 1.

35. "In Memoriam: Dr. Ray L. Jones, Teacher, Administrator, Advocate, Friend, 1917–1996," *Deaf Life Plus,* supplement to *Deaf Life* (December 1996): 1–2; Durrant, "Projects to Bring Full Blessings"; Cowan, *Church in the Twentieth Century,* 355–56; Stephen Gibson, "Needs Identified at Seminar for LDS Deaf," *Church News,* 19 August 1972, 7. Ray Jones' "impact on the Deaf LDS Church is still being felt today. And he is a man whose name should always be remembered and honored among the LDS Deaf." Jack Rose, "A Man with a Heart for the Deaf," *LDS Deaf Connection* (Spring 1991): 4–5.

36. "Needs Identified at Seminar," 7–12.

37. Cowan, *Church in the Twentieth Century,* 355.

38. "Materials for the Deaf," in Daniel H. Ludlow, ed., *Encyclopedia of Mormonism,* 4 vols. (New York: Macmillan, 1992), 1:364.

39. Ibid.

40. Ray L. Jones, "Now Therefore Ye Are No More Strangers and Foreigners, but Fellow Citizens with the Saints, and of the Household of God," talk given at the southern California area conference for the deaf, 21 October 1979, in "Projects to Bring Full Blessings," 3.

41. "Policies and Announcements," *Ensign,* May 1991, 110. The ASL translation of the endowment is available in all U.S. temples except those in Salt Lake City and Manti, Utah.

42. Minnie Mae Wilding-Diaz letter to the author, 16 October 1999; see Linda Hoffman Kimball, "Deaf Learn Skills at Conference," *Church News,* 9 May 1992, 11; Julie A. Dockstader, "Book of Mormon Available in Sign Language," *Church News,* 10 June 1995, 3.

43. Jack R. Rose letter; Wilding-Diaz letter; see Kimball, "Deaf Learn

Skills at Conference," 11; Matt Jamison, ed., *LDS Deaf Connection* (Summer 1991): 1.

44. Wilding-Diaz letter to the author, 22 January 2000; cf. Joseph Smith's instructions to the Twelve in Kirtland, 12 November 1835, as cited in Dahl and Cannon, *Teachings of Joseph Smith,* 380.

45. Wilding-Diaz, "Translation of the Book of Mormon into ASL," *LDS Deaf Connection,* Summer 1991, 2.

46. LeGrand Richards, in Conference Report, April 1976, 124; or *Ensign,* May 1976, 84.

47. Church Management Information, 11 January 2000: U.S. has 26 wards and 15 branches with "deaf" as their first classification, and Canada has 1 ward; U.S./Canada has 36 that "supports deaf"; international (non-U.S./Canada) has 6 units classified "deaf" or "supports deaf."

48. Douglas L. Hind, "Church Materials for the Deaf," *LDS Deaf News,* March–June 1989, 1; Hind, "Work to Move Forward among the Deaf in England," *LDS Deaf News,* February 1988, 1–2; Hind, "The Work Must Go Forth," *LDS Deaf Connection,* Winter 1993, 3.

49. Jones, "Now Therefore Ye Are No More Strangers," 1; "Deaf Singles Conference Held in Los Angeles," *Ensign,* October 1988, 79; Kimball, "Deaf Learn Skills at Conference," 11 (BYU has hosted the LDS Deaf Symposium a number of times); Cowan, *Church in the Twentieth Century,* 356; "Serving through Signing," *Ensign,* December 1997, 63–64; "North America Southwest Area: Communicate with Deaf," *Church News,* 10 July 1993, 12.

50. Greg Hill, "Conference Moments: Conference Dream," *Church News,* 8 October 1994, 24.

51. Jan Underwood Pinborough, "A Language beyond Sound: Making the Gospel Available to the Hearing-Impaired," *Ensign,* September 1991, 22–27; Connie Lewis, "Ideas for Teaching Deaf Children in Primary," *Ensign,* June 1986, 28, 54–55.

52. "Gospel for Deaf-Mutes," 102.

CHAPTER EIGHT

Latter-day Saints in the World Wars

ROBERT C. FREEMAN

One of the most tragic facts relating to the twentieth century is that its wars cost more lives and resulted in more devastation than all wars in the previous nineteen centuries combined. In particular, World Wars I and II were unequaled in history in terms of the amount of destruction inflicted upon mankind. These two great wars had a significant impact upon the Church and its members. Furthermore, the contribution of Latter-day Saints in both wars was important. An understanding of the experience of the Church and its members during the wars of the first half of the twentieth century should engender a greater appreciation for the sacrifice and faith of the disciples of peace who served valiantly to subdue the dictators of war.

The involvement of Latter-day Saints in twentieth-century wars was preceded by earlier contributions in the previous century. The first occasion for Church members to be involved in wartime military service came during the United States' war with Mexico. In 1846 the federal government called upon the Church to furnish approximately five hundred volunteers to form the Mormon Battalion, which actively served from July 1846 until July 1847. Battalion members marched two thousand miles from Ft. Leavenworth, Kansas, to San Diego, California, though they never engaged the enemy in battle.[1]

Robert C. Freeman is an assistant professor of Church history at Brigham Young University.

The most horrific war in American history was the one specifically prophesied by Joseph Smith.[2] In spite of its significance, the Civil War did not directly involve the Church and its members, as they were occupied with establishing a home in the Rocky Mountains. Additionally, Brigham Young had invoked a policy of isolation from the affairs of the United States during that period.

In 1896 a new era of cooperation between the Church and the federal government began when statehood was finally granted to Utah. When the Spanish-American War erupted just two years later in 1898, Utah stepped forward to provide support. Although the contribution of the newest member of the Union was modest, it included two artillery units primarily composed of Mormon volunteers. This war was historically significant because it was the first conflict in which Latter-day Saints died in military combat, the first being a young LDS infantryman named George Hudson.[3] In addition, the Spanish-American War saw the military appointment of the first LDS chaplain, Elias S. Kimball, son of Elder Heber C. Kimball.[4] Still, the impact of the Spanish-American War on the Church and its membership was comparatively limited. The actual number of Latter-day Saints involved in the war was a few hundred. Of this number, approximately a half dozen died. With the dawning of the twentieth century, however, Latter-day Saints would soon be called upon to make a greater sacrifice for their country.

WORLD WAR I

World War I was the first great war of the twentieth century. When hostilities erupted in Europe late in the summer of 1914, there were approximately 370,000 members of the Church worldwide. As in the nineteenth century, during the early twentieth century most members who joined the Church in areas outside of the United States eventually relocated to North America. At the beginning of the war, approximately 85 percent of all Church members were located in the United States with 65 percent of the Mormon population living in Utah. At this time only two stakes had been organized outside of the United States.[5] Hence, the story of the Latter-day Saints' participation in World War I is predominantly the story of Utah's involvement in the war.

Latter-day Saints in Uniform

While exact numbers are not known, approximately 22,500 U.S. Latter-day Saints served during World War I. Over the nineteen months of U.S. involvement, it is estimated that between six and seven hundred American LDS servicemen were killed. Less well known is the fact that approximately seventy-five LDS Germans also died in the war.[6] By comparison, the United States mobilized over 4,000,000 men, of whom 67,813 died. Included among the LDS contingent of servicemen were such future general authorities as Hugh B. Brown, Delbert L. Stapley, William J. Critchlow, and S. Dilworth Young.[7] President Joseph F. Smith had six sons who served in the war.

Five Latter-day Saints from the United States served as generals during the war: William E. Cole, Frank T. Hines, Briant H. Wells, Richard W. Young, and Edgar A. Wedgewood.[8] During the war, Wedgewood died from influenza, a disease that claimed more servicemen's lives than did combat. Also, three LDS chaplains were commissioned by the U.S. military during the war. They included Elder Brigham H. Roberts; Calvin S. Smith, son of President Joseph F. Smith; and Herbert Maw, future governor of Utah.[9]

Because of the strong concentration of Latter-day Saints in the Rocky Mountain region, the vast majority of United States LDS soldiers served in just a few units. The most significant of these was the 145th First Utah Field Artillery Regiment, which in 1918 reported that 1,016 of its 1,313 men were LDS. Those assigned to the 145th distinguished themselves from their peers as they established a record of exceptionally good health, obedience to military regulations, and dominance in competitions with other units. The 143d and 144th regiments were also both disproportionately LDS, as was the 65th Artillery Brigade of the 40th Division of the U.S. Army.[10] There were also a number of LDS servicemen who belonged to the 362d Infantry unit in the 91st Division, a unit which saw extensive action in France and Belgium during the war.

The Church and the War

The war greatly affected the Church's missionary program. In 1913, the year preceding the outbreak of war in Europe, the number of young men set apart for full-time missionary service was 858. In 1918, the last year of the war, the number was drastically reduced to a mere 245. At the beginning of World War I, approximately 433 full-time missionaries were serving in Europe. Most of the missionaries serving abroad were evacuated by the fall of 1914.[11] Even before the war, conditions in Germany had forced missionaries to conduct meetings and missionary discussions with investigators in secret. Elder James E. Talmage reflected on the difficult prewar years in Germany as he declared:

"Our missionary elders have time and again been imprisoned in Germany, and others have been forcibly banished from the empire of the boasted kultur, because they bore the message of freedom and individual agency. Formerly they went into that land with only the Scriptures and their own testimony of the truth as weapons in the conflict with sin. Now many of those selfsame men are on their way back wearing the uniform of the Nation, and with Browning guns as their instruments of persuasion."[12]

During the war the Church suspended full-time missionary work in countries such as France, Switzerland, and Germany—although the Church actually grew in Germany during the war. At the beginning of the war approximately 7,500 members of the Church lived in Germany, but by the time the Armistice agreement was signed, the number approached 8,000.[13]

As the conflict in Europe raged on, Church leaders spoke frequently on matters relating to the gospel and the war. President Joseph F. Smith, who presided over the Church during the war, subscribed to the U.S. policy of neutrality and frequently called upon the nations of Europe to cease their hostilities. He also spoke of the need to distinguish between the citizens of Germany and their corrupt leaders. Before the United States entered the fray, President Smith said:

"There is such a great prejudice wrought in the minds of some of the people against that country—not against the people; the people are innocent, the people are blameless. You must not condemn the people, however much you may judge and condemn their leaders, who place their people in jeopardy, and demand their life blood for their maintenance in position of prominence and power. Their leaders are to blame, not the people."[14]

While a spirit of tolerance was being taught, leaders were also predicting the eventual success of the Allied forces, using Book of Mormon teachings about the latter-day role of America. Elders

Heber J. Grant and Anthony W. Ivins were outspoken in their criticism of the German fascist regime. Elder Ivins even declared that German policy was the embodiment of the anti-Christ spirit.[15]

When events in Europe compelled the United States to enter the conflict on 6 April 1917, general Church leadership and individual members rallied to support the cause of the Allied nations. Church members responded enthusiastically by donating time to the American Red Cross, planting "victory gardens," and actively participating in rationing programs. Statistics on war-related efforts, such as agricultural and home canning production, were even reported in general conference. Near the end of the war, the general Relief Society delivered 250,000 bushels of badly needed wheat to the federal government. In response to this generosity, U.S. president Herbert Hoover wrote a personal letter of thanks.[16]

Church leaders actively encouraged members to support the war effort through the purchase of war bonds. The general priesthood, Relief Society, and youth programs made significant purchases of American Liberty bonds.[17] Elder Heber J. Grant served as chairman of the Liberty Loan Sales Committee for Utah and actively endorsed the purchase of bonds by Church members. In October 1917, a proposal was passed in general conference, "authorizing the Church to purchase $500,000 in Liberty bonds from the Federal government, which it promptly did."[18]

While the sacrifice was significant, the length of direct LDS involvement in the war was relatively short. On 11 November 1918, just nineteen months after the United States entered the conflict, the Axis powers signed the Armistice agreement, which effectively ended the war. In Utah, as well as throughout the United States, American citizens enthusiastically rejoiced at the end of the war. Remarking on Salt Lake City's celebrations, a jubilant Elder Heber J. Grant declared, "The city has simply gone wild with joy over the signing of the peace compact by the Germans. I never saw anything quite like it."[19] On 19 November 1918, just eight days after the end of the war, President Joseph F. Smith quietly passed away.

WORLD WAR II

Just twenty years after the guns of World War I were silenced, the world again became embroiled in conflict. As with World War I, the hostilities that resulted in the second great war began in Europe. When Germany invaded Poland on 1 September 1939, there were approximately 860,000 total members of the Church. Although the vast majority of all stakes were still located in the United States, since World War I thirteen new missions had been organized in the Church, the majority of which were located outside the United States.

Latter-day Saints in Uniform

As a result of the U.S. Selective Service Act of 1940, which mandated service for those of military age, many young men entered the draft over a year before the events at Pearl Harbor compelled the United States to enter the war. For instance, the first wave of Latter-day Saint draftees in Utah took the servicemen's oath on 18 November 1940. Records of the number of LDS active service personnel were not maintained until the spring of 1942. From that time they were kept for the duration of the war. These wartime estimates, based on ward and stake reports, indicated that the number of Latter-day Saints in uniform steadily increased through the years to a high of approximately 100,000 in 1945.[20] Several future general authorities served in the war, including a young army intelligence officer named Bruce R. McConkie, who later became the first World War II veteran called to be a general authority.[21]

According to the 1940 census, members of the Church constituted .5 percent of the citizenry of the United States. At the height of the conflict, however, they made up approximately 1 percent of the total U.S. military force.[22] Furthermore, Latter-day Saints from other Allied nations, including Canada, Britain, New Zealand, and Australia, provided distinguished service during the war. One of the lesser-known facts relating to the Latter-day Saint experience in World War II is that many Latter-day Saints fought for the Axis nations, including several thousand from Germany. By the end of the war, approximately five thousand Latter-day Saint servicemen from Allied and Axis nations had died.[23]

During the war President Heber J. Grant sent five grandsons into the conflict and only two returned. Future apostle Hugh B. Brown lost a son, a pilot who flew for the British Royal Air Force. Thousands of other Latter-day Saint families received tragic news of the loss of a loved one. One poignant example of such loss was the Borgstrom family, from northern Utah, who lost four sons in combat within six months.[24]

During the war numerous Latter-day Saints were honored for their heroism and courage. Five American Latter-day Saints received the most highly esteemed award of the United States military—the Congressional Medal of Honor. Included in this number were Mervyn S. Bennion (1942, posthumously), Leonard C. Brostrom (1945), William E. Hall (1943), Nathan K. Van Noy Jr. (1944, posthumously), and George E. Wahlen (1944). Additionally, Ed Michaels, a convert to the Church in the 1950s, also received the award. The experience of George E. Wahlen is illustrative of the bravery of those who were awarded the medal. Wahlen was honored for saving the lives of several wounded marines while seriously injured himself during the heat of battle on Iwo Jima.[25]

Latter-day Saints also rendered service of a different kind by administering priesthood blessings to fellow comrades. One such example was reported by a war correspondent who was present on an occasion when a priesthood blessing was given:

"Being a war correspondent, my boat was going in behind the first line of men, and we came upon . . . two wounded marines in the water. One, from the stain of red around him we could tell, was wounded badly; the other, wounded too, was holding the other's head above the water. . . . The one seemed too far gone to need much help, but the other refused aid until his wounded buddy was attended. But our help seemed insufficient, as we soon realized, and we announced our decision to his comrade. Then it happened. This young man, the better of the two, bronzed by the tropical sun, clean as a shark's tooth in the South Seas, slowly got to his knees. His one arm was nearly gone, but with the other, he lifted the head of his unconscious pal into his lap, placed his good hand on the other's pale brow and uttered what to us seemed incredible words—words which to this moment are emblazoned in unforgettable letters across the doorway of my memory: 'In the name of Jesus Christ, and by virtue of the Holy Priesthood which I hold, I command you to remain alive until the necessary help can be obtained to secure the preservation of your life.' Today the three of us are here in Honolulu, and he is still alive. In fact, we walked down the beach together today, as we convalesce. He is the wonder of the medical unit, for they say he should be dead. Why he isn't they don't know—but we do, for we were there, off the shores of Kwajulane."[26]

Throughout the war, many accounts of divine preservation were recorded. One involved a young LDS American pilot named Phil Shumway, who survived for nine days without any food rations on a small raft in shark-infested waters after his plane crashed in the Pacific Ocean near New Zealand. Shumway later recalled confronting the possibility that he would die before his rescue:

"I realized that the chances of my rescue were very, very slim indeed. . . . My greatest sadness, however, was the fact that I had left behind my wife of so short a time. Having been sealed in the Temple to her, realizing that she was still but a girl, I had great sadness at the prospects of life for her. I prayed constantly to the Lord in a different way than I had ever known before. I seemed to talk and to visit and received a great peace. I do not have recollection, and I am sure this is correct, that I never felt at any time anything but a peaceful feeling. Anxiety, yes, hope that a miracle could happen, but no hysteria. I was always grateful for the peace which I was able to feel."[27]

Another airman who felt divine intervention on his behalf during the war was Ken Schubert, a Mormon "bomb aimer" in the Canadian Royal Air Force who described being rescued and cared for after he was shot down one night over Belgium:

"When I landed, a Belgium farmer, who had been awakened by the gun battle, came across the field where I was trying to bury my chute. After some conversation in sign language, he took me home. He had a meager house and little food. . . . He had a wife, three daughters and a son. . . . These good people would have been shot for harboring me if I had been found. . . . To evade the Gestapo, I often hid in the attic where I sat and unstitched my parachute and my vest. The material was stuffed into pillows and after the war, was made into dresses for the three daughters. One day I was in the back yard and heard the father and mother excitedly speaking in loud tones in front of the house. I immediately headed for the field to hide, as I could not get into the attic. I realized this was a wide open area with no hiding spot available. So I immediately entered the goat shed, a small 6 x 7 foot square room in the work shed, where I squeezed myself (invisibly?) in the corner next to the door. The door opened and a big black boot came through, the goat lunged forward on her chain and the boot withdrew. When I had entered, the goat remained quiet, although she had never been a great friend of mine. Since then I hold all goats in high esteem as she, no doubt, saved me and the family from the Gestapo."[28]

Most Latter-day Saints serving in the war felt a dependence upon the Lord's protection and a desire to maintain their faith. Wherever Latter-day Saint servicemen could be found in sufficient numbers, the Church designated group leaders to conduct Church meetings. These meetings were often held under very adverse conditions. One group of servicemen meeting in the southwest Pacific reported using spent shell casings to administer the emblems of the sacrament. Another group convened meetings in a soggy pup tent. One group of soldiers, determined to have a more favorable meeting place, actually erected a brick chapel on a small island in the Mediterranean Sea. Where larger numbers of servicemen could be gathered, such as at military bases and other centers, LDS chaplains organized servicemen's conferences.[29]

The number of LDS chaplains in World War II was significantly larger than in World War I. Whereas in World War I there were only three LDS chaplains, by the end of World War II there were forty-six commissioned by the U.S. military.[30] The work of LDS chaplains was indispensable in facilitating contact between the Church and its servicemen. As part of their labors, chaplains would often employ creative ways to seek out individual soldiers. One group of especially creative "chaps" decorated their jeep with a beehive, an angel Moroni, and the word *Deseret*. They drove among the troops and were recognized by several LDS soldiers.[31] In addition, chaplains issued newsletters, visited the injured, corresponded with soldiers' families back home, and organized and spoke at religious services. Very often chaplains were found at the battlefront alongside the other men. Perhaps the most difficult assignment for the chaplains was to dedicate the graves of those who died in battle. One Mormon chaplain, Eldin Ricks, reported that he dedicated ten LDS graves in one day.[32]

The Church and the War

As with the previous world conflict, World War II had a dramatic impact on full-time missionary work. At the outset of the war, the Church evacuated all of the missionaries from Germany. Later all missionaries outside of the continental United States were called home. The story of the evacuation of the Mormon missionaries from Europe ahead of the war is one filled with miracles.[33] By the end of the war, full-time missionaries from the United States were only given assignments in the continental United States and the Sandwich Islands (now Hawaii).

The recall of American missionaries left local members to administer the programs of the Church alone, often in nations where the gospel was new and members struggled. The Church, however, went to great lengths to keep mission headquarters operating. At the beginning of 1942, Elder Thomas E. McKay, Assistant to the Twelve, reported that the headquarters of ten of the twelve European missions remained open. Under the leadership of local mission and district presidents, regular meetings were conducted and yearly district conferences were held.[34]

Over two years elapsed from the outbreak of the war in 1939 until the surprise Japanese bombardment of Pearl Harbor—on 7 December 1941—forced the United States into the war. One Latter-day Saint reported being present on that occasion:

"From the chapel grounds we watched the Japanese aircraft in formations of nine fly back and forth. Shells were bursting among them all the time but no planes fell. We decided, with the majority who were watching that it was 'M' day, and went on into Sunday School. On our way home a bomb burst a little way behind us. . . . After crossing a large part of the city we arrived home and for the first time heard the radio warning everyone—'The Japanese are attacking Pearl Harbor'—'Take cover'—and then came the warnings—'Keep off the streets'—'Take Cover'—'Be Calm.'"[35]

The author went on to describe how, immediately after the announcement, the station returned to its regular programming, which featured the Mormon Tabernacle Choir singing the phrase from the Latter-day Saint hymn "Come, Come, Ye Saints": "And should we die before our journey's through, Happy day! All is well!"[36]

As the United States became embroiled in the war, the Church had to adjust many of its programs and procedures. Within weeks of the U.S. declaration of war, on 17 January 1942, the Church issued a policy directing that all auxiliaries discontinue holding conferences and stake meetings in response to travel restrictions imposed by the federal government.[37] In early April of 1942 the Tabernacle was closed for the duration of the war. As a result, a celebration scheduled in the Tabernacle for the Relief Society's centennial anniversary was canceled. Only general authorities and stake presidencies were invited to attend general conferences, which were convened in the Assembly Hall adjacent to the Salt Lake Temple and in the temple itself.[38] Even the tradition of Christmas lights on Temple Square was suspended until after the war. Work on the Idaho Falls Idaho Temple was also halted during the war years.

An interesting side note to the war experience was that two liberty-class navy ships that were commissioned by the U.S. Navy were named for Latter-day Saint presidents. The U.S.S. *Brigham Young* launched on 17 August 1942, and the U.S.S. *Joseph Smith* was introduced to the naval fleet on 22 May 1943, both from California.[39] Local Church members delivered speeches and provided music for each of the christening ceremonies.

In October of 1942, the Church organized the General LDS Servicemen's Committee and named Elder Harold B. Lee as chairman. The purpose of the committee was to assist Latter-day Saints in uniform wherever they were stationed. Examples of such support included the issuance of pocket-sized scriptures and of the servicemen's edition of the *Church News*. A servicemen's directory was also issued, which included the addresses of Church meetinghouses and mission offices throughout the world.[40]

Hugh B. Brown, who served as president of the British Mission near the end of the war, was called to serve as the coordinator of the Servicemen's Committee.[41] President Brown and other leaders traveled regularly to meet with groups of servicemen. Brown also provided valuable reports to Church leaders in Salt Lake City about the welfare of LDS servicemen and the progress of the war. One memorable communication was his dramatic description written from England of the great number of British citizens "in silent supplication" at the time of the Allied invasion at Normandy on D-day. Two months later, President Brown reported on a series of bombing raids carried out on England that seriously damaged the British mission home in London.[42]

In addition to the support efforts initiated at Church headquarters, individual wards and stakes were also challenged to support their servicemen. Many wards maintained bulletin boards with soldiers' addresses and invited members to write to those away from home using V-mail, an economical type of letter used during the war. Such efforts were not without obstacles, however, as many letters from LDS servicemen arrived with return addresses which read "somewhere in the Pacific" or some other remote region. The success of wards and stakes in maintaining contact with servicemen varied greatly. A sampling from a recent survey of LDS veterans of World War II indicates that many received very little or no mail from local Church units, in part because of their isolated and constantly changing assignments.[43]

After six years of conflict, the war in Europe finally concluded on 8 May 1945. A prophet and ambassador of peace, President Heber J. Grant, died only days later on 14 May. As had his predecessor, President Grant died at the end of a terrible world war. Servicemen's committee chairman Elder Harold B. Lee commented on the apparent coincidence:

"That President Joseph F. Smith should have died just eight days after the ending of the so-called first World War in Europe and President Heber J. Grant just seven days following the ending of the second World War in Europe is not without deep significance. The ending of these great European conflicts apparently means also the beginning of a new era in the work of the Kingdom of God on the earth. Surely the reports of the stewardships of Joseph F. Smith and Heber J. Grant to the councils of heaven have and will make possible even more effective planning for the welfare of the Church of Jesus Christ of Latter-day Saints and its work of righteousness."[44]

On 15 August 1945, three months after the end of the war in Europe, the Japanese also surrendered after atomic bombs were dropped by the United States on Hiroshima and Nagasaki. While V-J (Victory over Japan) day was also welcomed by the world, many criticized the use of atomic weaponry as a means of ending the war. Two brothers who were convinced that the bombing of Japan saved their lives were twin brothers Cleve and Clyde Swenson of Spanish Fork, Utah, who trained as paratroopers to participate in an invasion of Japan in the event that the atomic bombs were either ineffective or not used. Cleve had a harrowing experience in connection with his training:

"In the summer of 1945 officers came to the different units asking for volunteers to join the paratroopers. Mr. Swenson and his brother thought it over and decided to volunteer. They soon found out that they were actually training soldiers who would parachute onto the island of Japan to try and stop the war. Mr. Swenson, along with many other soldiers, dove from the trooper plane at the mercy of their parachutes many times during training. On one particular jump Mr. Swenson describes his horrifying experience as he lunged from the plane to see that his chute did not open. Something malfunctioned, and he was sent helplessly falling to the earth. He somehow landed upon another trooper's chute and frantically tried to get his chute open. Rolling on the top of the trooper's chute like a helpless infant, he desperately tried to get off before it collapsed and killed both of them. As he rolled off, his chute opened, only a few seconds before he hit the ground."[45]

Plans for an invasion were aborted when Japan surrendered, sparing hundreds of thousands of servicemen and civilian lives. Still, the wars in Europe and the Pacific had exacted a terrible toll. Approximately twenty million soldiers, sailors and airmen died in combat worldwide, in addition to the nearly thirty million civilians who died. Nowhere was there a more dramatic measure of the devastation for Church members than in Germany. By the end of the war over six hundred German members died, including three acting mission presidents and three district presidents. Probably the most memorable German casualty was a young man by the name of Helmuth Hubener who was beheaded for his brave resistance to the Third Reich during the war.[46] Also, over twenty-five hundred members in Germany were listed as missing and 80 percent were left homeless.[47]

After the surrender of Japan, the tabernacle doors were once again opened when on 4 September 1945 the Church hosted a multi-denominational thanksgiving service celebrating the end of the war. The Church soon found itself in the more familiar role of administering humanitarian relief. On 3 November 1945 newly sustained Church president George Albert Smith met with U.S. president Harry S Truman to make arrangements to dispatch aid to destitute Latter-day Saints and others in Europe. At the request of the First Presidency, the newest apostle, Elder Ezra Taft Benson, traveled throughout Europe to oversee the effort. From February until December of 1946, Elder Benson traveled over sixty-one thousand miles and administered over four million tons of food and supplies to war-ravaged Europeans.[48]

Relief came not only from Church headquarters but from various Church units and individual members. One of the most poignant stories of the postwar period occurred as Saints from the formerly occupied Netherlands sent truckloads of potatoes to assist members in war-ravaged Germany. Later, during the American airlift to Berlin, Church member Gail S. Halvorsen organized regular candy drops to the children and was soon dubbed the "candy bomber."[49] In Japan, too, efforts were organized to provide relief. Much of the assistance in the Pacific came from Hawaiian Saints who contributed to the relief of stricken Saints in Japan. The healing process was greatly aided by such acts of Christian service and love.[50]

The Price of Peace and the Debt of Gratitude

In the first half of the twentieth century two great wars were fought—wars upon which the future of the entire world hinged. Looking back upon these sagas, it is clear that God's hand was ever-present in these periods of awful tragedy. Even in secular accounts of these wars, expressions of God's influence are abundant. As faithful LDS servicemen in the great world wars turned to their God, they sanctified their sacrifice—a sacrifice that was very real and in many cases ultimate. The response of young Latter-day Saints in World Wars I and II, as directed by inspired leaders, constituted a defense of righteousness reminiscent of the Book of Mormon title of liberty. These men of faith, armed with truth from their God and weapons from their nation, prevailed over tyrants and evil empires.

The Church responded admirably to world conflicts by providing support and direction to those at home and overseas. At the same time, the Church challenged the world to reject war and embrace the gospel message of peace. In the postwar period, the Church provided much needed humanitarian relief to many who suffered in distant lands.

Latter-day Saint involvement in war did not end with the close of World War II. In the second half of the century other conflicts, generally regional in nature, involved large numbers of Latter-day Saints. These wars have served as uncomfortable reminders of the continuing threat of war and of the devastation that accompanies such conflict. Still, even in the midst of worldly upheaval and turmoil, God's work has continued unabated. The gospel message has been spread to many distant corners of the world by military men and women who remembered that above all else they were soldiers of a heavenly army.[51]

In the new century, the threat of world conflicts will continue. Latter-day Saints today are obligated to learn from those who paved the way for their liberties and freedoms. A great debt is owed to those who laid their lives on the altar of liberty. Truly the names of Latter-day Saint servicemen should be held in sacred remembrance.

NOTES

1. Larry C. Porter, "The Mormon Battalion's Two-Thousand-Mile March," *Regional Studies in Latter-day Saint Church History* (Provo, Utah: Brigham Young University, 1998), 47. While twenty-three battalion members died from other causes, no combat related casualties occurred.

2. The Civil War, which commenced in 1861, resulted in the loss of more American lives than all other wars involving Americans from the Revolution to the end of the twentieth century. The revelation received by Joseph Smith on 25 December 1832 is recorded as section 87 of the Doctrine and Covenants.

3. Hudson died on 24 August 1898. A. Prentiss, ed., *The History of the Utah Volunteers in the Spanish-American War and in the Philippine Islands* (Salt Lake City: Tribune Job Printing Co., 1900), 418.

4. Joseph F. Boone, "The Roles of the Church of Jesus Christ of Latter-day Saints in Relation to the United States Military 1900–1975," master's thesis, Brigham Young University, 1975, 2:543. Elias S. Kimball was appointed as a chaplain in the army in June of 1898. Kimball served as army chaplain under Colonel Willard Young, son of Brigham Young in the second regiment of volunteer engineers.

5. The only two stakes outside the United States at that time were in Cardston, Canada, and Juarez, Mexico; both communities were colonized by Mormon pioneers in the 1880s. See *Deseret News Church Almanac 1999–2000* (Salt Lake City: Deseret News, 1998), 437–38.

6. Boone, "Roles of the Church," 1:223; Gilbert W. Scharffs, *Mormonism in Germany: A History of The Church of Jesus Christ of Latter-day Saints in Germany between 1840–1970* (Salt Lake City: Deseret Book, 1970), 58. During August of 1918, the Church publications *Improvement Era* and *Era* began a column entitled "Wounded in Action" and "Died in Service," which periodically listed the names of Latter-day Saints casualties during the war.

7. Boone, "Roles of the Church," 1:174. Hugh B. Brown later served as an apostle and member of the First Presidency. Delbert L. Stapley was

a member of the Quorum of the Twelve Apostles. William J. Critchlow served as an Assistant to the Twelve, and S. Dilworth Young was a Seventy.

8. Boone, "Roles of the Church," 1:220–21.

9. Boone, "Roles of the Church," 2:544–46.

10. *Deseret News,* 10 June 1918; Boone, "Roles of the Church," 1:231. Brigadier General Richard W. Young, a son of Brigham Young, was eventually installed as commander over the 65th Brigade.

11. *Church Almanac 1999–2000,* 553; Joseph F. Smith, in Conference Report, October 1914, 2.

12. Talmage, "Mormonism and the War," *Improvement Era,* October 1918, 1030.

13. Scharffs, *Mormonism in Germany,* 58.

14. Joseph F. Smith, in Conference Report, April 1917, 11.

15. Anthony W. Ivins, in Conference Report, October 1918, 50.

16. The Relief Society sold wheat to the government for a minimal price of $1.20 a bushel and deposited the proceeds in an account designated for future relief needs (see Boone, "Roles of the Church," 1:289).

17. Boone, "Roles of the Church," 1:198–201.

18. James E. Talmage, *Literary Digest,* 27 July 1918 (New York, 1918).

19. Boone, "Roles of the Church," 1:308.

20. Boone, "Roles of the Church," 1:335.

21. Conference Report, October 1946, 1. Elder McConkie was called in the October 1946 general conference to the First Council of Seventy and later served in the Quorum of the Twelve Apostles until his death in 1985. Other members of the current Twelve and First Presidency who also served in World War II include Thomas S. Monson (Navy), James E. Faust (Army Air Corps), Boyd K. Packer (Army Air Corps), L. Tom Perry (Marine Corps), David B. Haight (Navy), Russell M. Nelson (Navy), and Neal A. Maxwell (Army).

22. Boone, "Roles of the Church," 1:337. In June 1946, the First Presidency issued a statement advocating a no-draft policy during peacetime, and approximately a year later the number of Latter-day Saints in the armed forces was reduced from a wartime high of approximately 100,000 to around 13,000 in May of 1947.

23. Boone, "Roles of the Church," 1:354.

24. Thomas S. Monson, in Conference Report, October 1999, 23. On 26 June 1948 United States General Mark W. Clark presided at a service convened in Garland, Utah, to honor the four young men.

25. Allan Kent Powell, *Utah Remembers World War II* (Logan, Utah: Utah State University Press, 1991), 75–80.

26. This account was included in an LDS servicemen's newsletter

dated 1 July 1944, unpublished papers of Chaplain Eldin Ricks, in possession of Irene Ricks of Provo, Utah. The author of the account is not named in the newsletter.

27. Irene Ricks, "Leaves from My Journal" (self-published, 1984), 281.

28. Kenneth Schubert, unpublished personal written history, Canadian crew member of the aircraft Halifax, 9–10, in possession of the Schubert family.

29. *Deseret News-Weekly Church Edition,* 13 May 1944, 8; 3 February 1945, 8; 20 May 1944, 10. The servicemen's conferences varied both in their size and in their location. They were held in regions such as the Philippines, the Pacific Isles, Hawaii, Marianas, Italy, and Britain.

30. The military designation for chaplains was limited to Catholic or Protestant with LDS chaplains being grouped with the latter. Individual names of the chaplains are on file with the Military Relations Division of The Church of Jesus Christ of Latter-day Saints, Salt Lake City, Utah. Of the total number of chaplains who served during the war, only a single chaplain, Reed G. Probst, died in combat. A tribute to him was written by a Presbyterian chaplain and published in the *Deseret News,* 1 July 1944.

31. *Deseret News-Weekly Church Edition,* 2 September 1944, 10.

32. Ricks served in both northern Africa and in Italy. While stationed in Italy, he and several other Saints were received by the pope at the Vatican. During the visit, Ricks presented the pontiff with a copy of the Book of Mormon (Ricks family papers, in the possession of the Ricks family).

33. David Boone, "The Worldwide Evacuation of Latter-day Saint Missionaries at the Outset of World War II," master's thesis, Brigham Young University, 1981.

34. *Deseret News-Weekly Church Edition,* 17 January 1942, 4.

35. *Deseret News-Weekly Church Edition,* 28 November 1942, 1.

36. *Hymns of The Church of Jesus Christ of Latter-day Saints* (Salt Lake City: The Church of Jesus Christ of Latter-day Saints, 1985), no. 30.

37. Sheri L. Dew, *Go Forward with Faith: The Biography of Gordon B. Hinckley* (Salt Lake City: Deseret Book, 1996), 125. The policy was dated 17 January 1942.

38. Ibid., 126.

39. News of the inauguration of the U.S.S. *Brigham Young* and the U.S.S. *Joseph Smith* was carried in the *Deseret News-Weekly Church Edition,* 22 August 1942, 1; 29 May 1943, 2.

40. *Deseret News-Weekly Church Edition,* 13 March 1943; 15 May 1944; 27 March 1943.

41. *Church Almanac 1999–2000,* 136–37. One and a half years earlier,

in May of 1941, Hugh B. Brown had been assigned as LDS Servicemen's Coordinator.

42. *Deseret News-Weekly Church Edition,* 11 November 1944, 1; 8 July 1944, 8; 12 August 1944, 12.

43. Current research being conducted by the author and Dr. Dennis Wright of the Department of Church History and Doctrine disclosed that most received no mail from their local Church units during the time of their military assignments.

44. *Deseret News-Weekly Church Edition,* 30 June 1945, 12.

45. Jordon Nielsen, *Hometown War Heroes* (Spanish Fork, Utah: J Mart Publishing, 1999).

46. Scharffs, *Mormonism in Germany,* 116. Hubener's resistance came in the form of an effort to publish the truth about the plans of the Third Reich. He was assisted in his efforts by several fellow members in Germany, including Rudolf Wobbe, Karl-Heinz Schnibbe, and Gerhard Duwer. Hubener was beheaded for his part in the effort on 27 October 1942. See Alan F. Keele and Douglas F. Tobler, "The Fuhrer's New Clothes: Helmuth Hubener and the Mormons in the Third Reich," *Sunstone,* November-December 1980, 20–29.

47. *Church Almanac 1999–2000,* 324.

48. Frederick W. Babbel, *On Wings of Faith* (Salt Lake City: Bookcraft, 1972), 168.

49. *Church Almanac 1999–2000,* 138; Gail Halvorsen, *The Berlin Candy Bomber* (Bountiful, Utah: Horizon Publishers and Distributors, 1997).

50. Jill Mulvay Derr, Janath Russell Cannon, and Maureen Ursenbach Beecher, *Women of Covenant: The Story of Relief Society* (Salt Lake City: Deseret Book, 1992), 312.

51. Nations where the gospel was introduced by LDS servicemen during the twentieth century include Bermuda, 1953; Guam, 1944; Korea, 1951; Panama, 1941; Portugal, 1970s; Puerto Rico, 1947; Saipan, 1944; Spain, 1966; Taiwan, 1956; and Vietnam, 1964. See *Church Almanac 1999–2000,* 328–407.

CHAPTER NINE

THEODORE ROOSEVELT AND THE LATTER-DAY SAINTS

ARNOLD K. GARR

Prior to the twentieth century there was a considerable amount of interaction between the presidents of the United Sates and the Mormons, much of which was negative. Many of the presidents of that century were antagonistic toward the Mormons because they misunderstood or were skeptical of some of the Church's social, political, and economic institutions, particularly plural marriage. While a few, such as Polk, Fillmore, and Cleveland, were friendly, several presidents were hostile, notably Van Buren, Taylor, Buchanan, and Grant. At the beginning of the twentieth century, however, a man came to office who did more than any president before him to help diminish the public animosity toward the Mormons. That man was Theodore Roosevelt.

There were at least three episodes in Roosevelt's life that exemplified his friendly attitude toward the Mormons: first, a little-known friendship with Ben E. Rich, president of the Southern States Mission; second, his friendship with the apostle and U.S. Senator, Reed Smoot; and third, his activities relative to the anti-Mormon magazine crusade in the early twentieth century. The purpose of this essay is to briefly highlight Roosevelt's involvement in each of these episodes.

FRIENDSHIP WITH BEN E. RICH

Roosevelt first met Ben E. Rich in Rexburg, Idaho, in 1900 when Roosevelt was a vice-presidential candidate. Rich, then president of

---

Arnold K. Garr is an associate professor and associate chair of the Department of Church History and Doctrine at Brigham Young University.

the Southern States Mission, had gone west to attend the Church's October general conference in Salt Lake City. Roosevelt was to make a campaign speech in Rexburg, and Rich, chairman of the event, was to introduce the candidate. During the introductory speech, Rich predicted that Roosevelt would become the President of the United States. This obviously made an impression on the vice-presidential candidate, and after his speech he asked Rich if he would ride with him to Salt Lake City in his private rail car and tell him all about Mormonism and the story of the pioneers. Rich, of course, happily accepted the invitation. After boarding the train, Roosevelt invited Rich to his sleeping quarters. There they spent most of the night talking about the Church while Roosevelt sat up in bed in his pajamas.

Rich's biography states that Roosevelt asked hundreds of questions during the night. At the end of the discussion Roosevelt thanked Rich for the interview and told him "that he had never listened to a more interesting account of a great people and a great religion."[1] This, however, was not the end of their relationship.

In March 1902 Rich and John Henry Smith, a member of the Quorum of the Twelve Apostles, were sent as special envoys of the Church to see Roosevelt, who by this time had become President of the United States. The two men were sent to gain Roosevelt's support in suppressing a proposed amendment to the Constitution that would force the Mormons to stop practicing plural marriage; the sponsors of the bill claimed it was necessary in spite of the Church's 1890 Manifesto. As Thomas Kearns, the non-Mormon senator for Utah, introduced Elder Smith and Rich, President Roosevelt is reported to have interrupted the presentation and greeted them as friends who needed no introduction.[2] After visiting with the president, the two then met with Senator Hanna of Ohio and others friendly to the Mormons. Elder Smith reported to Church authorities on the meetings and indicated that the agitation for the proposed amendment would have no success and that "the policy adopted by the party leaders was silence."[3]

Later that year President Roosevelt was on a speaking tour in Chattanooga, Tennessee. There was a short parade from the president's hotel to the Chattanooga Auditorium, and the parade route had been roped off to keep the crowds from closing in on the president. Ben E. Rich was situated on the curb, behind the ropes, as the group marched by with President Roosevelt in the lead. As the president passed, Rich called out "How do you do, Mr. President?" Roosevelt turned around and recognized him. The president stopped the parade, went over to the curb, shook Rich's hand, and asked how he was doing in the mission field and if there were any more mobbings of his elders in the South. After a brief visit, Roosevelt said: "I think now by this recognition, you will have more friends in the South." Newspapers reported the incident, and afterward Rich was given greater respect in Chattanooga.[4]

On another occasion while Roosevelt was president, Ben E. Rich called on him at the White House. He received an immediate audience and when the president asked what he could do for him, Rich replied "that he did not have any request to make but had simply come to pay his respects. . . . Roosevelt said: 'You do not know how refreshing it is to meet a friend who does not want an office or support for this measure or that.'" Then he asked Rich if he would accept a photograph of the president as a gift. Rich said he would be honored and received the photograph, inscribed "To Ben E. Rich, Esquire, with regards of Theodore Roosevelt, March 7, 1903."[5]

In June 1903 Ben E. Rich's son was in Washington, D.C., and was introduced to the president by Senator Heyburn of Idaho. Roosevelt replied: "Ben Rich, my boy, are you related to my dear friend Ben E. Rich?" When informed that Ben E. Rich was his father, Roosevelt slapped him on the shoulder and said, "My boy, you have the finest dad of any man in the world. I hold him in deep affection. When I was running for Vice-President in Idaho, your father predicted that I would be the next President of the United States. I thought at the time his enthusiasm was probably getting away with him, but you see, now here I am."[6] Ben E. Rich also experienced further favorable interaction with the president in conjunction with the Reed Smoot case.

FRIENDSHIP WITH REED SMOOT

On 20 January 1903 the Republican-dominated Utah legislature elected Reed Smoot to the United States Senate. Smoot, however, was also a member of the Quorum of Twelve Apostles in the Church. This gave rise to protests by many non-Mormons that his election was a violation of the principle of separation of church and state. They also protested that Church officials were still preaching the practice of plural marriage, contrary to the law of the land.

A great deal of money was spent throughout the United States to arouse sentiment against Elder Smoot. By the time the Senate was finally in session, petitions against Smoot had flooded in from all over the country. When the Senate met on 5 March 1903, it was decided that Senator Smoot should be seated and that his case should be referred to the Committee on Privileges and Elections for investigation. The chairman of this committee was Julius C. Burrows of Michigan, whose grandfather had been excommunicated from the Church. Senator Burrows eventually voted against Senator Smoot.

Soon after he arrived in Washington, D.C., Elder Smoot called on President Roosevelt. A number of people had told the president that Smoot was a polygamist, but the senator assured him that he was not. The president then replied, "Senator Smoot, that is enough for me."[7]

Years later, in a national magazine, Roosevelt stated, "Senator Smoot . . . came to me of his own accord, and not only assured me that he was not a polygamist, but, I may add, assured me that he had never had any relations with any woman excepting his own wife; and I may also add that it was the universal testimony of all who knew anything of his domestic life that it was exemplary in every way." The president continued, "He also assured me that he had always done everything he could to have the law about polygamy absolutely obeyed, and most strongly upheld the position that the Church had taken in its public renunciation of polygamy and that he would act as quickly against any Mormon who nowadays made a plural marriage as against a gentile who committed bigamy." Roosevelt affirmed, "I did not interfere in any way as to his retention in the Senate, save that where Senators came up to speak to me on the subject, I spoke to them freely along the lines I have here outlined, taking the view [that] . . . if he had obeyed the law and was an upright and reputable man in his public and private relations, it would be an outrage to turn him out because of his religious beliefs."[8]

Although Roosevelt claimed he did not actively interfere in the Reed Smoot hearings, accounts by others involved indicate that he was much more active in the case than the above statement suggests. The following experience of Ben E. Rich illustrates.

When public animosity against Smoot increased, the leaders of the Church decided to send representatives to call on President Roosevelt privately and ask for his support. Ben E. Rich and John Henry Smith were selected, and when they met with Roosevelt, the president came right to the point. He asked, "Is Reed Smoot a polygamist, or has he ever been a polygamist?" After being assured that he was not, the president said: "By all that's holy, I say to you that Reed Smoot is entitled to his seat in the Senate under the Constitution, and the fact that he is a high church officer makes no difference. I shall do all in my power to help him retain his seat."[9] Roosevelt then suggested that the two Church leaders interview several prominent congressmen, among whom were Senators Aldrich from Rhode Island, Platt from Connecticut, Allison from Iowa, Frye from Maine, Foracker and Hanna from Ohio, Spooner from Wisconsin, Bailey from Texas, and Morgan and Pettus from Alabama.

Roosevelt also instructed Rich and Smith to tell "these senators that they had been sent to them by the President of the United States."[10] They interviewed all of the above-mentioned senators, thoroughly reviewing the Smoot case with each of them. According to Rich's biographer, President Joseph F. Smith declared that Rich's mission was "the greatest single factor in Smoot's victory to hold his seat in the Senate of the United States" and that "without Theodore Roosevelt's active support, Smoot probably would have lost."[11]

Another indication of the president's active support is a statement by Reed Smoot himself. In 1904 Smoot wrote to President Joseph F. Smith: "I called on President Roosevelt and asked him as a special favor to use his influence as far as possible to have my case decided at as early a day as possible. I told him I did not want it postponed, nor did I want a sub-committee to go to Utah for the purpose of taking testimony." Smoot further declared: "The President agreed with me and said that he would assist me in this matter in every way in his power. We considered the supposed attitude toward me of each of the members of the Committee, and he promised me that he would see the greatest number of them."[12]

Senator Smoot was well aware of the importance of President Roosevelt's support. In another letter to Joseph F. Smith, Smoot stated: "I have not called on the President, but I expect to to-morrow.

I am in hopes that he will be as friendly as ever, for without his friendship I am positive that it is impossible for me to win out."[13]

On another occasion the senator happily wrote to President Smith of a kindness Roosevelt had publicly done on his behalf: "Last evening Senator Dolliver [a new member of the Committee on Privileges and Elections] came to me and stated that the evening before he had been at a party with President Roosevelt, Senator Burrows, and a large number of senators and members of Congress; and that during the evening he asked Burrows how much longer he was going to keep me in suspense, and why he did not bring my case to a close and get the matter settled." Smoot continued: "Before Burrows could answer, the President took a hand in the conversation, and Senator Dolliver said that for nearly an hour the President told Burrows just what he thought of him and everybody else engaged in this unwarranted fight against me, and that during his remarks the President paid me a very high tribute."[14]

In his writings, B. H. Roberts suggested that President Roosevelt may have become involved in the Smoot case in still another way. At a time when developments on the hearings were at their peak, the president appointed Robert W. Tayler, the chief counsel for the complainants in the case, to be federal district judge in northern Ohio. This, according to Roberts, temporarily "threw the Smoot opposition into confusion,"[15] and hurt Smoot's opponents during an important time of the case.

Ultimately the majority of the Committee on Privileges and Elections, however, were not in sympathy with Senator Smoot and recommended that he was "not entitled to a seat as a Senator of the United States from the State of Utah." It is significant, however, that five of the thirteen members of the committee supported Senator Smoot. The minority report stated that there was "no just ground for expelling Senator Smoot or for finding him disqualified to hold the seat he occupies."[16]

The committee hearings were followed by a two-month debate on the Senate floor. Before the final vote was taken a humorous incident took place. Senator Boies Penrose was reported to have looked out over the floor and said, "I don't see why we can't get along just as well with a polygamist who doesn't polyg as we do with a lot of monogamists who don't monog!"[17] When the vote was finally taken in February 1907, twenty-eight opposed Senator Smoot, forty-two favored him, and twenty did not vote. Therefore, after more than three years of hearings and debate, it was finally decided that Senator Smoot could retain his seat.

Senator Fred Dubois of Idaho, Smoot's most relentless enemy during the case, recognized that it was because of Roosevelt's support that Smoot was victorious. During his final speech on the floor, just before the vote was taken, Dubois stated: "For the first time the Mormon question has been made a political one. The President of the United States is an open friend of the Senator from Utah. You all know it. The country knows it. The President wants him seated . . . but [the Mormon vote] has cost you the moral support of the Christian men and women of the United States."[18]

The leaders of the Church also realized that President Roosevelt was perhaps the person most responsible for the favorable outcome of the Smoot case. After the victory, President Joseph F. Smith wrote Senator Smoot and asked him to give a message of gratitude to President Roosevelt. In part, he stated: "Kindly say to the President in my behalf that God alone knows our heartfelt appreciation of his absolutely fair and kindly consideration of your case; and please say to him also that all we have to offer in return is the absolute assurance of the righteousness of our cause and the loyalty of our hearts."[19]

While Senator Smoot had to prove himself politically, his wife had to prove herself socially. President Roosevelt was helpful to Sister Smoot as well. One friend characterized Sister Smoot as a "proud and lonely woman" during her first years in Washington. "At one occasion, the wives of two congressmen reached over and began fingering the material of her dress, wondering aloud if Senator Smoot provided his other wives with such fine material." This type of rude behavior was not unusual during the first two or three years the Smoots were in Washington. Finally in 1907, at a White House reception, President Roosevelt made a gesture that put an end to the rudeness. "He spent a good share of the evening visiting with Sister Smoot." At the conclusion of the reception, as the president was leaving, he simply turned at the end of the hall and made a special point to say, "Good night, Mrs. Smoot."[20] With that simple gesture Roosevelt helped diminish her social exile.

All this suggests that President Roosevelt was a sincere friend to the senator-apostle and his family. Roosevelt also proved to be a good friend of the Latter-day Saints during a vicious anti-Mormon campaign carried on by some of the nation's leading magazines.

Answering the Anti-Mormon Magazine Crusade

In 1910 and 1911 several of the nation's prominent magazines published bitter essays against the Church. The articles raised the same old questions about plural marriage, and some also made personal attacks on the president of the Church, Joseph F. Smith. *Pearson's* published articles in September, October, and November of 1910. *McClure's* published similar essays in January and February of 1911. *Cosmopolitan* ran articles in March and April of 1911. It is difficult to determine what motivated the publication of the essays, inasmuch as the Smoot case had concluded three years before. At any rate, some of the articles also made false accusations against Theodore Roosevelt and his association with the Mormons. As a result Roosevelt published an open letter in *Collier's* that countered the anti-Mormon attacks and gave an unexpected boost to the public image of the Church.

Roosevelt first outlined some of the media's false accusations directed at him and at the Church. One magazine had stated that Roosevelt had made a bargain with the Mormon Church, promising to give his support to Reed Smoot and other Mormon causes in exchange for the Church delivering "the electoral votes of Utah, Wyoming, and Idaho." Roosevelt replied by saying that the story was "not merely an outrageous lie but one so infamous, so absolutely without the smallest particle of foundation, that it is utterly impossible that the men making the charge should be ignorant of the fact that they are lying." He continued his rebuke: "The accusation is not merely false, but so ludicrous that it is difficult to discuss it seriously. Of course, it is always possible to find creatures vile enough to make accusations of this kind. The important thing to remember is that the men who give currency to the charge . . . show themselves in their turn unfit for association with decent men when they secure the repetition and encouragement of such scandals."[21]

Concerning the subject of plural marriage, Roosevelt stated: "On one occasion a number of charges were made to the Administration

. . . that a number of our Federal officials had been polygamously married. A very thorough and careful investigation was made by the best men in the service into these charges, and they were proved to be without so much as the smallest basis in fact."[22]

The president then made a flattering statement about the Mormon people: "I have known monogamous Mormons whose standard of domestic life and morality and whose attitude toward the relations of men and women was as high as that of the best citizens of any other creed; indeed, among these Mormons the standard of sexual morality was unusually high. Their children were numerous, healthy, and well brought up."[23] With these statements in this public letter, the president once again demonstrated his friendship to the Mormons as he previously had done in his activities with Ben E. Rich and Senator Reed Smoot.

Members of the Church also made statements that indicated their high esteem for Roosevelt. After the Smoot case, Charles Wilson Nibley, presiding bishop of the Church, was so impressed with the president's attitude toward the Mormons that he advocated approaching Roosevelt about writing a book on the Church. Bishop Nibley maintained that Roosevelt should "write in his own clear and forceful style 'The Story of Mormonism' . . . which in my judgment would be the greatest book that has been published in a hundred years." The bishop felt the president could produce a book that would go on living even after Roosevelt's state papers had become obsolete.[24]

On one occasion when Senator Smoot was asked, "Who was the greatest statesman you met in your thirty-year career as Utah's Senator?" Smoot replied without hesitation, "Theodore Roosevelt."[25]

Years after Roosevelt died, the prophet Heber J. Grant complimented the deceased president saying, "I believe that Roosevelt felt that we were right. I think he was nearer converted to the truth than any man who ever occupied the presidential chair."[26]

President Theodore Roosevelt was an outstanding friend of the Mormons and did more than any president before him to improve the image of the Church. He befriended Ben E. Rich, president of the Southern States Mission; helped the Mormon apostle, Reed Smoot, retain his seat in the U.S. Senate; and publicly defended the Church during the anti-Mormon magazine crusade in 1910–11. All of this was done at a time when it was not popular or advantageous to sympathize with the Mormons. In return, many members of the Church, including some of its most important leaders, held Roosevelt in the highest esteem.

NOTES

1. Benjamin L. Rich, *Ben E. Rich, An Appreciation By His Son* (Salt Lake City, 1950), 24.

2. *Deseret News,* 19 March 1902, 1; Rich, *An Appreciation,* 24–25.

3. Journal History of The Church of Jesus Christ of Latter-day Saints, 3 April 1902, 5–6.

4. As cited in Rich, *An Appreciation,* 26.

5. Ibid., 27.

6. Ibid., 27–28.

7. Letter from Reed Smoot to Joseph F. Smith, 5 March 1905, in Reed Smoot Papers, Manuscript Section, Harold B. Lee Library.

8. Theodore Roosevelt, "Mr. Roosevelt to the Mormons," *Collier's,* 15 April 1911, 28.

9. Rich, *An Appreciation,* 25. Benjamin L. Rich seems to have confused this interview with Ben E. Rich's earlier, more publicized interview in 1902 when John Henry Smith was also present.

10. Ibid.

11. Ibid., 26.

12. Letter from Smoot to Smith, 8 January 1904, in Reed Smoot Papers.

13. Ibid., 24 November 1905, in Reed Smoot Papers.

14. Ibid., 9 March 1906, in Reed Smoot Papers.

15. B. H. Roberts, *A Comprehensive History of The Church of Jesus Christ of Latter-day Saints, Century One,* 6 vols. (Salt Lake City: Deseret News Press, 1930), 6:396–97.

16. *Proceedings Before the Committee on Privilege and Elections of the United States Senate in the Matter of Protests Against the Right of Honorable Reed Smoot, a Senator from the State of Utah, to Hold His Seat* (Washington: Government Printing Office, 1904), 4:498, 505.

17. *Reader's Digest,* June 1958, 142. A quotation from Francis T. Plimpton at Amherst College.

18. *Congressional Record Vol. VLI* (Washington: Government Printing Office, 1907), 3408.

19. Letter from Smith to Smoot, 23 February 1907, in Reed Smoot Papers.

20. Mary M. Bradford, "From Colony to Community, the Washington D.C. Saints," *Ensign,* August 1974, 22.

21. Roosevelt, "Mr. Roosevelt to the Mormons," 28.

22. Ibid.

23. Ibid.

24. Letter from Nibley to Reed Smoot, 2 December 1908, in Reed Smoot Papers.

25. M. R. Merrill, "Theodore Roosevelt and Reed Smoot," *Western Political Quarterly,* September 1951, 440.

26. Letter from Grant to Reed Smoot, 16 December 1924, in Reed Smoot Papers.

CHAPTER TEN

THE MIRACLE OF THE ROSE AND THE OAK IN LATIN AMERICA

MARK L. GROVER

In March 1831 Joseph Smith received a revelation directed toward Sidney Rigdon, Parley P. Pratt, and Leman Copley in which, among other things, events were described that would occur before the return of Christ to rule over the earth. "But before the great day of the Lord shall come, Jacob shall flourish in the wilderness, and the Lamanites shall blossom as the rose" (D&C 49:24). In this brief comment, not only is a beautiful metaphor of a flower given but also a description of a pivotal event of the last days that members of the Church await in great anticipation. It identifies a specific segment of the population of the Americas who will accept the gospel in great numbers, and it focuses attention on the many Book of Mormon prophecies concerning the descendants of Lehi.

The fulfillment of a promise of blossoming has been anticipated by prophets and Church members alike since the revelation was received. Joseph Smith and Brigham Young discussed their desire to take the gospel to the Native Americans of the United States, and missionaries were often sent specifically to them. The first mission to South America, undertaken by Parley P. Pratt in 1851, was an effort to go to the source of the Book of Mormon. Many early leaders believed Chile was the place Lehi landed. Early missionary activity in the Pacific Islands was motivated, in part, by the desire to fulfill the prophecies concerning the descendants of the Book of Mormon peoples.[1]

Mark L. Grover is bibliographer of Latin American Studies at Brigham Young University.

The anticipated blossoming has taken time. Nineteenth-century missionary activities among Native Americans in the United States resulted in some success but nothing that could be considered a fulfillment of the prophecy. Early missionary work in Mexico was similar in levels of success. Efforts in the United States extending into the middle of the twentieth century, under the direction of Elder Spencer W. Kimball, did not bear the expected results. The long-awaited success was to come not in the United States but in unanticipated places and with groups not expected. Most of the flowering was to occur south of the border of the United States and among a primarily mestizo, or mixed population.

There is a second prophecy concerning Latin America that is important. At a 4 July 1926 testimony meeting in Buenos Aires, Argentina, prior to returning to the United States from a six-month mission, Elder Melvin J. Ballard made the following statement concerning the Church in South America:

"The work of the Lord will grow slowly for a time here just as an oak grows slowly from an acorn. It will not shoot up in a day as does the sunflower that grows quickly and then dies. But thousands will join the Church here. It will be divided into more than one mission and will be one of the strongest in the Church. . . . The South American Mission will be a power in the Church."[2]

Elder Ballard's prophecy is significant. Though he was describing the Church specifically in South America, what he suggested occurred in all of Latin America. The growth of a young oak tree is deliberate and slow in comparison to other trees whose rapid growth in the beginning far overshadows that of the oak. Yet after the oak has reached maturity, it is one tree that can withstand the buffeting of winds and storms and the attack of predators and disease. That is what happened to the Church in Latin America. Many years of slow, laborious growth allowed for the development of strong members and leaders whose commitment and dedication to the Church stood up against the strong winds of opposition.

The Church in Latin America today is probably in the middle of the fulfillment of Joseph Smith's and Melvin Ballard's prophecies. The recent growth of the Church in Latin America has been miraculous and rates as one of the most significant events in the history of the Church in the twentieth century. In 1998 the membership of the

Church in Latin America numbered over three and a half million members, which was 38 percent of the total Church population (three quarters of the non-United States membership). More importantly, the number of baptisms occurring in Latin America was close to 60 percent of the Church's total baptisms. As shown in the following list of the twenty countries with the largest number of members, thirteen are Latin American countries (shown in bold type). Mexico, Brazil, Chile, Peru, Argentina, Guatemala, and Ecuador are seven of the ten largest.[3]

United States	4,923,000
Mexico	**783,000**
Brazil	**640,000**
Chile	**462,000**
Philippines	389,000
Peru	**312,000**
Argentina	**268,000**
Guatemala	**164,000**
Canada	151,000
Ecuador	**139,000**
England	133,000
Colombia	**122,000**
Japan	108,000
Bolivia	**100,000**
Australia	96,000
New Zealand	86,000
Honduras	**82,000**
Venezuela	**80,000**
El Salvador	**77,000**
Uruguay	**69,000**

LATIN AMERICA

Diversity and difference aptly describe the thirty-five independent countries of Latin America and the Caribbean. Mexico, Argentina, and Brazil are large countries blessed with extensive natural resources.

There are also many small island countries of the Caribbean with little natural resources beyond farmland and beaches. Five European languages are spoken in the region along with hundreds of native, creole, and pidgin languages. Some of the countries are populated with Native Americans and mestizos who maintain cultural and religious traditions that predate the European conquest.

Other countries, such as Argentina, have little indigenous influence. A few countries have a large segment of the population who are descended from Africa. As a result of the number of countries, cultures and customs in Latin America vary greatly. The taco and enchilada most Americans associate with Latin American cuisine can only be found in Mexico and a few Central American countries. They are replaced with potatoes in Bolivia, pasta and beef in Argentina, beans and rice in Brazil, and manioc in northern South America.

History

The Church of Jesus Christ of Latter-day Saints' expansion into Latin America and the Caribbean occurred primarily in the twentieth century and after World War II. A few missionaries went to Latin America in the nineteenth century, but they had limited success. The first attempts were short-lived, and missions to the Caribbean island of Jamaica in 1841 and 1853 were unsuccessful. These missions were limited to a few weeks in time and produced no baptisms. Missionaries did not return to this island until 1978, 165 years later.[4]

A second attempt to take Mormonism to Latin America was carried out by Elder Parley P. Pratt, who went to Chile in 1851. Accompanied by his wife and Rufus Allen, he spent five months in Chile with only limited success learning Spanish. They did not baptize any converts. Proselytizing was severely restricted by constitutional laws that limited the activities of non-Catholic religions in the country. Pratt returned to the United States convinced that the time had not yet arrived for the Church to go to Latin America.[5]

The only permanent nineteenth-century presence of the Church in Latin America was in Mexico. Three different groups of missionaries went to Mexico between 1875 and 1879, motivated primarily by a desire to explore for places of colonization and refuge and a desire to proselytize Native Americans. The last group was headed by Elder Moses Thatcher of the Quorum of the Twelve Apostles, who went to Mexico City in 1879 and established the first branch in Latin America.

Missionary work in Mexico was difficult, and missionaries had to leave several times during the succeeding fifty years, but a foundation was secured. That foundation was strengthened in 1885 when American members settled in several colonies in Northern Mexico.[6]

The next expansion into Latin America occurred after the turn of the century when Spanish-speaking missionaries went to Argentina in 1925 and German-speaking missionaries went to Brazil in 1928. The growth of the Church in these two countries was slow and was interrupted by a language change from German to Portuguese in Brazil in 1938 and by the second world war. Immediately after the war there came an additional expansion into Central America, Uruguay, and Paraguay. It was not until 1966 that all of the Spanish-speaking countries in South and Central America had missionaries. The last missionary effort occurred after 1978 when the Church began sending missionaries into the islands of the Caribbean. Cuba is the only major country in Latin America where the Church does not have missionaries.

The countries with the largest number of members are Mexico (783,000) and Brazil (640,000). Chile has about 500,000 members and Argentina and Peru close to 300,000. The 1997 growth rate shows that Brazil (46,000) and Chile (34,000) had a higher number coming into the Church than did Mexico (27,000). That difference in growth has been occurring for several years; if it continues Brazil will soon surpass Mexico in total number of members. It already has more stakes than Mexico.

The annual numbers of baptisms from 1996 through 1997 were as follows.

COUNTRY	NUMBER OF BAPTISMS	PERCENT OF LATIN AMERICAN BAPTISMS
Brazil	46,000	22 percent
Chile	34,000	17 percent
Mexico	27,500	13 percent
Peru	16,500	8 percent
Argentina	16,500	8 percent
Honduras	8,500	4 percent
Guatemala	8,000	4 percent
El Salvador	6,500	3 percent

One country in particular has experienced significant growth. Chile, a small thin country extending some twenty-six hundred miles along the coast of South America, has experienced significant economic change and development since the 1970s that has led to social changes and economic adjustments. Chileans are a deeply spiritual people who have historically been open to new ideas and change.[7] Missionaries went to Chile in 1955, and subsequent missionaries have had unusual baptismal success ever since. Chile's growth has resulted in a Church member population of over 3 percent of the total population of the country, the highest in the world with the exception of some of the small Polynesian islands.

RELIGIOUS GROWTH IN LATIN AMERICA

The growth of the Church in Latin America is remarkable, yet what is happening to the Church is not significantly different from what is occurring among other religions in the region. Mormonism's influence at present is limited. There is little recognition of the Church's growth among the general population, and there is a lack of interest in the Church in the media. Beyond the occasional anti-Mormon evangelical treatise, the infrequent Catholic antisect book, or brief articles in newspapers, little is written about the Church beyond our own publicity efforts. There are a few theses or dissertations that have been written about the Church, but these have generally been done by members. The LDS Church continues to be relegated to the category of "other churches" and doesn't seem to make people either mad or pleased. Even the academic left doesn't seem to be too concerned anymore about our supposed CIA connection, a popular false idea twenty years ago.[8]

One of the reasons for this apparent lack of interest is that the Church is but a minor player in the social and religious changes that are occurring in the region. Latin America is presently experiencing one of the most significant religious revivals ever seen in the modern world. Historically Latin America has been the Catholic Church's strongest region, but millions have been leaving the Catholic Church to join pentecostal, African, and a host of other churches. New religions are being founded, and evangelical churches are spreading throughout the continent at a surprising rate. Estimates of the number of Catholics in some of the countries of Latin America have dropped from above 90 percent to as low as 60 percent in fewer than twenty years.[9]

The present-day religious environment of Latin America is somewhat confusing and difficult to follow as people move from religion to religion looking for a church that is satisfying. There are remarkable similarities between what is happening in Latin America and what took place during the 1820s in New York when Mormonism began. Itinerant preachers are common, and a great variety of religious groups are found in all countries. This is not entirely bad for the Catholic Church. While it has had a decrease in total number of members, it has also experienced an increase in attendance and activity.

The reasons for this religious excitement are numerous and complex. A series of political and economic changes beginning shortly after World War II have encouraged people from all sectors and classes of society to begin looking for different religious experiences. Fluctuations in economies have left families with financial insecurity and struggles. A general democratization in most of Latin America has created feelings of freedom and liberation, encouraging many to leave what is traditional in society in search of new alternatives. Most countries have seen significant population shifts from rural to urban areas. These migrants have found themselves separated from traditional family and church ties at a time when they needed social and spiritual support. That support has often come from evangelical churches already in the neighborhoods where the new migrants are living.

The religions with the greatest success have been the evangelical churches and some alternative groups such as Afro-Latin religions. The Catholic charismatics have also had significant appeal. One of the important attractions of these religions is that they offer immediate spiritual experiences that are often lacking in the traditional Catholic Church. Probably the most aggressive and successful of the new religions in South America is the Brazilian church *A Igreja Universal* (the Universal Church), which is not only the fastest growing in South America, but is also expanding rapidly throughout the world, including in the United States. This church has very effective proselytizing techniques that include prayer and healing gatherings held in soccer stadiums, occasionally with over a hundred thousand people in attendance.[10]

The Church of Jesus Christ of Latter-day Saints has also grown, though not as much as other religions. Comparing LDS growth with that of other religions is enlightening. I have been able to obtain growth statistics for several traditional Protestant churches in the major countries of Latin America between 1986 and 1993. Statistics for the fastest-growing evangelical churches are not available. These figures for each religion were combined and arranged by countries. Based on these figures, the LDS Church during this time period grew more slowly than other churches in all countries, with the exception of Chile and Bolivia.[11]

The following statistics represent the Church's percentage of growth from 1986 through 1993.

COUNTRY	PROTESTANT GROWTH	LDS GROWTH	PERCENTAGE OF DIFFERENCE
Argentina	225.6	99.03	-126.57
Bolivia	100.21	119.10	18.89
Brazil	169.21	130.10	-39.11
Chile	101.33	104.14	2.81
Colombia	135.54	113.97	-21.57
Paraguay	367.62	113.33	-254.29
Peru	250.15	114.68	-135.47
Uruguay	127.57	49.99	-77.69
Venezuela	396.31	175.00	-221.31
Average	166.91	115.82	-51.09

I then isolated figures for the two churches that are traditionally grouped with the LDS Church—the Jehovah's Witnesses and Seventh-Day Adventists—to determine how the Church compared. The Church grew faster than the Jehovah's Witnesses but not faster than the Adventists. The following statistics are a comparison of the percentage of growth from 1986 to 1993: LDS, 115.82 percent; Jehovah's Witnesses, 88.08 percent; Seventh-Day Adventists, 156.67

percent. What these statistics suggest is that the LDS Church is not one of the faster growing churches in Latin America but is probably found in a group with slower growth. Such is the level of religious excitement and change occurring in South America.

CHARACTERISTICS OF THE CHURCH IN LATIN AMERICA

The LDS Church for the most part is an urban church with strength in national and regional centers. This is, in part, a function of the philosophy of missionary work that concentrates on cities with populations large enough to support branches, wards, and stakes before moving to the surrounding areas. As the numbers of missionaries being called to Latin America increases, this trend may adjust some, though probably not much. In 1998, 78 percent of Latin America was urban as compared to 31 percent in 1940. For the near future, the Church in Latin America will continue to be centered in the larger cities.[12]

Though most Mormons in the United States believe Latin America to be primarily Native American, or Lamanite, the Church has gone mostly to mestizos, or the descendants of European immigrants. Argentina, Uruguay, and Brazil have primarily a population of European descent. The number of Mormons with Native American ancestry is much higher in Mexico, parts of Central America, and the Andean countries of Peru, Bolivia, and Ecuador, though the percentage is not as high as might be expected. Brazil, the Dominican Republic, and Puerto Rico in particular, and to a limited extent Colombia and Venezuela, have many members who are of African descent.

True conversion to Mormonism has historically tended to create middle-class citizens. Though most of the new converts in Latin America come to the Church from the upper lower class, with baptism and conversion to the Church there appears to be a process of class change that occurs over a long period of time. This is due in part to the youth of new converts, many of whom are teenagers or recently married when they join. Many of these young men and women go on missions and return to positions of responsibility in the Church. Though there are struggles, in general there is a tendency among these young adults to seek for a higher level of schooling than would normally be expected. Economically they tend to do better than their parents.[13]

RETENTION

The growth of the Church has not come without struggles. In order for a person to be truly converted, Mormonism requires a significant commitment to change. For the early nineteenth century convert to the Church, becoming a Latter-day Saint generally meant gathering to Zion. Though the initial decision to move may have been difficult, the physical distancing from hostile family and friends to a place where there were other members with similar beliefs and experience facilitated the conversion process.[14]

While it is true that the Church is growing fast in Latin America, it is also true that the percentage who remain in the Church and become faithful members is lower than the baptismal rate. In Latin America the process of conversion tends to be complicated. Joining the LDS Church represents for many the rejection of national and religious traditions. The new member remains in the environment of family, work, and friends who often put pressure on new converts to stop going to church.[15]

The environment of rapid growth also complicates retention. Branch presidents and bishops tend to be young, often recently returned missionaries or converts of less than a couple of years in the Church. There are generally many teenagers in the wards and a high percentage of females. The number of complete families is occasionally low, and there are not enough members to adequately home and visit teach all the members.

RECOGNITION

The LDS Church in Latin America tends to be more recognized among the population than its numbers would merit. Unfortunately, often the perception of nonmembers is that the LDS Church is a wealthy American religion, due primarily to the visibility of the missionaries and the type of chapels built. Occasionally the Church has been the target of anti-American activities. These activities should not, however, be overemphasized. Mormons attract attention all over the world, and Latin America is no different.

Similarly, evangelical churches in Latin America have also been the target of revolutionary groups who have bombed their chapels and killed ministers. The Catholic Church periodically comes under attack from both the left and the right. Violence against the LDS Church is probably less than that which has occurred against other religions throughout the region. The one exception appears to be Chile, where in the 1980s our chapels were targeted for bombing by leftist revolutionary groups because of the Church's connection to the United States.

The association with the United States, however, is generally positive for the Church. The relationship with America may be questioned by leftist intellectuals, nationalists, and other churches, but for the population in general that connection is not considered different or significant. Foreign involvement in religion is accepted as a normal part of the religious environment. The Catholic Church historically has had a large number of foreign priests throughout Latin America. Protestant churches still maintain strong foreign connections. Many evangelical churches receive support from American religious organizations. Religions with African cultural elements are popular in Brazil. Asian religions are growing. Mormonism, in many ways, fits naturally into the religious environment of the region and is not seen as significantly different because of its American connection. For many, the attraction to America is what first interested them in the Church.

FUTURE

The future of the Church in Latin America is promising. There will probably not be a significant decrease in the growth rate for the next few years, as long as general population growth and urbanization continues. In all of Latin America, but particularly in Mexico, Guatemala, Chile, Argentina, Peru, Uruguay, and Brazil, there are large numbers of experienced and qualified leaders in the Church. They are young men and women in their late thirties and forties who have served missions, held responsible positions at early ages, and are occasionally prominent in their countries. These young leaders are different from their mothers and fathers, in part, because they were born and raised in the Church. They are talented, committed, and have an understanding of the Church that is unusual anywhere in the world. They have a respect for the Church in the United States and at the same time understand the environment in which the Church has developed in their own countries. They have been raised within an environment of growth and expansion. They know how to manage that growth and have anticipation for what the future holds.

CONCLUSION

America, both North and South, is a land of prophecy and miracles. It is a region that has been of particular interest to modern-day prophets. The growth and expansion of the Church in this part of the world is a fulfillment of prophecy. What is happening in Latin America is not a façade of growth. The miracle of growth and expansion of the Church in the last half of the twentieth century provides us with vision of what will happen in the twenty-first century when most of those prophetic predictions will probably come to fruition and the population of Latin America will "blossom as a rose." That blossoming has recently been emphasized by President Gordon B. Hinckley in a meeting in Venezuela on 3 August 1999:

"Where there are now hundreds of thousands, there will be millions and our people will be recognized for the goodness of their lives and they will be respected and honored and upheld. We shall build meetinghouses, more and more of them to accommodate their needs, and we shall build temples in which they may receive their sacred ordinances and extend those blessings to those who have gone beyond the veil of death."[16]

NOTES

1. For a summary history of missionary work with Native Americans, see "Native American," in Daniel H. Ludlow, ed., *Encyclopedia of Mormonism*, 4 vols. (New York: Macmillan, 1992), 3:981–85. For a discussion concerning Chile as the possible place Lehi landed, see Frederick G. Williams, *Did Lehi Land in Chile?: An Assessment of the Frederick G. Williams Statement* (Provo, Utah: Foundation for Ancient Research and Mormon Studies, 1988).

2. Bryant S. Hinckley, *Sermons and Missionary Services of Melvin Joseph Ballard* (Salt Lake City: Deseret Book, 1949), 100.

3. *Deseret News 1999–2000 Church Almanac* (Salt Lake City: Deseret News, 1998).

4. Andrew Jenson, in *Encyclopedic History of The Church of Jesus Christ*

of Latter-day Saints (Salt Lake City: Deseret News Publishing, 1941), 938–39.

5. A. Delbert Palmer and Mark L. Grover, "Hoping to Establish a Presence: Parley P. Pratt's 1851 Mission to Chile," *Brigham Young University Studies* 38, 4 (1999): 115–38.

6. F. LaMond Tullis, *Mormonism in Mexico: The Dynamics of Faith and Culture* (Logan, Utah: Utah State University, 1987).

7. Rodolfo Acevedo A., *Los Mormones en Chile* (Santiago de Chile: Impresos y Publicaciones Cumora, 1991).

8. For over twenty years I have been compiling a bibliography on the Church in Latin America and continue to be surprised at how little interest there is in the Church. Most descriptions and academic studies relegate the Church to a group with the Jehovah's Witnesses and Seventh-Day Adventists, which generally results in the Church being ignored.

9. David Martin, *Tongues of Fire: The Explosion of Protestantism in Latin America* (London: Basil Blackwell, 1990).

10. Edward L. Cleary and Hannah W. Stewart-Gambino, *Power, Politics, and Pentecostals in Latin America* (Boulder, Colo.: Westview Press, 1997).

11. Patrick Johnstone, *Operation World* (Carlisle: O. M. Publishing, 1995). The author provided introductory information for each country of the world and statistical data on Protestant churches, when available. I have no idea how accurate his figures are, although he is used by most scholars for statistical information on Protestantism worldwide.

12. This statistic was obtained from the Inter-American Development Bank at http://*www.iadb.org*.

13. Information on class change is not readily available for the Church in Latin America. One important study is Marcus Helvecio Tourinho de Assis Martins, "The Oak Tree Revisited: Brazilian LDS Leaders' Insights on the Growth of the Church in Brazil," Ph.D dissertation, Brigham Young University, 1996.

14. Tim Heaton, Stan L. Albrecht, and J. Randal Johnson, "The Making of British Saints in Historical Perspective," *Brigham Young University Studies* (Spring 1987): 119–35.

15. Mark L. Grover, "Mormonism in Brazil: Religion and Dependency in Latin America," Ph.D. dissertation, Indiana University, 1985, 137–58.

16. "Pres. Hinckley Urges More Missionary Effort in Venezuela," *Church News*, 14 August 1999, 3.

CHAPTER ELEVEN

A TIME FOR HEALING: OFFICIAL DECLARATION 2

JUAN HENDERSON

Being an African-American and a member of The Church of Jesus Christ of Latter-day Saints, I have been approached many times on the subject of blacks and the priesthood. In an effort to help those who have concerns, I have felt the need to study the revelation on priesthood, or Official Declaration 2.

From the days of Adam to 1978 there have been faithful black members of the Church who were unable to receive the priesthood. Now untold numbers of black men have received the blessings of the holy priesthood for themselves and for their families and others throughout the world. People of many nations have rejoiced at the infinite mercy of our Redeemer in extending the holy priesthood, by revelation, to all worthy male members of his Church.

Yet a few have felt unable to rejoice because of speculations concerning the prior priesthood restriction. For example, some have reasoned that the priesthood restriction did not originate with God, but resulted out of the prejudices of the early Brethren. Others have reasoned that the restriction did not begin with Joseph Smith, but only later became Church policy. And still others have reasoned that blacks were denied the priesthood because they were less valiant in the premortal life. Those who have sought to explain the restriction by the philosophies of men have impeded their ability—and sometimes the ability of others—to come unto their Heavenly Father in faith.

Juan Henderson is a doctoral candidate in educational leadership and an instructor in Church history and doctrine at Brigham Young University.

It is my hope that the words of the prophets, as well as the faithful accounts of other black Latter-day Saints, will aid such individuals in their search for peace. I bear witness that real peace can come only through the infinite mercy of the Lord Jesus Christ (John 14:27).

THE LONG-PROMISED DAY

In the 1978 general conference of The Church of Jesus Christ of Latter-day Saints, the following announcement was read:

"As we have witnessed the expansion of the work of the Lord over the earth, we have been grateful that people of many nations have responded to the message of the restored gospel, and have joined the Church in ever-increasing numbers. This, in turn, has inspired us with a desire to extend to every worthy member of the Church all of the privileges and blessings which the gospel affords.

"Aware of the promises made by the prophets and presidents of the Church who have preceded us that at some time, in God's eternal plan, all of our brethren who are worthy may receive the priesthood, and witnessing the faithfulness of those from whom the priesthood has been withheld, we have pleaded long and earnestly in behalf of these, our faithful brethren, spending many hours in the Upper Room of the Temple supplicating the Lord for divine guidance.

"He has heard our prayers, and by revelation has confirmed that the long-promised day has come when every faithful, worthy man in the Church may receive the holy priesthood, with power to exercise its divine authority, and enjoy with his loved ones every blessing that flows therefrom, including the blessings of the temple. Accordingly, all worthy male members of the Church may be ordained to the priesthood without regard for race or color. . . .

"We declare with soberness that the Lord has now made known his will for the blessing of all his children throughout the earth who will hearken to the voice of his authorized servants, and prepare themselves to receive every blessing of the gospel" (Official Declaration 2).

REACTION TO THE ANNOUNCEMENT

Church members—black and white—rejoiced. However, some viewed the revelation with skepticism.

Just hours after the public announcement was made, Elder David B. Haight of the Quorum of the Twelve Apostles was scheduled to preside at a stake conference in Detroit, Michigan. Elder Haight related the following experience:

"When my plane landed in Chicago, I noticed an edition of the *Chicago Tribune* on the newsstand. The headline in the paper said, 'Mormons Give Blacks Priesthood.' And the subheading said, 'President Kimball Claims to Have Received a Revelation.' I bought a copy of the newspaper. I stared at one word in that subheading—*claims*.

"Little did the editor of that newspaper realize the truth of that revelation when he wrote, ' . . . Claims to Have Received a Revelation.' Little did he know, or the printer, or the man who put the ink on the press, or the one who delivered the newspaper. . . . Little did they know what I knew because I was a witness to it."[1]

"Good Great and Holy Men"

President David O. McKay said: "The seeming discrimination by the Church toward the Negro is not something which originated with man; but goes back into the beginning with God."[2] Prophets both before and since that time have uttered the same thing. Yet some still believe that the restriction rose out of the prejudices of the early Brethren, particularly Brigham Young. In answer, I share an account of Jane Manning James, a faithful black sister in the Church.

When Jane joined the Saints in Nauvoo in 1843, having walked several hundred miles from her previous home in New England, Joseph and Emma Smith invited her to live with them. After the Prophet Joseph Smith was martyred, Jane was invited by Brigham Young to live with his family. Many years later, Jane testified: "I have seen Bro. Brigham, Bro's Taylor Woodruff and Snow, Rule this great work and pass on to their rewards and now Brother Joseph F. Smith. I hope the Lord will spare him if tis his holy will for many many years, to guide the Gospel ship to a harbor of safety, and I know they will if the people will only listen and obey the teachings of these good great and holy men."[3]

In my mind, this black sister's personal witness speaks volumes in dispelling any notion of prejudice on the part of the Brethren.

Policy from the Beginning

Others have reasoned that the priesthood restriction did not begin with Joseph Smith but only later became a Church policy. They cite the example of Elijah Abel, a black man who was ordained to the priesthood in the early days of the Church. In their opinion, Elijah Abel's ordination suggests that the Prophet Joseph Smith sanctioned ordaining black men to the priesthood. This opinion is not in harmony with the teachings of the Brethren.

In January 1970, the First Presidency of the Church issued this statement: "From the beginning of this dispensation, Joseph Smith and all succeeding presidents of the Church have taught that Negroes, while spirit children of a common Father, and the progeny of our earthly parents Adam and Eve, were not yet to receive the priesthood, for reasons which we believe are known to God, but which He has not made fully known to man."[4]

At a Brigham Young University devotional a few years before this statement was made, Elder Harold B. Lee stated: "Some are heralding the fact that there was one of colored blood, Elijah Abel, who was ordained a Seventy in the early days. They . . . hold that up as saying that we departed from what was started way back, but they forget that . . . President Joseph F. Smith is quoted in a statement under date of August 26, 1908, when he referred to Elijah Abel who was ordained a Seventy in the days of the Prophet and to whom was issued a Seventy's certificate. This ordination, when found out, was declared null and void by the Prophet himself and so likewise by the next three presidents who succeeded the Prophet Joseph. Somehow because of a little lapse, or a little failure to do research properly, some people reach a conclusion that they had wanted to reach and to make it appear as though something had been done way back from which we had departed and which now ought to be set in order."[5]

A QUESTION OF VALIANCE

Still others have reasoned that blacks were denied the priesthood because they were "less valiant" in the premortal life.

Following the announcement of the revelation on priesthood, Elder LeGrand Richards of the Quorum of Twelve Apostles said, "Some time ago, the Brethren decided that we should *never* say that. We don't know just what the reason was." And he further stated, "The Lord has never indicated that . . . black skin came because of being less faithful."[6]

Speaking of Pharaoh, king of Egypt, President David O. McKay said: "'Pharaoh, *being a righteous man,* established his kingdom and judged his people wisely and justly all his days, seeking earnestly to imitate that order established by the fathers in the first generations, in the days of the first patriarchal reign, even in the reign of Adam, and also of Noah, his father.' (Abraham 1:26).

"Now there was a noble man, righteous, fair in his judgment, seeking earnestly to guide the people according to the Priesthood which was given to Adam, a man who seems to have been worthy in every respect not only in regard to nobility of character, but also in regard to ability in leadership, but he could not receive the Priesthood."[7]

From President McKay's description, it seems to me that, as far as personal worthiness is concerned, this brother qualified for the priesthood.

President McKay also said: "It was the Lord who said that Pharaoh, the first Governor of Egypt, though 'a righteous man,' . . . 'could not have the right of priesthood.' Now if we have faith in the justice of God, we are forced to the conclusion that this denial was not a deprivation of merited right. It may have been entirely in keeping with the eternal plan of salvation for all of the children of God."[8]

The Lord taught us to be careful about making blanket judgments when he shared his understanding of the man blind from birth as recorded in the New Testament in John 9:1–2. Citing this story, Elder Neal A. Maxwell said: "There are clearly special cases of individuals with special limitations in life, which conditions we mortals cannot now fully fathom. . . . We must be exceedingly careful about imputing either wrong causes or wrong rewards to all in such circumstances. They are in the Lord's hands, and he loves them perfectly."[9]

REASON VERSUS REVELATION

In an interview printed in the *Daily Herald* on the tenth anniversary of the announcement of the revelation on priesthood, Elder Dallin H. Oaks, a member of the Quorum of the Twelve Apostles, was asked: "As much as any doctrine the church has espoused, or controversy the church has been embroiled in, this one seems to stand out. Church members seemed to have less to go on to get a grasp of the issue. Can you address why this was the case, and what can be learned from it?"

Elder Oaks responded, "If you read the scriptures with this question in mind, 'Why did the Lord command this or why did he command that,' you find that in less than one in a hundred commands was any reason given. It's not the pattern of the Lord to give reasons. We can put reason to revelation. We can put reasons to commandments. When we do we're on our own. Some people put reasons to the one we're talking about here, and they turned out to be spectacularly wrong. There is a lesson in that. The lesson I've drawn from that, I decided a long time ago that I had faith in the command and I had no faith in the reasons that had been suggested for it."

The interviewer continued, "Are you referring to reasons given even by general authorities?" Elder Oaks replied, "Sure. I'm referring to reasons given by general authorities and reasons elaborated upon that reason by others. The whole set of reasons seemed to me to be unnecessary risk taking. . . . Let's don't make the mistake that's been made in the past, here and in other areas, trying to put reasons to revelation. The reasons turn out to be man-made to a great extent. The revelations are what we sustain as the will of the Lord and that's where safety lies."[10]

SEEKING A CONFIRMATION IN FAITH

In his biography Elder Helvécio Martins, the first black general authority in the Church, shared how he received peace concerning the priesthood restriction. Six years before the announcement of the revelation (Official Declaration 2), missionaries tracted out his family. Elder Martins said, "The missionaries said they were representatives of the Lord Jesus Christ and that they had a blessing for our family if we would like one. I told them yes, but stated that I first had some questions I would like them to answer. First we talked in general terms about the Church. Then I asked a question I now realize God had prepared these young men spiritually to handle. I also realize now that God had prepared me and my family to hear their response.

"[I said,] 'Given that your church is headquartered in the United States . . . a country with a history of racial conflict, how does your religion treat blacks? Are they allowed into the church?' Elder McIntire initially went red in the face and nervously squirmed in his chair. Then, he asked our permission to have a prayer, which we agreed to, and afterward began giving what I now realize was the first missionary discussion. . . . Before we knew it, the hour was one in the morning, and those missionaries had given us, I again realize in retrospect, most of the missionary lessons. During that four-and-a-half-hour discussion, we dealt with the issue of blacks and the priesthood. The missionaries' explanation seemed clear to me and, more important, I accepted the practice as the will of the Lord [see Moroni 10:3–5]."[11]

When we petition the Lord in faith, he will hear our prayers and grant unto us the peace that we seek.

BUILDING UNDERSTANDING

Unfortunately, there have been times when members of the Church have either knowingly or unknowingly offended black members. I am reminded of the experience shared by Sister Lucille Bankhead, a faithful black sister in the Church. "Sometimes I've had to correct people who say things that aren't right. There was a [white] woman and every time she'd go to Relief Society somebody would ask her how she was doing. She'd say, 'Oh, I'm so tired, I've been working like a nigger.' I was determined to break her out of that saying. The next time I was at Relief Society and someone asked me how I was doing, I said, 'I'm so tired, I've been working like a nigger.' You could have heard a pin drop in the ward house. I just whipped her with her own stick. And I haven't heard that expression since."[12]

The insensitive behavior of some Church members toward people of color cannot be interpreted to be a part of the gospel of Jesus Christ. Elder Howard W. Hunter said: "The brotherhood of man is literal. We are all of one blood and the literal spirit offspring of our eternal Heavenly Father. Before we came to earth we belonged to his eternal family. We associated and knew each other there. Our common paternity makes us not only literal sons and daughters of eternal parentage, but literal brothers and sisters as well. This is a fundamental teaching of The Church of Jesus Christ of Latter-day Saints."[13]

THE INFINITE ATONEMENT

To those who have felt the pang of insensitive or prejudicial remarks on the part of some in the Church, I testify in the name of Jesus Christ that through his atoning sacrifice you can be healed. In the Book of Mormon we read: "And he shall go forth, suffering pains and afflictions and temptations of every kind; and this that the word might be fulfilled which saith he will take upon him the pains and the sicknesses of his people. And he will take upon him death, that he may loose the bands of death which bind his people; and he will take upon him their infirmities, that his bowels may be filled with mercy, according to the flesh, that he may know according to the flesh how to succor his people according to their infirmities" (Alma 7:11–12; see also D&C 19:16–19). There is no suffering that the Lord has not known himself.

Concerning Christ's sufferings Elder Boyd K. Packer said: "Before the Crucifixion and afterward, many men have willingly given their lives in selfless acts of Heroism. But none faced what the Christ endured.

"Upon Him was the burden of all human transgression, all human guilt. And hanging in the balance was the Atonement. . . . He, by choice, accepted the penalty for all mankind for the sum total of all wickedness and depravity; for brutality, immorality, perversion, and corruption; for addiction; for the killings and torture and terror—for all of it that ever had been or all that ever would be enacted upon this earth. In choosing, He faced the awesome power of the evil one who was not confined to flesh nor subject to mortal pain. That was Gethsemane!"[14]

TRUE TO THE FAITH

In conclusion may I relate the story of Samuel D. Chambers, another faithful black Saint in the early days of the Church. "In 1844, as a thirteen-year-old slave in eastern Mississippi, [Samuel] listened to the preaching of Preston Thomas and accepted baptism. . . . But, unlike other converts in the area who relocated to Nauvoo, . . . Samuel stayed behind. He was . . . a slave, not free to migrate. For a quarter of a century he had no further contact with the Church and no hope of ever joining the body of the Saints." Of that time, Brother Chambers said: " 'I was 21 years in bondage, during which time I never heard a word of the gospel. The spirit of God remained with me.' "[15]

After the Civil War, Samuel worked for four years before making the trek to Utah. In 1870 Samuel arrived in Salt Lake City with his wife and son. "The Chambers [family] settled in the Eighth Ward where they tithed and donated, received patriarchal blessings . . . and attended meetings. Samuel 'was appointed as assistant Deacon,' noted the ward records on May 1, 1873, but he received no priesthood. . . . Samuel represented his ward at monthly stake deacons quorum meetings. In January 1876, in appreciation for Samuel's service in the ward, 'A vote of thanks was unanimously rendered Br. Chambers for being so faithful in the discharge of his duties as Deacon. . . .' In the Wilford Ward they were well known and well liked. . . . The couple became known for their firm testimonies, their strict loyalty to Church leaders, their keeping of the Sabbath and generous church donations." Samuel lived the remainder of his life in Salt Lake City. He died in 1929, at age ninety-eight. To his death Samuel remained strong in the faith.[16]

Now why would a black man or black woman of that time want to join this Church, pay tithes, donate their time and talents, and sustain the leaders of the Church as men of God while the blessings of the holy priesthood were withheld from them? And why would they stay? The answer is simple: They knew the Church was true.

I bear my testimony with these faithful black brothers and sisters that The Church of Jesus Christ of Latter-day Saints is "the only true and living Church upon the face of the whole earth" (D&C 1:30). And I look forward to the day when what was said of the people of Fourth Nephi can be said of us: "There was no contention in the land, because of the love of God which did dwell in the hearts of the people. And there was no envyings, nor strifes, nor tumults . . . neither were there Lamanites, nor any manner of -ites; but they were one, the children of Christ, and heirs to the kingdom of God" (4 Nephi 1:15–17).

NOTES

1. David B. Haight, "This Work Is True," *Ensign,* May 1996, 23.

2. "Policy Statement of Presidency," *Church News,* 10 January 1970.

3. Biography of Jane E. Manning James, 1893, Special Collections, Harold B. Lee Library, Brigham Young University, Provo, Utah, 4.

4. "Policy Statement of Presidency."

5. Harold B. Lee, *Doing the Right Things for the Right Reasons,* Brigham Young University Speeches of the Year, Provo, Utah, 19 April 1961, 7.

6. LeGrand Richards, interview with Wesley P. Walters, Church

Office Building, Salt Lake City, Utah, 16 August 1978, Special Collections, Harold B. Lee Library, Brigham Young University, Provo, Utah.

7. David O. McKay, Remarks at Cumorah, Main Road Mowbray, Cape Town, South Africa, in Evan P. Wright, *A History of the South African Mission, Period III, 1944–1970* (Salt Lake City: Evan P. Wright, 1987), 458–60.

8. David O. McKay, *Home Memories of President David O. McKay* (Salt Lake City: Deseret Book, 1956), 227.

9. Neal A. Maxwell, "A More Determined Discipleship," *Ensign,* February 1979, 71.

10. "Apostles Talk About Reasons for Lifting Ban," *Provo Daily Herald,* 5 June 1988, 21.

11. Helvécio Martins, *The Autobiography of Helvécio Martins* (Salt Lake City: Aspen Books, 1994), 43–44.

12. Twila Van Leer, "Lucille Not Afraid To Speak Her Mind," *Deseret News,* 11 February 1997, 2.

13. Howard W. Hunter, "All Are Alike unto God," *Ensign,* June 1979, 72.

14. Boyd K. Packer, "Atonement, Agency, Accountability," *Ensign,* May 1988, 69.

15. William G. Hartley, "Saint without Priesthood: The Collected Testimonies of Ex-Slave Samuel D. Chambers," *Dialogue* 7, 2 (Summer 1979): 13, 18.

16. Hartley, "Saint without Priesthood," 13–14.

CHAPTER TWELVE

THE PIONEER SESQUICENTENNIAL CELEBRATION

BRIAN J. HILL AND MICHAEL N. LANDON

Historians rarely consider anniversary celebrations to be noteworthy, as scholarly attention is rightly focused on the historic events and peoples themselves. Ironically, however, perhaps the greatest force in bringing the Church out of obscurity internationally in the twentieth century has been the media attention generated during the 150-year celebrations of the founding of the Church and the pioneer treks west. In fact, worldwide coverage of the sesquicentennial reenactment of the 1847 Mormon Pioneer trail proved so extensive that Church leaders could not speculate about its far-reaching effects. Elder M. Russell Ballard said, "The Church's sesquicentennial celebrations were the most significant thrust in bringing the Church out of obscurity in its history."[1]

The 1997 pioneer sesquicentennial provided the real catalyst for an evolutionary paradigm shift in worldwide attention and attitudes toward The Church of Jesus Christ of Latter-day Saints. For much of the Church's history, its leaders, members, and doctrines received negative and inaccurate portrayals by print or broadcast media. Most people in the United States and, to an even greater degree, those outside of North America have been completely unfamiliar with the

---

Brian J. Hill is an associate professor and chair of the Department of Recreation Management and Youth Leadership at Brigham Young University.

Michael N. Landon is an archivist in the Department of Family and Church History of The Church of Jesus Christ of Latter-day Saints.

Church or its teachings. When President Gordon B. Hinckley assumed leadership of the Church, however, he encouraged a new approach to media within the Church and among Church leaders. His administration's policies toward the media and the pioneer sesquicentennial celebration coincided with resulting fundamental changes in media attitudes, or at least media coverage, of the Church.[2]

Media leaders anticipated centennial and sesquicentennial anniversaries in preparing feature articles covering the Church and its history during those events. The extra lead time fostered more extensive print and broadcast coverage during these celebration years. For example, *Time* magazine had a cover page treatment of the Church in July 1947 and again in August 1997, both in connection with pioneer anniversaries.[3] International attention, in particular, came as a result of pioneer reenactments with broadcast features of the 1997 wagon train in such places as England, France, Belgium, Spain, Japan, Russia, Hungary, Poland, the Czech Republic, and Ecuador. The critical difference, however, between the centennial and sesquicentennial events was in the magnitude and intensity of the media coverage.[4]

The effects of this pivotal change in positive attention and the pioneer celebrations of 1997 are far-reaching. During the pioneer sesquicentennial, the Church continued to foster good relations with various governments, particularly within the diplomatic corps.[5] Increased understanding of the Church by many U.S. government agencies, including the Bureau of Land Management, National Park Service, and U.S. Forest Service, resulted from their charge to manage public lands that the sesquicentennial wagon train crossed.[6]

Increasingly under pressure to accomplish more with fewer resources, many federal, state, and local government agencies quickly came to appreciate the value of voluntary service given by Church members and the ability of the Church to organize large groups of members on relatively short notice to accomplish specific service projects. The most visible example of Church-government cooperation came during the Heritage Day of Service on 19 July 1997, when many federal, state, and municipal governments were assisted by Church members in performing volunteer service projects for communities, national parks and monuments, and on other federal and state-owned lands.[7]

Finally, the impact on Church membership is incalculable. Many historical documents, some unknown previously and others thought to have been lost or destroyed, have come out of obscurity and been made available to Church historians. A great creative outpouring of literary, musical, artistic, and dramatic works were developed in celebration of our pioneer heritage. A feeling of pride in the remarkable Mormon history memorialized by the media brought many less-active members of the Church out of self-imposed obscurity and into renewed Church activity. Nonmembers with Mormon pioneer ancestry spoke up proudly in public about their forefathers. Ancestral pioneer families separated because some chose to stay behind in Iowa or Nebraska reunited after many years through these vitalizing events. Missionary work increased in many areas and some new converts point to sesquicentennial events as essential elements in their Church investigation and ultimate conversion.

While the sesquicentennial of the pioneers was a onetime event, the process of the Church "coming out of obscurity" is ongoing. The pioneer sesquicentennial events and the media attention they generated have served as a basis for a new visibility of the Church, a visibility that is increasing as we move into the twenty-first century.

HISTORICAL MEDIA ATTITUDES

Since the earliest days of the Church, anti-Mormon literature and negative media reporting have targeted perceived flaws in Latter-day Saint doctrinal tenets, the Church's wealth and power, or the character of Church leaders. Such negative stereotyping often made it difficult for the Church to fairly portray the Latter-day Saint experience and message. Reports about positive Latter-day Saint values and traits, including a deep commitment to family, healthy living, honesty, sacrifice, and a strong work ethic, were overshadowed by negative or sensational accounts.[8] The image of the Church in the minds of the public had improved steadily by the mid-twentieth century, but from the 1960s into the early 1980s issues surrounding blacks and the priesthood and the Equal Rights Amendment again brought negative media coverage. In the 1980s and early 1990s, public perceptions of the Church were also affected negatively by the events surrounding the Mark Hoffman forgeries and, to some degree, by increased focus on the Church's financial activities and business holdings.[9]

While negative publicity presented its own challenges, of even greater concern was the general lack of knowledge about the Church, nationally and internationally. A survey conducted in the early 1990s indicated that more than 70 percent of Americans knew almost nothing about the Church, and the case was similar internationally.[10] Now the great challenge before the Church was not only to be portrayed objectively by press and broadcast media but also to be considered by organizations disseminating information to the public.

In 1996 a fundamental shift began to appear both in terms of the Church's public visibility as well as in the manner in which the press treated the Church. This revolutionary shift in public relations came from the tenor of President Gordon B. Hinckley's new administration and a worldwide celebration of the pioneer sesquicentennial.

Public Affairs Revolution

Two particularly profound events, occurring together, created a public relations revolution for the Church. First and foremost was the calling and installation of Gordon B. Hinckley as the president of The Church of Jesus Christ of Latter-day Saints. President Hinckley has spent his life immersed in media and public relations for the Church. His educational studies in classical literature, his first job in Church media, and his many years as a counselor in the First Presidency have helped him prepare to face and embrace public exposure and the press. Never before has a Church president been so familiar and comfortable in front of the public eye.

Interviews with Mike Wallace of *60 Minutes* and an appearance on the *Larry King Live* show, among other appearances, have displayed the skill and aplomb of President Hinckley in public forums. From the very beginning of his administration, at a very open press conference announcing the formation of the new First Presidency, it was clear that media relations would be different. President Hinckley shifted the prevailing attitudes of general Church leadership toward public discourse rather than away from it.[11]

In what might be called providential or at least a fortuitous coincidence, the pioneer sesquicentennial occurred just two years after

President Hinckley's installation as Church president. Celebrations of the 150th anniversary of the pioneer exodus from the Midwest into the Salt Lake Valley captured the attention of media institutions of every description all over the globe. As the Church reached milestones in total membership and international growth, and as President Hinckley made himself available more than ever to a curious press, the sesquicentennial provided a hinge point to tell the story of The Church of Jesus Christ of Latter-day Saints. Articles and broadcasts that began with the story of the reenactment wagon train invariably included stories about the Church's history, doctrines, and phenomenal growth, as well as feature stories about the current charismatic prophet, President Hinckley. Unprecedented positive media coverage of the Church throughout the world was the result of these powerful coinciding events.

PIONEER SESQUICENTENNIAL MEDIA ATTENTION

The Public Affairs Department of The Church of Jesus Christ of Latter-day Saints made a concerted effort to collect representative media coverage from throughout the United States and around the world during the pioneer sesquicentennial celebration. Public affairs specialists forwarded newspaper and magazine articles focusing on the Church and local celebrations to Church headquarters. These clippings were placed in twenty-three scrapbook volumes representing 2,763 scrapbook pages. The collection does not represent all print media attention, and the length of articles on each scrapbook page varies from a two-column inch clipping to several related articles to a multiple page magazine cover feature.

A cursory content analysis of these scrapbooks presented in Table 1 and Table 2 (at the end of this chapter) suggests very broad and deep media attention focused on the Church from all across the United States and the world.[12] One highlight in the scrapbooks focuses on media coverage of the Heritage Day of Service scheduled for 19 July 1997. The *Church News* reported that on that day alone, three million hours of service contributed by twenty thousand Church units benefitted local communities around the globe. Media interest in that effort did much to bring the Church out of obscurity as an organized and powerful service provider.[13]

National and international broadcast media coverage was

extensive, perhaps even eclipsing print media. Newscasts and documentaries were produced and shown in places where the Church's presence was extremely small and knowledge about the Church had been very limited. Not only were wire clips picked up by international news but also production crews from at least fifteen foreign nations came to film and broadcast news stories and documentaries about the wagon train and the Church. Mike Otterson, media relations director for Church Public Affairs, told the Public Relations Society of America, "The amount of news coverage generated during the sesquicentennial is impossible to calculate accurately. . . . News clippings have been pouring into headquarters and our offices around the world. At one time, our Frankfurt office was reporting fifty clippings a day. The director there asked if they could stop measuring their clips by column inch and start weighing them by the pound!"[14]

ADDITIONAL PIONEER SESQUICENTENNIAL IMPACTS

Among many notable impacts, the sesquicentennial also brought increased interaction and cooperation between officials of various U.S. government agencies and the Church or Church members. One of the most significant contributions of this increased cooperation was the publication of a number of trail guides to the Mormon Pioneer Trail or historic sites along the trail. A map of Mormon trail sites in the North Platte Valley was produced by a number of Wyoming and Nebraska agencies. A Mormon trail guide for Nebraska was published by the state Division of Tourism.

In 1996 the state of Iowa, the Iowa Mormon Trails Association, and Dr. Susan Easton Black of Brigham Young University combined efforts to produce a Mormon Trail guide for Iowa. A trail guide for the entire length of the Mormon Trail was produced by the National Park Service and Bureau of Land Management with cooperation from the Church and a number of private trails organizations, including the Mormon Trails Association in Utah and the Crossroads Chapter of the Oregon-California Trails Association.

Another significant contribution during the sesquicentennial was the assistance by Church members in helping the BLM prepare the Martin's Cove site for visits by the public. The use of Church members in worthwhile community service projects will undoubtedly increase as the demands placed upon state and federal agencies charged with preserving our historic past outpace the resource base they are given to perform their work.

Regardless of the notoriety produced by the pioneer sesquicentennial celebrations, perhaps the spiritual impact on individuals was the greatest and most meaningful. Individuals experienced a significant increase of personal faith as they celebrated and reverenced the heritage of faith left by early Church pioneers.

This increase in faith prompted many Church members to look at their own family history, and many made decisions about preserving important historical records. Impressed by the events of the sesquicentennial, one family brought the journal of James G. Bleak "out of obscurity" and donated it to the Church archives so it would be available for the edification of all. Bleak's journal was significant because it was one of the few Martin Handcart Company journals not written retrospectively, but penned by the always optimistic Bleak during the tragic events of the winter of 1856.[15]

Artistic expressions within the Church throughout its history have focused on the unique pioneer experience of its early members. The sesquicentennial, however, provided an opportunity for a particular outpouring of pioneer-based art and scholarship. Visual arts, performing arts, literature, and scholarship enjoyed banner years during the celebration. Some examples include special exhibits at the Smithsonian Institution and the Museum of Church History and Art, programs such as "Barefoot to Zion" and "Trail of Dreams," the nationally broadcast documentary "Trail of Hope," and new musical releases from the Mormon Tabernacle Choir, Merrill Jenson, Dan Carter, and other songwriters. Literary contributions to the pioneer sesquicentennial included numerous books about the trail and its significance.[16] Scholarly efforts were encouraged through conferences and symposia in Omaha, Nebraska; Des Moines, Iowa; and Provo, Utah.[17]

The national and local media attention also seemed to touch the hearts of many that have long been estranged from the Church. While Brian Hill was serving as a stake president in Nebraska, he noted that a number of Church members who had previously avoided missionaries or other Church members came forward into the community pleased to claim Church membership and rejoin the Saints in their worship and activity.

Another unexpected result of the pioneer celebrations was the reuniting of families separated since pioneer times. The Oliver family typified such a reuniting. In the early 1860s, while traveling to Utah, they broke a wagon axle in central Nebraska and were forced to stay the winter. In the next emigration season, the father of the family pressed on to Utah, but the mother and children stayed behind to homestead along the Wood River and remained out of the Church. Not until the pioneer sesquicentennial did the Utah and Nebraska arms of this family take the opportunity to reunite. In 1997 letters came forward that revealed that rather than abandoning the family, the husband had sent money to his wife over the years and begged her to come west and be with him.[18]

The hearts of the children were turned to their fathers in other ways as well. Announcing a proclamation that established a Mormon Pioneer Heritage Day in Nebraska, Secretary of State Scott Moore surprisingly and proudly revealed his own early Mormon ancestry. Family history interests were particularly sparked along the Mormon Trail. Elder Jeffrey R. Holland noted in one interview, "People have gone back in great numbers, even massive numbers, in the last several months—really in the spirit of the sesquicentennial activities—to do family history research."[19]

Not only did Church members become active in doing family history, but internationally Church members celebrated the pioneer heritage, making the Church much more visible than it had ever been before. As an example, Church members in South America donated more than thirty thousand hours of service during the Heritage Day of Service.[20]

From the Church's perspective, the most meaningful of all the sesquicentennial effects were the positive influences of the celebration that caused people, in and out of the Church, to change their lives for the better. Such influences often lead to individual conversions. In connection with the wagon train reenactment, several members of the train and others touched by its powerful spirit received baptism. Most noteworthy was the well-known teamster, Larry "Turbo" Stewart, who was baptized at This Is the Place State Heritage Park by Elder Hugh W. Pinnock the day the wagon train arrived. He subsequently had a wagon accident that has kept him in a coma to the year 2000.

CONTINUING TO COME OUT OF OBSCURITY

Although only a few short years have passed since the pioneer sesquicentennial celebrations, it appears that the positive Church attention generated during the event will continue. President Hinckley remains as available as ever, evidenced by a second international interview on *Larry King Live* on Christmas Eve 1999 and a second scheduled appearance before the Washington Press Club.

In 1997 Elder Ballard told Associated Press members, "I would guess by the end of this year we will have had more favorable press in one year than perhaps in the entire history of the church."[21] The positive impact of the sesquicentennial is, indeed, a tribute to the pioneering successes of those who first embraced the faith and carried it forward in their difficult journey to a promised land. Those who participated in the sesquicentennial as well as those honored by it can rejoice that such a celebrated event has and will continue to bring a deep, abiding faith out of obscurity for the benefit of all mankind.

PUBLIC AFFAIRS SCRAPBOOKS OF DOMESTIC PRINT COVERAGE OF PIONEER SESQUICENTENNIAL

STATE	SCRAPBOOK PAGES	HERITAGE DAY PAGES
Alabama	6	4
Arizona	28	12
Arkansas	1	1
California	194	104
Colorado	4	
Connecticut	11	5
Florida	25	18
Georgia	17	18
Hawaii	5	2
Idaho	82	7
Illinois	22	
Indiana	4	2

STATE	SCRAPBOOK PAGES	HERITAGE DAY PAGES
Iowa	52	4
Kansas	2	
Louisiana	6	2
Massachusetts	6	
Michigan	4	6
Minnesota	2	
Missouri	9	1
Montana	2	1
Nebraska	425	
Nevada	11	2
New Mexico	7	2
North Carolina	17	10
North Dakota		1
Ohio	9	7
Oklahoma		1
Oregon	2	4
Pennsylvania	12	3
Rhode Island	1	
South Carolina	19	6
South Dakota	2	
Tennessee	8	1
Texas	16	3
Utah	745	11
Virginia	10	2
Washington	16	4
Wyoming	122	
National Media	12	
Totals	1916	244

PUBLIC AFFAIRS SCRAPBOOKS OF INTERNATIONAL PRINT COVERAGE
AND BROADCAST COVERAGE OF
PIONEER SESQUICENTENNIAL

COUNTRY	SCRAPBOOK PAGES	HERITAGE DAY PAGES	BROADCAST PRODUCTION
Africa	2	4	
American Samoa	16		
Argentina		1	
Australia	26	27	
Austria	12		Documentary
Belgium	46		News
Canada	4	4	
Chile		2	
Czech Republic			Documentary
Dominican Republic	2		
Ecuador			Documentary
France	30	5	News
Germany	92	48	Documentary (3 Networks)
Honduras		3	
Hungary	3		Award-Winning Documentary
Italy	24	2	Documentary
Japan	20		News
Korea	8		
Mexico		2	
Netherlands		1	
New Caledonia	2		
New Zealand	19	25	

Country	Scrapbook Pages	Heritage Day Pages	Broadcast Production
Papua New Guinea	1		
Philippines			Documentary
Poland	2		Documentary
Portugal	2	1	
Romania			Documentary
Russia	10		Documentary
Solomon Islands	1		
Spain	8	10	News
Switzerland	38	1	
Tahiti	10	8	
Tonga		1	
United Kingdom	42	27	News Documentary
Western Samoa	6	5	
Totals	426	177	

PIONEER SESQUICENTENNIAL MEDIA HIGHLIGHTS

Time magazine's cover feature, "Mormons, Inc."
New York Times cover page feature
Washington Post cover page feature
Los Angeles Times feature and column
Atlanta Journal-Constitution feature
"CBS This Morning"
"Good Morning, America"
"Today Show"
"Fox National News"
"BBC World Service"
CNN clip of wagon train wreck
Newsweek
Wall Street Journal

BBC one-hour documentary

PBS documentary, "Trail of Hope"

Odyssey channel "Legacy West"—thirteen thirty-minute TV productions on the Mormon Trail Wagon Train

News service coverage from Associated Press, Reuters—Britain, Agence France Presse—France, Deutsche Presse Agentur—Germany, and Kyodo News Service—Japan

Extensive daily, local coverage by KSL, *Salt Lake Tribune,* and others

NOTES

1. "In Hallmark Year, Sesquicentennial Touches the World," *Church News,* 30 August 1997, 3.

2. Evidence of President Hinckley's approach to the media began at a press conference in March 1995 shortly after becoming president of the Church in which he allowed reporters to ask questions, the first time that had been done by a president of the Church in more than twenty years. Continuing from that point, he has been the leading example in making the Church more visible, with highly publicized appearances on the CBS news program "60 Minutes" with Mike Wallace on 7 April 1996, and appearances on CNN's "Larry King Show" on 24 December 1999.

3. "Utah: A Peculiar People," *Time,* 21 July 1947, 3; "Mormons, Inc.," *Time,* 4 August 1997, 8.

4. Attendance at Salt Lake City's 1947 "Days of '47 Parade" commemorating the pioneers proved so large it was held twice, but the focus of the 1947 centennial events was on Utah and its development since the pioneers arrived. The importance of the Church's message to a national or international audience was not emphasized in the same degree as was done in the sesquicentennial. Perhaps the most significant pioneer centennial event was the dedication of the "This Is the Place" monument, which drew a crowd of fifty thousand people, about the same as in the sesquicentennial. For a history of the monument, see T. Edgar Lyon, *This Is the Place Monument Story and History* (Salt Lake City: n.p., 1955). For a review of pioneer centennial events in Utah, see *Deseret News,* Centennial Edition, 19 July 1947, 16; *Deseret News,* 23 July 1947, 21.

5. Beginning in the mid-1980s, the Church's International and Government Affairs Office began to invite the Washington D.C. diplomatic corps to a number of events, including formal dinners, the "Festival of Lights" at the Washington D.C. Temple during the Christmas season, and western-style barbecues. Similar activities have been conducted for diplomats serving in consular offices in the San Francisco area. In 1996 the Church hosted eighty-three ambassadors. See "Diplomats Welcomed by Elder Maxwell to Festival of Lights," *Church*

News, 10 December 1994, 6–7; "In Hallmark Year, Sesquicentennial," 3; *The Latter-day Herald,* April 1999 (Washington, D.C.), 1.

6. Particularly in Wyoming, representatives of the Bureau of Land Management and U.S. Forest Service interacted with Church members through efforts to mark and preserve specific historic sites, including Martin's Cove, Rocky Ridge and Rocky Ford, and Simpson's Hollow. The relationship established during the pioneer sesquicentennial continues as officials of the BLM have subsequently invited LDS representatives to speak in a series of lectures held in Rock Springs and Green River commemorating not only the Mormon Pioneer Trail, but the California Trail as well. In addition, the National Park Service's decision to move the Long Distance Trails Office from Denver to Salt Lake City greatly enhanced the contact between NPS officials and Latter-day Saints interested in preserving the Mormon Pioneer Trail. Information from correspondence from Mike Brown, BLM, Rock Springs, Wyoming, to Mike Landon, Historical Department Archives, The Church of Jesus Christ of Latter-day Saints, Salt Lake City.

7. For a sampling of service projects see "Worldwide Day of Service," *Church News,* 26 July 1997, 8–10.

8. A few examples of sensationalism in titles of anti-Mormon literature include Eber D. Howe, *Mormonism Unvailed* (Painesville, Ohio: Eber D. Howe, 1834); Joshua V. Himes, *Mormon Delusions and Monstrosities,* (Boston: Joshua V. Himes, 1842); Fanny Stenhouse, *The Tyranny of Mormonism* (London: Sampson Low, Marston, Searle, & Rivington, 1888); *Expose of Polygamy in Utah: A Lady's Life among the Mormons* (New York: American News Company, 1872); Steven Naifeh and Gregory White Smith, *The Mormon Murders* (New York: Weidenfeld and Nicolson, 1988). Motion pictures also used sensationalism in titles such as the 1922 film *Trapped by the Mormons.* For an overview essay on treatment of Latter-day Saints in published material, see William O. Nelson, "Anti-Mormon Publications," in *Encyclopedia of Mormonism,* edited by Daniel H. Ludlow, 5 vols. (New York: Macmillan, 1992), 1:45–52.

9. The Mark Hoffman forgery case, besides receiving intense newspaper and broadcast media attention, generated a flurry of books examining the event from every perspective. Interest in Church financial and corporate activity also was heightened by the publication of John Heinerman's, *The Mormon Corporate Empire* and articles in the *Wall Street Journal* (8 November 1983, 91) and *Arizona Republic* (30 June–2 July 1991, 43–45). Interest in the Church as a corporate entity continues to be a popular media theme, as evidenced by the title of *Time* magazine's 4 August 1997 cover story, "Mormons, Inc." (4 August 1997, 8).

10. Church Public Affairs representative Mark Tuttle not only indicated the percentage of Americans unfamiliar with the Church but also stated, "When respondents were asked to rate their knowledge of

religions, American, English, and French respondents ranked Mormonism last. The religion tied for last in Australia and was second to last in New Zealand" ("Media 'Wise Men' Charting PR Path for LDS Church," *Salt Lake Tribune,* 23 August 1997, B1–2).

11. For a frank discussion of attitudes toward the media by Church leaders before and after Gordon B. Hinckley became Church president, see the interview by Rod Decker on the local Salt Lake City television show with Elder M. Russell Ballard. In the interview Elder Ballard stated, "I think it's a wonderful thing that we have President Gordon B. Hinckley who is so willing to meet the press [and] let people ask him questions. Members of the Council of the Twelve are doing that now where, maybe ten years ago, there was a little hesitancy to do that" ("Take Two," KUTV, 22 June 1997, Salt Lake City).

12. Pioneer Sesquicentennial Committee International media coverage scrapbooks 1996–1997, Historical Department Archives.

13. "Worldwide Day of Service," 8–10.

14. Talk given by Michael Otterson to the BYU International Society, August 1997, Provo, Utah, 17.

15. James G. Bleak, Journal, February 1854–February 1860, Historical Department Archives.

16. Books that were published about the Mormon Pioneer Trail and other western trails just prior to or during the pioneer sesquicentennial include Maurine Jensen Proctor and Scot Facer Proctor, *The Gathering: Mormon Pioneers on the Trail to Zion* (Salt Lake City: Deseret Book, 1996); Richard Neitzel Holzapfel, *Their Faces Toward Zion: Voices and Images of the Trek West* (Salt Lake City: Bookcraft, 1996); William W. Slaughter and Michael Landon, *Trail of Hope: The Story of the Mormon Trail* (Salt Lake City: Shadow Mountain, 1997); Arthur King Peters, *Seven Trails West* (New York: Abbeville Press, 1996); William E. Hill, *The Mormon Trail: Yesterday and Today* (Logan, Utah: Utah State University, 1996); James B. Allen and John W. Welch, eds., *Coming to Zion* (Provo, Utah: BYU Studies, 1997); Richard E. Bennett, *"We'll Find the Place": The Mormon Exodus, 1846–1848* (Salt Lake City: Deseret Book, 1997); Susan Easton Black and William G. Hartley, eds., *The Iowa Mormon Trail: Legacy of Faith and Courage* (Orem, Utah: Helix Publishing, 1997); Carol Cornwall Madsen, *Journey to Zion: Voices from the Mormon Trail* (Salt Lake City: Deseret Book, 1997); Roderic Korns and Dale L. Morgan, eds., *West from Fort Bridger: The Pioneering of the Immigrant Trails across Utah, 1846–1850,* revised by Will Bagley and Harold Schindler (Logan, Utah: Utah State University Press, 1994); Peter H. DeLafosse, ed., *Trailing the Pioneers: A Guide to Utah's Emigrant Trails, 1829–1869* (Logan, Utah: Utah State University Press, 1994). For a review of each of these published works, see Craig S. Smith, "A Legacy of the Sesquicentennial: A Selection of Twelve Books," *Journal of Mormon History,* Fall 1999, 152–63.

17. A Mormon Trail Symposium was held in May 1996 in Des Moines, Iowa, sponsored by the State History Department of Iowa; the Iowa Mormon Trails Association; the Mormon History Association; Nauvoo Restoration, Inc.; Brigham Young University Department of Church History and Doctrine; Joseph Fielding Smith Institute for Church History, also at Brigham Young University. The Mormon History Association also held their 1997 annual conference in Omaha, Nebraska, with a focus on the exodus west. Brigham Young University also sponsored a conference in September 1997 commemorating the exodus of the Saints to the Salt Lake Valley.

18. Information on Oliver family reunion in files of Brian Hill.

19. "Sesquicentennial Is Celebration of Beliefs," *Church News*, 26 July 1997, 6.

20. "33,000 Hours of Service Given in South America Area," *Church News*, 6 September 1997, 10.

21. Ballard, Associated Press release, "LDS Church Basks in Glow," *Salt Lake Tribune*, 21 July 1997, D1.

CHAPTER THIRTEEN

THE CHURCH IN AFRICA

E. DALE LEBARON

Until the 1990s most members of the Church knew little or nothing about the Church in Africa. Few were aware that President Brigham Young had sent missionaries to South Africa in 1852. Only a few missionaries served at any one time, and they proselytized only among the white population. For sixty-five years no full-time missionaries served there at all. The Church in South Africa was extremely isolated, and growth was slow. Being ten thousand miles from Salt Lake City and five thousand miles from the nearest mission or stake, it was a full century before any general authority visited there. When President David O. McKay visited South Africa in 1954, he brought new hope and faith to the Saints. This resulted in increased growth and the organization of the first stake in 1970.

While establishing the seminary and institute programs in South Africa in 1973, I was privileged to hear President Spencer W. Kimball, then President of the Quorum of the Twelve Apostles, offer a dedicatory prayer on that land and its people. It was a powerful and prophetic prayer that brought increased hope and confidence about the future growth of the Church in South Africa. President Kimball's blessing focused on such things as accelerated missionary work, wards and stakes to cover the land, and even a temple. Less than a month after visiting South Africa, President Kimball became the president of the Church. His inspired leadership brought a powerful focus and explosive growth for the Church in all of Africa.

E. Dale LeBaron is a professor of Church history and doctrine at Brigham Young University.

While presiding over the South Africa Johannesburg Mission in 1978—then the only mission on the continent of Africa—I witnessed events that would forever affect the Church, especially in Africa. First and foremost was the revelation on the priesthood received in June 1978, which opened the door for the gospel to go to the entire African continent. It is impossible to describe the flood of emotions I felt at that time, but they are forever frozen in my memory. To me it seemed to be an essential part of the restitution of all things. For the people of Africa it may well be the most important event since the restoration of the Church.

Although the revelation blessed people throughout the world, no continent was affected as greatly as was Africa. Prior to the revelation, missionaries were not able to proselyte the black people in Africa. In Nigeria and Ghana thousands of converts were waiting and pleading for Church membership for up to fourteen years, but they had been told that they must wait because without the priesthood they could not preside or perform ordinances. In South Africa apartheid laws prevented blacks from attending white worship services and vice versa.

For decades the South African government had restricted the number of foreign church missionaries that could serve in the country at one time. Although there needed to be several missions to properly service the vast area of South Africa and Zimbabwe, there were not sufficient missionaries to even service one. Through the leadership of Elder David B. Haight of the Quorum of the Twelve Apostles, and under the inspired direction of President Kimball, arrangements were made for me to meet with the South African Ministry of the Interior in August 1978 to discuss this rigid quota.

The Saints and missionaries fasted and prayed. Through a sequence of miracles, the Spirit of the Lord touched hearts, and two months after the revelation allowing the blacks to receive the priesthood, the quota was removed. The number of missionaries and converts multiplied. Today there are many times more missions, stakes, and members as there were prior to the revelation.

Another historic event occurred in October 1978 when an area conference was held in Johannesburg, South Africa, with President Kimball presiding. This was only the second time in our history that a president of the Church had visited the Saints in Africa.

Accompanying the prophet were President N. Eldon Tanner and Elders Gordon B. Hinckley, Neal A. Maxwell, and James E. Cullimore. It was the first time that more than one general authority had been in Africa at the same time. It was the experience of a lifetime for the five thousand Saints who attended the conference, many traveling more than fifteen hundred miles to be there. These events did much to bring the Church in Africa out from under the blanket of obscurity and darkness.

From the time the gospel was first preached in Africa, many people perceived the Church as evil and something to be afraid of. This was illustrated to me as a new missionary when I began door-to-door proselyting in East London, South Africa, in 1956. After we identified ourselves to an elderly woman, she ran to her kitchen, grabbed her broom and rushed back swinging it at us while screaming, "I know who you are! You are Mormons and you are here to take our young girls back to Salt Lake City to hide them in the walls of your temple and make them your plural wives." We jumped off the steps because her swing was as vicious as her cursing. I was stunned! Unfortunately, in Africa such misconceptions about the Church were widespread until recent decades. Some people have observed that Satan has had control over the "dark continent" for so long that he will not give it up without an all-out battle. I thought then, and I believe more strongly now, that the adversary will do everything possible to deceive and to blind men and that the war in heaven never ended; it just changed battlegrounds (Moses 4:4; D&C 76:29).

In the 1950s Church leaders became aware that interest in the Church was growing in the west African countries of Nigeria and Ghana. In these countries, the Africans themselves were sowing the seeds of the restored Church. The gospel message was spread primarily by devout Christians who, in their search for truth, had gained a testimony of the gospel from the Book of Mormon and other Church literature obtained while living or traveling overseas. Upon returning to Africa, they shared the message with others who then sent hundreds of letters to Church headquarters requesting literature and baptism.

What began as a comparative trickle of requests in the early 1950s became a flood by the 1960s. More letters requesting Church literature were received from Nigeria and Ghana than from all the rest of the world combined.[1] The Church responded by sending literature, but the demand was so great that some Africans even established LDS bookstores. Since there were no priesthood holders to preside and provide priesthood ordinances, however, those asking for baptism were told, "The time is not yet. You must wait." As they waited, they shared their knowledge and testimony of the gospel with others and organized congregations. It was reported that in the 1960s there were over sixty congregations in Nigeria and Ghana, with more than sixteen thousand participants, none of whom was baptized.[2]

This was a paradox for the Church. With an army of missionaries eager to go to the ends of the earth to teach and baptize, there were thousands in Africa pleading to join the Church who were not able to be baptized. This created a unique challenge for the Church, as well as for the unbaptized converts.

The early converts in black Africa, thousands of whom waited up to twenty years for baptism, experienced persecution and public attacks against the Church from the very beginning. Joseph W. B. Johnson, one of the earliest pioneers in Ghana, was converted through the Book of Mormon and then devoted his time, talents, and energies to sharing the gospel message with others. Although he had always shared his belief in Jesus Christ with others, he never faced opposition until he began teaching about the restoration of the gospel. He noted:

"Each time we preached we were challenged. The people did not believe that there was any other book equal or similar to the Bible. . . . I remember once while preaching in the post office square in Accra, a crowd came and shouted at us. They said we were anti-Christs, and adding to the Bible. . . . A group of people came and passed out anti-Mormon literature and we were booted out. . . . There was a paper in Ghana which had pictures of our prophets and they wrote filthy statements about them with the intent to sway us from the Church. However, we were undaunted, we knew they were telling us false things."[3]

In 1960 President David O. McKay assigned South Africa mission president Glen G. Fisher to visit Nigeria as the first Church representative. He met with several unbaptized converts. One group consisted of over 5,600 participants in many congregations. President Fisher told the First Presidency that he received a royal welcome because the native converts had been preparing themselves and their congregations for baptism for years. Their continued plea was for membership in the true Church.[4] He was also impressed with their sincerity. Even though they were extremely poor, they never mentioned financial help.

The intensity of their pleadings continued to increase, as reflected in this letter to President David O. McKay from a pastor in Nigeria who had made several previous requests for baptism. He wrote:

"I have to say that my heart will not rest . . . until I achieve my objective to be a baptized member of The Church of Jesus Christ of Latter-day Saints, to receive the gift of the Holy Ghost . . . and to be fully instructed in the gospel as restored [through the] Prophet, Joseph Smith . . . in order to be able to preach the true gospel to my people and win for my Savior, hearts that should otherwise perish in the darkness."[5]

Such letters received President McKay's attention and concern, not only because of their fervent plea but also because of their letterhead, which read, "The Church of Jesus Christ of Latter-day Saints, Nigeria Branch." The prophet did not know there were branches of the Church in Nigeria.

In 1961 President McKay assigned LaMar Williams, secretary to the Church Missionary Department, to go to Nigeria on a month-long fact-finding mission, to determine if the people were sincere and willing to accept the Church without holding the priesthood. Although Brother Williams had been responding to the flood of letters from Africa, he was not prepared for what he found there. He was met at the airport in Port Harcourt, Nigeria, by ten pastors with whom he had been corresponding. He was surprised to discover that not only did each pastor operate independently but they were not even aware of each other. Despite the poverty of the people, Brother Williams was treated like royalty and given celebrity status.[6]

The first official Church meeting in black Africa was held 22 October 1961 in a small mud hut in Opobo District, Nigeria, where Brother Williams met with a pastor and 110 followers. No one came by car. Many, including eight mothers with small children, had begun their day before 4:00 A.M. and walked twenty-five miles or more to be there. After teaching them for two hours, Brother Williams prepared to end the meeting. He recorded:

"It was hot as blazes. . . . My suit was wringing wet. . . . When I turned the meeting back to [the pastor], I heard a murmur all through the congregation . . . and [the pastor] . . . said to me, 'They don't want to go home. They have something to say.'

"Then for three hours . . . these people were standing up bearing testimony to the truthfulness of the Church and how they believed in the Prophets. I could not believe what I was hearing.

"One elderly gentleman said: 'I keep hearing you say, "if we are sincere." 'Elder Williams, I want you to know that I am sincere. I am an old man. . . . I am sick. But when I heard you were going to be here, I walked 16 miles this morning to see you and to hear what you have to say. I still have to walk 16 miles to get back home, and I am not well. I want you to know that I am sincere or I would not be here. I have not seen President McKay. I have not seen God. But I have seen you. And I will hold you personally accountable to tell President McKay that I am sincere.'"

Brother Williams reported to President McKay that he felt thousands were ready for baptism. President McKay called Brother and Sister Williams to preside over the first mission in black Africa, but the Nigerian government refused to issue the necessary visas, and their assignment was eventually canceled.[7]

Brother Williams turned over fifteen thousand names and addresses of unbaptized African converts to Elders Spencer W. Kimball and Gordon B. Hinckley, both of whom were on the Church Missionary Committee.[8]

The visas for the missionaries were not granted primarily because of bitter media reports in Nigeria, such as a lengthy article titled "Evil Saints," demanding that the Church not be allowed into the country. These articles referred to the Church's priesthood restriction to blacks as "religious apartheid."[9] These articles were written by Nigerian students attending universities in California in the early 1960s when civil rights was a volatile issue. They became incensed upon learning that blacks could not receive the priesthood, and they took immediate steps to prevent the Church from entering their country. This delayed the Church's entrance into west Africa for more than fifteen years.

Those who waited many years to join the Church, however, were wonderfully patient and faithful. When asked if they were angry with

God for having to wait so long for baptism, they each declared their gratitude for Heavenly Father's goodness to them. The rapid growth in Nigeria and Ghana is evidence of their feelings.

In just twenty years from the time the first missionaries arrived in Nigeria in 1978, membership there grew to over thirty-seven thousand with nine stakes and three missions. Ten years after missionaries arrived in Nigeria, Church membership surpassed that of South Africa. Nigerians are currently serving in leadership positions on every level, including three area authority seventies and a counselor in the Africa West Area presidency.

The priesthood revelation's impact on the present growth of the Church in Africa is phenomenal. After 125 years of missionary work in Africa, membership reached just over 7,000. In the next twenty years it rose to more than 120,000. The average number of baptisms per year is more than ninety times what it was prior to the revelation. There is also a similar increase in the number of missions and stakes. Africa's first stake was organized in Johannesburg, South Africa, in 1970—117 years after the missionaries first arrived. The first stake in black Africa was organized just over nine years after the missionaries arrived, whereas in the Philippines it took more than twelve years after missionary work commenced in 1961 before a stake was created.[10] In Africa the number of stakes jumped to thirty in just twenty-two years after the revelation, with virtually all the growth coming from black African converts. In South Africa, where many white members emigrated to other countries when a black government was established, it is reported that more than 90 percent of convert baptisms are among the blacks.

The explosive growth of the Church in Africa is largely due to the great faith and courage of the African Saints. In Africa, religion is a favorite topic of discussion, and people find it as nonthreatening as talking about the weather. Once converted to the gospel, African Saints are anxious to discuss their new faith. Reuben Onuoha, of Nigeria, is just one example of how quickly the gospel message spreads amongst the family and friends of African converts. The Sunday after he, his wife, and nine children joined the Church in 1985, a Church unit was organized in his home so they would not have to travel so far to meetings. Brother Onuoha was ordained a priest and set apart as president of that unit. That day Brother

Onuoha introduced the gospel to two other families, who joined the Church three weeks later.

Within four months they had eighty members. Their home was too small to accommodate such a large group so they moved to a larger facility, a branch was created, and he was set apart as the branch president. In just over two years that number had increased to over two hundred and a chapel was built to accommodate them. By then, Brother Onuoha was serving in the district presidency. One of the hundreds that he brought into the Church was a nationally recognized surgeon who, less than a year after his baptism, was called to the high council of the Aba Nigeria Stake, the first stake organized in black Africa. When Elder Neal A. Maxwell organized this stake, he noted that this was a historic day for the Church "in this dispensation, and in any dispensation."[11] It was the first stake in known history in which all the priesthood leadership was black.

Prior to organizing the stake, Elder Maxwell interviewed many in the district and called those who were to serve within the new stake, including Brother Onuoha. Elder Maxwell asked him if he would be willing to accept any position in the stake that the Lord called him to. Brother Onuoha answered that he would. Elder Maxwell then told Brother Onuoha that the Lord wanted him to serve as a stake patriarch and asked if he would accept that important calling. Brother Onuoha replied humbly, "Yes, I will accept the calling, but I have a question. What is a patriarch?"[12]

Another significant factor for Church growth in Africa is its strong base of priesthood leadership, many of whom are well educated by African standards. When Elder Boyd K. Packer organized the first stake in Ghana, he observed that it was also the first stake he remembered organizing in his thirty years as a general authority in which all of the stake presidency, high council, and bishops were college graduates.

The faithfulness of African Saints is also reflected in their church attendance and service in spite of the challenges imposed by poverty. When the Benin Nigeria Stake was organized, the presiding general authority noted that, in spite of the great distances many had to travel, there was 87 percent attendance with only eight cars in the parking lot—and some of those were brought by Church leaders and missionaries.

As the Church in Africa grows in numbers and faithfulness, it increases "in favor with God and man" (Luke 2:52) and is thereby brought out of obscurity and out of darkness. This was recently illustrated to me when I was asked to host a prominent dignitary from Ghana who is not a member of the Church. He served as minister of finance in Ghana and is a prominent international representative on African affairs. During a meeting with a member of the Quorum of the Twelve Apostles, he explained how he brought about significant financial stability to Ghana (a near impossible feat in African nations) and in the process gained a great appreciation for the Church.

The first step in his mammoth undertaking was to try to identify all forms of corruption in the government. To do so, he began by watching and testing the many top government officials to see if they would accept bribes or in other ways be dishonest. He said he found only two officials who did not show any signs of dishonesty. It was during his recent visit to Salt Lake City that he learned that they are both Latter-day Saints. Needless to say, in his mind the Church now stands as a beacon of light and truth.

His experience has particular significance when we realize that just ten years earlier, while this gentleman was serving in the government of Ghana, his government expelled all foreign LDS missionaries and banned the Church from functioning in Ghana. The anti-Mormon video *The Godmakers* was shown over national television twice. The government minister who made the announcement expelling the Church declared that the Mormon Church would never return to Ghana. All Church property was impounded and members were arrested if they met in groups beyond their own family. Two brethren were arrested and put in jail for administering to a sick child.

The faithful members continued meeting in their own homes and fasting and praying for the ban to be lifted. Both Church and U.S. government leaders worked hard to help Ghanaian officials see that the Church had been misunderstood and maligned. Former U.S. president Jimmy Carter, a Baptist, was involved in that process. Eighteen months after the ban was imposed, the Ghanaian government rescinded it, and less than four months later Ghana's first two stakes were organized by President Boyd K. Packer and Elder James E. Faust. The Ghanaian head of state made an official apology to

President Gordon B. Hinckley during President Hinckley's historic visit to Ghana in February 1998.

Although the Church has experienced considerable opposition from other Christian churches in Africa, we also owe them a great debt of gratitude for their many sacrifices and great service in bringing Christianity to Africa. Since the sixteenth century the Catholic and Protestant churches have sent missionaries, priests, and nuns to Africa, and a high percentage of them never returned to their homelands because of the high mortality rates due to malaria and other problems. They have built schools and hospitals and have provided employment for many Africans.

During the twentieth century, Christianity in Africa increased from 10 million to 350 million followers, causing one historian to refer to it as "the missionary success story of all time."[13] This service has been a blessing of great value in preparing the people for the gospel. Although less than half of Africa's population is Christian, of the 733 Latter-day Saint pioneers I have interviewed in Africa, more than 98 percent of them came from Catholic or Protestant churches. If these Christian churches had not accomplished what they did, surely Africa would not now be so ready for the gospel.

Another area of concern for the Church in Africa is the temporal needs of the people. Covering one fifth of the world's land mass, Africa incorporates some of the world's poorest and most struggling nations. Hundreds of millions of people suffer from sickness, disease, lack of education, and political unrest.

Because of the temporal help received from other churches, some converts expected similar benefits when the missionaries first came. One of the early mission presidents in Nigeria, Elder Robert E. Sackley of the First Quorum of the Seventy, was confronted by a delegation of about fifty brethren at one of his first district conferences. They handed him a long list of demands for temporal benefits that they wanted the Church to provide. His response was: "While I would like to rescue you economically, and I certainly have a great interest in that, my first motive will be to attempt to return you to the Celestial Kingdom even if it is on an empty stomach. That will take priority over anything else I do."[14] To this primary objective, most of the converts have responded with great zeal.

During the past two decades, the Church has provided

humanitarian aid to many areas of the world, especially Africa. This has been a major focus of the Church and has blessed the lives of countless people without regard to church affiliation. For many years the Church has contributed generously and compassionately, especially following natural disasters, war, or famine. In 1985 the First Presidency requested the North American Saints to hold two special fasts, from which nearly eleven million dollars was contributed to relieve suffering in Africa.[15] Soon thereafter the American Red Cross honored the Church for its relief efforts.[16]

Church media has also helped bring the Church in Africa out of obscurity and darkness. Latter-day Saints throughout the world learn of these faithful converts through television, the printed word, and videos like *Ensign to the Nations* shown at October 1997 general conference. But it was President Gordon B. Hinckley's historic visit to Africa in February 1998 that really focused a spotlight on Africa for Church members. He traveled 24,700 miles, nearly the equivalent of circling the earth, and met with thirty-five thousand faithful Saints in five African nations. Who can forget the pictures of the prophet standing before a vast sea of white shirts and handsome black faces in a priesthood meeting in Nigeria?

Although the Church's growth in Africa has been amazing, the future looks even brighter, as President Hinckley assured the Saints in Kenya: "Where there are now hundreds, there will be thousands, there will be tens of thousands. . . . We've barely scratched the surface of what will come. I haven't the slightest doubt of that."[17] The retention and activity of African Saints is described by general authorities as excellent.

President Spencer W. Kimball stated that the historic revelation allowing all worthy males to hold the priesthood brought "one of the greatest changes and blessings that has ever been known."[18] It might be compared to the restoration of the Church as far as black Africa is concerned. The coming forth of this revelation and the events surrounding Church growth in Africa is a wonderful illustration of the Lord bringing the Church out of obscurity and out of darkness. In concluding his visit to Africa two years ago, President Gordon B. Hinckley testified: "This is the work of the Lord and it is going to go on and grow and grow and grow in a mighty and powerful and wonderful way. This is a time of prophecy fulfilled."[19]

Perhaps the greatest evidence of Church growth in black Africa is President Hinckley's surprising announcement, while in Ghana in 1998, that a temple would be built in that land. Two years later, in April general conference 2000, he announced that a temple would be built in Nigeria. Never in recorded history have two nations on the same continent been privileged to receive temples in such a short time after missionary work first commenced—fewer than twenty years in Ghana and fewer than twenty-two years in Nigeria. Truly the coming forth of the Church out of obscurity and darkness in black Africa has been explosive and inspiring.

NOTES

1. Edwin Q. Cannon Jr. interview with Gordon Irving, 10 January 1980, Historical Department Archives, The Church of Jesus Christ of Latter-day Saints.

2. Author's interview of LaMar Williams, Salt Lake City, 12 February 1988. Because of the fluctuating numbers of followers and the lack of organization and regular contact, it is difficult to have accurate numbers of participants. In 1965 LaMar Williams of the Church Missionary Department knew of more than fifty congregations and fifteen thousand people who wanted to join the Church in Nigeria alone. In Ghana there were at least twelve congregations with about twelve hundred people waiting for the missionaries.

3. Author's interview of Joseph W. B. Johnson.

4. E. Dale LeBaron, *Glen G. Fisher: A Man to Match the Mountains* (Edmonton, Alberta: Fisher House Publishers, 1992), 145–46.

5. Letter of 29 July 1961, copy on file with the author.

6. Ibid., 10–12.

7. Ibid., 10–12, 25–27.

8. Williams interview, 7, 20–21, 35.

9. *Nigerian Outlook,* 5 March 1963, 3, photocopy in the author's possession.

10. *Church Almanac 1999–2000* (Salt Lake City: Deseret News, 1998), 437–38, 374, 364–65.

11. "Western Africa's Short Mission History Filled with Success Stories," *Church News,* 21 May 1988, 7.

12. Author's interview of Elder Neal A. Maxwell, on file with the author.

13. Jon P. Kirby, "Cultural Changes and Religious Conversion in West Africa," *Religion in Africa,* ed. Thomas D. Blakely, Walter E. A. vanBleek

and Dennis L. Thompson (Provo, Utah: David M. Kennedy Center, Brigham Young University, 1994), 57.

14. Author's interview of Elder Robert Sackley.

15. Isaac C. Ferguson, "Freely Given," *Ensign,* August 1988, 10.

16. "American Red Cross Honors Church Relief Efforts," *Ensign,* May 1988, 93–94.

17. "'This Work Will Grow and Grow in This Land,'" *Church News,* 28 February 1998, 3.

18. Spencer W. Kimball, *The Teachings of Spencer W. Kimball,* ed. Edward L. Kimball (Salt Lake City: Bookcraft, 1982), 451.

19. "Members Urged to Build Up Homeland," *Church News,* 28 February 1998, 5.

CHAPTER FOURTEEN

THE SIMPLIFICATION AND REDUCTION OF CHURCH CURRICULUM

JOHN P. LIVINGSTONE

In the mid-1970s Church leaders began to be concerned with the sheer volume of Church material being produced in the English language. By April 1979 they presented the problem to Church curriculum writers in an interesting way. They had gathered up one of everything printed by the Church. It took two trucks to carry it from the distribution center. Staff members were challenged to go back to their department and see if they could reduce the amount of material generated for Church use. Josiah Douglas, who was in that meeting, said, "We were told that the Church could not go to all the parts of the world with all the *'stuff.'* We were told that the Church had attempted in the past to reduce and simplify the printed and audiovisual material but the effort had not gone far enough. President Spencer W. Kimball said, 'This is a perilous problem and must be solved.'"[1]

Could this same volume of material be translated into the exploding number of languages in which the Church was beginning to produce materials? It was clear that in order to help establish the Church around the world, a more streamlined and "continuous" (that is, from the most embryonic to the most mature of Church units) curriculum was necessary. This need coincided with the efforts made by the Church's Lamanite and Minorities Committee to use simplified

---

John P. Livingstone is an associate professor of Church history and doctrine at Brigham Young University.

curriculum materials on Native American Indian reservations and among clusters of Asian refugees from the Vietnam conflict. It was felt that such a basic curriculum could be useful in many other places in the world where the Church was growing. Efforts to distill the most essential doctrines and principles into manuals and materials that were easy to read and teach from paved the way for the simplification and reduction of curriculum Churchwide.

Priesthood correlation had been in place long enough that the need for a Churchwide curriculum department was becoming evident. Auxiliary and priesthood departments had long been producing their own materials independently, and a unified curriculum department would help the right hand know what the left hand was doing. Centralizing the writing, translation, and production of curriculum in the Church soon became a reality.

The first manual produced by the centralized curriculum department was the well-known *Gospel Principles* manual in 1978. Members loved its simple, direct language, although few of the general membership were aware of the companion priesthood and Relief Society basic manuals that followed shortly thereafter. These simplified lesson books, which became familiar in small branches throughout the Church, formed the foundation of a curriculum that could meet a wide variety of Church organizational needs. They also formed the core of a more easily translatable gospel curriculum.

In a variety of Church scenarios, from a newly baptized family alone in Mongolia, to a small struggling branch in inner-city Detroit, to a fully developed 150-year-old ward in the heart of Utah itself, the gospel could now be taught using fully "correlated" resources. An effectual door was thereby opened, and the work could go forward in a major way. Now the gospel could be taught simply and directly, and the Church could be established wherever missionaries were allowed to go. Because not all cultures and settings encountered by missionaries were similar to the social, financial, and educational development found in North America, stories and materials, as well as the complexity of organization reflected in the mainstream Church curriculum, were often confusing and more complicated than necessary for new and developing areas. Thus the need for simplified and reduced materials that were faithful to Church teachings, but not culture specific, became obvious.

To illustrate, imagine an extended Latter-day Saint family (brothers and sisters and children) being transplanted to somewhere like the Canadian Northwest Territories, or Libya, or any other remote setting. If the Church was not formally organized there previously, what kind of Church unit would that family represent? How many Melchizedek Priesthood holders would they have in this little Church unit? Would there be enough to have a full branch presidency? What about an elders quorum presidency? How many Young Women would they have? Would there be any deacons? How big would the Relief Society be? Would the Primary be large or small? What would be the best configuration for this new unit of the Church? How much of the full Church program could they reasonably handle?

The Church along the Wasatch Front is mostly composed of members who are familiar with a ward and stake organization rooted in a sturdy LDS pioneer heritage. Growing families, a few newcomers, along with mature children returning from university training and business pursuits around the country make its growth like that of a living cell, dividing itself again and again over time. Yet, Church growth in the United States is actually outpaced by diverse frontier growth in regions far removed from the culture of western America. Establishing the Church in less-developed parts of the world raises very interesting challenges.

Primarily as a result of missionary work among Native Americans, Church leaders realized that not all cultures were prepared to implement the full Church program as it had evolved from pioneer days. Clearly, the development of the Church following the days of the great trek west to Utah featured deeply committed individuals and families whose forebears paid a heavy price to establish the Church in the semiarid climate of the Great Basin. Some of the first institutions developed were schools, and education became a primary feature of the new LDS presence. A firm foundation of nation-building, self-sacrificing pioneers created complex Church organizations based on strong gospel commitment and missionary efforts that brought converts from afar. This pioneer Church in the Great Basin wilderness would grow to become the engine of spectacular worldwide growth.

A leadership tradition and heritage evolved through practical experience. Bishops, stake presidents, and other leaders often served for decades. For many years, leaders gathered at each semiannual general conference as well as auxiliary conferences and enjoyed leadership training directly from apostles and prophets, creating an umbilical leadership connection with general authorities. This direct training allowed a tradition of leadership to emerge that was consistent from unit to unit and year to year. The homogeneity of the post-pioneer membership in the West, however, generally meant there was little variation from unit to unit.

As missionary work expanded into new parts of the world and fewer members emigrated to Utah, it became evident that the mushrooming diversity required organizational and curricular modification. The steadily increasing missionary numbers ensured that investigators were well taught, even if missionaries doubled as ecclesiastical leaders in some units. Helping new members to assume responsibility and leadership of their own units became desirable and necessary. This leadership training occurred mostly in the context of "dependent Sunday Schools," which were organized in areas where a new membership nucleus was forming. These Sunday Schools were affiliated with and reliant upon larger, independent units some distance away.

With Church membership surpassing the 2.5 million mark in 1970, it was becoming apparent that leaders would not always be able to gather at general conference to be instructed personally at Church headquarters. "Gathering" itself was redefined in 1972 by Elder Bruce R. McConkie when he said the following to the Saints of Mexico and Central America at an area general conference: "The place of gathering for Mexican Saints is in Mexico; the place of gathering for the Guatemalan Saints is in Guatemala; the place of gathering for the Brazilian Saints is in Brazil; and so it goes throughout the length and breadth of the whole earth. Japan is for the Japanese; Korea is for the Koreans; Australia is for the Australians; every nation is the gathering place for its own people."[2]

It was becoming clear that the decentralization of much that the Church did was inevitable. It was also obvious that it would not be possible to simply transplant the complex American Church around the world. Of course, the pioneering period of Church establishment in other countries would not necessarily require the same amount of time, energy, and isolation that characterized the early days of the

Church in the United States. Missionaries, traveling general authorities, and the growing staff of workers in the Church Educational System, Welfare Services, and other Church departments could greatly reduce development time for new Church units around the world.

As curriculum writers like Wayne Lynn, Ron Knighton, and Josiah Douglas were wrestling with notions of a reduced curriculum, men like Stewart Durrant, secretary to the Church's Lamanite Committee, were being encouraged by general authorities to envision less complex Church units that would not require years of experience to lead and manage. Concurrently, individuals in charge of curriculum translation were asking questions about *what* should and should not be translated into *which* foreign language based upon *what* criteria.

All of these issues seemed to converge in the mid-1970s. And so did the solutions. It became clear that the reduced curriculum could not only accommodate American Indians, but many other countries and cultures throughout the world. The simplified organizational and curriculum resources that preceded the full-blown Church program could also set the pattern for the translation of Church material. Church attendance levels could guide the production and distribution of needed materials in other languages.

Cultural considerations affected curriculum, too. Some societies were better prepared for complex materials than others. Local and general Church officers could determine the curriculum and organizational needs of units in each country of the world. Thus a pattern was established that allowed for the orderly development of Church materials in a prioritized way throughout the world. Newer and simpler units would have basic materials, while more developed and more numerous units in a particular language would have more complex materials. As newer units gained experience and additional members, they could move to more complex organization and materials, if appropriate.

As Church leadership configurations evolved and area presidencies were organized from the First Quorum of the Seventy in 1984, general authorities began to reside within their geographical assignments outside of the U.S. and Canada. With local and general Church leaders in greater proximity to each other, more frequent observation and training gave local leaders better contact with their priesthood leaders and facilitated faster consultation on the organization and development of units. General authorities on site could better assess conditions and more easily recommend necessary organizational and curriculum adjustments.

THE CURRICULUM DEPARTMENT

In April of 1961, Elder Harold B. Lee announced the creation of the All-Church Coordinating Council, which was "to formulate policy which will govern the planning, the writing, coordination, and implementation of the entire Church curriculum."[3] Three correlation committees, each led by a general authority, were created to prepare materials for children, youth, and adults. These correlation committees also included representatives from the relevant priesthood groups and auxiliaries.

Prior to this time, Church manuals and curriculum materials were produced by the individual auxiliaries and departments of the Church. Each produced what they felt was needed in order to help members lead, teach, and learn. Sometimes an overlapping and duplication took place where different organizations within the Church were producing similar materials. Over time, the writing and production preparation for all manuals, handbooks, and lesson materials was shifted over to the Curriculum Department. Some leaders, of course, were reluctant to let go of their curriculum development responsibility, but over time all materials for auxiliaries and departments began to go through a process of sifting and filtering called Church Correlation. This process subjected all official Church written material and graphics to assessment for doctrinal accuracy as well as integration into the "unified, balanced, and standardized curriculum, marked by stability and expansiveness."[4]

In 1972 the Internal Communications Department was organized and given responsibility for producing Church curriculum. This department had four subareas, one of which was the instructional materials group, headed by Daniel H. Ludlow. Under Brother Ludlow, the first leader of curriculum planning was Dean L. Larsen, who was later called as a general authority. He would be replaced as planning leader in 1974 by Wayne B. Lynn, who had been serving in the children's curriculum area under Elder Larsen and his committee.

These two brethren had years earlier served in a bishopric together in Viran, Wyoming, and later been involved in Indian seminary together. Under Wayne Lynn, curriculum planning charts were drawn up to show what doctrines and principles were being taught in the various Church manuals among adults, youth, and children.[5] These charts outlined for curriculum writers the times at which certain doctrines were introduced in the various manuals produced by the Church through auxiliaries and other groups. Efforts were then made to establish a correlated system of lessons ensuring that essential doctrines and principles were uniformly presented in each age group.

As the curriculum planning charts were adjusted for the addition of material, when needed, and edited when overlap was apparent, the new correlated outline or blueprint began to emerge. Simultaneously, this blueprint also became the foundation prioritizing which doctrines and principles were most important and which were less vital in arranging a correlated Church curriculum.

THE SIMPLIFICATION AND REDUCTION EFFORT

Designing a basic curriculum that could be easily translated into a variety of languages for the various developing nations and cultures began to be discussed. The curriculum planning charts presented an outline, and work began on a basic manual that would bring together under one cover those doctrines and the principles that derived from them. Care was taken to make the language and sentence structure plain and simple for ease of reading and translation. The result was the book *Gospel Principles*, which is now used in the Sunday School class for those investigating the Church.[6] Virtually every new member receives a copy of this manual. In areas of the world where Latter-day Saint scriptures are not yet available in a particular language, a similar manual entitled *Gospel Fundamentals* was developed that did not use direct scripture quotes but cited references only, to avoid any later conflict in wording that might occur once scriptures, or selections of scriptures, were published in that language.

The development of the *Gospel Principles* manual became the foundation for additional basic manuals. Two rudimentary priesthood manuals, both entitled *Duties and Blessings of the Priesthood*, were also developed. The first manual was named "Part A" and the second "Part B." They were to be used in alternating years. Likewise, in Relief

Society, *The Latter-day Saint Woman,* Parts A and B appeared. In addition, a children's manual, *Walk in His Ways,* Parts A and B was produced.

A correlated foundation for general Church curriculum was now beginning to emerge. The foundation doctrines of the Church were articulated, prioritized, and coordinated throughout the children, youth, and adult manuals and materials in such a way as to expose the individual member to the essential teachings of the Church at a calibrated rate over their lifetime.

All of these simple manuals, written at a sixth-grade level or below, laid out gospel doctrine so succinctly and directly that relatively inexperienced members in developing areas could teach effectively, focusing on the most essential doctrinal elements. This reduced dependency on missionaries for Church teaching and more deeply embedded gospel doctrine into the hearts of members. Of course, this same simplicity greatly facilitated translation into other languages and made the gospel understandable to peoples of many different lands and cultures.

This meant missionaries were somewhat freed up to focus on proclaiming the gospel and were able to bring investigators to Church meetings led and taught by indigenous members. This shift in responsibility helped place the stewardship of the local Church into the hands of the local members, rather than full-time missionaries. In terms of actually *establishing* the Church, this shift of custody from missionaries to members placed the burden of Church development more squarely upon those who ought to have the greatest interest in forging a vibrant, effective Church unit. With the aid of the manuals, Church members learned effective ways of teaching the gospel for the benefit of themselves, their families, and friends.

A further aid was the concurrent development of simplified guidebooks that established the basic principles of Church leadership such that new converts could be called to preside in local units.[7] Even senior couples serving as missionaries could act in more of a consulting role, rather than having to assume priesthood responsibility for the leading and teaching of members. With this shift, more of their time could be spent in contacting, teaching, and fellowshipping the less-active members that had fallen away during previous years of missionary-run units. One of the great challenges in implementing the new curriculum was to help missionaries realize the existence and purposes of the simplified materials to avoid misguiding members to use the fully developed curriculum rather than the simplified manuals.

These basic manuals also allowed new converts to understand the gospel more rapidly. The manuals acted as a supplement to missionary teaching. New members could read on their own, in their own language, and thereby find conversion more quickly and perhaps more deeply than had been the case previously. It thus enabled them to take more responsibility for their own gospel growth, by having additional resources they could refer to as they were motivated. The manuals also contained lessons that dealt with issues basic to personal and family preparedness that would help new members and those from developing areas better organize their lives according to gospel principles.

A CONTINUOUS CURRICULUM

In 1992 the First Presidency issued a letter to priesthood leaders suggesting phases of curriculum for Church units. An introductory phase, followed by phase 1, phase 2, and phase 3 were outlined. These phases provided "a systematic approach for teaching the gospel so that the needs of members in any circumstance [could] be appropriately addressed."[8] Attached to the letter were instructions on which materials could be used in each phase. Sunday meeting blocks of time and activity were outlined also.

While the family is undoubtedly *the* most basic unit of the Church, the following items became the entire Church curriculum for small units made up of just a few families or individuals: scriptures, *Gospel Principles* book, *The Prophet Joseph Smith's Testimony;* these became the introductory curriculum for very small developing units of the Church. A basic list of Church items each LDS family should have was listed also. The curriculum was designed to be able to expand to the capacity and number of members in various Church units. Priesthood and Relief Society manuals were added at the point when there were enough priesthood holders and women to warrant holding these meetings. Thus unit development was triggered by an increase in numbers of active priesthood holders.

The flexibility of the curriculum allowed youth to be taught from the same manuals as the adults, and in perhaps the same classes depending on the availability of teachers. As parents and priesthood leaders felt the need, and members were willing and able, children's classes were also added. Similarly, if units decreased in size, for whatever reason, classes could be collapsed again so that members would not be taxed beyond their capacity in trying to maintain the full range of classes.

In introductory and phase 1 units, all lessons for youth and adults were taught using the *Gospel Fundamentals* manual (for non-English-speaking units) or *Gospel Principles*. Priesthood brethren met for a few minutes only to "plan service activities and discuss other priesthood duties." No lesson time was outlined. While the men met in their shortened priesthood meeting, women and Young Women also held an abbreviated meeting to "plan service and homemaking activities and to discuss their roles in building the kingdom of God." Children under twelve all met together and were taught using *Gospel Fundamentals* (or *Gospel Principles*) and the Church magazines, where available.[9]

In phase 2 units, the Primary was organized if enough children warranted and teachers were available. Children were taught from the *Walk in His Ways* manual, which had several pictures and songs at the back and was basically self-contained, not needing additional resources beyond those provided. In 1992 the suggestion from Church headquarters was that the new *CTR B* Primary manual be used in alternating years with *Walk in His Ways*. The Church magazines and the scripture readers—a colorful, pictorial rendering of the Old Testament, New Testament, Book of Mormon, and Doctrine and Covenants—were the only additional resources recommended.

Youth in phase 2 units could meet with adults or separately, depending on numbers of youth and teachers. It was also suggested that two new manuals for youth, *Aaronic Priesthood 1*, and *Young Women 1* be used where youth met separately from adults during the priesthood and Relief Society time block. All priesthood boys would meet together rather than in quorums. The same was true of Young Women classes. It was recommended that some priests and Laurels be invited to teach lessons.

Melchizedek Priesthood and Relief Society in phase 2 were instructed to use *Duties and Blessings of the Priesthood* and *The Latter-day*

Saint Woman, respectively. Parts A and B were to be used in alternating years. Units usually moved from phase one to phase two when there were enough Melchizedek Priesthood holders to make an elders quorum president possible.

It should be understood that as units grew in size or maturity, introductory units could move toward phase 1 status, and phase 1 units toward phase 2. As phase 2 units grew, it would be possible to gradually begin to use more phase 3 materials as priesthood holders and teachers became available. Phase 3 represents the full program of the Church. These would be found in most wards. Thus the development of Church units could be pictured as being on an uninterrupted continuum, without necessarily needing to meet strict criteria to move from phase to phase. As membership strength and experience warranted, units could grow, adding new curriculum components as necessary.

On the other hand, units that did not experience this kind of growth could remain at a comfortable level without multiplying Church assignments to individuals for the sake of accommodating the regular Church curriculum. After all, the most essential aspects of the Church have to do with covenants and the ordinances that make those covenants official. While homes and temples are essential, buildings, programs, and curriculum are negotiable and flexible. One does not need to live in a full phase 3 unit to qualify for exaltation. This leads us to look at the conditions that may facilitate a phase 1 or 2 unit.

In some areas of the world where the Church was new, unit development was augmented by the use of phase 1 and phase 2 materials that were translated as numbers of members and local conditions warranted. It also allowed the "dependent Sunday School" model of Church development to be replaced by a system that called for the creation of smaller units with an indigenous priesthood leader who was not necessarily dependent on another unit for support.

In a sense, priesthood keys were now available to leaders of smaller units who could conduct their own sacrament meetings, order Church materials, and conduct affairs much more independently than before. This meant that these same priesthood keys were put into the hands of local leaders much sooner than might previously have been the case. This facilitated an on-the-job leadership training setting for new branch presidents over small units and created the possibility of greatly accelerated unit growth and development, depending on the inspiration and direction of these new local leaders.

The reduced curriculum did not create a second-rate branch of the Church but simply focused on the essentials and eliminated some of the negotiable aspects of Church organization and curriculum. After all, exaltation was not dependent on what curriculum phase was used in any given unit. Covenants and ordinances could still be contracted as long as homes and temples were accessible. Even a meetinghouse was negotiable in some circumstances.

When Church growth and strength allowed, phase 3 materials were introduced, thus facilitating an orderly evolution of curriculum materials production and distribution. The translation of curriculum in new languages proceeded at a reasonable pace, and a minimum criteria at which basic curriculum materials would be produced in each language was set. It became clear which manuals and guidebooks would be produced in *which* language at *what* time. Tithing resources would be conserved thereby, and unnecessary expenditures were avoided by such a pattern of curriculum production.

One challenge of applying the reduced curriculum around the world comes when members or missionaries from North America or other phase 3 units encounter the simplified manuals. Often they are unfamiliar with them and will unwittingly encourage the use of phase 3 Church manuals and guidebooks. New members or those aware of the more complex curriculum may feel the missionary knows best and that somehow the more complex curriculum is better or more advanced. Educating members and missionaries to the continuous Church curriculum and the fact that materials exist that are appropriately customized to certain developing languages, nations, and cultures can avoid confusion and misunderstanding. When members or missionaries who have only been exposed to the full Church curriculum learn about the simplified materials, they can have a greater effect in developing units and prevent members from feeling they are "drinking from a fire hose" as they are introduced to the Church and its programs.

Understanding the opportunity for leadership among indigenous leaders that the phase 1 and 2 curriculum and organization offers can be critically important to the establishment of the Church in a developing area. Avoiding a long period of initial missionary ecclesiastical leadership affords new members the opportunity to learn and exercise priesthood leadership early. The unit experiences a potential kick-start toward firmly establishing the Church by having leaders grow with the unit, rather than having them assume leadership after missionaries or other seasoned members have perhaps unwittingly fashioned a premature phase 3 unit.

The Church's decision to translate curriculum in a graduated manner through the phases makes this scenario much less uncertain than it was previously. Even some units in North America, however, could benefit from the reduced curriculum, avoiding multiple Church calling circumstances common when a few members are trying to carry the full Church program.

As the general membership of the Church becomes more familiar with the phase 1 and 2 curriculum, fewer instances of mismatched curriculum and burned-out volunteers will occur, and units will enjoy a more manageable organization. The benefits of giving indigenous leaders responsibility for the unit as early as practical will also become evident. In addition, missionaries will begin to see the importance of a balanced proselyting effort, seeking potential priesthood holders in addition to women and children who may be more naturally inclined to listen to their message. This type of unit building will do more toward establishing the Church on a firm foundation of indigenous priesthood leadership than having missionaries trying to manage branches made up primarily of women and children. As the simplified materials and organizational guidebooks were developed and honed, and basic pilot studies completed, President Spencer W. Kimball said in the April 1979 general conference: "Now, my brothers and sisters, it seems clear to me, indeed, this impression weighs upon me—that the Church is at a point in its growth and maturity when we are at last ready to move forward in a major way. Some decisions have been made and others pending, which will clear the way, organizationally."[10]

The continuous spectrum of Church curriculum, from the newest phase 1 branch to the most mature of phase 3 units, truly adds to this effort inasmuch as "the keys of the kingdom of God are committed unto man on the earth, and from thence shall the gospel roll forth unto the ends of the earth, as the stone which is cut out of the mountain without hands shall roll forth, until it has filled the whole earth" (D&C 65:2).

NOTES

1. Author's interview of Josiah Douglas, Salt Lake City, 9 October 1998.

2. Bruce R. McConkie, *Missionary Preparation* (Salt Lake City: The Church of Jesus Christ of Latter-day Saints, 1996), 5.

3. Harold B. Lee, in Conference Report, October 1961, 80.

4. Wayne B. Lynn, "Curriculum," *Encyclopedia of Mormonism,* edited by Daniel H. Ludlow, 5 vols. (New York: Macmillan, 1992), 1:352.

5. Ibid., 1:351.

6. Author's interview of Wayne B. Lynn, Centerville, Utah, 19 July 1998.

7. *Priesthood Leader's Guidebook, Branch Guidebook, Family Guidebook* (Salt Lake City: The Church of Jesus Christ of Latter-day Saints, 1992).

8. First Presidency letter on Church curriculum, 6 April 1992.

9. "Instructions for Priesthood Leaders on Curriculum for Non-English-Speaking Units and Appropriate English-Speaking Units" (Salt Lake City: The Church of Jesus Christ of Latter-day Saints, 1992), 1.

10. Spencer W. Kimball, in Conference Report, April 1979, 114.

CHAPTER FIFTEEN

THE INTERNATIONALIZATION OF THE CHURCH

VICTOR L. LUDLOW

In recent years many Latter-day Saints have been inspired by special declarations of the First Presidency and the Quorum of the Twelve Apostles, especially those commonly called "the proclamation on the family" and the "apostles' testimony of Christ." Officially titled "The Family: A Proclamation to the World" and "The Living Christ: The Testimony of the Apostles," these statements have been translated into many languages and are often framed and hung in the homes and apartments of Latter-day Saints throughout the world.

An earlier statement of the First Presidency that has especially impressed me as a specialist in Near Eastern Studies was given on 15 February 1978. It is titled "God's Love for All Mankind." This statement highlights the doctrine that all men and women are brothers and sisters both through our blood relationship as descendants of Adam and Eve and also through our spiritual relationship as literal spirit children of an Eternal Father. "God's Love for All Mankind" also declares that moral truths were given in times past by God to great religious leaders and philosophers "to enlighten whole nations and to bring a higher lever of understanding to individuals."

In addition, it also claims that God has given and will yet give to all peoples "sufficient knowledge to help them on their way to eternal salvation." Expressing "special love and concern for the eternal welfare of all men and women, regardless of religious belief, race, or nationality," this statement by the Church leaders indicates the

Victor L. Ludlow is a professor of ancient scripture and coordinator of Near Eastern Studies at Brigham Young University.

sensitivity of the First Presidency to the spiritual needs of all people. "God's Love for All Mankind"[1] highlights the divinely inspired moral truths and gospel preparations that are helping peoples throughout the world.

Given toward the middle of President Spencer W. Kimball's administration, "God's Love for All Mankind" was one of many major indicators by President Kimball that The Church of Jesus Christ of Latter-day Saints was expanding into a worldwide religion. On 3 May 1975, "the First Presidency announced the creation of an area supervisory program and the assignment of six Assistants to the Twelve to oversee Church activities while residing outside of the United States and Canada." In 1977 presiding bishopric area supervisors for eight areas outside the United States and Canada were announced. During the same year, in response to continued growth in membership worldwide, the geographic subdivisions of the Church were reorganized and renamed. On 9 June 1978, just a few months after "God's Love for All Mankind" was issued, "the First Presidency announced the revelation that worthy men of all races would be eligible to receive the priesthood."[2]

On 1 April 1981 plans to build eight temples in Central America, Asia, Africa, and Europe were announced. In 1983, for the first time in Church history, two temples were dedicated within a week's time in Tonga and Samoa and "the first of a series of multi-stake (later known as regional) conferences was held in London, England."[3] In addition to the revelation on the priesthood, perhaps the most noteworthy benchmark of President Kimball's administration was his strong encouragement of missionary work as he admonished the Saints to "lengthen your stride" and to take the gospel "unto all the world." In fact, the latter became the title of his famous video that showed how missionary work would expand from area centers of strength into all the corners of the earth.[4]

This article and presentation, with a number of charts and statistical facts, highlights how President Kimball's vision of the internationalization of the Church has seen fulfillment since the "God's Love for All Mankind" statement of the First Presidency was issued in the beginning of 1978. Eight different aspects of the Church were analyzed to determine how rapidly each of these particular dimensions of the Church moved toward the 50 percent level, where at least half the numbers would be international—that is, outside the United States and Canada. The eight aspects, in alphabetical order, are as follows:

- Book of Mormon sales (number of copies sold in all other languages compared to number of copies sold in English)
- CES seminary and institute students (international enrollment compared to USA-Canada)
- General authorities of the Church (according to their place of birth)
- Membership of the Church (baptized members outside USA-Canada compared to inside)
- Missionaries (full time) of the Church (according to their country of origin)
- Missions of the Church (all other nations compared to inside USA-Canada)
- Stakes of the Church (all other nations compared to inside USA-Canada)
- Temples of the Church (all other nations compared to inside USA-Canada)

During the months the data was being compiled, I was curious to know how Latter-day Saints perceived the internationalization of the Church. How aware were we—especially at BYU with its large returned missionary and international student body—as to how worldwide the Church was becoming? Thus, an informal survey was prepared that identified how many Latter-day Saints at Brigham Young University and a few other Latter-day Saints in Idaho, Texas, Arizona, Nevada, and California perceive the internationalization of the Church. The following is a sample of the survey.

Survey Sample: Internationalization of the Church

The findings of this survey indicated that most Latter-day Saints think that four areas are already above the 50 percent level of internationalization: Book of Mormon (67%), membership (64%), missions (60%), and stakes (59%). They felt that two areas were close to the 50 percent level: missionaries (49%) and temples (48%). CES enrollment (25%) and general authorities (12%) were considered to be the least international.

The actual results of our study into Church statistics indicate the following ranking of internationalization at the end of 1999: missions (68%), Book of Mormon (53%), membership (51%), CES enrollment (45%), temples (40%), stakes (40%), missionaries (24%), and general authorities (10%).

Most people were fairly accurate in predicting the three highest areas of missions, copies of the Book of Mormon sold, and membership. These top three categories were often not in the correct order, but the three of them were at the top of most people's lists. Most people also accurately identified the category of general authorities as being the least international. Many were quite far off, however, in evaluating the strength of CES enrollment; most ranked it 6, 7, or even 8 instead of 4. In the opposite direction, many people overestimated the percentage of international full-time missionaries, assuming that they were close to or already over the 50 percent rate instead of the 24 percent current figure.

It should be stated that the purpose of this presentation is *not* to determine how accurately Latter-day Saints perceive the internationalization of the Church. This informal information just helps set the context for the facts and evaluations that follow. The purpose of this year's Sperry Symposium is to analyze the status of the Church as a new millennium begins. The role of this presentation is to review how international the Church has become. The primary emphasis is upon the Church's impressive international growth during the time period since "God's Love for All Mankind" was given by the First Presidency at the beginning of 1978.

With valuable help from my research assistant, Carli Anderson, and various individuals at the Church Office Building, we have assembled a variety of statistics regarding the international status of the Church at the end of 1977 and compared them to similar statistics for the end of 1999. To appreciate the rate of increase during that twenty-two-year period, similar figures and rates for the previous twenty-two-year period from 1955 to 1977 were prepared. We wanted to see how worldwide the Church was in 1955 and then see how much international growth had occurred in the twenty-two-year period leading up to the time when "God's Love for All Mankind" was given.

We then studied how much international growth had occurred in the twenty-two-year period after that statement was given by the

First Presidency. As much as is possible for each of the eight areas, we started with the base year of 1955 and then determined the growth rate in twenty-two-year increments. Thus we basically looked at three benchmark years—1955, 1977, and 1999—and evaluated the international growth rates for the time periods between them. The results are fascinating.

To provide some historical continuity and simplified order, we will discuss each of the eight dimensions in the order of their international ranking at the end of 1999. That is, we will start with the missions of the Church with their international percentage of 69 percent and move through the topics towards the general authorities of the Church who now have an international percentage of 10 percent. Grouped according to percentage figures, these eight areas appear like a tree, as illustrated below.

68%
Missions

51–53%
Book of Mormon—Membership

40–45%
CES students—Temples—Stakes

24%
Missionaries

10%
General authorities

We'll start with the top of the tree and work down to the roots.

FULL-TIME MISSIONS OF THE CHURCH

Since early in Church history, the number of organized international missions has almost always been greater than the number of organized missions in the United States and Canada.[5] While the first missionary efforts of the Church were directed to the northeast United States and eastern Canada, the first organized mission with a president was in Great Britain in 1837. The next missions to be organized were in the eastern United States (1839) and the Society Islands of the South Pacific (1844). As the Saints moved to the Rocky

Mountains in 1847, three of the five missions were outside USA-Canada. In the early 1850s, eleven of the thirteen existing missions of the Church were established in areas outside the United States of America and Canada.

When the U.S. Army under Colonel Albert Sidney Johnston entered Salt Lake in 1858 and then remained in Utah for four years, all the missions in the United States and some international missions were closed. From May 1860 to March 1864 the only missions of the Church in operation were outside USA-Canada. Early in 1864 only six missions were active: British; Scandinavian; Swiss, Italian, and German; Australasian; South African; and European. Gradually, some missions were reestablished and new ones organized until, by the end of 1900, eleven out of the worldwide total of nineteen missions were international, for a 60 percent ratio.

After a hundred years of existence, the Church in 1930 had thirty missions, with nineteen (63 percent) of them headquartered outside of USA-Canada. With the Great Depression and World War II, some international missions were discontinued. As seen in the chart below, however, the international rate at the end of 1955 was still well above the 50 percent mark. Since 1955 it has increased from 55 percent to the current 68 percent ratio as noted below.

International Missions

AT YEAR ENDING	TOTAL MISSIONS	OUTSIDE U.S. AND CANADA	PERCENTAGE INTERNATIONAL
1955[6]	44	24	55
1977[7]	158	101	64
1999[8]	333	226	68

International Missions Net Increase

YEARS	NEW MISSIONS	NEW INTERNATIONAL MISSIONS	PERCENTAGE INTERNATIONAL
1956–77	114	77	68
1978–99	175	125	71

In summary, the full-time international missions ratio was already quite high at 55 percent in 1955, especially when compared to the other seven areas of focus. Gradually it has increased another 13 percent. In the year 2000 nearly seven out of every ten full-time missions of The Church of Jesus Christ of Latter-day Saints are headquartered outside the United States and Canada.

BOOK OF MORMON SALES

Until the mid-1980s the great majority of the copies of the Book of Mormon that were sold and distributed were printed in English. From 1985 through 1989 the foreign language ratio of Book of Mormon copies sold gradually increased annually from 38 to 49 percent. In 1990, 3,541,709 of the 6,558,383 copies sold were in foreign languages—54 percent. During the decade of the 1990s, the foreign language copies averaged 53 percent per year. Carli and I ran into some major challenges in trying to gather the figures for the years before 1981. The precise number of copies of the Book of Mormon sold each year was not recorded. Some estimates have been made, but it has been even more difficult to calculate what percentage of the sales were in foreign languages. Our best estimates, with some help from the Church Historical Department and other Church offices, are shown below.

Book of Mormon Foreign Language Sales

YEAR OF SALES	TOTAL COPIES SOLD/DISTRIBUTED	PERCENTAGE ENGLISH	PERCENTAGE FOREIGN LANGUAGES
1955	300,000	80	20
1977	750,000	65	35
1999	5,440,310	47	53

Another way to compare Book of Mormon language sales from 1955 through 1999 would be to note the number of foreign languages into which the Book of Mormon was translated and available in the benchmark years of 1955, 1977, and 1999. In 1955 the Book of Mormon was available in twenty foreign language editions.[9] By 1977 the Book of Mormon was available in seven additional languages.[10] At the end of 1999, the complete Book of Mormon was available in fifty-one different languages, including two Braille editions (English and Spanish). In addition, "Book of Mormon Selections" were available in some of the fifty-one languages mentioned above and also in thirty-six additional languages. Of the 2,881,027 foreign language copies sold in eighty-five different languages during 1999, one-half of them were in Spanish and one-fifth were in Portuguese. The 1999 statistics are shown in the chart below.

Book of Mormon Foreign Language Sales in 1999

LANGUAGE(S)	COPIES SOLD	PERCENTAGE OF SALES
English	2,559,283	47
Spanish	1,450,905	27
Portuguese	573,436	10.5
French	125,276	
Tagalog	120,009	4.5
Russian	97,979	
German	87,049	
Chinese	66,754	
Japanese	61,977	
Italian	45,489	
Cebuano	44,220	
Korean	33,531	8
35 languages with 1,000–16,000 copies each[11]	165,782	3
40 languages with 2–980 copies each (mostly "Book of Mormon Selections")[12]	8,620	.2
Total copies sold in 1999	5,440,310	100

It should be noted that of the 2,559,283 English copies of the Book of Mormon sold in 1999, many of them were in English-speaking countries outside USA-Canada, such as the British Isles, Australia, and New Zealand. As a contrast, copies of the Book of Mormon in many foreign languages were sold and distributed in the United States and Canada during 1999.

Even with the lack of precise data, it is obvious that the distribution of the Book of Mormon into different languages, nations, and cultures has expanded greatly since 1955, with the most notable increases coming during the past fifteen years. It is estimated that 92 percent of the total world population now has the Book of Mormon or the "Book of Mormon Selections" available in their native language. The foundation is truly laid for even greater sales and distribution of the Book of Mormon among many millions of people during the coming years.

MEMBERSHIP OF THE CHURCH

With this third area of comparison, we will see a pattern of remarkable growth typical of the Church since 1955—that is, a doubling of numbers in each twenty-two-year period. Although the precise international numbers for the earlier years were not recorded, the chart below shows a consistent growth pattern as the percentage of international Church membership usually doubled from one benchmark year to the next (from 11 percent to 21 percent to 51 percent).

International Membership

AT YEAR ENDING	TOTAL CHURCH MEMBERSHIP	TOTAL INTERNATIONAL MEMBERSHIP	PERCENTAGE INTERNATIONAL
1955	1,357,274	150,000 (approx.)	11 (approx.)
1977	3,969,220	831,505	21
1999	10,752,986	5,483,002	51

INCREASE DURING YEAR	NEW MEMBERS	NEW INTERNATIONAL MEMBERS	PERCENTAGE INTERNATIONAL
1955	55,034	9,500 (approx.)	17 (approx.)
1977	226,471	156,449	69
1999	397,983	305,552	77

NET INCREASE DURING YEARS	TOTAL CHURCH MEMBERSHIP	INTERNATIONAL MEMBERSHIP	PERCENTAGE INTERNATIONAL
1956–77	2,611,946	681,505 (approx.)	26 (approx.)
1978–99	6,783,766	4,651,497	69

It was in the winter of 1999, probably during January, when the international Church membership surpassed the numbers inside the United States and Canada.[13] Assuming the Church grows at the same rate in the next twenty-two years as it has in the past twenty-two years, over 60 percent of the more than thirty-three million Latter-day Saints in 2021 would be living outside USA-Canada. To put it in another perspective, more than twice the total Church membership of today would be living abroad. If the rate of increase continues growing as it has since 1955, however, then we could have triple the total Church membership of today living in countries outside USA-Canada by the end of 2021.

CES SEMINARY AND INSTITUTE STUDENTS

This fourth area of Church growth in the international arena is the biggest surprise to most Latter-day Saints. They assume that the seminary and institute program is primarily a USA-Canada phenomenon. They are aware of some elementary school programs for LDS children in the South Pacific and some other underdeveloped areas, but they have no idea how rapidly the CES seminary and institute enrollment has exploded throughout the world. As we look at our benchmark years, it is easy to see why this CES enrollment is such a "sleeper." In 1955 CES international seminary and institute student enrollment was at zero with no foreign students enrolled in these CES programs. By the end of 1977 more than 83,000 of the 301,000 seminary and institute students were enrolled outside USA-Canada, and the international numbers have continued their rapid growth, as shown in the following chart.

International CES Growth

END OF SCHOOL YEAR	TOTAL ENROLLMENT	TOTAL INTERNATIONAL ENROLLMENT	PERCENT INTERNATIONAL
1955–56	43,843	0	0
1977–78	301,439	83,174	28
1998–99	659,137	298,093	45

Growth During Years	Enrollment Increase	International Increase	Percentage International
1955–56	1,396	0	0
1977–78	13,136	15,448	118*
1998–99	16,429	19,678	120†

*Enrollment in USA-Canada lost 2,312
†Enrollment in USA-Canada lost 3,249

Net Increase During Years	Total Increase	International Increase	Percentage International
1956–78	257,596	83,174	32
1978–99	357,698	214,919	60

Assuming a CES growth rate comparable to the past twenty-two years, it will be seven to ten years before the international ratio would reach 50 percent. With the growth rate of the last few years of the 1990s continuing into the next millennium, we could assume an increase of twenty thousand students a year with over 90 percent of them being outside USA-Canada; then the 50 percent international ratio could be reached as early as the 2002–3 school year. It will be interesting to note how this international CES student body strengthens the numbers of full-time missionaries, stakes, and other areas of international development of the Church in the coming decades.

TEMPLES OF THE CHURCH

With the great numbers of the new, smaller-design temples being announced and built since 1998 April general conference, Latter-day Saints are usually not surprised that almost 50 percent of the temples are outside the United States and Canada. Although only 40 percent of the sixty-eight temples dedicated by the end of 1999 were international, twenty-eight (or 60 percent) of the additional forty-seven newly announced temples are being built being outside USA-Canada. When they are all dedicated, 48 percent of the temples of the Church will be international. As with the Church membership figures, which doubled every twenty-two years, the following chart shows how the international temple ratio almost doubled from 1955 to 1977, and then more than doubled from 1977 to 1999.

International Temples

END OF YEAR	TOTAL OPERATING TEMPLES*	INTERNATIONAL TEMPLES	PERCENTAGE INTERNATIONAL
1955	9	1	11
1977	16	3	19
1999	68	27	40

*Nauvoo and Kirtland Temples not in use

INCREASE DURING YEAR	NEW TEMPLES	NEW INTERNATIONAL TEMPLES	PERCENTAGE INTERNATIONAL
1955	1	1*	100
1977	0	0	0
1999	15	4	27

*Bern Switzerland Temple, September 1955

NET INCREASE DURING YEARS	TOTAL TEMPLES BUILT	INTERNATIONAL TEMPLES	PERCENTAGE INTERNATIONAL
1956–77	7	2[14]*	29
1977–99	52	24[15]	46
2000–01[†]	47	28[16]	60
Future[‡]	115	55	48

*Hamilton New Zealand, 1958; London England, 1958
[†]Announced but not yet completed
[‡]When all announced temples are dedicated

Assuming that not as many new temples will be announced in the next couple of years, especially when compared to 1998 through 1999 but also assuming that 60 percent of them will be international, then as soon as twenty-one more new temples are announced, 50 percent of the temples of the Church (68 of 136) would be outside the United States and Canada. This could take place as early as 2001, but more likely will occur sometime during 2002 or 2003.

One interesting observation about temples in the Church has been to evaluate the ratio of LDS temples to LDS stakes through the years.

From 1884, when the second Utah temple was dedicated, until after the end of World War II in 1946, there was usually one temple in operation for every fifteen to twenty stakes of the Church. At that time the growth rate of stakes was much faster than that for temples, so that by 1955 there were twenty-five stakes per temple in the Church. In 1977 there were fifty-five stakes per temple, and the ratio peaked at the end of 1982 when there were seventy stakes per temple throughout the Church.

It is noteworthy that these ratios have been essentially the same within USA-Canada and internationally, although the ratio now slightly favors the areas outside USA-Canada. For example, at the end of 1977 there were fifty-three stakes per temple internationally, compared to fifty-six stakes per temple in the United States and Canada. With the temples dedicated and announced by the end of 1999, the international ratio will be about twenty stakes per temple, while USA-Canada ratio will be about twenty-six stakes per temple when all these temples are completed.

STAKES OF THE CHURCH

In 1955 there was only one LDS stake and one temple outside the United States and Canada. The stake was located in the Mormon colonies in northern Mexico, and the temple was in Bern, Switzerland. By the end of 1999 there were one thousand twenty international stakes and fifty-five international temples dedicated or announced. Obviously, the growth of international stakes is a strong sign of growing Church strength in many countries as the Church programs and strong Melchizedek Priesthood leadership are developed. The following statistics show how the percentage of stakes has risen from less than .5 percent in 1955 to 40 percent in 1999.

International Stakes

AT YEAR ENDING	TOTAL LDS STAKES	STAKES OUTSIDE U.S. AND CANADA	PERCENTAGE INTERNATIONAL
1955	224	1	.4
1977	885	159	18
1999	2,542	1020	40

Growth During Year	New Stakes	New International Stakes	Percentage International
1955	6	0	0
1977	87	40	46
1999	39	22	56

Net Increase During Years	Total New Stakes	New International Stakes	Percentage International
1956–77	661	158	24
1978–99	1,657	862	52

Because of the large number of stakes in the United States and Canada, it could be a number of years before over half of the LDS stakes will be international. As examples, if the growth rate of the past few years continues and 55 percent of the future stakes organized by the Church were international, three thousand more stakes would need to be established before the 50 percent international ratio would be reached. In other words, we would have to more than double our current number of stakes. At a 60 percent growth rate, it would require twenty-five hundred more stakes (close to the current total number of stakes) before the 50 percent international level would be reached. At a 70 percent growth rate, it would take "only" one thousand more stakes to reach the 50 percent level.

In 1999 Church leaders were so strict in their requirements for the organization of new stakes that only thirty-nine new stakes were established during the year. This was less than half the average number of seventy-seven new stakes organized annually from 1978 to 1988. If only fifty new stakes are organized each year, it would take over twenty years before the majority of stakes would be outside USA-Canada. With one hundred new stakes a year and 70 percent of them being international, however, the 50 percent international level could be reached in ten years.

FULL-TIME MISSIONARIES OF THE CHURCH

For much of Church history, the great majority of full-time missionaries came from the United States and Canada. After World War II the Latter-day Saints were encouraged to stay in their homelands to build the Church there, but it was still the general expectation that missionaries would be provided by the North American Saints. This is highlighted in the 1955 figures, which show that only .33 percent of the 4,706 full-time missionaries serving at the end of that year came from countries outside the United States and Canada.[17] This percentage increased to 11 percent in 1977 and then more than doubled by 1999, as shown in the following chart.

International Missionaries

At Year Ending	Total Full-Time Missionaries	International Missionaries	Percentage International
1955	4,607	14	.3
1977	27,173	3,085	11
1999	58,593	13,817	24

Net Increase During Years	Total Increase in Missionaries	International Increase	Percentage International
1956–77	22,566	3,071	14
1978–99	31,420	10,732	34

If the pattern of doubling the international percentage, which we have seen in other areas of Church growth, continues in the missionary program, then some time during the 2020s over one-half of the full-time missionary force of the Church will come from countries outside the United States and Canada.

GENERAL AUTHORITIES OF THE CHURCH

Throughout Church history, a small percentage of LDS general authorities were born outside USA-Canada. For example, one early apostle and later president of the Church, John Taylor, was born in England. The following shows all the international general authorities.

General Authorities Born Outside USA-Canada

AT YEAR ENDING	TOTAL GENERAL AUTHORITIES SERVING	INTERNATIONAL GENERAL AUTHORITIES	PERCENTAGE INTERNATIONAL
1955	33	3	9
1977	63	4	6
1999	103	10	10

CALLED DURING YEAR	NEW GENERAL AUTHORITIES	NEW INTERNATIONAL GENERAL AUTHORITIES	PERCENTAGE INTERNATIONAL
1955	0	0	0
1977	4	2	50
1999	2	1	50

NET INCREASE DURING YEARS	GENERAL AUTHORITIES CALLED	INTERNATIONAL GENERAL AUTHORITIES CALLED	PERCENTAGE INTERNATIONAL
1830–1955	167	15*	9
1956–77	48	4†	8
1978–99	146	22‡	15

*International General Authorities Called, 1830 to 1955

Date Called	Name	Country
1838	John Taylor	England
1841	William Law	N. Ireland
1844	Edwards Steven	Spain
1859	Christian D. Fjelsted	Denmark
1866	George Reynolds	England
1877	Brigham H. Roberts	England
1882	George Teasdale	England
1887	John R. Winder	England
1889	Anthon H. Lund	Denmark
1904	Charles W. Penrose	England
1907	Charles W. Nibley	Scotland
1918	John Wells	England

1941	Marion G. Romney	Mexico
1951	John Longden	England
1952	Carl W. Buehner	Germany

†International General Authorities Called, 1975 to 1977

Date Called	Name	Country
1975	Charles Didier	Belgium
1976	Jacob de Jager	Netherlands
1977	F. Enzio Busche	Germany
1977	Yoshihiko Kikuchi	Japan

‡International General Authorities Called, 1978 to 1999

Date Called	Name	Country
1981	Angel Abrea	Argentina
1984	John Sonnenberg	Germany
1985	Hans B. Ringger	Switzerland
1985	Helio da Rocha Camargo	Brazil
1987	Douglas J. Martin	New Zealand
1988	Robert E. Sackley	Australia
1989	Carlos H. Amando	Guatemala
1989	Horacio A. Tenorio	Mexico
1990	Eduaro Ayala	Chile
1990	Helvecio Martins	Brazil
1990	Kenneth Johnson	England
1991	Julio E. Davila	Colombia
1991	Jorge A. Rojas	Mexico
1991	Han In Sang	Korea
1992	Lino Alvarez	Mexico
1992	Augusto A. Lim	Philippines
1992	Kwok Yuen Tai	Hong Kong
1994	Dieter F. Uchtdorf	Germany
1994	Claudio R. M. Costa	Brazil
1996	Francisco J. Vinas	Uruguay
1998	Athos M. Amorim	Brazil
1999	Adhemar Damiani	Brazil

The following figures show how the strong international numbers of the recently appointed area authority seventies increase the international mix of Church leaders.

Area Authority Seventies Serving at End of 1999

AT YEAR ENDING	TOTAL AREA AUTHORITIES SERVING	INTERNATIONAL AREA AUTHORITIES	PERCENTAGE INTERNATIONAL
1999	150	90	60

General and Area Authorities Serving at End of 1999

AT YEAR ENDING	TOTAL AUTHORITIES SERVING	INTERNATIONAL AUTHORITIES	PERCENTAGE INTERNATIONAL
1999	253	100	40

It will be interesting to note how soon and how many of these international area authorities will be called into the levels of general authority leadership of the Church.

One additional area of The Church of Jesus Christ of Latter-day Saints reflects the strong, growing international dimension of the Church. Although not one of the original eight areas of evaluation, the growth and increasing international dimension of the Church communications systems with general conference and other satellite broadcasts is shown in the following chart.

General Conference Broadcasts

1955	MEDIUM	RANGE
USA and Canada	Radio and television	In 9 states in Western USA
International	None	None

1977	MEDIUM	RANGE
USA and Canada	Radio and television	All 50 states
International	Radio satellite	In Latin America; Australia; Philippines; parts of Africa, Europe, and Asia

Continued on next page

Continued from previous page

1977	MEDIUM	RANGE
	Oceanic cable	In 7 countries in Europe
	Taped copies	In 2 languages

1999	MEDIUM	RANGE
USA and Canada	Radio, television, and cable	All 50 states
	Satellite transmission	At 3,400 sites across North America
International	Satellite transmission	At 220 sites in Europe, 70 in Latin America In 16 languages
	Taped copies	In 43 languages

It is worth noting that after the 3 October 1981 announcement that the Church would place five hundred satellite dishes outside of Utah, the communication capacity of the Church has expanded greatly throughout the world. The use of the worldwide web on the Internet and other communications facilities will only enhance and enlarge the Church's capacity to reach out to the world.

SUMMARY

Although The Church of Jesus Christ of Latter-day Saints has always had a strong emphasis on international missions, at the end of 1955 only 12 percent of the Church membership was outside the United States and Canada. Only one stake and one temple were outside USA-Canada. No CES seminary or institute students were enrolled outside of North America. The general conference and other Church broadcasts did not reach beyond the western United States.

Only a small percentage of foreign language copies of the Book of Mormon were being sold and distributed. Some general authorities and very few missionaries were being called from foreign lands. The Church in 1955 was clearly a North American institution.

By the time the First Presidency issued the statement "God's Love for All Mankind" in February 1978, the Church was beginning to expand worldwide in almost every dimension. The international Church membership had doubled to 25 percent, and roughly one-fourth of the CES students were in foreign lands. Nearly one-fifth of the stakes and temples were outside USA-Canada. General conference broadcasts by radio were beginning to reach outside of North America. About one-third of the copies of the Book of Mormon sold and distributed were in foreign languages. Over one out of ten full-time missionaries were being called from foreign countries. A clear pattern of international growth was being established.

Both the raw numbers and the growth rates, however, have greatly increased since the administration of President Kimball when the "God's Love for All Mankind" statement of the First Presidency was issued. As the year 2000 signals the approach of a new millennium, the Church has the majority of its members outside of North America. Soon the majority of its CES students and temples will be abroad. The general conferences and other Church broadcasts are available at LDS stake centers throughout the world. With the Internet, Church broadcasts and other gospel materials will soon be available to Latter-day Saints and others worldwide. The majority of the copies of the Book of Mormon distributed in the world are in an increasingly larger number of foreign languages. Within a few decades, the number of LDS stakes will surpass those in the United States and Canada, and the number of full-time foreign missionaries will outnumber those from North America.

The statement "God's Love for All Mankind" from the First Presidency declares that the gospel of Jesus Christ provides the only way to happiness and joy forever. It expresses the concern of Church leaders for all of God's children on earth. The events of the past twenty-two years have demonstrated the commitment of the Church to fulfill its calling to take the gospel to every nation, kindred, tongue, and people.

Now in the year 2000, we are standing at a pivotal point in

Church history as increasingly more dimensions of the Church are becoming truly international. But let us not lose sight of the fact that the Church still has plenty of room to grow in North America. As expressed in the book *World Religions in America,* The Church of Jesus Christ of Latter-day Saints, as international as it may be, maintains a strong presence and a growing influence in the United States and Canada.[18] In fact, in another book called *The American Religion,* the author states his belief that The Church of Jesus Christ of Latter-day Saints will be one of the two most influential organizations in the United States during this newly-opened twenty-first century.[19]

Eventually, the Church will have a similar major influence in more and more nations of the earth as it continues to grow internationally. The great and eternal blessings that the gospel and the Church of Jesus Christ bring into the lives of more and more people throughout the earth truly demonstrate God's love for all mankind.

NOTES

1. "Based upon ancient and modern revelation, The Church of Jesus Christ of Latter-day Saints gladly teaches and declares the Christian doctrine that all men and women are brothers and sisters, not only by blood relationship from common mortal progenitors but also as literal spirit children of an Eternal Father.

"The great religious leaders of the world such as Mohammed, Confucius, and the Reformers, as well as philosophers including Socrates, Plato, and others, received a portion of God's light. Moral truths were given to them by God to enlighten whole nations and to bring a higher level of understanding to individuals.

"The Hebrew prophets prepared the way for the coming of Jesus Christ, the promised Messiah, who should provide salvation for all mankind who believe in the gospel. Consistent with these truths, we believe that God has given and will give to all peoples sufficient knowledge to help them on their way to eternal salvation, either in this life or in the life to come.

"We also declare that the gospel of Jesus Christ, restored to his Church in our day, provides the only way to a mortal life of happiness and a fulness of joy forever. For those who have not received this gospel, the opportunity will come to them in the life hereafter if not in this life.

"Our message therefore is one of special love and concern for the eternal welfare of all men and women, regardless of religious belief, race, or nationality, knowing that we are truly brothers and sisters because we are sons and daughters of the same Eternal Father." (Compare 2 Nephi

29:7, 12; 30:8; Mosiah 3:13; Alma 29:8; D&C 11:22; 109:54–58; Ezekiel 47:22–23.)

2. *1997–1998 Church Almanac* (Salt Lake City: Deseret News, 1996), 497–98.

3. Ibid., 499–500.

4. "Go Ye into All the World," Brigham Young University, 1975.

5. Only for two brief periods of time (May 1839–April 1844 and July 1897–January 1898) did the number of missions in USA-Canada barely reach the 50 percent rate (1 out of 2 and then 9 out of 18 total Church missions).

6. During 1955 all three of the newly created missions were international (100 percent).

7. During 1977 eight of the eleven new missions were international (73 percent).

8. During 1999 both of the two new missions were international (100 percent).

9. These twenty foreign languages, in order of translation, were: Danish, German, French, Italian, Welsh, Hawaiian, Spanish, Swedish, Maori, Dutch, Samoan, Tahitian, Turkish, Japanese, Czech, Armenian-Western, Portuguese, Tongan, Norwegian, and Finnish.

10. Rarotongan, Chinese, Korean, Afrikaans, Thai, Indonesian, and Aymara.

11. Full Book of Mormon: Hungarian, 10,822; Thai, 10,369; Dutch, 10,095; Swedish, 10,065; Bulgarian, 9,272; Croatian, 7,348; Polish, 7,288; Czech, 6,057; Samoan, 5,015; Finnish, 4,290; Vietnamese, 4,278; Tongan, 4,098; Ilokano, 3,712; Ukrainian, 3,665; Arabic, 3,479; Fijian, 3,438; Albanian, 3,000; Haitian-Creole, 2,905; Afrikaans, 2,838; Danish, 2,792; Greek, 2,023; Indonesian, 1,602; Norwegian, 1,501; Tahitian, 1,427; Hindi, 1,249.

Mostly "Book of Mormon Selections": Romanian, 15,948; Hiligaynon, 12,179; Cambodian, 4,418; Marshallese, 2,319; Waray, 2,138; Kiribati, 1,353; Papiamento, 1,277; Fante, 1,207; Armenian, 1,048; Navajo, 1,035.

12. Full Book of Mormon: Armenian-West, Aymara, Catalan, Hawaiian, Icelandic, Kekchi, Maori, Pangasinan, Rarotogan.

Mostly "Book of Mormon Selections": Bengali, Bikolano, Bislama, Cakchiquel, Chamorro, Efik, Guarani, Hmong, Kisii, Kuna, Laotian, Lingala, Malagasy, Mam, Maya, Niuean, Palauan, Pampango, Persian, Pohnpeian, Quechua-Bolivia, Quechua-Peru, Shona, Sinhala, Swahili, Tamil, Trukese, Turkish, Tzotzil, Urdu, and Zulu.

13. The Church membership outside the U.S. exceeded the membership within the U.S. during late February or early March 1996 (see "Over Half LDS Now outside U.S.," *Church News*, 2 March 1996, 3).

14. Hamilton New Zealand, 1958; London England, 1958

15. Twenty-four international temples dedicated 1977 through 1999: Sao Paulo Brazil, 1978; Tokyo Japan, 1980; Apia Samoa, 1983; Nuku'alofa Tonga, 1983; Santiago Chile, 1983; Papeete Tahiti, 1983; Mexico City D.F. Mexico, 1983; Sydney Australia, 1984; Manila Philippines, 1984; Taipei Taiwan, 1984; Guatemala City Guatemala, 1984; Freiberg Germany, 1985; Stockholm Sweden, 1985; Johannesburg South Africa, 1985; Seoul Korea, 1985; Lima Peru, 1986; Buenos Aires Argentina, 1986; Frankfurt Germany, 1987; Hong Kong China, 1996; Preston England, 1998; Colonia Juarez Chihuahua, 1999; Madrid Spain, 1999; Bogota Colombia, 1999; Guayaquil Ecuador, 1999.

16. Twenty-eight additional international temples announced by end of 1999: Accra Ghana; Adelaide Australia; Brisbane Australia; Campinas Brazil; Caracas Venezuela; Ciudad Juarez, Chihuahua, Mexico; Cochabamba Bolivia; Copenhagen Denmark; Fukuoka Japan; Guadalajara Mexico; The Hague Netherlands; Hermosillo, Sonora, Mexico; Kiev Ukraine; Melbourne Australia; Merida, Yucatan, Mexico; Monterrey, Nuevo Leon, Mexico; Montevideo Uraguay; Oaxaca Mexico; Perth Australia; Porto Alegre Brazil; Recife Brazil; San Jose Costa Rica; Santo Domingo, Dominican Republic; Suva Fiji; Tampico Mexico; Tuxtla Guiterrez Mexico; Veracruz Mexico; Villahermosa, Tabasco, Mexico.

17. In fact, eight of the fourteen international missionaries came from the Mormon colonies in Northern Mexico, so that only six came from outside the traditional areas of LDS strength in North America. Also, six of the fourteen were sister missionaries.

18. See Danny L. Jorgensen, "The Latter-day Saint (Mormon) Religion in America and the World" in Jacob Neusner, ed., *World Religions in America,* rev. and exp. (Louisville, Ky.: Westminster John Knox Press, 2000), 205–19.

19. Harold Bloom, *The American Religion* (New York: Simon and Schuster, 1992), 110–11, 122–23, 126–27, 256–57, 269–71.

CHAPTER SIXTEEN

PROCLAIMING THE GOSPEL IN THE TWENTIETH CENTURY

ROBERT E. LUND

The Lord declared to Joseph Smith, "I call upon the weak things of the world, those who are unlearned and despised, to thrash the nations by the power of my Spirit" (D&C 35:13). During the restoration of the gospel, the Spirit of the Lord filled the Prophet's heart with a desire to testify of the truth so that every human soul might have salvation. Immediately after the Church was organized, Joseph Smith called his brother, Samuel Smith, to preach the gospel. Samuel had no formal training before his mission and no missionary lessons to refer to during his mission. He simply went forth with his testimony of the restored gospel, copies of the Book of Mormon, and a love in his heart for people.

Throughout the nineteenth century, missionaries followed the faithful example of Samuel Smith, accepting mission calls from the pulpit, often with no advance warning and without missionary discussions to rely upon. Like Samuel, early missionaries used their own personal knowledge and experiences for proselyting dialogue. They simply followed the counsel of Church leaders and taught the first principles of the gospel as their missionary discussions. On 9 April 1844 Hyrum Smith directed the departing elders:

"Preach the first principles of the Gospel—preach them over again . . . you will then be able to make them plainly understood by those you teach, so that you meet scarcely any honest man who will not obey them, and none who can oppose. Adduce sufficient reason to

---

Robert E. Lund is a seminary principal in Farmington, Utah.

prove all things, and you can convert every honest man in the world."[1]

During the twentieth century, three major changes affecting missionary work would occur. First, many missionary materials were developed, including several systematic missionary lessons or discussions to unify the doctrines taught. Second, centers of training were erected to increase the effectiveness of missionaries. Finally, materials were produced for the radio and television to aid missionaries in this great work.

THE DEVELOPMENT OF MISSIONARY MATERIALS

During the first part of the twentieth century a negative image of Mormons was propagated throughout the country.[2] Because of this negative image, much of the early missionary material focused on defending the restored gospel. By the middle of the twentieth century, due to the great increase of missionaries after World War II, each mission had developed its own particular missionary lessons to train newly called missionaries. In the later part of the century, standardized missionary discussions were created to unify the missionary force and teach missionaries how to rely on the Spirit as they proclaimed the gospel.

Defending the Faith: Missionary Lessons from 1900–1930

In an effort to better prepare missionaries to defend the restored gospel, changes were recommended by the First Presidency and the General Church Board of Education concerning missionary discussions and the training of missionaries. By 1900 a missionary preparation course was introduced at Brigham Young Academy and other Church schools. The course lasted six months and was tuition free. These early missionary training courses used Elder James E. Talmage's book *Articles of Faith* as their text. In addition, the course included subjects on the Book of Mormon, Church history, and biblical history.[3]

From 1900 to 1930 many of the early Church leaders provided published materials for these faithful missionaries to use. Elder James E. Talmage wrote *The Great Apostasy* and *Jesus the Christ*. Other prominent works included twelve tracts entitled *Rays of Living Light*, by Elder Charles W. Penrose, a member of the Quorum of the Twelve Apostles;[4] *New Witness for God in America, The Mormon Character, On*

Tracting, and *Why Mormonism?* by B. H. Roberts, president of the Eastern States Mission and a member of the First Council of the Seventy; and finally, *Friendly Discussion,* by Ben E. Rich, which presented the gospel as a dialogue between an investigator and a missionary.

The combined styles of *Friendly Discussion,* with its dialogue format, and *Rays of Living Light,* with its logical outline of the gospel, would eventually develop into the format of missionary discussions used later in the century. Additional instructions were written in *The Successful Missionary* by Elder John A. Widtsoe, president of the European Mission and member of the Quorum of the Twelve Apostles.

In addition to the above missionary teaching aids, at the beginning of the twentieth century there were two leading missionary guidebooks published to assist missionaries in presenting the gospel. In 1906 the Eastern States Mission published a small guidebook called The *Elders' Reference.* Although the majority of the book contained rules and regulations of mission life, it did give some general direction as to what the elders should teach while on their missions. For instance, it counseled: "Get an understanding of the Gospel, and teach it as the Spirit directs. . . . You are sent out to preach the first principles of the Gospel, and call all men to repentance."[5]

Other Church missions had publications similar to the *Elders' Reference* to help their missionaries. In the early twentieth century, missions were not completely unified regarding lesson content and missionary methods. A shift toward unification came, however, in 1918 when the First Presidency published the *Elders' Manual.* Its preface stated, "This Manual is a compilation from previous Manuals used in other Missions . . . with necessary additions to make it suitable for use in all the Missions of the United States. In this little book a number of helpful suggestions and instructions have been compiled."[6]

The *Elders' Manual* was the first step the Church took toward a unified missionary system. Although the rules were now similar, the missionary lessons used to teach investigators were guided by materials written by individual missions. The most successful missionary lessons for teaching investigators were developed by the Southern States Mission.

Sharing the Gospel: Missionary Lessons from 1930 to 1952

Between 1933–37 LeGrand Richards served as president of the Southern States Mission and recognized the need for a systematic method of teaching the gospel. He said, "I shall attempt to outline what I feel would be a proper presentation of OUR message under twenty-four separate headings or subjects, each suitable for one night's discussion and sufficient for six months at one night a week."[7]

President Richard's discussions were called *The Message of Mormonism.* He saw, like most mission presidents, that the inexperienced elder would benefit from being prepared to teach specific gospel topics. The gospel message had an orderly flow of subject headings that began with the First Vision and continued through other gospel events and topics.[8] Soon other missions adopted and adapted the Southern States Mission plan. For instance, *Helps for Missionaries,* compiled and written by two missionaries in the East Central States Mission, followed the same topics but had only nineteen lessons instead of twenty-four. Later, *The Message of Mormonism* was revised by LeGrand Richards and published as *A Marvelous Work and a Wonder.*[9]

In 1937 President Heber J. Grant directed the publication of *The Missionary's Hand Book,* which brought uniformity to all the missions throughout the Church as far as missionary guidelines were concerned but still left unresolved the uniformity of missionary lessons. The handbook was to "supersede all other previous publications of a similar nature."[10] Although it did not contain a set of missionary lessons, it did have dialogue to be used while tracting. It also included several suggested discussions for cottage meetings and public addresses.

By the end of World War II, the Church's full-time missionary force soared from 477 in 1945 to 2,244 in 1946.[11] Because of a dramatic increase in the number of untrained missionaries entering the mission field, there was a great need for standardized missionary lessons, or discussions. This demand for missionary lessons was met by many missionaries, but the most widely used missionary plan was provided by a young missionary named Richard L. Anderson. After being released from the armed forces, Richard applied for a mission. He told his experience as follows:

"I was interviewed for my mission by Elder Joseph F. Merrill. There was a blank on the missionary form that would indicate the missionary's preference of where he wanted to go. I don't know if he was even going to ask me the question, but I took the initiative to say to Brother Merrill, 'I have spent a huge amount of time in the service preparing for my mission and I feel that I am ready from day one to knock on a door and start missionary work and not just learn about it.' I also said that I felt it would be very advantageous for me to use this momentum in an English-speaking mission. If I went to a foreign mission where I would have to learn another language . . . it could have stifled my momentum. I felt impelled and a very strong sense of calling at that point that I wanted to go on an English-speaking mission! When the call came through, it was for the Northwestern States Mission."[12]

When Elder Anderson arrived in the mission field, he wrote his own missionary lessons patterned after his experiences in Florida as a stake missionary. Elder Anderson's mission president, Joel Richards, soon realized how blessed he was to have Elder Richard Anderson in his mission. After seeing Elder Anderson's success, President Richards interviewed the new missionary and exclaimed, "This is exactly what I have been looking for!" President Richards initiated the new missionary lessons immediately in the Northwestern States Mission and they proved to be a superb success.

Soon the news spread that the Northwestern States Mission had a triumphant missionary plan, and other missions began requesting it. The plan was officially called *A Plan for Effective Missionary Work*. It was, however, more commonly known as the "Anderson plan." At one time the plan was used by 60 percent of the missionaries in the Church. Many missions were given permission or just took the liberty to make their own copies. Other missions modified the original "Anderson plan," and at one time there were about twenty-five variations in existence. In addition, other plans were being developed. Willard A. Aston of the Great Lakes Mission developed his own plan in 1948. This prompted the Church to direct Gordon B. Hinckley, as executive secretary of the Missionary Committee, to take the best ideas from each of these plans and write a uniform plan that the whole Church would use.[13]

Teaching by the Spirit: Missionary Plans from 1952–1999

The Missionary Committee wrote the *Systematic Program for Teaching the Gospel*, which was published in 1952. It was the first official set of missionary lessons used by the entire Church. This was the first major missionary publication of this kind since the organization of the Church. Its effects were far reaching, because by standardizing missionary plans the Church relieved mission presidents of the burden of developing and publishing missionary lessons, a responsibility that has stayed with the Missionary Committee.

Standardized missionary discussions would unify the mission force. The *Systematic Program for Teaching the Gospel* contained only seven lessons. It reflected many of the same topics as the "Anderson plan." It also contained a suggested dialogue that could be used in each lesson, similar to what had been done in the tract *Friendly Discussion*. The publication declared "that which is given here is by way of suggestion. It should not be memorized. Every missionary should pray and live for the inspiration of the Lord and should feel free to make such adaptation as he feels desirable."[14] This feeling that the missionary lessons should not be memorized, however, soon changed.

A new set of missionary lessons was written in 1961. It was entitled *A Uniform System for Teaching Investigators* and was presented at the first-ever worldwide seminar for all mission presidents. This plan was to be adopted by every mission, replacing any former missionary lessons. This new plan had six *discussions* instead of seven *lessons* and required word-perfect memorization![15] In addition, this new plan introduced visual aids consisting of a flannel board and pictures that would help the investigators visualize gospel concepts. Specially prepared cutout strips and characters were to be used with each discussion.

Furthermore, the new discussions came on the heels of a challenge issued by President David O. McKay, who stated, "Every member a missionary! You may bring your mother into the Church, or it may be your father; perhaps your fellow companion in the workshop. Somebody will hear the good message of truth through you."[16] Now every member was commissioned to bring at least one other individual into the fold. This dramatically increased convert baptisms.[17] Eventually, the emphasis on perfect memorization decreased, and a change was again made.

In 1973 the Church announced a new set of missionary discussions: *A Uniform System for Teaching Families.*[18] This plan contained the same doctrines and many of the features from the previous plan, but it stated, "At first memorize the discussions as they appear. As you use them more and more, you may be more comfortable and effective using your own words." The missionaries were not, however, to deviate from the spirit and intent of the discussion. It further instructed the missionaries: "Keep in mind how you want the family to feel. Do not force them to say what you want them to say—TEACH THEM—help them feel good about the gospel. . . . People do not often express their real doubts or objections at first. Seek to understand their real reservations. Deal with the problem, not the symptom. Encourage the family to express their feelings honestly."[19]

The *Uniform System for Teaching Families* included other changes: a set of full-color pictures in a notebook, specific tracts to be read between visits, a special discussion called the "Baptismal Challenge," and flexibility in the order of presenting the missionary discussions. In addition to the missionary discussions, missionaries had several pamphlets to distribute: *The Joseph Smith Testimony, The Plan of Salvation,* and *Why Stay Morally Clean?*

In April 1985 the Church held a special worldwide missionary seminar inviting all mission presidents to attend. One of the purposes of the conference was to announce new missionary discussions. After a year of refining, the Church published *The Uniform System for Teaching the Gospel.* Its introduction states: "Your goal is to help investigators become converted by the Spirit and be baptized into the kingdom of God. To do this, you must help them feel and recognize the influence of the Spirit (see D&C 50:14–22). As they feel the Spirit, you will be able to help them make and keep the commitments that lead to conversion and baptism. These discussions are based on a simple pattern for helping investigators make and keep the basic commitments."[20]

This new set of missionary discussions is based upon a commitment pattern. The format of the discussions focuses on creating an atmosphere where the Spirit of the Lord can be felt and recognized by the investigator. When the investigator feels the Spirit, the missionary should invite him to make a commitment to be baptized, attend church, pay tithing, and so on. These discussions include new visuals, examples, and tracts or pamphlets for each discussion to leave with investigators between visits.

The 1985 discussions stress that missionaries are to "master" the principles taught in the discussion, rather than memorize them. Perhaps the greatest strength of the new discussions is the insistence of open-ended questions from the missionary. This allows the investigators a chance to share their feelings about the subject. When investigators are encouraged to share their feelings, the Spirit has a greater opportunity to testify to the investigator of the truthfulness of the message. The emphasis on recognizing the Spirit during a discussion is an intentional effort to make the discussion a powerful spiritual experience for the investigator and the missionary. These missionary discussions continually counsel missionaries to "prepare investigators to feel the Spirit, for conversion to the gospel comes through the Spirit."[21]

Although missionary plans have changed in content, length, and methods of presentation, the essential elements of the conversion process have remained the same over the past century. The most recent set of missionary discussions, *The Uniform System for Teaching the Gospel,* focuses on carrying out the scriptural charge of "thrashing the nations by the power of my Spirit" (D&C 35:13).

In addition to missionary discussions coming forth during the twentieth century, the increase of missionaries created a need to train them before sending them into the mission field.

THE DEVELOPMENT OF MISSIONARY TRAINING CENTERS

From about 1900 to 1925 missionaries reported directly to their assigned mission after being set apart by a general authority. In 1925, however, the first missionary training center was built in Salt Lake City. From that time forward, missionaries called from the United States or Canada first reported to the Salt Lake mission home for a week before traveling to their assigned mission. Eventually, the mission home was succeeded by the Missionary Language Institute, Language Training Missions, and finally Missionary Training Centers.

"Box B", a Call to Serve

During the first part of the century, a letter with the return address of "Box B" signified a call from the First Presidency to serve a mission. Often married men were called to leave their families and report directly to the mission field to serve the Lord. One of those missionaries was President Ezra Taft Benson's father. His story captures the great faith these missionaries possessed. President Benson recounts:

"I cannot help but think of the example of my own father. I recall vividly how the spirit of missionary work came into my life. I was about thirteen years of age when my father received a call to go on a mission. As Father drove the horse homeward, Mother opened the mail, and, to their surprise, there was a letter from Box B in Salt Lake City—a call to go on a mission. No one asked if one were ready, willing, or able. The bishop was supposed to know, and the bishop was Grandfather George T. Benson, my father's father. As Father and Mother drove into the yard, they were both crying—something we had never seen in our family. We gathered around the buggy—there were seven of us then—and asked them what was the matter. They said, 'Everything's fine.' 'Why are you crying then?' we asked. 'Come into the living room and we'll explain.' We gathered around the old sofa in the living room, and Father told us about his mission call. Then Mother said: 'We're proud to know that Father is considered worthy to go on a mission. We're crying a bit because it means two years of separation. You know, your father and I have never been separated more than two nights at a time since our marriage.'"[22]

Calls were issued from Box B, and mission presidents received the missionaries with the responsibility to train them regarding every aspect of missionary work. As missionary work progressed, however, the First Presidency purchased and remodeled a home in Salt Lake City as a place for missionaries to be trained.

The Mission Home

In 1925 the Church Missionary Home and Preparatory Training School, commonly called "the Mission Home," was dedicated by President Heber J. Grant. The Mission Home accommodated up to ninety-nine missionaries and was devoted entirely to training missionaries. This training included gospel lessons from the Church leaders—usually general authorities—Church procedures, missionary methods, and proper manners.[23] For more than thirty-five years the Mission Home trained outgoing missionaries. The increase of missionaries, however, required the need for other facilities.

Language Training Missions

Missionaries were experiencing lengthy delays obtaining visas for Mexico and Argentina, and so in 1961, the Missionary Language Institute (MLI) was opened. After the usual week at the Mission

Home in Salt Lake City, missionaries were sent to Provo and housed in a local hotel or in dorms on the BYU campus. Ernest J. Wilkins, president of BYU, was the MLI's first director. He explained that the goal was "to place a missionary in the field ready to speak the language."[24]

In 1963 the Church fully endorsed this idea and granted mission status to the MLI, made Wilkins a mission president, and changed the name to the Language Training Mission (LTM). At first, only Spanish was taught, but soon Portugese and German were added to the curriculum.[25]

Thirteen more languages were added by 1968 and other Church schools were needed to accommodate the missionary training demand. Other LTMs were soon created. The LTM located on the Ricks College campus was to teach Dutch and Scandinavian languages. Another LTM at the College of Hawaii campus was directed to teach Polynesian and Oriental languages.

The Missionary Training Centers

By 1978 the Church consolidated all language training, or LTMs and English-speaking training into one multimillion-dollar complex adjacent to the BYU campus. The facility was renamed the Missionary Training Center (MTC) to more appropriately reflect the comprehensive training involved.

Although missionaries in the United States and Canada now had training at the Provo MTC, usually missionaries from other countries serving outside the United States or Canada still reported directly to the mission field without formal training. In order to include and train all missionaries, by the end of the twentieth century there were over fourteen MTCs in South America, Europe, Asia, and the Pacific, all adjacent to temples.[26] In addition to the inspirational training for missionaries, other aids were being developed by the Church to assist in the proselyting effort.

MISSIONARY AIDS

At the beginning of the twentieth century, the number of visitors to Salt Lake City increased. This prompted the Church to establish a bureau of information in 1902, which was its first visitors' center. The success of this effort on Temple Square inspired the Church to create successive visitors' centers throughout the United States and the world. The premier visitors' center, however, still remains Temple Square, which was incorporated into its own mission with scores of missionaries serving therein. In addition to visitors' centers assisting in proselyting work, Mormon pageants have also been a successful means of proclaiming the restored gospel.

As radio broadcasting developed in the 1920s, the Church was quick to use this medium to proclaim the gospel. In 1922 President Heber J. Grant delivered the first message by radio. In 1924 James H. Moyle, president of the Eastern States Mission, instituted a series of radio programs about Latter-day Saint beliefs. Throughout the remainder of the century the Church continued to use radio spots and programs to communicate their message, the most famous being the weekly Mormon Tabernacle Choir broadcast.

Perhaps the earliest visual missionary aids emerged in 1924 when the Church prepared slides for the missionaries to use. Soon after, in 1928, President Moyle produced sixteen-millimeter movies on the ruins of Central America to support the Book of Mormon. Powerful movies such as *The First Vision* would eventually follow. Some missionary films were developed for specific events, such as *Man's Search for Happiness* originally produced for the 1964 New York World's Fair. In the 1970s the Church developed several filmstrips, such as *Christ in America* and *Families Are Forever,* to assist in the missionary effort. During this decade the Church also produced the award-winning *Homefront Series*—commercial spots for television designed to communicate Latter-day Saint values.

With the advent of VCRs in the 1980s came missionary videos. Besides converting the old filmstrips to videos, in 1985 the Missionary Department began producing several Direct Gospel Messages (DGMs). The first was *Our Heavenly Father's Plan* (1987)—a video that portrayed a young man who discovered his relationship to God and the role of Jesus Christ in the plan of salvation. These DGMs were often shown during prime time television hours in selected areas followed by instructions on how to receive more information. After the success of the first DGM, others soon followed: *Together Forever* (1988), *What Is Real* (1989), *Labor of Love* (1989), *Prodigal Son* (1990), *On the Way Home* (1992), *Family First* (1992), and *Family Answers* (1996).

Along with DGMs were commercials discussing and advertising

the Book of Mormon. This led to the creation of the telecenter at the Provo MTC. The telecenter did not receive initial inbound calls from viewers, but rather missionary operators at the MTC were used to handle follow-up calls to see if individuals had received the requested video or copy of the Book of Mormon, how they felt about it, and if they desired to receive more information.

In the mid-1990s worldwide missionary firesides were held in February presided over by a member the Quorum of the Twelve Apostles. The first of these, entitled *We Believe in Christ,* was held in February 1995 and featured Elder Jeffrey R. Holland. Other missionary open houses included *Witness of Christ* (1996), *Strengthening Families* (1997), and *The Plan of Happiness* (1998), featuring Elder M. Russell Ballard, Elder Dallin H. Oaks, and Elder Henry B. Eyring, respectively.

Notwithstanding the use of modern technology to spread the gospel message, the content of the message remained the same. The direction given by Hyrum Smith in 1844 to "Preach the first principles of the Gospel—preach them over again. . . . Adduce sufficient reason to prove all things, and you can convert every honest man in the world"[27] remained the common thread.

CONCLUSION

The development of the missionary discussions, training centers, and missionary aids throughout the twentieth century brought unity and clarity to the message preached by missionaries; nevertheless, however pure and perfected the message has become, inspired messengers are still needed.

The faithfulness of Samuel Smith and the spirit of "Box B" demonstrated by President Ezra Taft Benson's father is essential for missionaries today. Elder David B. Haight explained:

"Today, that call—in the spirit of 'Box B'—has been extended to all young men. They are prepared from an early age to serve the Lord. Thousands upon thousands have responded. The spirit of 'Box B'— the call to serve—rests not only on all young men and dedicated young women who desire to serve, but now it has also been extended—and has been for some time—to mature couples."[28]

At the beginning of the Restoration, missionaries were sent forth "to preach my gospel by the Spirit, even the Comforter which was sent forth to teach the truth" (D&C 50:14). From the Restoration to today, successful missionaries have followed this commission.

NOTES

1. Eastern States Mission, *Elders' Reference* (Brooklyn, New York: The Church of Jesus Christ of Latter-day Saints, 1913), 35–36. This was the first missionary publication that attempted to compile into one book guidelines on how missionaries should deal with members of the opposite sex, distribute tracts, and care for oneself, along with several priesthood ordinances and how to perform them. In addition, the appendix of the *Elders' Reference* contains over fifty brief doctrinal statements from the Prophet Joseph Smith.

2. For example, "In February 1898 the *Alcorn Democrat* of Corinth, Mississippi, urged the lynching of elders in Jackson 'quicker than . . . the most poisonous reptile which ever crawled upon the earth.' The man who protected a Mormon elder or failed to guard his household was not only a 'disgrace to the state but a menace to civilization,' said the paper" (Thomas G. Alexander, *Mormonism in Transition: 1890–1930* [Urbana, Illinois.: University of Illinois Press, 1986], 223).

3. Alexander, *Mormonism in Transition,* 214.

4. "The most widely distributed and longest continually used literature ever published by the church were Penrose's twelve *Rays of Living Light* tracts. The pamphlets covered basic principals by taking the reader through a systematic program of gospel study. The first tract included a discussion of the need for true religion. . . . Tract Number 2 dealt with the nature of God and the Godhead. Continuing the discourse on the first principles, tracts Numbers 3 and 4 discussed the doctrine of repentance, baptism, the gift of the Holy Ghost, and other spiritual gifts. Tract Number 5 dealt with the nature of authority and outlined the difference between the Melchizedek and Aaronic priesthoods. Number 6 considered the apostasy from the primitive church and emphasized the [prophecies] of this apostasy by Christ and the Apostles. Number 7, 8, and 9 dealt with the restoration, the story of the Book of Mormon, and the need for continuous revelation in the church. Numbers 10 and 11 discussed work for the dead, the mercy of God, and [eternal families]. Tract number 12 considered the positive aspects of the public image of the Mormons" (Alexander, *Mormonism in Transition,* 221).

5. *Elders' Reference,* 16–17.

6. *Elders' Manual* (Salt Lake City: Missions of The Church of Jesus Christ of Latter-day Saints, 1918), preface. The eight current mission presidents contributed to this publication under the direction of Elder Stephen L Richards and Athon W. Ivins of the Quorum of the Twelve Apostles and the First Presidency. It contained instructions on how to perform marriages and excommunications, both of which were dropped

from subsequent missionary publications, and by the end of the century, missionaries were generally discouraged from being involved in either marriages or excommunications. The only exceptions were when the missionary served as a branch president.

7. LeGrand Richards, *The Message of Mormonism* [n.p., n.d.], 2.

8. Ibid., 3–21.

9. See *Church Almanac 1999–2000* (Salt Lake City: Deseret News, 1998), 120–21.

10. Missionary Literature Committee, *The Missionary's Hand Book* (Salt Lake City: 1937), 3. In the preface, all the other works to be replaced were mentioned, including George S. Romney, *Missionary Guide;* Council of the Twelve, *Instructions to the Missionaries;* European Mission, *District Supervision and Branch Supervision;* John A. Widtsoe, *Successful Missionary;* B. H. Roberts, *On Tracting;* and the *Elders' Manual.* It was the predecessor of the "little white Bible" or *Missionary Handbook* currently in use by missionaries today.

11. Richard O. Cowan, *The Church in the Twentieth Century* (Salt Lake City: Bookcraft, 1985), 279.

12. Author's interview of Richard L. Anderson, 12 March 1993. After high school, Richard L. Anderson joined the navy to assist the United States in World War II. He desired to serve a mission after being released from his military duties, so he prepared for his mission during his service in the navy. Part of Richard's preparation included interviewing returned missionaries and asking them about their missions. He then took notes on what he felt successful missionaries were doing. While in the military service, Richard was assigned to Jacksonville, Florida, and was called as a stake missionary. He proselyted in Florida with other local missionaries. Richard's part-time missionary experiences in Florida fanned his desire to further his missionary education. He keenly observed in great detail how successful missionaries taught in order to better his ability to proclaim the gospel.

13. Sheri L. Dew, *Go Forward with Faith: The Biography of Gordon B. Hinckley* (Salt Lake City: Deseret Book, 1996). This biography describes President Hinckley's deep involvement as executive secretary of the Missionary Committee. He had the responsibility of "essentially everything relating to missionary work, . . . the call and training of missionaries and mission presidents; the preparation and distribution of mission literature and other teaching materials" (p. 144). President Hinckley's involvement with the editing of the first set of missionary lessons cannot be overstated: "Gordon B. Hinckley of the Missionary Committee helped formalize a standard plan in 1952 that was used Churchwide" (*1999–2000 Church Almanac,* 120–21).

14. *Systematic Program for Teaching the Gospel* (Salt Lake City: The Church of Jesus Christ of Latter-day Saints, 1952), 6. This first

missionary plan contained seven lessons entitled: 1. The Godhead, 2. The Apostasy, 3. The Restoration, 4. The Book of Mormon, 5. The First Principles of the Gospel, 6. The Plan of Salvation, and 7. Call to Repentance.

15. *A Uniform System for Teaching Investigators* (Salt Lake City: The Church of Jesus Christ of Latter-day Saints, 1961). These six discussions included: 1. The Church of Jesus Christ, 2. A New Witness for Christ, 3. Ye Shall Know the Truth, 4. The Gift of God Is Eternal Life, 5. The Law of Eternal Progression, and 6. Be Ye Therefore Perfect.

16. David O. McKay, in Conference Report, April 1959, 122.

17. Cowan, *Church in the Twentieth Century*, 282.

18. *The Uniform System for Teaching Families* (Salt Lake City: The Church of Jesus Christ of Latter-day Saints, 1973). The seven proselyting discussions included: 1. The Restoration, 2. Eternal Progression, 3. Continuing Revelation and Individual Responsibility, 4. Truth versus Error, 5. Obedience to the Lord's Commandments Brings His Blessings, 6. Our Relationship to Christ, and 7. Membership in the Kingdom.

19. *A Uniform System for Teaching Families*, A-1.

20. *Instructions for the Discussions* (Salt Lake City: The Church of Jesus Christ of Latter-day Saints, 1986), 1. With one less discussion than the previous set, the six titles included: 1. The Plan of Our Heavenly Father, 2. The Gospel of Jesus Christ, 3. The Restoration, 4. Eternal Progression, 5. Living a Christlike Life, and 6. Membership in the Kingdom.

21. *Instructions for the Discussions*, 2–3.

22. Ezra Taft Benson, "Godly Characteristics of the Master," *Ensign*, November 1986, 46.

23. *Church History in the Fulness of Times* (Church Educational System Religion 341–43 manual, 1989), 503.

24. Cowan, *Church in the Twentieth Century*, 284.

25. Richard O. Cowan, "Missionary Training Centers," *Encyclopedia of Mormonism*, edited by Daniel H. Ludlow, 4 vols. (New York: Macmillian, 1992), 2:913.

26. Cowan, "Missionary Training Centers," 2:914.

27. *Elders' Reference*, 35–36.

28. David B. Haight, in Conference Report, April 1987, 70.

CHAPTER SEVENTEEN

WHEN THE PRESS
MEETS THE PROPHET

W. JEFFREY MARSH

In 1846 and 1847 President Brigham Young led the vanguard pioneer company of 148 people and their wagons into the wilderness and out of the public limelight. One hundred and fifty years later, with the reenactment of the Mormon trek west, President Gordon B. Hinckley began leading the Church, as had been prophesied, out of obscurity and out of darkness (see D&C 1:30; 101:93–95). Many recent events have contributed to the miraculous fulfillment of this prophecy, including the reemphasis on the Book of Mormon—which the Lord declared would cause the "eyes of the blind [to] see out of obscurity, and out of darkness" (Isaiah 29:18)—the international growth of the Church; the emergence of media and telecommunications; and the technological explosion (including the advent of e-mail and the Internet) that has occurred during President Hinckley's administration.

Although press conferences with LDS leaders have been held from time to time, President Gordon B. Hinckley's administration has received more media opportunities and has been more openly receptive to them than ever before. At his inaugural introduction as the fifteenth president of The Church of Jesus Christ of Latter-day Saints, President Hinckley invited questions from the press for the first time since President Spencer W. Kimball had done so in 1973.

For thirty minutes the prophet responded to a variety of inquiries. Few of those in attendance realized it had been twenty-one years since such a meeting with the press had occurred, but almost everyone

W. Jeffrey Marsh is an associate professor of ancient scripture at Brigham Young University.

recognized that "what they were seeing was rare and that a statement was being made." Thus began what has become an almost commonplace occurrence wherever President Hinckley has traveled throughout the world. President James E. Faust expressed a sentiment shared by many: "I don't know of any man who has come to the Presidency of this Church who has been so well prepared for the responsibility."[1]

President Hinckley's ability to put people at ease, his sense of humor, and his comfort with the press have also led to some very important interviews with the media that have most certainly helped to bring the Church "out of obscurity and out of darkness." Mike Wallace has written that as a result of his interviews with President Hinckley, "We came away with a fascinating profile of a genuinely remarkable man. . . . This warm and thoughtful and decent and optimistic leader of the Mormon Church fully deserves the almost universal admiration that he gets."[2]

The purpose of this presentation is to briefly review President Hinckley's lifelong preparations to interact with the press, to catalog some of his interviews with the media, to summarize what questions were asked most frequently, and to share a few of his responses to those questions.

PREPARATION OF THE PROPHET

President Hinckley has been well prepared to lead the Church in the modern era of telecommunications. Beginning with his call to serve on the Radio, Publicity, and Mission Literature Committee immediately following his return from Great Britain as a missionary in 1935, through his overseeing and pioneering work to expand Bonneville International into the media and communications conglomerate it is today, Gordon B. Hinckley's life has been filled with one opportunity after another to interact with the media. He graduated from the University of Utah with a degree in English. He was called to serve in the European Mission, with headquarters in London, where he wrote articles for the *Millennial Star* and produced slide presentations. He intended to pursue a graduate degree in journalism from Columbia University when he returned from his mission but accepted an invitation to work for the Church instead, where he immediately found himself in the center of all the Church's media efforts.

He served as the executive secretary, and then for forty years as a member of the General Missionary Committee, as an Assistant to the Quorum of the Twelve, and as a member of the Quorum of the Twelve Apostles. He helped initiate Church broadcasts on radio and television, planned the exhibits for the 1939 and subsequent world's fairs, and wrote and produced numerous radio shows about the Church. He was named to the board of directors and as a member of the executive committee of the Radio Service Corporation of Utah (or KSL) as well as the Bonneville International Corporation. On 12 March 1995 President Hinckley was ordained as the president of The Church of Jesus Christ of Latter-day Saints, thus becoming the Lord's chief spokesman on the earth (see D&C 1:38; 21:5).

At the close of the April 1996 general conference, President Hinckley referred to the prophecy that was given by the Prophet Joseph Smith in the dedicatory prayer of the Kirtland Temple—that the kingdom of God would one day fill the whole earth and that the Church would "come forth out of the wilderness of darkness, and shine . . . [as] clear as the sun" (D&C 109:73). He then testified, "We are witnessing the answer to that remarkable pleading. Increasingly the Church is being recognized at home and abroad for what it truly is."[3]

"Many of his General Authority colleagues believed that he himself was integral to the fulfillment of that prophecy. 'President Hinckley is helping to lead the Church out of obscurity,' Elder Neal A. Maxwell stated. 'The Church can't move forward as it needs to if we are hidden under a bushel. Someone has to step out, and President Hinckley is willing to do so. He is a man of history and modernity at the same time, and he has marvelous gifts of expression that enable him to present our message in a way that appeals to people everywhere.'" Elder Joseph B. Wirthlin added: "President Hinckley is lifting the Church to a new height of admiration in the world. He knows how to present our message to people not of our faith. His instincts tell him what to say, how to say it, and when to speak up."[4]

MEETING THE PRESS

One immediate consequence of the spotlight shining more brightly on the Church and its members in these latter days is that the unique beliefs and teachings of the Church will also come under more intense scrutiny. There will obviously be more than casual glances given to the doctrines of the Restoration. As people begin to ask more questions about what Latter-day Saints believe, how best can we respond to their inquiries? What kinds of questions are most likely to be asked? What should we say? As the presiding leader of the Church, President Hinckley's dealings with the press help us understand how best to respond. He turned ninety this year, 2000, but he has been blessed with strength, energy, and a quick wit, which is readily apparent during media interviews.

President Hinckley shared his philosophy about engaging the media when he addressed a conference of the Association of Latter-day Saint Public Relations Professionals. He said, "We have a responsibility to stand tall and speak out with clarity and with decency and not with boasting, but factually and honestly and candidly." He noted that he approaches these news media interviews with humility, "with some trepidation and a prayer. But [reporters] don't scare me," he said. "I just look upon them as somebody next door. They have just as many troubles as I do and a few more. And you just be honest with them, check your facts, be sure of your facts so that nobody can dispute what you say, and speak up to them."[5]

President Hinckley's press conferences often present a panoramic view of the Church and the doctrines of the Restoration, but he also focuses on the importance of the individual. To journalists assembled for the forty-ninth annual convention of the Religion Newswriters Association in 1997, he said, "We speak of large numbers, 10 million of us, but our responsibility is to deal with individuals. There is something of divinity in everyone."[6]

In his closing remarks made to the National Press Club in Washington, D.C., he said: "We are a church, a church in whose name is the name of the Lord Jesus Christ. We bear witness of Him and it is His example and His teachings we try to follow. We give love. We bring peace. We do not seek to tear down any other church. We recognize the good they do. We have worked with them on many undertakings. We will continue to do so. We stand as His servants. We acknowledge that we could not accomplish what we do without the help of the Almighty. We look to Him as our Father and our God and our ever-present helper, as *we seek to improve the world by changing the hearts of individuals.*"[7]

One reporter who was in attendance at a convention of the Religion Newswriters Association made this observation:

"When President Hinckley entered the room it was a similar feeling to being in a session of General Conference. As he was ushered in, a hush fell over all of us. Everyone stood up. I have never seen reporters do that before. President Hinckley was extremely warm and extremely genuine. He is so different from politicians whom reporters are used to interviewing. His answers are clear, direct, and responsive to the questions being asked without trying to deflect the discussion in other directions. Reporters are used to seeing 'plastic' personalities or hearing 'teflon' responses. But President Hinckley has a refreshing ability to endear people with his wit and charm. His self-deprecating humor puts everyone at ease. He has moved beyond a posture of having to defend the Church from persecution, or feeling as if apologies have to be continually made for the past. He presents a genuine message that says, 'Let me tell you about the Mormons and why you should be one.' He has a wonderful demeanor, a great sense of humor, and a terrific presence on camera."[8]

In his inaugural press conference, held 13 March 1995, President Hinckley met a large contingent of local, national, and international press. Beside him sat presidents Thomas S. Monson and James E. Faust. Seated behind him were the eleven members of the Quorum of the Twelve Apostles.

"All were positioned against a magnificent backdrop: a heroic-sized statue of the Prophet Joseph Smith that seemed to preside over the occasion. . . .

"President Hinckley responded to a variety of inquiries that focused principally upon the condition and future of the Church. Quietly in command of the situation from the outset, he revealed his warmth, wit, and vast range of knowledge. It was quickly apparent that this was a man who thoroughly understood the large, multi-faceted organization over which he now presided. One prominent reporter called the experience 'exhilarating'; another described President Hinckley's 'debut' as impressive. Taken in concert, his responses not only underscored his faith in and devotion to the work in which he had been engaged for nearly sixty years, but also revealed the unique traits, strengths, and attitudes that he brought to his new calling."[9]

This was the first of what has since grown into many dozens of press interviews and media opportunities. Though not anxious to do so, President Hinckley has always been willing to meet with the press. Mike Wallace, reflecting on the day he met President Hinckley at the Harvard Club in New York City when he invited him to be interviewed on *60 Minutes,* said that he had been "trying for decades to get some top Mormon leader, any top Mormon leader" to talk with him on camera. He said that "President Hinckley's bespectacled eyes literally twinkled" when asked for an interview.[10]

The religion editor for the *Deseret News* observed that "President Hinckley's ease in working with, and accessibility to, reporters for major media outlets worldwide has generated unprecedented publicity for the LDS Church since 1995." His interviews "seem to have broadened the audience for his messages, which center around simple principles of the LDS gospel."[11]

THE MOST PRESSING QUESTIONS

When President Hinckley is interviewed by the media, what questions do reporters ask? What is it they want to know? How has President Hinckley responded? In this study, answers to these questions are limited to twenty-five published interviews—the most easily accessible in public sources (listed at the end of this chapter). The questions from those twenty-five interviews are, nevertheless, of sufficient variety and number to provide ready answers for people curious to know what happens when the press meets the prophet.

All totaled, there were 295 questions in these 25 printed interviews. From reading the transcripts, it was obvious that there were numerous other questions asked by the media and answered by the prophet that were not included in the printed text of the articles. Therefore, the conclusions drawn in this portion of the study should not be taken as the final word about what the media is most interested in finding out about the Church—that would only be possible if every question posed to President Hinckley had been printed. With the information available, however, we do get a glimpse.

Also, the reader should note that the subject matter of the questions being asked seemed to flow with the breaking news and current events of the day. So the fact that a lot of questions were asked about President Hinckley's views on President Bill Clinton in some interviews had more to do with the impeachment trial that was then under way than with how interested reporters are in the Church's view of the White House.

Overall, however, there is a general pattern to the questions asked. The topics that were of significant interest to the media (averaging about one out of every fifty questions) included Brigham Young University, the welfare program, excommunication from the Church, forgiveness, race relations, spouse or child abuse, revelation, temples and temple rites, and the health code in the Mormon faith (the Word of Wisdom).

The topics that were of a moderate interest (averaging about one out of every one hundred questions) included Brigham Young, the future of the world, the role of men in the Church, families, baptism for the dead, Salt Lake City, whether political pressures affect Church policy, Joseph Smith, the Book of Mormon, prayer, temple clothing, the 2002 Winter Olympics, cloning, access to LDS historical documents, thoughts about Christmas, polygamy, the next life (after death), and abortion.

The topics of absolute highest interest, the questions asked by the media more often than others (averaging about one out of every ten to thirty questions), included Church beliefs (LDS doctrines and practices), personal questions about President Gordon B. Hinckley and his life, the astounding growth of the Church and the Church as a worldwide organization, the role of women in the Church, Mormon relations with people of other faiths, tithing and Church finances, moral issues, the Clinton family, the role of a living prophet, missionaries and missionary work, media relations with the Church, and family history.

THE PROPHET'S RESPONSE

Space does not permit all of President Hinckley's responses to be given, but following are some of the answers he provided to the most often-asked questions.

Regarding Church Beliefs

Many questions were asked about LDS practices and doctrines. When asked what Latter-day Saints generally believe, President Hinckley responded: "We are Christians. No church in the world speaks up with a stronger witness of the divinity of the Lord Jesus

Christ as the Son of God and the Redeemer of the world than does this Church, which carries His name—The Church of Jesus Christ of Latter-day Saints. And His gospel is the gospel we teach. And the spirit of love which we exemplify is the spirit in which we try to work."[12]

Personal Questions about President Gordon B. Hinckley

Dozens of questions were asked about President Hinckley's travels, his personal thoughts, and greatest personal challenge. To a question on his greatest personal challenge, he responded: "Finding enough time to do what I have got to do. I've been trying to get out among our people around the world. That is my disappointment that I don't have more time."[13] "When recently asked about his secret to staying so vigorous, President Hinckley replied in his trademark humor, 'The idea that I try to follow is to go to bed every night and be sure to get up in the morning.'"[14]

When asked about the kind of legacy he desired to leave, for what he would want his own grandchildren and great-grandchildren to remember him, the prophet answered: "I would hope that I might be held in remembrance as a man who tried to do some good in the world, to make the world a better place, to improve it. And as a man who walked with integrity with his associates, both those in the Church and out of the Church, with love and appreciation for the goodness that he saw in people wherever he went."[15]

Church Growth throughout the World

In response to a question about the greatest challenge facing the Church, President Hinckley said:

"Well, one word sums it up, and that is growth. Now the three great challenges are to increase the momentum of the work, which I think we can do, I am confident we can do. Secondly, to accommodate the growth with new buildings, which are required wherever we go. And the training of local leadership. All of our local congregations are presided over by volunteer workers not compensated financially in any way. As we grow it becomes necessary to train leaders, and that is a challenge. That is the same challenge that Brigham Young faced. We have faced it all through the years and will continue to face it as the Church grows across the world. But thus far we have met that challenge and, I think, handled it very, very well. We are building buildings in many countries, at the rate of about 375 new buildings a year across the world, which is really phenomenal. We have a tremendous program for training local leadership. Those are the challenges as I see them."[16]

The Role of Women in the Church

When asked whether the Church is sensitive to the rights of women in roles of leadership, President Hinckley said:

"We have probably the largest women's organization in the world—over three million members—with their own leadership, with their own program, with their own courses of study, their own officers. I don't know of any other religious organization in the world that gives women as great an opportunity as they have in The Church of Jesus Christ of Latter-day Saints. I believe that my wife is just as important as I am in the plan of the Lord. In the Mormon way, the wife walks neither behind nor ahead of her husband, but at his side as his companion, his equal. I have three daughters and two sons. I love my daughters as much as I love my sons—maybe a little more so, they are so kind to me. But, I think our Father in Heaven regards His daughters the same way. I don't apologize for one minute for the Church's program for women. We have women sitting on the board of trustees of Brigham Young University; women spoke in the last general conference of the Church; they speak in our worship services, they offer prayers, they have all the advantages that the Church has to offer."[17]

Mormon Relations with People of Other Faiths

Mike Wallace recalled his first meeting with President Hinckley. His requests for interviews with others about the prophet and the Church had been regularly turned down, "So I was totally unprepared," he said, "for a cordial, even a sunny greeting from Gordon B. Hinckley at the luncheon. And I was still hesitant when, following his postprandial remarks, he threw the floor open for questions from any and all of us. Timorously, I wondered aloud to him whether he might entertain the notion of an interview-cum-profile for *60 Minutes*. President Hinckley's bespectacled eyes literally twinkled as he good-naturedly allowed that it sounded like an appealing notion; after all, he really had nothing to hide, and he imagined he'd have little difficulty handling whatever queries I loosed at him. He'd heard and answered worse, he was sure, during his young missionary years in London, where he'd taken on whatever the skeptics and nonbelievers had thrown at him in his Hyde Park appearances and/or confrontations."[18]

During the ensuing interview, President Hinckley was asked "How do you view non-Mormons?" His response was: "With love and respect. I have many non-Mormon friends. I respect them. I have the greatest of admiration for them. . . . To anybody who is not of this Church, I say we recognize all of the virtues and the good that you have. Bring it with you and see if we might add to it."[19]

Tithing and Church Finances

Mike Wallace asked if it was expensive to be a Mormon. President Hinckley answered: "Oh, it isn't expensive. We are living by the law of the Lord—tithing." Then he explained what tithes and offerings were used for:

"Building chapels . . . [about 400] new buildings each year to accommodate the needs of the growing membership. [The funds are also] used for education. We maintain the largest private, church-sponsored university in the world, Brigham Young University, with its 27,000 students on that campus, as well as other campuses. We maintain a tremendous institute of religion program, where we have off-campus connections with [students in] the major universities of America. You will find institutes at UCLA, USC, Harvard, Yale, Princeton, the University of New York, the University of Massachusetts, the Massachusetts Institute of Technology, and so forth. When it comes to the financial circumstances of the Church, we have all funds carefully audited. We have a corps of auditors who are qualified CPAs who are independent from all other agencies of the Church and who report only to the First Presidency of the Church. We try to be very careful. I keep on the credenza behind my desk a widow's mite that was given me in Jerusalem many years ago as a reminder, a constant reminder, of the sanctity of the funds with which we have to deal. They come from the widow; they are her offering as well as the tithe of the rich man, and they are to be used with care and discretion for the purposes of the Lord. We treat them carefully and safeguard them and try in every way that we can to see that they are used as we feel the Lord would have them used for the upbuilding of His work and the betterment of people."[20]

In his remarks given at the National Press Club in Washington, D.C., President Hinckley said, "You ask how all of this has been accomplished. It takes money, you say. Where does it come from? It comes from observance of the ancient law of the tithe. . . . This law is set forth in 35 words in our scripture. Compare that with the rules and regulations of the IRS."[21]

Moral Issues

"You also have a moral code?" Mike Wallace asked. President Hinckley replied: "We believe in chastity before marriage and total fidelity after marriage. That sums it up. That is the way to happiness in living. That is the way to satisfaction. It brings peace to the heart and peace to the home."

Mr. Wallace asked a follow-up question: "Some of the students we've talked to say that the health code is easy compared to no premarital sex. . . . They say that not smoking or not drinking is a clear line but that the sexual line is somewhere—[well,] they are confused, some of them anyway, about where that line is."

The prophet responded: "Oh, I think they know. Any young man or woman who has grown up in this Church knows where that line is. When you see yourself slipping, begin to exercise some self-discipline. And if it is a serious problem, take it to the Lord. Talk with God about it. Share your burden with Him. He will give you strength. He will help you. They know that. I am confident they know that."[22]

President William Jefferson Clinton

Larry King asked, "What, President Hinckley, are your thoughts on President Clinton?" His response: "Well, I feel very sorry for him in the first place. Here's a man of great talent and capacity who has evidently just hurt himself so seriously that it must be a terrible thing for him. Personally, I forgive him. The Lord has said, I, the Lord will forgive whom I will forgive. But of you, it's required to forgive all men. And in that sense I forgive him of any offenses committed against me. But he still has accountability. He's accountable to the Congress. He's accountable to the people of the United States who elected him. He's accountable to God. I believe that. And that's what he must face."[23]

Role of the Living Prophet

"What is your role? You're the leader of a major religion. What's your role?" Larry King asked. President Hinckley answered, "My role is to declare doctrine. My role is to stand as an example before the people. My role is to be a voice in defense of the truth. My role is to stand as a conservator of those values which are important in our civilization and our society. My role is to lead."[24]

Mike Wallace observed that "the Mormons, Mr. President, call you a 'living Moses,' a prophet who literally communicates with Jesus. How do you do that?" President Hinckley responded:

"Let me say first that there is a tremendous history behind this Church, a history of prophecy, a history of revelation, and . . . decisions which set the pattern of the Church so that there are not constant recurring problems that require any special dispensation. But there are occasionally things that arise where the will of the Lord [is needed and] is sought, and in those circumstances I think the best way I could describe the process is to liken it to the experience of Elijah as set forth in the book of First Kings. Elijah spoke to the Lord, and there was a wind, a great wind, and the Lord was not in the wind. And there was an earthquake, and the Lord was not in the earthquake. And there was a fire, and the Lord was not in the fire. And after the fire a still, small voice, which I describe as the whisperings of the Spirit. (See 1 Kings 19:9–12.) Now, let me just say, categorically, that the things of God are understood by the Spirit of God, and one must have and seek and cultivate that Spirit, and there comes understanding and it is real. I can give testimony of that."[25]

Missionaries and Missionary Work

When queried about the missionaries and missionary work the Church is engaged in, President Hinckley said:

"The work is strenuous; it is difficult. It isn't easy to go to New York or London or Tokyo and knock on doors and face people you have never met before. But it does something for you. . . . It creates in the first place a feeling of reliance upon the Lord. . . . It builds within [a young man] something of strength and capacity. . . . There is nothing like it. . . . I can walk down the streets of Salt Lake City with you and meet people who speak fluently in Japanese and Chinese and Swedish and Norwegian and Finnish and Spanish and Portuguese and who have love in their hearts for the people among whom they served.

" . . . We believe that the Lord meant what He said when He said, 'Go ye into all the world, and preach the gospel to every creature' (Mark 16:15). We believe in that mandate. We think it rests upon us to try to fulfill it. We are doing that with all of the energy and resources that we have."[26]

Family History

In 1995 President Hinckley visited the White House to present the president of the United States with a copy of his family history. Later, while talking to Larry King about family histories, the prophet said: "We have many other [buildings, including a] great family history resource, used by people all over the world."[27] It is worthy to note that the LDS Internet Genealogy Service (*www.familysearch.org*) received its three billionth hit less than a year after it was launched, making it one of the most popular sites on the web (see LDS Church press release, 19 May 2000).

OUT OF OBSCURITY

The Church is coming out of obscurity. To be obscured is to be hidden from view, or to have something's importance or glory dimmed. But the Lord has promised—and is now in the process of fulfilling his promise—to bring to the world things "they have never considered" (D&C 101:94). He has described the unfolding work of the Restoration as a "marvelous work and a wonder" that will cause the wisdom of the wise to perish and the understanding of even the most prudent men to be hid (see Isaiah 29:14; 1 Nephi 22:8, 12). The Restoration is real and it is now gathering steam to fulfill its ultimate destiny. According to the National Council of Churches, The Church of Jesus Christ of Latter-day Saints "continues to be the fastest growing mainstream church in the United States."[28] President Hinckley has pointed the entire Church to the future with buoyant optimism:

"The centuries have passed. The latter-day work of the Almighty, that of which the ancients spoke, that of which the prophets and apostles prophesied, is come. It is here. For some reason unknown to us, but in the wisdom of God, we have been privileged to come to earth in this glorious age. . . .

"We stand on the summit of the ages, awed by a great and solemn sense of history. This is the last and final dispensation toward which all in the past has pointed. I bear testimony and witness of the reality and truth of these things. . . .

" . . . Say good-bye to a millennium. Greet the beginning of another thousand years.

"And so we shall go forward on a continuing path of growth and progress and enlargement, touching for good the lives of people everywhere."[29]

The major implication of the Church coming "out of darkness" is that it will be brought "into the light"—meaning that it will be noticed more often and become more noted for its accomplishments throughout the world than in previous generations. On 6 April 1845, the Quorum of the Twelve Apostles issued a proclamation declaring that as the work of restoration "progresses in its onward course [it will become] more and more an object of political and religious interest and excitement" that will eventually catch the attention of every "king, ruler, or subject . . . community or individual."[30]

As the Church continues to move out of obscurity and becomes more and more an object of political and religious interest, all members will need to know how to respond to questions about our faith— especially the questions that are most frequently asked. President Hinckley's example and wisdom in these matters can be a great benefit and blessing to us all. In his own words, President Hinckley testified of how challenging, yet how important it is to always be ready to respond and to do as the apostle Peter counseled: "Give an answer to every man that asketh you a reason of the hope that is in you with meekness and fear" (1 Peter 3:15).

President Hinckley has wisely counseled: "As I have gone about the world, I have had opportunity for interviews with representatives of the media. This is always a worrisome undertaking because one never knows what will be asked. These reporters are men and women of great capacity, who know how to ask questions that come at you like a javelin. It is not exactly an enjoyable experience, but it represents an opportunity to tell the world something of our story. As Paul said to Festus and Agrippa, 'This thing was not done in a corner' (Acts 26:26). We have something that this world needs to hear about, and these interviews afford an opportunity to give voice to that."[31]

TWENTY-FIVE MEDIA INTERVIEWS WITH
PRESIDENT GORDON B. HINCKLEY

DATE GIVEN	PRINTED	DESCRIPTION
7 April 1980	*Go Forward with Faith,* 370–71	Interview with Tom Brokaw on the *Today Show,* Fayette, New York
23 October 1985	*Go Forward with Faith,* 430–32	Press conference regarding the Mark Hoffman forgeries and bombings, Salt Lake City
13 March 1995	*Go Forward with Faith,* 1–5	Summary of inaugural interview after ordination as president of the Church, Salt Lake City
12 May 1995	*Go Forward with Faith,* 576–78	Interview by Phil Reisen, KUTV Television, Salt Lake City
17 July 1995	*Go Forward with Faith,* 578–79	Interview by Gustav Niebuhr, *New York Times*
28 August 1995	*Go Forward with Faith,* 579–80	Interview with Lawrence Spicer, London News Service
9 September 1995	*Deseret News*	Interview with British media representatives from the BBC radio and television, London News Radio and a Liverpool newspaper
13 November 1995	*Go Forward with Faith,* 537–39, 581–82	Press conference at the Harvard Club, New York City
13 November 1995	*Deseret News*	Interview with Lee Davidson, *Deseret News* Washington correspondent, after President Gordon B. Hinckley presented President Bill Clinton with his family history

Date Given	Printed	Description
18 December 1995	Conference Report, October 1996, 66–71	Interview with Mike Wallace, Salt Lake City
10 March 1996	Conference Report, October 1996, 71–72	Second interview with Mike Wallace, Salt Lake City
18 May 1996	*Go Forward with Faith,* 587–88	Media luncheon and press conference, Tokyo Miyako Hotel, Japan
22 May 1996	*Go Forward with Faith,* 589–91	Press conference in Seoul, Korea
13 July 1996	*Go Forward with Faith,* 591–92	Press conference in conjunction with Grand Encampment celebration. Council Bluffs, Iowa
2 December 1996	*Church News,* 7 December 1996	Interview with reporters after a fireside in Washington, D.C., stake center
6–7 March 1997	*Church News,* 15 March 1997	Interview with media after President Hinckley's address at the World Affairs Council dinner, Los Angeles
13 April 1997	*San Francisco Daily Chronicle*	Interview with Don Lattin, *Chronicle* religion writer, San Francisco
13 May 1997	Online transcript, ksl.com	Televised interview with Duane Cardall of KSL during President Hinckley's visit to New Zealand and Australia
18 July 1997	*Online* newsletter, pbs.org/newshour	Interview with Richard Ostling, *Time* magazine's religion correspondent
8 September 1998	Online transcript, ldschurch.org	CNN transcript of *Larry King Live*

DATE GIVEN	PRINTED	DESCRIPTION
4 October 1998	Conference Report, October 1998, 90–93	Review of some questions asked during the *Larry King Live* interview
18 December 1998	*Deseret News*	Interview with Ted Capener, KUED TV, Salt Lake City
9 May 1999	*Los Angeles Times*	Interview with Teresa Watanabe, Los Angeles
24 December 1999	*Church News,* 1 January 2000	Interview with Larry King on *Larry King Live* in the Salt Lake Tabernacle, Salt Lake City
8 March 2000	National Press Club	The National Press Club, Washington, D.C.; posted on the Web and used with permission of the Church Public Affairs Department

NOTES

1. Sheri L. Dew, *Go Forward with Faith: The Biography of Gordon B. Hinckley* (Salt Lake City: Deseret Book, 1996), 510–11.

2. Mike Wallace, Foreword to Gordon B. Hinckley, *Standing for Something: Ten Neglected Virtues That Will Heal Our Hearts and Homes* (New York: Random House, 2000), viii.

3. Gordon B. Hinckley, in Conference Report, April 1996, 115.

4. Dew, *Go Forward with Faith,* 535–36.

5. "This Thing Was Not Done in a Corner," *Church News,* 26 October 1996, 10.

6. "Pres. Hinckley Addresses Journalists," *Church News,* 20 September 1997, 5.

7. National Press Club, Washington, D.C., 8 March 2000, published on the web and used with permission of the Church Public Affairs Department.

8. Author's discussion with the religion editor of the *Deseret News,* 7 February 2000.

9. Dew, *Go Forward with Faith,* 3.

10. "Pres. Hinckley, King on Air Again Dec. 24," *Deseret News,* 8 December 1999.

11. "Pres. Hinckley Writes Book Aimed at General Readers," *Deseret News*, 1 September 1999.

12. Mike Cannon, "Pres. Hinckley Testifies of Christ to British Media," *Deseret News*, 9 September 1995.

13. "President Hinckley Responds to Questions about Church," *Church News*, 15 March 1997, 7.

14. "President Hinckley Will Host 90th-Birthday Celebration," *Church News*, 20 May 2000, 5.

15. Dew, *Go Forward with Faith*, 578.

16. Ibid., 591–92.

17. Ibid., 588.

18. Wallace foreword in Hinckley, *Standing for Something*, viii.

19. Gordon B. Hinckley, in Conference Report, October 1996, 71.

20. Ibid., 69.

21. Remarks given 8 March 2000.

22. Hinckley, in Conference Report, October 1996, 68.

23. *Larry King Live* interview, 8 September 1998, CNN transcript.

24. Gordon B. Hinckley, in Conference Report, October 1998, 90.

25. Hinckley, in Conference Report, October 1996, 70–71.

26. Ibid., 70–71.

27. *Larry King Live* transcript.

28. "Fastest Growing U.S. Mainstream Religion," *Church News*, 20 May 2000, 6.

29. Gordon B. Hinckley, in Conference Report, October 1999, 94–95.

30. As cited in Ezra Taft Benson, in Conference Report, April 1980, 46.

31. Hinckley, in Conference Report, October 1996, 66.

CHAPTER EIGHTEEN

RICHARD L. EVANS, A LIGHT TO THE WORLD

LLOYD D. NEWELL

At the first session of the April 1972 general conference, President Harold B. Lee, first counselor in the First Presidency, conducted. In his opening remarks, he extended cordial greetings and then spoke of one who was missing. "It is with subdued hearts that we remember our beloved Richard L. Evans. His voice, his spirit, and his admonitions and counsel were one of the highlights of his association as a General Authority of the Church. Richard L. Evans didn't just belong to the Church; he belonged to the world, and they claimed him as such. We know that there are heavenly choirs, and maybe they needed an announcer, and one to give the Spoken Word. If so, maybe the need was so great that he is called to a higher service in that place where time is no more."[1]

President Lee's words must have comforted those who had been mourning the death of Richard L. Evans. He was beloved by members of the Church and millions more throughout the world. One of the best known and most respected Mormons of the twentieth century, Richard L. Evans helped to build bridges of understanding around the world. As a broadcaster and a public figure, his life's work brought immeasurable recognition to the Church. Countless people of many faiths and countries admired his teaching, writing, and speaking. As a member of the Seventy and then a member of the Quorum of the Twelve Apostles, Richard L. Evans devoted his life to building the kingdom and bringing the Church out of obscurity. For

Lloyd D. Newell is an assistant professor of Church history and doctrine at Brigham Young University and the announcer and a writer for Music and the Spoken Word.

forty of his sixty-five years, Richard L. Evans was a famous man. Yet, few of his admirers knew of his humble, even inauspicious beginning.

EARLY YEARS

A descendant of hardworking, faithful pioneer ancestors, Richard Louis Evans was born in Salt Lake City on 23 March 1906. He was the ninth child of goodly parents, John and Florence Evans. His father had worked up the ranks from errand boy at the *Deseret News* to the position of general manager. Ten weeks after Richard was born, his father returned from a late meeting, tried to get off a streetcar just before it reached a full stop, missed his footing, and fell to the ground. With a brain concussion and other injuries, he died several weeks later. Richard's widowed mother was left behind with nine children under eighteen years of age. Although Richard never knew his father, his mother always taught the children that their father was still with them as the head of their eternal family.[2]

Richard and his siblings learned to work hard in a variety of jobs to help support the family. From the early years of grade school to the time he left on his mission, he delivered newspapers, sold flowers, washed dishes, drove truck, and worked as a traveling salesman, to name but a few of many jobs. At an early age, he learned about thrift, frugality, and the value of hard work. He excelled in school, was the editor of his high school newspaper and yearbook, a champion debater, and recipient of the Heber J. Grant scholarship award.

Just after Richard turned eleven years old, he was wounded in a mock battle with neighborhood playmates. Unbeknownst to Richard, one of the boys was playing with a loaded BB gun. A pellet struck Richard in his left eye. With blood streaming down his face, he ran home, pleading with his sister, "Don't cry; pray for me." He lost the eye and was fitted with an artificial eye. Few knew he was blind in one eye for the remainder of his days. That disability seemed to give him an extra measure of spiritual sensitivity and empathy for those who struggled with challenges and those burdened by adversity.

Throughout his life Richard was known for his loving devotion to his mother. The circumstances of his birth and his father's death established a special bond and deep mutual affection between them. When eleven years old, he wrote this poem to his dear mother:

Patient Mother long ago,
As patient now if not more so.
All the years she has faithfully served;
Whether tired or not, she is like a sweet bird.

She is the dearest thing in the world to me
If not for her, a stranger I would be
To this wide world—everything and everybody
She says to me, "You are still my baby."

I owe her all I own, if not more.
It matters not in the future whether I am rich or poor;
I will go through every kind of strife
To keep her safe throughout my life.[3]

Years later, as a grown man, he would speak of his mother on the Tabernacle Choir broadcast:

"The Lord God had given her to me, and me to her, and she seemed to be as the extended arm of His influence. . . . She had nourished and sheltered me in infancy; nursed me in illness; heeded my cries and quieted my fears; had taught and counseled and encouraged, and dulled the sharp edge of disappointments. . . . We thank mothers for life given and for lessons learned, and for the constancy of their sacrifice and service. And best we honor them when we become the best of what they have taught us to be."[4]

At his mother's knee, Richard was taught the principles of the gospel and the importance of strong faith. When he was sixteen years old, an inspired patriarch blessed him that he had a "bright career" ahead of him, that he would "stand in holy places and mingle with many of the best men and women upon the earth." He was told that he would serve the Lord in "distant lands, travel much and see many wonderful things." The patriarch also blessed him that his "tongue [would] be loosened and become as the pen of a ready writer in dispensing the word of God and in preaching the gospel to [his] fellow men."[5]

MISSION TO THE BRITISH ISLES

At twenty years of age, Richard L. Evans was called to the British Mission, where he served for nearly three years. As a missionary, he worked hard and continued to have opportunities to learn and serve.

While on his mission, he was called to be the associate editor of the *Millennial Star,* first under Elder James E. Talmage and later under Elder John A. Widtsoe (both of the Council of the Twelve Apostles). Elder Widtsoe also appointed Elder Evans to be secretary of the European Mission and persuaded him to write the centennial history of the mission—which he did during and after his mission, publishing it in 1937.[6] He was rigorously taught, lovingly mentored, and warmly embraced by these two giants in Church history.

Richard L. Evans continued a close association with Elder and Sister Widtsoe until their deaths. He became as a son to them, the Widtsoes having lost their last surviving son only a few months before arriving in England. When he said goodbye to the Widtsoes at the conclusion of his mission, he wrote in his journal:

"This morning I parted company with the best man I have ever known. . . . Before we parted, he gave me the most wonderful blessing I have ever had and promised long, full service, health and achievement and told me in certain terms that the Lord was pleased with my labors. We put our arms around each other and parted as father and son."[7]

The Widtsoes gave Richard a key to their home, which he carried in his pocket until the day he died—as a symbol of what they had meant to him.[8]

BEGINNING LIFE'S CAREERS

During the years after his mission and continuing through his thirties, opportunities and blessings poured into Richard's life, as he worked hard and prepared for all that lay ahead. He married Alice Thornley from Kaysville, Utah, in 1933 and together they had four sons. He earned bachelor's and master's degrees, with honors, from the University of Utah. He got a job as an announcer with radio station KSL, began announcing the Tabernacle Choir broadcast, and became editor of the *Improvement Era.*

At age thirty-two, he was called by President Heber J. Grant to fill the vacancy occasioned by the death of J. Golden Kimball and became a member of the First Council of Seventy, the youngest man called as a general authority of the Church in more than thirty years. (The average age of the other six members at that time was sixty-five; the youngest was fifty-seven.) In his address given at general conference in October 1938, immediately after being called as a general authority, he said:

"I spent a sleepless night Thursday night, burning old bridges and building new ones. I think that perhaps this call would have come easier to me a little later in life, after I had had a better opportunity to make substance of more of my dreams, but perhaps this is not so. Perhaps I must just exchange old dreams for new dreams. . . . Furthermore, it is all part of a great plan. The Lord still chasteneth whom he loveth, and all those things which come into our lives in spite of our best laid plans, are part of the education and enriching experience of every child of God who walks the earth."[9]

Richard's various assignments allowed him to develop a close relationship with President Heber J. Grant. On one occasion, prior to his call as a general authority, Richard spoke with him about his desire to work on a doctorate and possibly pursue job opportunities in broadcasting that had opened up to him in several large eastern cities. Richard reported that when he asked President Grant's advice, the prophet looked at him with a twinkle in his eye and said, "I think I'd stick around if I were you." And so he did.[10] Richard's brother commented that "as his life unfolded, Richard recognized that . . . the President's advice had changed his whole life—and for the better."[11]

Indeed, many years later he would say on the *Spoken Word:*

"No man ever lived his life exactly as he planned it. There are things all of us want that we don't get. There are plans all of us make that never move beyond the hopes in our hearts. There are reverses which upset our fondest dreams. . . . There are many things in life beyond the present power of anyone to alter or to answer or to understand. And what we cannot understand we shall have to accept on faith—until we do understand. In any case, rebellion isn't the answer. But neither is hopeless resignation. Resignation may retreat too far. But somewhere between bitter rebellion and beaten resignation there is an effective fighting ground where a man can make the most of whatever is; where he can still face each day and do with it whatever can be done."[12]

MUSIC AND THE SPOKEN WORD

His longest association began in the spring of 1930, when he was just twenty-four years old. While employed at KSL he was assigned to announce the weekly nationwide Tabernacle Choir program that had begun broadcasting over the NBC network the year before. (Two years later the program would switch to the CBS radio network, where it remains to this day.)

THE CHOIR AND BROADCAST

In addition to the weekly broadcasts, Richard L. Evans accompanied the choir as it traveled to sing in concert halls throughout the world. As the choir announcer, he would introduce the music and add well-chosen words of commentary and humor. His love for the choir and *Music and the Spoken Word* was deep; he rarely missed a broadcast.

For many years, as a member of the Twelve, he had supervision of the choir. Upon his passing, Elder Gordon B. Hinckley—another man who loves the choir and its broadcast—was assigned to take his place and has retained direct supervision of the choir to this day.

The Tabernacle Choir has played a vital role in bringing the Church out of obscurity. Known as "America's choir," the choir has sung at four presidential inaugural ceremonies and numerous worldwide telecasts and special events, appeared at thirteen world's fairs and expositions, and performed throughout the United States and Canada, South and Central America, Europe, Asia, Israel, the South Pacific, and in numerous other nations.[13]

Today, the choir continues to tour the world, spreading goodwill wherever they go. Usually concert halls are filled as people travel great distances to see and hear this beloved and impressive choir. Stories are legion about how people want to know more about the Church after hearing the choir or listening to their more than 150 recordings, films, and videotapes. In fact, letters have been received at the choir offices with no more of an address than "Choir USA" or "Crossroads of the West."

One of the countless stories that could be told captures the impact of the choir on people around the world. A missionary who served in Norway recalls how a family they had been teaching asked the missionaries to stop visiting them. He and his companion tried everything to warm the family's hearts but to no avail. The missionary felt impressed to leave with the family a note expressing their testimonies and love and a tape of the Tabernacle Choir. Several days later, the father invited the elders back and explained that the choir's beautiful music had helped them feel the Spirit again and want to learn more of the gospel message. They were later baptized. One tape, with music not sung in their native language, had touched their hearts.[14]

Volumes could be filled with similar experiences. The choir is a powerful, effective means of bringing the Church out of obscurity and opening hearts to further light. Using the universal language of music, the choir speaks to individuals and nations as it travels the world representing the Church. Richard L. Evans understood the choir's magnitude and was its advocate and spokesman from 1930 to 1971.

MESSAGES OF HOPE

For forty-one years, until his death, Richard L. Evans continued as announcer, writer, and producer of *Music and the Spoken Word*. As a result, his name and voice became familiar to millions around the world. The words he wrote many decades ago continue on the broadcast today: "within the shadows of the everlasting hills," "from the crossroads of the West," and "May peace be with you this day and always." Recordings of his *Spoken Word* messages are still carried by several radio stations across the country. For example, in 1997, twenty-six years after his death, the *Wall Street Journal* carried a front-page article and picture about the enduring appeal of Richard L. Evans, who has been featured prominently on radio station KMOX in St. Louis drive-time programming. In response to a question from management, listeners called and wrote in by the hundreds telling the station to continue broadcasting Richard L. Evans's taped inspirational messages—as they have done for several decades.[15]

One writer expressed his regard for Richard Evans this way, "His deep, soothing voice and his genius for composing moving messages have made him famous and well loved in countries throughout the world. His expressed thoughts have seemed to be exactly what people wanted and needed to hear, and the response of so many has been, 'He seemed to be talking only to me.'"[16]

Richard L. Evans spoke on a wide variety of subjects, but each message was filled with hope and truth—the good news of the gospel. He often spoke of such principles as work, gratitude, duty, industry, civility, happiness, and love. With simple eloquence and uncommon wisdom, he wrote and spoke about faith, mercy, and God's goodness. He stood for timeless values, and constantly urged his vast audience to focus their lives on the everlasting things. He said on the broadcast, "Life is largely a reflection of what people believe plus what they have the courage and conviction to stand for, to live for."[17] His voice and the broadcast were a constant in good and bad times.

Like trusted friends, Richard L. Evans and "*Music and the Spoken Word* ha[ve] seen its audience through war and depression, peace and prosperity. . . . [They] ha[ve] steadied troubled hearts, assuaged disappointments, added upon joys, lightened loads, and led one generation after another to God."[18] Of the millions who listened weekly or read his many writings, no one can count how many people were moved to change their lives for the better; no one knows how many wanted more information about the "church of Richard L. Evans." What is known is that each year, still today, many hundreds of letters are received regarding the broadcast—a request for a message, a personal question, a note of appreciation.

Since 1990 when I started with the broadcast, I have received countless letters—mostly from non-LDS individuals—expressing gratitude for the program. Frequently, nearly three decades after his death, the letter writer expresses love and admiration for Richard L. Evans and remembers, with fondness, his voice and his messages. He was so closely connected with the broadcast for so many years that even today untold numbers cherish his memory and honor his name.

In 1954, to commemorate its twenty-fifth year of weekly broadcasts, *Life* magazine editorialized on the program's legacy with these words:

"Those who know this program need no arguments for listening to it, or no introduction to its producer and commentator, Richard L. Evans, . . . or to the disciplined voices. . . . Millions have heard them, and more millions, we hope, will hear them in years to come. It is a national institution to be proud of, but what matters more is that Americans can be linked from ocean to ocean and year to year by the same brief respite from the world's week, and by a great chord of common thoughts on God and love and the everlasting things."[19]

From its beginning on 15 July 1929, *Music and the Spoken Word,* (now in its seventy-second year) remains the longest continuously broadcast network program in the world. It is produced and distributed internationally to some twenty-three hundred television, radio, and cable stations by Bonneville Communications (a division of Bonneville International, which is the holding company for the Church's broadcast properties). Today the Church owns and operates several radio and television stations across the country.

THE CHURCH AND BROADCASTING

The Church has been involved in broadcasting since the early 1920s, when it assumed majority ownership of radio station KSL. "Beginning in 1923, radio was used to broadcast General Conference to overflow crowds of some 4,000 people who gathered on Temple Square. By April 1926, the Conference Report noted there were an estimated 50,000 people listening to the proceedings."[20] Today, millions of people (members of the Church and others not of our faith), hear and see general conference, Tabernacle Choir broadcasts, and many other Church programs and satellite broadcasts because of the miracles of mass communication.

Not only do these efforts strengthen the Saints, but they also assist in creating a positive public image for the Church, dispelling misconceptions, opening doors, and softening hearts to receive further gospel light. On any given day, millions of people are hearing a message from the Church through public service announcements (such as the Homefront series), or an interview with President Hinckley on international radio or television, or a broadcast of the Tabernacle Choir. The Lord has said, "For, verily, the sound must go forth from this place into all the world, and unto the uttermost parts of the earth—the gospel must be preached unto every creature" (D&C 58:64). The Church, from its earliest periods, has used communication vehicles of the day to promote and spread the gospel message. And Richard L. Evans played a vital role in bringing the Church, mass communication, and broadcasting outreach and technology together.

A PUBLIC SERVANT

Richard L. Evans understood the awesome power of broadcasting and other media to shape opinions and spread goodwill, and he worked tirelessly to share these gifts. In addition to the weekly choir broadcast, for five years he wrote a syndicated newspaper column for William Randolph Hearst's King Features Syndicate that was circulated to millions of homes and had one of the largest readerships in the nation. He wrote articles for *Reader's Digest, Encyclopedia Britannica,* and was asked to write an article for *Look* magazine to define the Church's beliefs.[21] The article appeared in October of 1954 under the title "What is a Mormon?" and according to one writer, "Was one of the best statements about the Mormons and their beliefs to appear in the national press up to that time, and it further established Richard as an authoritative writer for the Church as well as its best-known voice through his Tabernacle Choir broadcasts. The *Look* article was later reprinted and widely used as a missionary tract."[22]

He wrote seventeen books, most of them compilations of his messages and quotes nationally published by Harper and Brothers. His books were read by millions and reviewed by the most prestigious media outlets of the time, including this *New York Times* review: "[They] reveal an Addisonian charm which lifts them into literature. . . . Here is a classic, an example of how to put ancient realities to a modern world." Or this from the *Los Angeles Times:* "There is a classic simplicity here which makes meaning clear, and an eloquence which drives home a point." The *Baptist Sunday School Board* issued this review: "Many of the subjects would make excellent topics for sermons and devotions. Most public speakers could profit by studying these essays as models for great thoughts put into beautiful but simple language."[23]

He also was busy with civic affairs, most notably with the Rotary Club. Over three decades he rose from local offices to become president of Rotary International in 1966. During that year he and his wife addressed audiences in sixty countries on every continent and in twenty-five states in the United States. He traveled to a total of ninety countries in his years of service to Rotary. As Rotary leadership opportunities continued to come to him, he became concerned about the increasing time commitment to Rotary. He counseled with President David O. McKay, who encouraged him to accept leadership responsibilities within Rotary as they came.[24]

It would be impossible to calculate the goodwill he generated for the Church as he traveled, spoke, and met with dignitaries and officials from around the world. Not only was he familiar to many of them from his broadcasting and writing, but the people with whom he met understood that he was a "high-ranking official" in the LDS Church, and over many years of service and contribution, they came to love and trust him—and his church.

CALL TO THE APOSTLESHIP

His greatest honor came at age forty-seven after serving fifteen years in the First Council of Seventy. President McKay announced his name at the October 1953 general conference of the Church as the newest member of the Quorum of the Twelve Apostles with these words, "Elder Evans, whom you know and have known because of his work on the radio and his service in the stakes, and whom the entire nation knows,—Richard L. Evans,—will now speak to us."[25]

The new apostle came to the pulpit in the Tabernacle and said:

"I have frequented these beloved walls for a period now approaching a quarter century in many situations and assignments. But this is the most difficult thing that I have here had to do. It seems that this chapter was not in the script which I had written for myself. In the brief, but in some respects too long a time since first I became aware of this possibility, I have measured the full measure of my life many times over. There are those here who know much better than I the weight of this work. There is none here who knows better than I my own limitations, inadequacies, and imperfections, and the feeling of smallness which I have. But if you and my Father in heaven will accept me as I am, with your help and his, I shall earnestly endeavor to be better than I am or have ever been."[26]

As a special witness of the Lord Jesus Christ to the world, Elder Evans would take on new and demanding activities and assignments. Elder Marion D. Hanks wrote:

"To his calling as an apostle, Elder Evans gave the full measure of his strength and devotion and great faith. His already heavily scheduled life took on added dimensions, and his service broadened and his influence deepened in the spirit of his new calling. His trained mind and great capacity became even more widely known, as did his delightful sense of humor, and his seasoned understanding of problems and difficulties and his love for people won for him the love, trust, and loyalty of both old and young."[27]

People often wondered how he could do all that he did. They

attributed his accomplishments to talent and genius. He had much God-given ability, to be sure, but those who knew him best "recognized the working garments in which the genius was clothed."[28] He was an extremely hard worker, seldom rested from his labors, and often rose between 3:00 and 5:00 A.M. to work for a few hours before going to the office.

THE PASSING OF A GIANT

Richard L. Evans's death was unexpected. He was only sixty-five years old when he died just after midnight on 1 November 1971. He worked vigorously, as usual, up to his final days, when he became ill from a viral infection. Just before Elder Evans died, he lay in his hospital bed and the Sunday morning broadcast came on. His voice and words, on nationwide broadcast, encouraged faith in the future.

"There are times when we feel that we can't endure—that we can't face what's ahead of us; . . . that we can't carry the heavy load. But these times come and go . . . and in the low times we have to endure; we have to hold on until the shadows brighten, until the load lifts. . . . There is more built-in strength in all of us than we sometimes suppose. And what once we said we couldn't do or couldn't live with or couldn't carry, we find ourselves somehow doing and enduring."[29]

Richard L. Evans endured well. Elder Marion D. Hanks, a close friend who had been mentored for many years by Elder Evans, wrote at his passing:

"To millions he was the image of the Church. To multitudes of persons who were not well acquainted with the theology of The Church of Jesus Christ of Latter-day Saints, he was the only church they knew and the only religion they formally experienced. Countless others arranged their worship around his broadcasts. The impact of his personality was, if anything, even greater as he stood in person before numerous audiences across the earth and in his own inimitable way taught men the meaning of life and called them to repentance and to a greater sense of responsibility to themselves, to each other, and to God."[30]

Upon his death, the Council of the Twelve issued a statement to commemorate his life and contribution:

"Numerous people the world over have happily boasted that 'Richard Evans is my church.' For forty-two years, under intense pressures, Elder Evans has returned to the microphone nearly every week with a message of depth and faith and freshness and inspiration. As limitless approaches are made with the people all over the world by missionaries and others of us, we are greeted with the statement: 'I listen every Sunday morning to Richard L. Evans.' This apostle touched the hearts of millions."

The First Presidency continued with this expression of love and admiration:

"Above all else, however, we admired him for his firm testimony of the truthfulness of the gospel of Jesus Christ, and for the way in which he bore testimony to the world. He was a special witness of the divinity of the Savior, and it was in this role that he rendered his greatest service and received his greatest personal satisfaction and sense of fulfillment. While others may be raised up to shoulder part of the heavy load he carried, there will never be one to take the place of Richard L. Evans, apostle, philosopher, thoughtful friend, wise counselor, loving husband and father."[31]

Richard L. Evans was the face and voice of the Church for four decades of the twentieth century, admired and beloved by millions. He was integral in helping the Church become known, respected, and trusted. His untiring work to build the kingdom and bring gospel light to a darkening world will be appreciated by generations yet unborn. Today, as members of the Church, we are reaping the benefits of what he started, what he worked on all his life, what he wore his life out for. The Lord raised up this honored man for a crucial period in Church history to help bring it out of obscurity. "The name and life and ministry of Richard Evans will not be forgotten. He is and will be tenderly, gratefully remembered 'this day, and always.'"[32]

NOTES

1. Harold B. Lee, in Conference Report, April 1972, 3.

2. David W. Evans, *My Brother Richard L.* (Salt Lake City: Beatrice Cannon Evans, 1984), 2.

3. Evans, *My Brother Richard L.*, 3.

4. Richard L. Evans, *From within These Walls* (New York: Harper and Brothers, 1946), 229–30.

5. Richard L. Evans Jr., *Richard L. Evans—The Man and the Message* (Salt Lake City: Bookcraft, 1973), 23.

6. Richard L. Evans, *A Century of Mormonism in Great Britain* (Salt Lake City: Deseret News Press, 1937).

7. Evans, *Richard L. Evans,* 35.

8. Evans, *Richard L. Evans,* 36.

9. Richard L. Evans, in Conference Report, October 1938, 90.

10. Evans, *Richard L. Evans,* 45–46.

11. Evans, *My Brother Richard L.,* 27.

12. Richard L. Evans, *Tonic for Our Times* (New York: Harper and Brothers, 1952), 43–44.

13. "The Church and Society," *Selections from the Encyclopedia of Mormonism* (Salt Lake City: Deseret Book, 1992), 341–44.

14. Story told to author.

15. *Wall Street Journal,* 12 February 1997, A1, A11.

16. Gerald A. Petersen, *The Mormon Tabernacle Choir: More Than Music* (Provo, Utah: Brigham Young University Press, n.d.), 51.

17. Richard L. Evans, *May Peace Be with You* (New York: Harper and Brothers, 1946), 20.

18. Lloyd D. Newell, "A Trusted Friend," *Music and the Spoken Word,* 15 September 1996.

19. Richard L. Evans, *From the Crossroads* (New York: Harper and Brothers, 1955), 14.

20. Bruce L. Olson, "'Out of Obscurity and Out of Darkness,'" *Ensign,* January 2000, 47.

21. *Look,* 5 October 1954, 67–68; *Reader's Digest,* June 1955, 143–46.

22. Evans, *My Brother Richard L.,* 51.

23. Evans, *May Peace Be with You,* book jacket.

24. See Evans, *Richard L. Evans,* 69.

25. David O. McKay, in Conference Report, October 1953, 128.

26. Richard L. Evans, in Conference Report, October 1953, 128.

27. Marion D. Hanks, "Elder Richard L. Evans, Apostle of the Lord," *Ensign,* December 1971, 5.

28. Ibid., 7.

29. Evans, *Richard L. Evans,* 85.

30. Hanks, "Elder Richard L. Evans," *Ensign,* December 1971, 2.

31. Ibid., 11.

32. Ibid., 9.

CHAPTER NINETEEN

COMPUTERS AND THE INTERNET IN THE CHURCH

RUSSELL C. RASMUSSEN

In the late 1950s the Borg-Warner Corporation issued an advertisement in a national magazine. It featured a Ripley's "Believe It or Not" article that declared that in 1830 the head of the U.S. Patent Office predicted there could be no more worthwhile inventions and suggested that his office be closed. The Borg-Warner advertisement followed this declaration by stating that since 1830 more than 2.5 million patents had been issued and ten billion dollars had been invested yearly in research.[1]

To add to this irony, today there are approximately 6.5 million patents, and yearly research investments have risen above the trillion dollar mark.[2]

It comes as no surprise to us that during the 1830s the inventive wisdom and intellect of the world increased significantly. When Heavenly Father and Jesus Christ appeared to Joseph Smith, the lines of communication between man and the ultimate source of wisdom were once again opened. Light and knowledge were being disseminated from above, and the whole of mankind was benefiting.

I have marveled at the gradual, many-stepped, almost miraculous creation of the computer as we know it today. How have we gone from electrical volts turning on and off, to 1s and 0s, to alphanumeric characters displayed on a screen, to full-motion video on that same screen? To me it is absolutely astounding, and I work in the computer industry on a daily basis. But humans are interesting

Russell C. Rasmussen is a doctoral candidate in instructional psychology and technology and an instructor in ancient scripture at Brigham Young University.

274

creatures. Success, creativity, invention, and discovery focus our attentions inward and propel us toward pride and dangerous levels of independence. No matter how brilliant our creations, our ideas are not our own. We may be bright moons but only because of the light of the sun (Son).

President Brigham Young said: "All true wisdom that mankind have they have received from God, *whether they know it or not*. There is no ingenious mind that has ever invented anything beneficial to the human family but what he obtained it from that One Source, whether he knows or believes it or not. There is only one source from whence men obtain wisdom, and that is God, the fountain of all wisdom; and though men may claim to make their discoveries by their own wisdom, by meditation and reflection, they are indebted to our Father in heaven for all."[3]

I no longer wonder about the source of the wisdom and intelligence behind the invention of such an amazing device as the computer.

Elder Russell M. Nelson expressed it thus: "Consider the genius to create the computer. Then consider the man who created the computer. Then consider the Creator of the mind of the man who created the computer. Then you get some little inkling of the infinite wisdom of our Creator. To me, it's really inspiring because I think the development of the computer is a drop in the bucket compared to the infinite wisdom of the Lord."[4]

OUT OF OBSCURITY

It is marvelous that this symposium is focused on the ways in which The Church of Jesus Christ of Latter-day Saints has climbed out of obscurity and presented itself as a "city that is set on an hill [that] cannot [and will not] be hid" (Matthew 5:14).

You might ask, what is so wrong with being obscure or hidden or unknown to the world? Why would we, a "peculiar people," want to be brought out of obscurity? Aren't we simply happy to live peaceably and let the world go along as it will? No. We are not happy to sit idly by. We have a divine injunction, a command to share our knowledge of the truth (see D&C 42:58), to proclaim that which has been revealed from the heavens, and to be the steadfast oak in the midst of a mighty wind.

In terms of ourselves as individuals being known to the world, there really is no value. Self-aggrandizement only serves to benefit the individual, and once the party is over it leaves him desperately alone. But in terms of The Church of Jesus Christ of Latter-day Saints as a whole being known to the world, there are blessed eternal ramifications. The Church as the kingdom of God on earth provides the knowledge, the truths, and the covenants that will be a rock and a foundation for mankind. In fact, the most sublime truth, the necessity of the atonement of Jesus Christ and the covenants that give us full access to that atonement, are found only within The Church of Jesus Christ of Latter-day Saints. That is not a presumptuous statement. It is not a proverbial sticking out our tongue at the rest of humanity. God has declared it as such, and so we merely restate his words.

"Not all truths are of equal value."[5] The fact that my shirt is white, while unquestionably true and possibly mildly interesting, has absolutely no salvational importance for us. The truths that will change us as individuals and draw us nearer to being like God are the truths of the gospel. Knowledge, especially knowledge of truth, has tremendous power.

"And in that day shall the deaf hear the words [truths] of the book, and the eyes of the blind shall see out of obscurity and out of darkness" (2 Nephi 27:29; Isaiah 29:18).

The brunt of the responsibility rests on us to make sure that none can claim deafness or blindness. The world cannot believe what it has never had the opportunity to know. This is why it is our duty and even a command to share the gospel with all the ends of the earth.

THE MISSION OF THE CHURCH: PROCLAIMING THE GOSPEL

"And I give unto you a commandment that ye shall teach [the knowledge of truth and the scriptures] unto all men; for they shall be taught unto all nations, kindreds, tongues and people" (D&C 42:58).

"For, verily, the sound must go forth from this place into all the world, and unto the uttermost parts of the earth—the gospel must be preached unto every creature" (D&C 58:64).

In an oft-quoted talk about the need for sharing the gospel through many mediums, President Spencer W. Kimball said this about the use of technology:

"Technology will help spread the gospel. We need to enlarge our field of operation. . . . I have faith that the Lord will open doors when we have done everything in our power.

"I believe that the Lord is anxious to put into our hands inventions of which we laymen have hardly had a glimpse. . . .

"I am confident that the only way we can reach most of these millions of our Father's children is through the spoken word over the airwaves, since so many are illiterate. . . .

"Even though there are millions of people throughout the world who cannot read or write, there is a chance to reach them. . . . We can preach the gospel to eager ears and hearts. These should be carried by people in the marketplaces of South America, on the steppes of Russia, the vast mountains and plains of China, the subcontinent of India, and the desert sands of Arabia and Egypt.

" . . . We shall use the inventions the Lord has given us to awaken interest and acquaint people of the world with the truths, to ease their prejudices and give them a general knowledge."[6]

Though he was a man of small physical stature, President Kimball could see above and beyond the vision of most men and women. His visions of technology as a means of spreading the gospel have come true and are continuing to come true. Never before has the Church used so many mediums to disseminate the truth of the gospel.

Please note that at the time of this writing there are literally handfuls of proposals within the Church for new ways to utilize the current technology, so what is covered here may have been long since implemented by the date of the symposium.

COMPUTERS AND THE INTERNET

Some have complained that when it comes to new technologies, the Church is always watching and pondering, but rarely acting. Elder Jeffrey R. Holland gives us some insight into the reasons for the Church's seemingly reluctant progress:

"We are not breathlessly smitten by the Internet, nor are we in any way underestimating its possibilities. We are just moving steadily, and we think wisely, to consider it along with every other way we know to communicate with each other, teach the gospel and further the work of the Lord." The Church's involvement with the Internet is and will continue to be reviewed "carefully and methodically."[7]

There is an interesting phenomenon you may want to observe sometime. You can almost always tell when the Lord has inspired the creation of something that can be used for good and for the building and sustaining of the kingdom of God, and determine its value in this work by how masterfully it is used in the hands of evil individuals.[8]

Lehi spoke of this doctrine of opposition: "For it must needs be, that there is an opposition in all things. If not so . . . righteousness could not be brought to pass" (2 Nephi 2:11). Television, satellite and the Internet are three timely examples of such powerful creations. And yet if something is being used effectively for evil purposes, then *there must be an equal and opposite potential for good.*

Church leaders do not harbor any mistaken or ill-advised notions that technology is inherently evil simply because it has been used by many of those furthering some of Satan's pet projects. They are not going to overestimate or underestimate this potential for good and are continually seeking ways to best utilize its power and pervasiveness.

Elder Joseph B. Wirthlin commented, "There are two things that make communications so critical for the Church now. First, growth has given the Church higher visibility. . . . And second, the revolution in the way we communicate. The multiplicity in television channels and the Internet give us the ability now to communicate with each other and various audiences in ways that weren't with us a short 10 years ago."[9]

"The Lord has inspired skilled men and women in developing new technologies which we can use to our great advantage in moving forward this sacred work," said President Gordon B. Hinckley at the launch of the *familysearch.org* website.[10]

Next we will focus on some of the ways the Church is currently using technology, specifically computers and the Internet, to expand its reach and project the gospel message.

COMPUTER PROGRAMS

Numerous computer programs currently assist Church leaders in maintaining different arms of the Church as an organization. I have chosen to outline four programs in particular: Financial Information System, Membership Information System, Technology Assisted

Language Learning, and Wide Area Network and Local Area Networks.

Financial Information System (FIS)

The FIS program is used to handle all financial details on an individual ward and stake level. It gives clerks quick and easy access to the financial status of the ward. It was released in the United States and Canada from 1988–91, replacing a more tedious process of typed receipts and manual ledgers. The transfer of financial information is handled via modem to Church headquarters. Virtually all units outside of the United States and Canada, however, still use a manual tracking system.

Membership Information System (MIS)

The MIS program handles the tracking of individuals at a ward and stake level. Ward clerks are able to transfer and request membership records. This process, which once took weeks or even months, is now usually accomplished within twenty-four hours. MIS also tracks home teaching and visiting teaching companionships and visits and allows members to generate an almost limitless number of reports, from ward phone and address directories to lists of individuals with or without callings in a ward.

In 1975 Church headquarters moved its membership tracking to an automated system. Since 1986 MIS has been introduced in the United States and Canada. While international membership records have been automated at Church headquarters, MIS has yet to be integrated internationally within local meetinghouses.

Technology Assisted Language Learning (TALL)

The TALL program does not perform a maintenance role within the Church but rather serves as a means of training and supporting missionaries. The Provo Utah Missionary Training Center developed TALL to assist outgoing missionaries in learning new languages. First developed in the early 1990s, this program has had a tremendous positive impact in its ability to train new missionaries. TALL has received numerous accolades for its ingenuity and effectiveness.

Wide Area Network and Local Area Networks (WAN/LAN)

While WAN/LAN is not a computer program, it includes an extensive wide area network with major data centers in Salt Lake City,

England, and Australia. Connected to these data centers are many local area networks that allow for ward and stake buildings and temples to communicate with Church headquarters.

Internet Websites

The Internet has never been more popular or widely used than it is today. This global network allows individuals to access hundreds of millions of websites and billions of pages of information within seconds. Used mainly as a source of information, entertainment, and more recently commerce, the Internet offers varied opportunities for the Church, some of which I will discuss.

www.lds.org

The website *www.lds.org* was launched unannounced in early December 1996 and is a marvelous resource for both nonmember and member. Nonmembers can read about the basic tenets of the Church, order a free Book of Mormon, or read about ways to strengthen family relationships. Web users can read news releases from the Church, get ideas for family home evenings, or read general conference reports back to April of 1997. It is a heavily trafficked site, receiving 750,000 hits a day.

www.ldschurchnews.com

For years members of the Church have enjoyed the *Church News,* published every Saturday as a supplement to the *Deseret News* newspaper. In December 1995 the *Church News* went online. The supplement's two main articles are featured on the site's opening page, but access to the complete articles and features is restricted to registered users. The site also contains searchable *Church News* archives dating back to the early 1980s.

www.ldscatalog.com

Online since the middle of 1999, *ldscatalog.com* is an electronic version of the more familiar Salt Lake Distribution Center catalog. Access is currently limited to wards and stakes who request a password. Part of *ldscatalog.com* is available through *familysearch.org* and allows individuals to purchase family history–related materials and software. It is projected that the majority of the website will be open to the general public sometime in late 2000.

www.generalconference.com

In late 1999 Millennial Star Network Inc. (MSTAR)—a Church-owned company—launched *www.generalconference.com*. Brigham Young University's own Newsnet did the first English audio broadcast of general conference in April 1997. Since that time these two entities have teamed up on successive general conferences to provide audio broadcast over the Internet in fourteen languages, and in October 1999 they provided the first successful conference video broadcast. Audio archives for general conferences back to April 1999 are available on this website.

Building Construction Website

This site is not available to the general public but is used to connect Church headquarters with those involved in the building of meetinghouses and temples. Previously, computer-assisted design (CAD) drawings had to be printed and mailed to and from architects and construction companies, a process which could take weeks. Now, departments at Church headquarters can immediately upload accessible drawings and specifications for buildings in a matter of minutes.

Scriptures and Church Magazines Online

Currently in beta testing is a website that will allow individuals to search and read all parts of our standard works, from the footnotes to the topical guide and gazetteer. Also in the planning stages is an on-line source for the *Ensign, New Era,* and *Friend* magazines, with search capabilities extending back to magazines dating from the 1970s.

MSTAR (Millennial Star Network Inc.)

As the new electronic media provider for the Church, MSTAR will be in the forefront of development for Church-related electronic materials. Plans are in the works for a Church web portal to be developed that will provide access to all Internet enterprises developed by and for the Church. Sometime in the future, ward and stake buildings may receive Internet connections and programs that function specifically over the Internet.

FAMILY HISTORY

President Howard W. Hunter stated, "The role of technology in this work has been accelerated by the Lord himself, who has had a guiding hand in its development and will continue to do so. However, we stand only on the threshold of what we can do with these [technological] tools. I feel our most enthusiastic projections capture only a tiny glimpse of how these tools can help us and of the eternal consequences of these efforts."[11] Below is a list of the currently available computer-based tools relating to family history.

CD-ROMs

Several compact disks are available containing databases of information, censuses, and vital records indexes. Since the emergence of familysearch.org, the Pedigree Resource File, an international family history record has been generated from submissions from around the world and saved on CD-ROMs. Approximately 1.2 million new names are submitted each month.

Personal Ancestral File (PAF) Software

This is a free software package available from the *lds.org* and *familysearch.org* websites that helps individuals organize their personal family history records.

TempleReady Software

TempleReady allows members to prepare ancestral names that can be taken directly to the temple for the completion of temple ordinances.

www.familysearch.org

After a month of beta testing, the *www.familysearch.org* website was officially launched on 24 May 1999 at a news conference that linked Salt Lake City and Washington, D.C., by satellite. In November of 1999, 240 million names were added to an already massive database of 640 million names. The site's popularity is evident in the amount of traffic that it generates: on the day *www.familysearch.org* was launched, service was impaired for several hours because of the volume of individuals attempting to access the website. Though the site's initial novelty has worn off, it continues to receive roughly 8.5 million hits a day. In October 1999 *familysearch.org* surpassed 1.5 billion hits on the site. It promises to be a powerful force for good.

Elder D. Todd Christofferson of the Seventy summed it up this way: "The Internet service has developed a tremendous reservoir of goodwill for us. People are grateful the information is available for them where they can get at it."[12]

LOOKING TO THE FUTURE

It is my hope that we would be humble and submissive as we take opportunities to create and develop technological tools to assist us in strengthening the Church. In our efforts to build the kingdom of God, we must combine reason with knowledge of gospel truths found in the scriptures, all the while seeking the guidance of the Holy Spirit. Let me share a tremendous story told by Elder Russell M. Nelson that illustrates this point:

"When I started medical school, we were taught that one must not touch the heart, for if one did, it would stop beating. But I also pondered the scripture that tells us that 'All kingdoms have a law given. . . . And unto every kingdom is given a law; and unto every law there are certain bounds also and conditions' (D&C 88:36, 38). I believe sincerely the scripture that certifies: 'When we obtain any blessing from God, it is by obedience to that law upon which it is predicated.' (D&C130:21).

"Knowing these scriptures while concentrating on the 'kingdom' of and the blessing of the beating heart, I knew that even the function of this vital organ was predicated upon law.

"I reasoned that if those laws could be understood and controlled, perhaps they could be utilized for the blessing of the sick. To me this meant that if we would work, study, and ask the proper questions in our scientific experiments, we could learn the laws that govern the heartbeat.

"In 1949 our group of researchers presented at the American College of Surgeons the report of the first successful use of the artificial heart-lung machine in sustaining the life of an animal for a thirty-minute period of time, without its own heart powering its circulation.

"In the decade of the 1950s, successes in the animal laboratory were extended to human beings. Now, with many of those laws learned, the heartbeat can be turned off while performing delicate repairs on the damaged valves or vessels, and then turned on again—provided the laws are obeyed upon which that blessing is predicated. Over 200,000 open-heart operations are performed in this country annually, and many more worldwide, thereby extending life for many. But you should know that it was through the understanding of the scriptures and 'likening' them to this area of interest, that the great field of heart surgery as we know it today was facilitated for me."[13]

Referring to his training as a physician, Elder Russell M. Nelson also said:

"I did not hesitate to communicate with the Lord in great detail, even about the technical steps in a new operative procedure that was to be performed. Often just the process of rehearsing it in my mind while engaged in prayer allowed divine direction for me to see a better way."[14]

"In your quest for personal righteousness, go periodically to the mountain of the Lord's house—his holy temple. There, learn of him. Covenant with him. There and wherever you are, pray to our Heavenly Father in the name of the Son. Merge your faith with your scholarship to give a spiritual depth of focus to all of your righteous desires."[15]

The invention of the printing press has had far-reaching effects on the world at large. In fact, its inventor, Johannes Gutenberg, has recently been hailed by many organizations as the most influential person of the millennium.[16] This device was the impetus for sharing the word of God. God inspired that invention so that his work could go forth. As technologies have continued to expand under God's inspiration and tutelage, many new mediums have come forth as possible tools to assist in our great task of taking the gospel to all the world. The ability to transfer signals across the world that carry voice, picture, sound, and data is absolutely amazing.

While these new inventions are unarguably awe-inspiring, their importance pales in comparison with the significance of the goodness and greatness of God. It is in their roles as means to spread the eternal truths of the gospel that they find true merit. It is the word of God that builds foundations, straightens ideologies, quells fears, and sets individuals on a course that will lead them closer to God and life eternal. My hope is that we create and use wisely and well the technological advances that God has inspired and given us for the building of the kingdom, for in the words of President John Taylor, it truly is "the Kingdom of God or Nothing."[17]

NOTES

1. Delbert L. Stapley, "Man, a Child of God," Brigham Young University Speeches of the Year (Provo, 10 January 1962), 6.

2. Numbers calculated by the author from *http://www. patents.uspto.gov.*

3. Brigham Young, *Journal of Discourses,* 26 vols. (London: Latter-day Saints' Book Depot, 1854–86), 13:148; emphasis added.

4. Russell M. Nelson, "Computer Aids Scripture Study," *Church News,* 23 April 1988, 13.

5. Ezra Taft Benson, *A Witness and a Warning: A Modern-day Prophet Testifies of the Book of Mormon* (Salt Lake City: Deseret Book, 1988), 10.

6. Spencer W. Kimball, *The Teachings of Spencer W. Kimball,* ed. Edward L. Kimball (Salt Lake City: Bookcraft, 1982), 587–88.

7. Jeffrey R. Holland, in "Church Enters World Wide Web 'Carefully and Methodically,'" *Church News,* 1 March 1997, 6.

8. Elder Jeffrey R. Holland made a similar comment when speaking about the Internet. He said, "Anything that has the potential for good almost always has the potential for damage and danger as well" ("Church Enters World Wide Web," 6).

9. Joseph B. Wirthlin, in "Bursting Forth from Obscurity," *Church News,* 23 October 1999, 10.

10. Gordon B. Hinckley, in "Technology Helps Church Spread Gospel," *Church News,* 29 May 1999, 5.

11. Howard W. Hunter, 1994 Centennial celebration of the Genealogical Society of Utah, as cited in "Technology Helps Church Spread Gospel," 4.

12. D. Todd Christofferson, in "Bursting Forth from Obscurity," *Church News,* 23 October 1999, 7.

13. Russell M. Nelson, "Begin with the End in Mind," in *Brigham Young University 1984–85 Devotional and Fireside Speeches* (Provo: Brigham Young University, 1985), 14.

14. Ibid., 16.

15. Russell M. Nelson, "Reflection and Resolution," in *Brigham Young University 1989–90 Devotional and Fireside Speeches* (Provo: Brigham Young University, 1990), 66.

16. For more information, see Agnes Hooper Gottlier, Henry Gottlier, Barbara Bowers, Brent Bowers, *1,000 Years, 1,000 People: Ranking the Men and Women Who Shaped the Millennium* (New York: Kodansha America).

17. John Taylor, in *Journal of Discourses,* 6:18.

CHAPTER TWENTY

THE KOREAN WAR AND THE GOSPEL

HONAM RHEE

Let me begin by sharing with you three stories that are very close to my heart. These stories have something quite simple, but remarkable, in common: miracles of humanity.

All the stories take place during the Korean War, and before I start with the stories, I would like to provide a brief background of the war to give you a sense of the hardships endured. One of the greatest tragedies Korea suffered in the past century is the Korean War. It lasted for three long years, from 1950–53. The war broke out with North Korea invading South Korea in hopes of capturing the South and ruling it under Communism. The savage blows of the war claimed millions of innocent lives, annihilated homes and villages, and left millions of people without loved ones and separated from their families.

I remember the summer of 1950, the year the war broke out. My family, like most other families in the country, had very little food to eat. There was no sign of relief anywhere. We were a family of ten, with eight kids. It wasn't long before we were having to go to bed hungry and wake up hungry. One night, it was late and all the children had gone to bed, and I was unable to fall asleep from hunger.

Soon I found myself eavesdropping on my parents' conversation. My father was persuading my mother to trade her only, and might I add, most treasured, Singer sewing machine in exchange for some rice. He was comforting her and convincing her that this was truly

Honam Rhee is a professor of Asian and Near Eastern language at Brigham Young University.

our last resort. "Think of the children," he whispered, as if she needed to be reminded. She often did not eat her portion so the children could have just a morsel or two more of whatever was edible on the table. She agreed of course, thinking of her eight children—and her sewing machine.

The next morning before anyone was awake, my father put the sewing machine on the back of his bicycle and took off to where the farms were—to the countryside. He returned in the evening to his family eagerly awaiting at least a week's supply of rice. He pulled out a sackful of potatoes only. We counted eighteen small potatoes. My mother didn't, or perhaps couldn't, eat. I approached her late that night and delivered my resolution like a soldier: "Mom, I'm going to buy you a brand-new sewing machine one day. I promise." She thanked me in tears.

Years later, much later than I had anticipated, I was able to fulfill that promise. To this day, however, I cannot approach a potato without a deep prayer of gratitude and a long memory of sadness. As the horrors of war carried on, we felt as if we were going to be buried alive. Yet, I saw with my very own eyes and felt in my heart true miracles of humanity amidst the ruthless and irrational horrors of war.

STORY ONE

On 28 September 1950, General Douglas MacArthur made the famous Inchon Landing to take back the capital city, Seoul, from the North Koreans who had been occupying it. The city was chaotic, to say the least.

My youngest brother, Bonnam, was five years old at that time. Amidst chaos, dislocation, and military occupation, he panicked one evening and ran away without knowing where he was going. Because things were not the same, he could not recognize enough paths to find his way home.

At home we were panicked ourselves, not to mention shocked, to find that the little boy, our youngest, had been missing for hours. We looked for him everywhere, but he was nowhere to be found. Oh, how painful it was to think he might have died; and all the while I couldn't help but fancy the worst, that one of the North Korean soldiers somehow got to my brother. I made my way to where the dead bodies were and looked through the bodies under the covers. With each body uncovered, I became that much more certain that my little brother had died.

A few weeks passed. One of our neighbors came over one afternoon shouting, "Bonnam is alive! Bonnam is alive!" I was sure she had the wrong child, as I had made firm peace with myself only by believing that he was dead and must be in a better place than the one we were living in. We all rushed out in disbelief. Before us, there was an elderly gentleman holding Bonnam's tiny hand. It was as if I had seen an angel. Bonnam rushed into our arms, crying happily.

We learned that the man had spotted my little brother washing his feet at the nearby Samchung Dong Canal. He found it a bit odd that a little boy was washing his feet all alone. Furthermore, he could see that the little boy was crying. Rather than assuming—as most people may have been inclined to do—that it was a little child in tears from having been chastised by his parents, this gentleman decided to go over and inquire about this peculiar encounter.

It was wartime, after all, and this boy could be lost, homeless, or without family, he thought. Or maybe he just hurt his foot playing. Whatever the case may be, he simply couldn't take the chance—this boy could be without a home or a family. Sure enough, most of his suspicions were confirmed—the little boy was lost, hungry, and had been roaming for hours, scared and hopeless. He was too young to be able to give the exact address of where he lived; besides, there was such chaos all around the city, it was hard to reference landmarks the way we used to.

Bonnam was taken into this man's home, his own family agreeing to welcome, feed, and shelter this little child without knowing how long and perhaps without knowing how they would feed another mouth given the extreme and ubiquitous scarcity of food. In those days, everything was scarce, but especially food. Having one more mouth to feed was no easy task and certainly more than a mere act of charity. Everywhere, the horrors of war turned our stomachs and deadened our hearts. This man's decision—of complete and whole-hearted sacrifice—restored life in our hearts. To think your loved one dead and then to see your loved one in the arms of a stranger, and all this amidst an ongoing war—this was a miracle as real as any other miracle stories I had heard before. But this time, it wasn't a miracle of some supernatural force or a miracle of some goddess. This was a miracle born and created amongst each other, amid humanity of kindness and love.

"A certain man went down from Jerusalem to Jericho, and fell among thieves, which stripped him of his raiment, and wounded him, and departed, leaving him half dead.

"But a certain Samaritan, as he journeyed, came where he was: and when he saw him, he had compassion on him,

"And went to him, and bound up his wounds, pouring in oil and wine, and set him on his own beast, and brought him to an inn, and took care of him.

"And on the morrow when he departed, he took out two pence, and gave them to the host, and said unto him, Take care of him; and whatsoever thou spendest more, when I come again, I will repay thee.

"Which now of these three, thinkest thou, was neighbour unto him that fell among the thieves?

"And he said, He that shewed mercy on him. Then said Jesus unto him, Go, and do thou likewise" (Luke 10:30, 33–37).

STORY TWO

The war continued relentlessly. More American soldiers came to rescue South Korea while the Chinese Communist Army became involved on the side of North Korea. It was 1951, and the Chinese army was gaining strength and began to reoccupy the Kyung-Gi-Do area in the south. My father decided to move the family (we were in Seoul at the time) to escape the war zone. After days of traveling, we finally found an empty, abandoned house. It was mid-winter, fiercely cold, and the wind as unrelenting as the cruelties of war. We decided to spend the night there and continue on to our destination the next day.

What we didn't realize was that this house had once been the house of the director of an anti-communist organization. Within hours of our arrival, the Chinese army moved into the area and began a full search of all the houses and buildings in the area. Needless to say, we were discovered and interrogated. Upon searching the house, the Chinese soldiers found an identification card.

They were able to understand, through their interpreter, that this ID belonged to the director of an anti-communist organization.

My father was immediately apprehended and accused of being the director of the anti-communist party. My father's execution was ordered at once. My mother began to tremble. My little brother, Bonnam, somehow sensing that something was terribly amiss, began to cry, and before any of us could stop him, he ran to the Chinese sergeant whose order it was to execute my dad and clung to his leg with all his might. There was a long pause as the soldier stared down at my little brother, who was shaking him and begging him "not to hurt my daddy!" We were sure the Chinese sergeant would fling him off his leg with contempt. We tried to get him, but we were stopped by the surrounding soldiers.

A conversation took place between the interpreter and the sergeant. The Korean interpreter approached my dad and allowed him to explain his disclaimer as to the ID found in the house. My father explained that this ID was not his, that he lived in Seoul and his name was Chong Suk Rhee. He explained that we were planning to leave the next day to move into a region where the fighting wasn't so severe. But strangely enough, when my father was giving his name, he felt compelled to qualify his last name by explaining that by ancestry he was of the Won-Ju Rhee clan. In Korea, each last name has several different clan heritages; that is to say, two people can have the same last name of *Rhee* but they can be of different clans.

Koreans identify strongly with the ancestry of clans, and when this North Korean interpreter learned that my father was a member of the Won-Ju Rhee clan, he began to listen discerningly. His tone of voice softened, almost sounding respectful. Next thing we knew, the interpreter was talking to the sergeant and my father was released.

We never stopped talking about this incident, as it was our strong hunch that the interpreter was also of the Won-Ju Rhee clan. When on his deathbed, my father told me, "There is an old saying, Honam, 'Blood is thicker than water' and if the North and the South should ever unite, I want you to go to the Ham Kyung Do area in North Korea. It's known to be rife with Won-Ju Rhees. I want you to inquire after this man, who served as an interpreter for the Chinese army. I'm sure he was one of us. Even the Communist ideology must bow to the spirit of ancestry and family."

I've always agreed with my father, but I have often wondered differently about why the Chinese officer chose to react the way he did toward my little brother. It wasn't unusual to witness soldiers clubbing and striking people, even children, during this time. During the war human relations were preempted by war relations. He could have easily flung the little boy off his leg under wartime protocol. What moved this Chinese Communist officer? Was it the naive courage of this boy? Was it that he was reminded of his own little child back in China? Was it the tears streaming down those chapped red cheeks? Or could it have been the human touch, wrapped so tightly around his leg, with a language which has no words, but knows a courage that is full of so much love that it speaks to the heart? Whatever his reasons were, for me it was a moment of miracle, a miracle of humanity that decried the paradigms of war.

STORY THREE

My last story is a fiction story called "Dong Heng" (Go Together) written by Korean novelist Il-Nam Choi about a black American soldier in Korea. Private Thorpe had lost his unit. It had been two days, and two days of walking. He did not want to walk anymore, and he was almost unable to continue. The more he continued, the more he seemed to be lost; there were mountains upon mountains, hills upon hills, and no sign of life anywhere. He was desperate for something, for anything to happen, life or death. He no longer wondered where he was; he just knew that he was alive. Just then, a house came into view. He proceeded cautiously and investigated the house for any sign of life. A dog began to bark as it heard Thorpe enter its territory, but it was clear that no one lived there. It was an abandoned house.

Just as the dog ceased barking, a baby bellowed as if to take up its turn. Private Thorpe was surprised but tried to stick to his initial conclusion that there was nothing for him there. He found himself, however, entering the room where the baby was wrapped in a blanket. Thorpe began noticing the baby's lips, how they stretched and pinched. He even thought about how cute the baby was. He immediately got up to leave in order to dismiss the thought, but as he got up the baby cried louder. It seemed to have sensed his intentions. At that moment, Private Thorpe was overwhelmed with a peculiar and undeniable feeling of closeness to this baby—it was as if this baby was his own flesh and blood.

The next chapter opens and closes with the sun shining, incandescent and oblivious to all but a small lump of snow around which a dog sniffs, circles, and barks as if to try its hand at recalling life. One thing is clear. The baby is swathed tightly and firmly in the bosom of a soldier. They are in deep snow, in all white.[1]

MIRACLES OF HUMANITY

I remarked earlier that in all three stories there is something quite simple but remarkable in common: miracles of humanity. What do I mean by miracles of humanity? What miracles do we perform or possess? Is this the secret answer to all our questions and problems? Hardly.

But let us leave that question and let the stories stew for a bit. I would like you to think back to those happy days when you began to acquire language and reason about almost anything and everything. I'm sure most of you can remember one of the first lines of inquiry being "why?" If you can't recall, try holding an extended conversation with any four-year-old, and pretty soon you will be locked into an infinite sequence of innocent but unrelenting "but why?" questions.

We soon learn that the wonders of *why* don't go away simply because we get older or wiser. Rather, we are able to pursue our line of inquiry in different ways to effect a better and a more meaningful understanding as well as to strengthen our knowledge. In school for example, as students and as teachers, we are encouraged to ask the question "why?" in different scholarly disciplines, such as science, literature, philosophy, and many others. But in our everyday lives, I can think of times when we are compelled to ask "why?" perhaps in the same way a child is guilelessly compelled to ask why. But this time, we ask not out of mere curiosity but out of sheer inability to understand, after all—out of sorrow, out of anger, out of hopelessness, and perhaps, out of desperation: "Why this pain?" "Why this suffering?" "Why my loved one?" "Why would God let this happen?"

I don't profess to have the answers to these questions. I cannot tell you why this pain exists in your heart, why you are suffering the way you do, why there is such cruelty in this world, why our loved ones die. What I can share with you are experiences and stories of how we are able to live in spite of this pain, hardship, and suffering. In each story, we can hear the cries of "Why?" At the same time, however, in each story there is a response. Not an answer, but a response—a human response. As human beings, we have the capacity for a human response, despite overwhelming realities of despair and hopelessness that readily render us numb. But more than that, the miracle I referred to earlier is actualized precisely when this human capacity is exercised.

Even though we may not be able to supply ourselves with satisfactory answers to our questions of *why*, we can certainly ground ourselves in the *how* of life: How will I go on? In these stories, it is our noble but fundamental ability to be human that is able to subdue even the horrors of war. The human response infuses even the most desolate moment with such life: the stranger who took the little boy's hand, the soldiers who allowed sympathy, and the private who did not ignore the human bond.

All of you possess this gift of human courage and love. Moreover, every day you have the opportunity to exercise this gift amongst each other. But you have an even greater advantage and blessing as Mormons—the knowledge of the gospel. The gospel not only guides our *how's* in this world to be righteous and humble, full of meaning and purpose, but the gospel also helps us attain a richer and higher understanding of the *why's* of this world. Again, the gospel doesn't hold a mathematical answer for all the questions of despair we put to ourselves and loved ones, but it does bring us to a higher plane of being that supplies us with an understanding of the larger plan at work.

I was blessed with this knowledge through an example of a man by the name of Calvin Beck, who was serving in the army during the Korean War. I was an interpreter during that time, with what little English I knew then. I noticed Calvin Beck right away. He was always polite and courteous to everyone, and it was clear that he was genuine and true in his interactions with people. I never heard him swear. I never heard him raise his voice or get angry with anyone, and I never saw him on Sundays. He was always going somewhere on Sundays, and he was gone first thing in the morning.

You can imagine, when Calvin invited me to attend church with him one day, I was so eager and felt so privileged. I thought to myself, "Can a man be this good, even during a war like this? I must get to know him." I was determined to acquaint myself with a man who seemed so angelic to me. I went to church with him one Sunday. It was a place and feeling I had never known before.

Afterward, Calvin sat down with me for twenty-five minutes and within that period of time he was able to explain the plan of salvation with three circles. That day I told Calvin, "In Korea the teachings of Confucius are well respected and known. He said, If you discover the truth today, you can die tomorrow. Calvin, I can die tomorrow." I was the happiest and richest man alive, I said to myself. I was baptized on 5 September 1954 by Allen Potts, who was a soldier stationed in Korea.

Ironically, it was right after the war that the gospel of The Church of Jesus Christ of Latter-day Saints was introduced to Koreans struggling through the war. What is more ironic is that it was not through the full-time missionaries but through a few American Latter-day Saint soldiers that the teachings of the Church were spread. These soldiers came to fight on the soil of Korea, but they also sowed the seeds of the gospel in the hearts of the Korean people. Their examples were invaluable. Some of these soldiers were later called to serve in Korea as mission presidents and temple presidents.

I can't think of a better gift for my people after the Korean War than the gift of the gospel. The people of Korea embraced the gospel so gratefully for the truth it brought but also for the way it fit into the everyday lives of the people. We could see that this gospel delivered God's truth, which was not distant or abstract, but which was with us at all times to guide us through prayer and teachings of the Church. I would like to share a story that is very dear to me about a boy in Korea who applied the teachings of his seminary classes to his life.

A good friend of mine, who was also a member of the Church, was approached by his co-worker. The co-worker wondered if everything was okay at home, financially speaking. My friend thought it strange that he would be asked such a question. He answered graciously, "Yes, everything's fine, but why do you ask?" My friend learned that the co-worker had spotted Tae Wan, my friend's son, selling newspapers on the street. My friend was shocked to hear this news, since he had no idea about any of this and wondered if Tae Wan was in trouble of some kind.

That evening he approached Tae Wan, who was in his early teens, and asked him if everything was fine. "Yes, Dad, everything is fine." "Do you have enough money, I mean is the allowance we give you enough?" "Sure, Dad, it's fine. I don't really spend money so it's quite enough." "Let me ask you, then, are you selling newspapers on the street?"

Tae Wan began to tell his story. There was a kid in his classroom whose family was very poor. He hardly had anything for lunch, and he sold newspapers to help out at home. But more than that, he had no money for tuition (in Korea you bring the tuition to school quarterly), so he was behind in his tuition payment. To top it all off, this boy fell sick and was not able to sell newspapers or come to school. Tae Wan decided to get his friends and help this boy out. They all decided to sell newspapers after school and help the boy pay for his tuition. Upon sharing this story with his wife, my friend learned that Tae Wan had been asking his mom to pack him double the usual amount for lunch, telling her that he's been getting hungrier than usual. Of course, she was happy to pack him as much lunch as he wanted. He then had plenty to share with the boy.

My friend could not help but be proud, especially when he learned from Tae Wan that he was inspired to help his classmate after a seminary class he had attended that had impressed him to do so. "The best thing," my friend said, "is that not only was he inspired to do good, but he also got his friends to work with him on helping this boy out. Now, that is conversion."

I can recall my own son coming home after his seminary class sharing with me his thoughts on what he learned that day. Once, after a long discussion, he said to me, "The best thing about seminary class, Dad, is that it teaches me things that I can do. It's like learning how to live." That is what the gospel brought to the people of Korea who had lost means, ways, and hope in life. We were guided in our hearts and minds as to the *why's* and *how's* of life.

Korea rose from the ashes of war and now enjoys economic prosperity and political stability. The Church has grown strong in the past fifty years and there are about eighty thousand members with seventeen stakes and four missions in Korea. A temple was dedicated in 1985 and has saved millions of Korean ancestors. We don't have all the answers, but we have each other, brothers and sisters. We have each other despite whatever hardships we all bear, and it is in reaching out to others that we renew and infuse our hearts with what it means to be human.

As partakers of the gospel, we are further reminded of what it means to be a child of God for ourselves as well as for other people who may be in need. I would like to close with a scripture that has stayed close to my heart, especially in times of struggle and pain:

"My son, despise not thou the chastening of the Lord, nor faint when thou art rebuked of him:

"For whom the Lord loveth he chasteneth, and scourgeth every son whom he receiveth. If ye endure chastening, God dealeth with you as with sons; for what son is he whom the father chasteneth not?

"But if ye be without chastisement, whereof all are partakers, then are ye bastards, and not sons.

"Furthermore we have had fathers of our flesh which corrected us, and we gave them reverence: shall we not much rather be in subjection unto the Father of spirits, and live?

"For they verily for a few days chastened us after their own pleasure; but he for our profit, that we might be partakers of his holiness.

"Now no chastening for the present seemeth to be joyous, but grievous: nevertheless afterward it yieldeth the peaceable fruit of righteousness unto them which are exercised thereby" (Hebrews 12:5–11).

NOTE

1. Il-Nam Choi, "Dong Heng," *Hyundae Munhak* (Seoul, Korea: Hyundae Munhak, 1959), 81–90.

CHAPTER TWENTY-ONE

THE CHANGING FACE OF THE QUORUM OF THE SEVENTY

MATTHEW O. RICHARDSON

In 1831 it was revealed that the Lord's servants "might have power to lay the foundation of this church, and to bring it forth out of obscurity and out of darkness" (D&C 1:30). Within four years, Joseph Smith saw in a vision[1] quorums "building up the church and regulating all the affairs of the same in all nations, first unto the Gentiles and then to the Jews" (D&C 107:34). One of the quorums given this responsibility was the Quorum of the Seventy.

The First Quorum of the Seventy was established 28 February 1835 in Kirtland, Ohio, under the direction of Joseph Smith. As outlined in section 107, the Quorum of the Seventy, also known as the First Council of the Seventy, was presided over by seven presidents (see D&C 107:93–98). The duties of the Quorum of the Seventy included preaching the gospel, being especial witnesses unto the Gentiles and in all the world, acting in the name of the Lord under the direction of the Twelve, building up the Church, and regulating all its affairs in all nations (see D&C 107:25–26, 34). "Their words," Joseph Young, the presiding president of the First Quorum of the Seventy, said concerning the Seventy, "will be as the words of God to the people, in strengthening their hands and cheering their hearts to persevere, until Zion is built up and perfected on the earth."[2] Clearly, since its

Matthew O. Richardson is an assistant professor of Church history and doctrine at Brigham Young University.

inception, the Quorum of the Seventy was intended to take an active role in bringing the Church out of obscurity and out of darkness.

Over the years, the Quorum of the Seventy greatly influenced the growth of the Church. While a growing membership is a great blessing, it also presents unique challenges—especially administratively. The ever-changing Church membership, both in size, geography, and spiritual maturity, greatly influenced the function, role, and administration of the Quorum of the Seventy. Overall, there were very few changes in the quorum during the first one hundred years. Other than debates concerning the purpose, authority, and administration of the Quorum of the Seventy, it was "business as usual." During the twentieth century, however, significant changes and modifications began to occur.

1883—REVELATION FROM TIME TO TIME

The quorums rapidly flourished and by the early 1880s there were seventy-six quorums of seventy. Some of the Saints wondered how the present organization and structure could effectively meet the needs of a burgeoning membership. This rekindled discussions about the purpose and authority of the Seventy and in 1883, John Taylor petitioned the Lord to "show unto us Thy will, O Lord, concerning the organization of the Seventies."

On 14 April 1883 John Taylor received a revelation giving further instruction regarding the Seventy. Perhaps what should have been the most salient point of these instructions was the Lord's concluding remarks. "Fear me and observe my laws, and I will reveal unto you, from time to time, through the channels that I have appointed, everything that shall be necessary for the future development perfection of my church, for the adjustment and rolling forth of my kingdom, and for the building up and the establishment of my Zion. For you are my Priesthood and I am your God."[3]

Thus, that which is *necessary* for the development of the kingdom (bringing the Church out of obscurity and darkness) will be *revealed* from *time to time* through appointed channels. When one considers the changes in the Quorum of the Seventy during the twentieth century *together*, rather than as isolated events, it becomes clear that these changes were linked steps—one step leading to the next. Through this "line upon line" approach (2 Nephi 28:30), the Lord revealed necessary changes, from time to time, regarding the Quorum of the Seventy that would accommodate unprecedented growth, meet the member's needs, and maintain doctrinal integrity.

1941—Assistants to the Twelve

Even after the 1883 revelation, not much changed regarding the quorums of the Seventy. Missionary labors continued to be the emphasis, and in hopes of making their efforts more effective, B. H. Roberts provided a manual of study in 1909 for the Quorum of the Seventy entitled *The Seventy's Course in Theology.*

Although the seventies contributed to the growth through their missionary efforts, it became increasingly clear that what seemed to work well for 8,835 members in 1835 was not working as expected for the 900,000 members by 1941. "The expanding Church," Elder John A. Widtsoe wrote, "has made it difficult, if not impossible, for the Council of the Twelve to perform, to their full satisfaction, the many duties placed upon them."[4] As a result, on 6 April 1941 five men, all high priests, were called as Assistants to the Twelve.[5] The newly called assistants were expected to minister throughout the Church as general authorities under the direction of the Quorum of the Twelve Apostles. Thus, they presided over stake conferences, spoke, toured the Church, and directed missionary labors.

Elder Widtsoe later commented: "This action shows the adaptability of the Church to changing, increasing conditions, without violating in the least the divinely established order and organization of the Church."[6] This historic change in administration could actually be viewed as a *prelude,* or initial step, to later changes to the Quorum of the Seventy. The direct correlation between the Assistants to the Twelve and the Quorum of the Seventy could not actually be seen until changes were made within the quorum in 1976.

The addition of the Assistants to the Twelve not only helped alleviate the administrative burdens of the brethren, it also helped bring about further investigation regarding the Seventy. In this light, the Lord was revealing "everything that shall be necessary for the future development . . . and rolling forth of my kingdom" from time to time and, it seems, point by point.

1961—High Priests and Seventies

Perhaps one of the most significant steps influencing the direction of future changes in the quorum began on 11 June 1961. In order to make the seventies "more serviceable and effective in their work," members of the First Council of the Seventy—the seven presidents of the quorums of the Seventy—were ordained high priests.[7] Previously, those serving in Quorums of the Seventy were ordained as seventies.

President David O. McKay explained that "members of the First Council of the Seventy are now given the authority of high priest to set in order all things pertaining to the stake and the wards, under the direction of the Twelve Apostles."[8] Not long afterward, on 12 January 1964, the seven presidents were also given sealing authority.

Some felt that ordaining the presidents of the Seventy as high priests was stirring up the fighting and debates that had occurred when the Quorum of the Seventy was formed. The quarreling in 1835 over this matter finally reached a point that it was taken before Joseph Smith for mediation. Joseph decided to separate those who were high priests from the First Quorum of the Seventy. In addition, he declared that it was contrary to the order of heaven that a high priest should be in the position of the Seventy.[9] Some felt that Joseph's comments set the doctrinal precedent and thus invalidated the First Presidency's ability to ordain the seven presidents (former seventies) as high priests in 1961.

Without considering the circumstances of the time, one may jump to conclusions by forming a hasty opinion. According to Brigham Young, for example, Joseph was more interested in keeping peace among the brethren than declaring precedent and doctrine. "I can tell you," Brigham taught, " it was to satisfy the continual teasing of ignorant men who did not know what to do with authority when they got it." He continued: "I believe there were none of the whisperings of the spirit suggesting that movement."[10] Perhaps Joseph's declaration of "contrary to the order of heaven" was directed more to issues of practical government at that time than establishing doctrine.

After 1961—A Presiding Quorum

More important, however, is the absolute need to remember that the restored gospel is contingent upon current revelation. The

Prophet Joseph taught: "This is the principle on which the government of heaven is conducted—by revelation adapted to the circumstances in which the children of the kingdom are placed."[11] Thus, when considering the order of heaven, one must consider the *revealed* order of heaven. "Had you ever thought," Elder Harold B. Lee mused, "that what might have been contrary to the order of heaven in the early 1830s might not be contrary to the order of heaven in 1960?" He concluded: "Sometimes we forget that today, here and now, we have a prophet to whom the Lord is giving instruction for our good."[12]

This point is important to remember even when it doesn't seem to fit or make sense. Joseph also taught that we "may not see the reason thereof till long after the events transpire."[13] Although the changes to the Quorum of the Seventy were revelatory, learning to understand the reasons for the changes required diligent investigation, pondering, discussion, and patience. Perhaps this is why the event of 1961 was so important to the future of the Seventy. The debate between the authority of the high priests and the Seventy has been lengthy, but as a result John Taylor, B. H. Roberts, George Albert Smith, Harold B. Lee, and Boyd K. Packer, among others, spent considerable time studying the responsibilities and ministry of the Seventy. The fruits of their investigations have not only provided a more complete understanding of the Quorum of the Seventy, but they also led to the next inspired changes.

What was once appropriate in the early formation of the Church foundered over the years. The growing Church, the international constituency, circumstances, a deepening spiritual maturity, and that which was necessary to facilitate continued growth required changes to the structure of the Quorum of the Seventy. It cannot be said that the changing Church required a *new* structure, for that is not true. What it required was a *restored* structure—the structure originally revealed to the Prophet Joseph in 1835.

For those who understood priesthood doctrines and procedure, it became plain that this 1961 event and the ensuing discoveries concerning the role of the Quorum of the Seventy would require changes with the Assistants to the Twelve, the First Quorum of Seventy, and with local quorums of seventy. It is important to note, however, that even with this understanding and the anticipation of forthcoming changes, the Lord directed the changes in his own due time and in accordance with the circumstances of the Saints.

1975—THE FIRST QUORUM OF THE SEVENTY

On 3 October 1975 President Spencer W. Kimball announced that three new general authorities were added to the First Quorum of the Seventy to "assist in the carrying forth of the work of the Lord, especially in the missionary area."[14] It was intended that this quorum would gradually increase in size with the potential of seventy members. Each member of the First Quorum of the Seventy was considered a general authority, whose service would be lifelong. This was the first step in reorganizing the Quorum of the Seventy as a presiding quorum as outlined in Doctrine and Covenants 107.

1976—CONSOLIDATING ASSISTANTS TO THE TWELVE AND THE FIRST QUORUM OF THE SEVENTY

When the reorganization of the First Quorum of the Seventy was announced in 1975, it was clear that event necessitated other changes in current Church hierarchy. As a presiding quorum, the First Quorum of the Seventy was to act under the direction of the Twelve. In fact, the Twelve were to "call upon the Seventy, when they need assistance, to fill the several calls for preaching and administering the gospel, *instead of any others*" (D&C 107:38, emphasis added).

With this in mind, the role of the Assistants to the Twelve came into question. On 1 October 1976 President Spencer W. Kimball announced changes that set the presiding quorums "in their places as revealed by the Lord."[15] Central to these changes was the consolidation of the Assistants to the Twelve and the First Quorum of the Seventy. The former Assistants to the Twelve were called as part of the First Quorum of the Seventy along with four new members. This action brought the total membership of the quorum to thirty-nine, providing a majority of the quorum and allowing them to do business.

President Kimball taught that these changes concerning the Quorum of the Seventy were considered as early as 1941 but the "scope and demands of the work at that time did not justify the reconstitution of the First Quorum of the Seventy." Obviously changes in Church membership—3.7 million in 1976—and its broadening scope justified a needed reconstitution. President Kimball felt that these key changes would "make it possible to handle efficiently the present heavy workload and to prepare for the increasing expansion and acceleration of the work."[16]

1978—EMERITUS STATUS

In October 1978 President N. Eldon Tanner said, "The very rapid growth of the Church across the world, with the attendant increase in travel and responsibility, has made it necessary to consider a change in the status for some of the Brethren of the General Authorities."[17] At this time, it was announced that those members of the First Quorum whose age or health prevented their full participation would be designated as emeritus members of the First Quorum of the Seventy. Since the calling to the First Quorum of the Seventy was a lifelong calling, those emeritus members would not be released but excused from active service. On that very day, seven members of the First Quorum of the Seventy were given emeritus status.

1984—THREE-TO-FIVE-YEAR TERMS OF SERVICE

The events of 1984 could be considered another *prelude,* or step, toward other changes in the future, namely those in 1989. In April 1984 six new members of the First Quorum of the Seventy were sustained to the quorum for a period of three to five years rather than for lifetime service. President Gordon B. Hinckley explained:

"In the case of the Seventy, we are putting into effect the practice long generally followed and accepted in the Church with reference to other offices. Members of the First Quorum of the Seventy are General Authorities in every sense: in calling, in responsibility, in power and authority. Theirs have been permanent appointments, and those presently serving will continue to serve. However, tenure of appointment is not important insofar as the work is concerned." This change would also provide an "infusion of new talent and a much widened opportunity for men of ability and faith to serve in these offices."[18]

1986—STAKE QUORUMS OF SEVENTY

Prior to his call as a general authority, Boyd K. Packer engaged in an exhaustive study of the priesthood and the offices of the priesthood. Sometime after his calling as an apostle in April 1970, Elder Packer was asked by the Brethren to prepare a document briefly detailing all the past discussions and decisions regarding the seventies. He consulted the scriptures, historical records, and personal notes of John Taylor, George Albert Smith, and Harold B. Lee.

With this strong comprehensive background, Elder Packer reviewed Doctrine and Covenants 107 again and became particularly interested in verse 10: "High Priests . . . have a right to officiate . . . in administering spiritual things, and also in the office of an elder, priest, . . . teacher, deacon, and member." Although this verse did not mention the Seventy specifically, Elder Packer felt verse 10 was "a verse on the Seventy that should be added to the others." He concluded that this verse clearly declared that while a high priest could officiate as a deacon, teacher, priest, and elder, he "could not officiate in the office of a Seventy." He took his discovery to Elder Bruce R. McConkie and found that he too had never considered verse 10 in that light.[19]

Prior to this time the order of priesthood government had always been listed as deacon, teacher, priest, elder, seventy, high priest, *seventy* (typically meaning the First Quorum of the Seventy), and apostle. According to this list, it was assumed that a priest, for example, could officiate in the duties of a priest, teacher, and deacon. Likewise, an apostle could officiate in the duties of apostle, *seventy,* high priest, seventy, elder, priest, teacher, and deacon. This hierarchical ordering logically prohibited a deacon from officiating in any office *above* his own. One can easily see that the early arguments between the seventies and high priests regarding who was "greater" was based on this hierarchical listing of priesthood offices.

This insight was more than a clarification of who could officiate in what office. It reconstituted the entire foundation for priesthood government in general and required a new way to think of Church government and priesthood advancement. It became clear, in light of Doctrine and Covenants 107, that the Lord had always intended, since 1835, for priesthood government to be ordered as deacon, teacher, priest, elder, high priest, seventy, and apostle. With this understanding and combined with other scriptural references regarding the Quorum of the Seventy, it became obvious that the Lord intended the Quorum of the Seventy to be a *presiding* quorum like the First Presidency and the Quorum of the Twelve (see vv. 22–26).

With this new perspective of priesthood organization it would be impossible, even contrary to the order of heaven, for a high priest to officiate as a Seventy (meaning general authority) by virtue of his office in the priesthood alone. It would, however, be possible for a Seventy (a member of the presiding quorum) to officiate as a high priest, elder, priest, teacher, and deacon. Naturally, this perspective necessitated certain changes to the local quorums of seventy.

A monumental change regarding the Quorum of the Seventy occurred on 4 October 1986. This change, unlike so many previous changes concerning the Quorum of the Seventy, seemed to be less linked to the increasing numbers and administrative needs of a growing church than it was the final change to a movement officially started in 1975. With the move to make the First Quorum of the Seventy a presiding quorum, as revealed in 1835, it became increasingly clear that the stake quorums of seventy must be changed.

Thus, almost eleven years after the changes to the First Quorum of the Seventy were initiated, it was announced that the "seventies quorums in the stakes of the Church are to be discontinued, and the brethren now serving as seventies in these quorums will be asked to return to membership in the elders quorums of their wards."[20] Any man ordained to the office of seventy from this point forward would be a member of the presiding hierarchy of Church government.

1989—THE SECOND QUORUM OF THE SEVENTY

As President Gordon B. Hinckley turned the time to President Thomas S. Monson for the sustaining of general Church officers on 1 April 1989, he said: "This will include some business of great significance and interest to all of us."[21] After sustaining members of the First Presidency and Quorum of the Twelve Apostles, President Monson announced: "With the continued rapid growth of the Church, the First Presidency and the Quorum of the Twelve have determined that the time has come to take additional steps to provide for the expansion and regulation of the Church. We announce, therefore, the organization of the Second Quorum of the Seventy to become effective immediately."[22]

Since April 1984 the number of men called into the First Quorum of the Seventy as nonlifetime servants increased to thirty. Similar to the transition in 1976 where the Assistants to the Twelve were made members of the First Quorum of the Seventy, twenty-eight members of the First Quorum of the Seventy, all called in temporary service, were sustained as new members of the Second Quorum of the Seventy along with eight newly called members. These men were to be considered general authorities serving under a five-year call.[23]

President Hinckley later referred to members of this new quorum as "wise and mature men with long experience in the Church and with freedom to go wherever circumstances dictate."[24]

This historic announcement of forming a second Quorum of the Seventy is completely in line with the 1835 revelation: "And they shall have seven times seventy in accordance with the needs and growth of the Church" (D&C 107:96). After the formation of the Second Quorum of the Seventy in 1989, it was hard to imagine any other possible changes to the Quorums of the Seventy. It seemed that all things had been properly reconstructed according to the designs of the Lord as was revealed in both scripture and through the living prophets.

1997—AREA AUTHORITY SEVENTIES

In October 1967, under the direction of President David O. McKay, 69 regional representatives of the Twelve were called to "carry counsel to and to conduct instructional meetings in groups of stakes or regions as may be designated from time to time."[25] By 1997 the number of regional representatives had grown to an unwieldy 284. On 1 April 1995 President Gordon B. Hinckley announced that on 15 August 1995 all regional representatives would be released and that area authorities would be chosen from experienced high priests.[26]

The final significant change to the Quorum of the Seventy in the twentieth century occurred on 5 April 1997. It was determined that area authorities were to be ordained seventies. As such, they would belong to a quorum presided over by the Presidents of the Seventy and under the direction of the Quorum of the Twelve Apostles, Presidents of the Seventy, and the area presidencies where they live. These new seventies, now known as area authority seventies, are to serve in a voluntary capacity in their area of residence for a "period of years."[27] This meant that these men would maintain their own residence and employment and at the conclusion of their service, they would return to their respective wards and stakes and meet with their high priests group.

Three new quorums of area authority seventies were organized. Presently, every geographical area of the world is assigned to a particular quorum of area authority seventies:

Third Quorum of Seventy: Europe, Africa, Asia, Australia, and the Pacific.

Fourth Quorum of Seventy: Mexico, Central America, and South America.

Fifth Quorum of Seventy: United States and Canada.

President Hinckley outlined the responsibilities of the area authority seventies as: "(a) preside at stake conferences and train stake presidencies, (b) create or reorganize stakes and set apart stake presidencies, (c) serve as counselors in Area Presidencies, (d) chair regional conference planning committees, (e) serve on area councils presided over by the Area Presidency, (f) tour missions and train mission presidents, and (g) complete other duties as assigned."[28]

With the newly established quorums of seventy, the growth of the Church and the effective link from members to presiding quorum will not be limited or ineffective.

CONCLUSION

The changes to the Quorum of the Seventy in the twentieth century have been a wondrous witness of continued revelation to the modern Church. When the changes concerning the Quorum of the Seventy during the twentieth century are considered together, a deeper appreciation for Elder Widtsoe's 1941 comment is realized. He said: "This action [not just the change in 1941 but all the changes during the century] shows the adaptability of the Church to changing, increasing conditions, without violating in the least the divinely established order and organization of the Church."[29]

No wonder President Gordon B. Hinckley, nearing the close of the twentieth century, could testify with assurance that "the Lord is watching over His Kingdom." He then said, "He is inspiring leadership to care for its ever growing membership."[30] With inspiration guiding diligent study, contemplation, and prayerful investigation, we remain in the light of divine direction and, as a result, the quorums of the seventy, especially as presently constituted, still serve to bring the Church out of obscurity and out of darkness.

NOTES

1. Joseph Young Sr., *History of the Organization of the Seventies* (Salt Lake City: Deseret News Steam Printing Est., 1878), 1–2; D&C 107; Joseph Smith, *History of The Church of Jesus Christ of Latter-day Saints,* ed. B. H. Roberts, 7 vols. 2d ed. rev. (Salt Lake City: The Church of Jesus Christ of Latter-day Saints, 1932–51), 2:182n.

2. Young, "Enoch and His City," in *History of the Organization of the Seventies,* 12.

3. John Taylor, in James R. Clark, comp., *Messages of the First Presidency of The Church of Jesus Christ of Latter-day Saints,* 6 vols. (Salt Lake City: Bookcraft, 1965–75), 2:354.

4. John A. Widtsoe, "Assistants to the Twelve," *Improvement Era,* May 1941, 288.

5. Marion G. Romney, Thomas E. McKay, Clifford E. Young, Alma Sonne, and Nicholas G. Smith.

6. Widtsoe, "Assistants," 288.

7. Harold B. Lee, in Conference Report, October 1961, 81.

8. David O. McKay, in Conference Report, October 1961, 90.

9. Smith, *History of the Church,* 2:476.

10. Brigham Young, in *Deseret News,* 6 June 1877.

11. Smith, *Teachings of the Prophet Joseph Smith,* sel. Joseph Fielding Smith (Salt Lake City: Deseret Book, 1976), 256.

12. Lee, in Conference Report, October 1961, 81.

13. Smith, *Teachings,* 256.

14. Spencer W. Kimball, in Conference Report, October 1975, 3.

15. Spencer W. Kimball, in Conference Report, October 1976, 10.

16. Ibid.

17. N. Eldon Tanner, in Conference Report, October 1978, 23.

18. Gordon B. Hinckley, in Conference Report, April 1984, 4.

19. Lucille C. Tate, *Boyd K. Packer: A Watchman on the Tower* (Salt Lake City: Bookcraft, 1995), 236.

20. Ezra Taft Benson, in Conference Report, October 1986, 64.

21. Gordon B. Hinckley, in Conference Report, April 1989, 22.

22. Thomas S. Monson, in Conference Report, April 1989, 22.

23. John K. Carmack and Hans B. Ringger, who were originally called as members of the First Quorum of the Seventy with three-to-five-year terms, were extended lifetime callings in the First Quorum of the Seventy on 1 April 1989. In the early stages, the time of provisional

service was announced as three to five years. After 1987 it was often announced as a five-year calling. As late as April 1997, however, the length of service was again said to be three to five years.

24. Gordon B. Hinckley, in Conference Report, April 1997, 4.

25. Harold B. Lee, in Conference Report, October 1967, 105.

26. Gordon B. Hinckley, in Conference Report, April 1995, 71.

27. Gordon B. Hinckley, in Conference Report, April 1997, 4.

28. Ibid.

29. Widtsoe, "Assistants to the Twelve," 288.

30. Hinckley, in Conference Report, April 1997, 5.

CHAPTER TWENTY-TWO

RELIEF SOCIETY IN THE TWENTIETH CENTURY

BARBARA B. SMITH AND SHIRLEY W. THOMAS

From the time the Church was organized in 1830, its members were plagued by persecution. Brigham Young was happy to bring his followers to the arid valley of the Great Salt Lake, a place no one else wanted to settle, where they could be a people apart and have the freedom to establish their way of life in peace. But near the turn of the century many of the leaders began to recognize that "the Church could not survive, let alone expand, if it retained its identity as a kingdom separate from the world."[1] Typical of problems resulting from their isolation was the debate still festering in the U.S. Senate (1903 to 1907) over the question of whether to seat the recently elected Utah senator, Reed Smoot, who was also a member of the Quorum of the Twelve Apostles. Church leaders saw a need for greater association with those not of our Church, and they urged the members to reach out in kindness to others.

It was time for the Latter-day Saints to find their place in the world. Having laid the foundation for the Church, they needed now to "bring it forth out of obscurity" (D&C 1:30). Women of Relief Society were to play a distinctive and important role in helping bring this to pass. Recounting here some of the specific ways they have helped will highlight a wheat storage program, leadership excellence

---

Barbara B. Smith served as general president of the Relief Society of The Church of Jesus Christ of Latter-day Saints from 1974 to 1984. Shirley W. Thomas served with her as second counselor in the Relief Society general presidency from 1978 to 1983.

in national and international women's organizations, and enthusiasm for political success in the Lord's cause.

WHEAT STORAGE PROGRAM

The Relief Society began a wheat storage program in the fall of 1876, at the request of Brigham Young; by the beginning of the twentieth century, their granaries were filled and waiting for the "time of need" President Young had advised might come. A report of the first annual meeting of the Central Grain Committee in 1877 reveals some of the ways the women acquired their supply:

"The aggregate amount of grain reported in good condition stored within the year, since Nov. 17, 1876 up to the present time is 10,465 bushels. Of this wheat 299 1/2 bushels were gleaned by the sisters of the Relief and Young Ladies' Societies. Fifty bushels were bought with Sunday eggs saved by the good sisters of Deweyville, Box Elder County. . . . There is also a quantity of flour stored and held in trust . . . besides many articles, such as quilts, carpets, and other products of the labors of the sisters in their organizations as Societies, which they intend disposing of to purchase wheat."[2]

The sisters' wheat was lent to farmers whose crops had failed and also to bishops for the use of the poor. Then, at the time of the earthquake and fire in San Francisco, in 1906, a carload of flour was promptly dispatched to aid the distressed. Relief Society wheat was reportedly the first to arrive in the stricken city.[3] Other Relief Society shipments followed. The next year a famine in China signaled the shipment of another carload. In 1918 during World War I, at the request of the United States government and at a price set by it, the Relief Society sold its wheat to the government with the consent and approval of the First Presidency and presiding bishopric.

Clarissa Williams, writing in the *Relief Society Magazine* of August 1918, said: "The Relief Society has turned over to the United States Government over two hundred thousand bushels of wheat. Grain that was gleaned in aprons, bought with the difficult dimes and nickels of the faithful sisters, stored in their own or hired granaries for nearly half a century against a time of famine."[4]

On the floor of the House of Representatives, Utah Congressman M. H. Welling gave glowing tribute to the sisters of the Relief Society for their 205,518 bushels of wheat. His remarks were carried in hundreds of newspapers throughout the United States. Then on Thursday, 18 September 1918, while stopping in Salt Lake City, President and Mrs. Woodrow Wilson called on General Relief Society President Emmeline B. Wells and extended thanks to her on behalf of the United States government for the Relief Society wheat.[5]

The sisters' response to a prophet's call to store wheat allowed them to meet the needs of the hungry, while helping to make known in the world the work of the Lord. At the time Relief Society was organized, Sister Emma Smith, president, said to the women, "We are going to do something *extraordinary* . . . we expect extraordinary occasions and pressing calls."[6] Feeding the hungry of San Francisco, of China, and of large areas of the United States with wheat gathered and stored by this relatively small group of women living in scattered settlements on the western frontier *was* extraordinary. Clearly it was an evidence of uncommon faith and works.

The Relief Society Building in Salt Lake City is adorned with golden sheaves of wheat on the window panels. More than just a decoration, the wheat represents grain gathered and stored by the women of Relief Society for over a hundred years, in response to the call of a prophet. And in a way, it symbolizes all the work of Relief Society women—the work of nurturing life.

NATIONAL AND INTERNATIONAL WOMEN'S ORGANIZATIONS

In quite another way, Relief Society helped to bring the Church out of obscurity during the tenure of President Belle S. Spafford. Her nearly thirty years as general president were marked by many outstanding accomplishments. Even one role that she undertook quite reluctantly resulted in bringing great distinction and recognition to her—and thereby to the Church. The Relief Society had participated in the National Council of Women since 1891—the days of Zina D. H. Young.[7] Yet when Sister Spafford first became general president, she was of the opinion, and indicated to her counselors, that the national council no longer had anything to offer the Relief Society, and they should withdraw their membership. Belle Spafford's first visit as a representative to the council had not been a pleasant one, and this may have contributed to her adverse feelings.

At the time of that visit she was not the general president but a Relief Society general board member. She seems to have gone alone to the meetings, and "at luncheon [she] attempted to find a place to sit at several tables where there were empty chairs, but at each table, the women, knowing she was a Mormon from Utah, told her the seats were taken. After being refused a seat at every available table, Belle approached the Council president 'Where would you like me to sit? It seems that all the chairs are taken.' The president, assessing the situation, graciously asked Belle to sit next to her at the head table."[8] It was not an easy experience.

Sister Spafford made the proposal to terminate their membership in the national council to her advisor, President George Albert Smith. She may have been a little surprised at his response: "Do you always think in terms of what you get? Don't you think it's well to think in terms of what you have to give?" He then urged, "I think Mormon women have something to give to the women of the world and they may also learn from them. Rather than to terminate this membership, I suggest that you take two or three of your ablest board members and go to these meetings. . . . Go back and make your influence felt."[9] This she did and became one of the most dedicated members of the group.

Keeping in mind President Smith's advice, Belle Spafford gave generously of her time and talent to help further the well-being of women through this organization. During her many years on the National Council of Women, she served in their most important committees and delegations and made a significant difference in the work. When she was nominated to be president, however, she turned the nomination down, believing that she could not serve effectively as president of both the national council and the Relief Society.[10] She was obliged, though, to reverse her decision at the recommendation of Church president David O. McKay. Dutifully accepting the nomination, she was unanimously elected president.[10]

Belle was pleased with the council's accomplishments during the two years she served as president. Then, "she chaired the Constitutional Revision Committee that reviewed and rewrote the constitution and bylaws of the organization."[11] Again, the words, "Let your influence be felt," rang clearly. After more than twenty-nine years of representing Relief Society as its president on the National Council of Women, Belle Spafford was released from her Church calling. This changed her role on the council, though she continued her affiliation.

On one memorable occasion, the president, seeing the familiar face in the crowd of women awaiting the start of a meeting, hurried over and asked Sister Spafford to come sit at the head table. But Belle declined since she had been released from the Relief Society presidency and thus from the executive board of the council. The president, however, insisted. So Belle found herself seated at the long table with the dignitaries, notable women from many countries, and representing prominent women's organizations.

"As the meeting began, the president introduced each of the women by name, country, and organization; but when she came to Belle, she simply said, 'You all know our dear Belle.' The women at the long table rose to give Belle a standing ovation."[12] The Mormon woman from Utah who was shunned by many of the women when she first attended a council meeting and could find none who would invite her to join them at their luncheon table, had, through succeeding decades, served them in the most responsible positions, even directing the rewriting of their constitution and bylaws. In all these years of working with the women of the council, who are themselves leaders of other women, her influence had indeed been felt. Along with the love so evident in the president's introduction, she was respected and admired and, as on this particular day, honored with the collective tribute of esteemed women from throughout the world.

POLITICAL SUCCESS

In much the way Belle Spafford had been advised by President George Albert Smith to participate with the National Council of Women and make her influence felt, Barbara Smith was charged by the brethren with another kind of responsibility. She was to proclaim the Church's position regarding the highly controversial Equal Rights Amendment to the Constitution of the United States. She would carry the word throughout the nation in Relief Society meetings, women's conferences, and similar gatherings, for the intent that the proposed law would not be ratified by the states. Although Church leaders were in favor of equal rights for women, they held that this amendment to the constitution was not the way to achieve that end.

Indeed, they believed that the establishment of such a law would prove a disadvantage to women and a threat to the home.

Barbara B. Smith had succeeded Belle Spafford as general president of Relief Society in 1974. Only weeks after being sustained, she was called into the Special Affairs Committee of the Church to discuss this assignment and the amendment itself, and particularly its potential danger to the home. This meeting was the beginning of a long season in which efforts were directed toward informing people of the dangers and the problems that could come about with the ratification of this proposed amendment. Sister Smith gave scores and scores of talks and traveled thousand of miles as she defended the Church's position. She said that at one point she was feeling sorry to have to spend so much time with this issue, then she realized how important it was that the Church had taken a stand and how critical it was to the safety of the homes of the Saints.

Her efforts, along with those of other like-minded people, had mattered, for in the end, the proposed amendment did not receive enough support for ratification. Because the equal rights matter was so much debated and had far-reaching implications, it received wide media coverage. Through this, the Church and its beliefs became known to many—the flood of mail received in the Relief Society building over this issue testified of that. Some other experiences that were a part of this effort also clearly gave the Church greater visibility.

One day the program director of the *Phil Donahue Show* called Barbara Smith to ask her to appear on this popular television talk show. Sister Smith and Beverly Campbell, a public affairs representative for the Church in Washington, D.C., appeared together in a one-hour show presenting the Church's position. The resulting avalanche of mail and deluge of phone calls continued long afterward. The show, which was frequently rebroadcast over the next two years, introduced many to the Church and some of its beliefs. By actually seeing Barbara Smith and Beverly Campbell, people seemed to identify with them and their cause.[13]

Another equal rights related experience had the effect of opening doors for the Church. It was associated with the dedication of the Relief Society Monument to Women in Nauvoo, Illinois. In a beautiful garden setting, eleven statues created by Dennis Smith of Alpine,

Utah, and two more by Florence Hansen, each representing a facet of a woman's life, are combined to create a monument to women. This garden was established in Nauvoo to commemorate the founding of Relief Society there in 1842.

It was in June of 1975 that the dedication was to be held. A three-day event was planned to include every possible feature to make it memorable. It would be attended by thousands of Relief Society women and many special guests. Among those to be invited was Roslyn Carter, wife of United States president, Jimmy Carter, and Sister Smith would make this invitation personally. The proper arrangements having been made, Barbara called at the White House. The First Lady was gracious, friendly, and warmly supportive of the event. Because of the Church's position and active opposition to the Equal Rights Amendment, however, it was politically inappropriate for Mrs. Carter to attend, she being in support of the ERA. She arranged for the lovely wife of a senior senator to go in her place.[14]

More than that, Mrs. Carter and her husband invited Sister Smith to serve on the National Advisory Committee for the White House Conference on Families. This was a group of twenty-one men and nineteen women selected from across the country who met in several planning sessions to assure that truly cogent discussion groups were arranged for the larger White House Conference on Families. As a result of service on this committee, Sister Smith became even better acquainted with Mrs. Carter and her husband, who continued to remain friends of the Church.[15]

One more Equal Rights Amendment–Nauvoo monument incident brought a woman of the media a clearer understanding of and appreciation for the Church. She was a smartly dressed, young, career reporter who covered the monument dedication for the United Press. After attending the dedicatory events and observing the women, conversing with many, she wrote of her personal reactions to the three-day event in a letter. She pointed out that she had always thought Mormon women were slaves to their homes and families, living benighted lives in this modern day of freedom; she now understands that Mormon women know exactly what they are doing. They see clearly the alternatives available to women in this day. They have *chosen* to stay in their homes because they believe that is the place they can make the greatest difference with their lives. She ends, "I only wish I had that same commitment in my life."[16]

WOMEN HELPED BRING THE CHURCH OUT OF OBSCURITY

These have been examples of how, during the twentieth century, women helped to bring the Church out of obscurity while fulfilling Church assignments. They are only representative; other instances could be mentioned. Some will remember the five concerts in 1982 featuring highly accomplished Latter-day Saint women, including a Metropolitan Opera soprano, a young cellist prodigy, and so many more, performing in five leading concert halls across the country from Constitution Hall in Washington, D.C., to Dallas, Los Angeles, Oakland, and Abravanel Hall in Salt Lake City.

The current Church audience is aware of the thousands of Relief Society-made quilts having been sent to war-ravaged countries, an ongoing literacy program that changes lives, and goodwill efforts to unite women in the work of the Lord.[17]

"Bringing forth out of obscurity" is a work women do well. An army of sixty thousand missionaries spread across the globe, coming largely from Latter-day Saint homes with Latter-day Saint homemakers is witness to this. Woman is forever Eve. She nurtures, heals, and helps love grow. She is the mother of all living. This is true with people, and in the Church it has been true with programs. The Primary and Young Women began in Relief Society; so also did the making of sacred clothing, now Beehive Clothing Manufacturing. Most of the Church social services—department by department—found a beginning with Relief Society until they grew big enough to leave their Relief Society home. This has been true also with the wheat.[18]

The Relief Society wheat storage had continued actively or in trust for over a hundred years. Each general Relief Society president accepted the charge from the last, considering it a sacred trust. Then in October 1978, the following action was taken in the welfare meeting of general conference, as the Relief Society wheat became part of a Church Welfare Services, worldwide grain storage program.

President Barbara B. Smith, speaking in the Tabernacle said, "The Relief Society General Presidency has prayerfully considered the matter of their wheat stewardship and has decided that this responsibility has now been fulfilled. It is time to include the Relief Society wheat in the worldwide Church grain storage program." She continued, "We wish to propose that the 266,291 bushels of Relief Society wheat now be made a part of the grain storage plan of Welfare Services for the benefit of all the Church and that the *wheat fund [$1,651,157] be used exclusively for purchase of grain.* This action is unanimously supported by the Relief Society General Board. We have also written to other stakes and missions recorded as holding wheat certificates . . . and have received their unanimous support."

Sister Smith concluded, "With President Kimball's permission, I would like to ask the sisters present in this meeting also to affirm this action. All sisters in favor of joining with us in the decision to include the Relief Society wheat in the worldwide Church grain storage program, please signify." (All voted in the affirmative.)

In response, President Kimball urged, "Let this gift from the Relief Society today be an example of the cooperative effort and harmony that can enrich our lives in the Church and in the home."[19]

The Relief Society wheat had already brought attention to the Lord's work with the 1918 visit of President and Mrs. Woodrow Wilson. As a part of the welfare grain storage it enjoyed the visit of another United States president on 11 September 1982. On this day President Ronald Reagan, in an effort to learn from the Church's successful practices in taking care of its own, visited an operating Church Welfare Center in Hooper, Utah.

The giving of the wheat marked the end of an era for the Relief Society, but in each age women have responded to needs as they have become aware of them. In the late 1970s, as more and more matters concerning women required answers, the Relief Society presidency with the approval of their advisors and the cooperation of Brigham Young University, established a Women's Research Institute. Located on the BYU campus, the institute staff researched topics of importance to students and faculty of the university as well as the Relief Society general presidency and board.

At this period also the Relief Society joined with women of Brigham Young University in organizing women's conferences. Held each year at BYU, these featured a wide array of gospel-related lectures and classes of particular interest to women. Women's conferences, while starting modestly, grew to become a major event each year hosting tens of thousands of women, many coming from long distances. They offered extraordinary learning opportunities for the women with classes taught at a university level, often by BYU and LDS institute of religion faculty.

These educational advances reflected a new emphasis on learning and especially gospel learning for Relief Society women and another way for them to have influence in the world about them. The impact defies measurement, but one can imagine the effect of thousands of women who come to learn at the women's conferences each year and then go back to their homes, families, wards, neighborhoods, and communities as living witnesses of what increased knowledge, and hopefully, a greater understanding of how to implement the gospel in their lives can mean.

Finally, a word about Relief Society's well-known "charity never faileth," or, as it has been rendered in Spanish, "the love that never ceaseth to be" (1 Corinthians 13:8). The Prophet Joseph Smith taught the sisters from 1 Corinthians, and soon afterward they selected the beginning phrase as their motto.[20] It is hoped that charity—loving kindness, the pure love of Christ—may color all that women of Relief Society do.

President Gordon B. Hinckley, in a general conference near the end of the century, called particular attention to the need for charity. He mentioned the matter of some "other faiths who do not regard us as Christians" and pointed out that this need not concern us since it is how we regard ourselves that matters. But then he made the case for kindness: "Love and respect will overcome every element of animosity. *Our kindness may be the most persuasive argument for that which we believe.*"[21] Treating people with loving kindness can persuade them of one's belief in Christ.

As the early Church leaders in this century urged their members to reach out to others in kindness, so our prophet at the century's close has that counsel for members today. Peter, too, knew that in this way we show "forth the praises of him who hath called [us] out of darkness into his marvellous light" (1 Peter 2:9).

NOTES

1. Jill Mulvay Derr, Janath Russell Cannon, and Maureen Ursenbach Beecher, *Women of Covenant: The Story of Relief Society* (Salt Lake City: Deseret Book, 1992), 153.

2. *History of Relief Society 1842–1966* (Salt Lake City: General Board of Relief Society, 1966), 110.

3. Derr, Cannon, and Beecher, *Women of Covenant,* 166.

4. *History of Relief Society,* 110.

5. Ibid.

6. In Derr, Cannon, and Beecher, *Women of Covenant,* 31.

7. Ibid., 137.

8. Janet Peterson and LaRene Gaunt, *Elect Ladies* (Salt Lake City: Deseret Book, 1990), 155.

9. Derr, Cannon, and Beecher, *Women of Covenant,* 336.

10. Ibid., 337.

11. Ibid., 338.

12. Peterson and Gaunt, *Elect Ladies,* 145.

13. Barbara B. Smith, *A Fruitful Season* (Salt Lake City: Bookcraft, 1988), 163–69.

14. Derr, Cannon, and Beecher, *Women of Covenant,* 262–64.

15. Peterson and Gaunt, *Elect Ladies,* 177.

16. Personal letter in author's files.

17. Smith, *Fruitful Season,* 197.

18. *History of Relief Society,* 42, 47, 65, 93, etc.

19. Barbara Smith, in Conference Report, October 1978, 114–16.

20. *History of Relief Society,* 43.

21. Gordon B. Hinckley, in Conference Report, April 1998, 3–4; emphasis added.

CHAPTER TWENTY-THREE

"TO TAKE THE TEMPLES TO THE PEOPLE"

JOHN C. THOMAS

When the twentieth century opened, The Church of Jesus Christ of Latter-day Saints operated four temples. All four stood in Utah, and all had been commenced during the life of Brigham Young. At the October 1999 general conference, as the century drew to a close, President Gordon B. Hinckley reviewed progress toward the goal of having one hundred temples in service by the end of the year 2000. He reported that sixty-eight temples would be dedicated to their sacred purposes by the close of 1999, with as many as forty-two more ready in the following year, so that the goal might well be surpassed. In fact, the Boston Massachusetts Temple, the one hundreth temple, was dedicated on 1 October 2000.

Reflecting on the "tremendous undertaking" launched in 1998, he said, "You cannot believe what is involved in it unless you are closely associated with the process." In spite of the challenges, however, President Hinckley affirmed that the Church would go on building temples "for as long as the Lord wills that it be done." The proliferation of temples marked not only the Church's growth in numbers but also "the increase of faith and obedience to the principles of the gospel" by Latter-day Saints around the globe. The remarkable acceleration of temple building in the twentieth century was unprecedented, but it was foreseen in prophecy and directed by revelation.[1]

John C. Thomas is a professor of religious education at Brigham Young University–Idaho.

NINETEENTH-CENTURY GLIMPSES OF THE
FUTURE OF TEMPLE BUILDING

The Saints struggled mightily to complete six temples in the nineteenth century, including those left behind in Kirtland and Nauvoo. In the course of their struggles, their concept of the relationship between building temples and building Zion evolved. In 1884, for example, Erastus Snow recalled how his vision of the work had developed:

"The time was that we looked for one temple. The early revelations given to the Latter-day Saints predicted *a* temple in Zion, and Zion in our minds at that time was a little place on the Missouri River in Jackson County. . . . Our ideas of Zion were very limited. But as our minds began to grow and expand, why we began to look upon Zion as a great people, and the Stakes of Zion as numerous. . . . We ceased to set bounds to Zion and her Stakes. We began also to cease to think about a single temple in one certain place. Seeing the different Stakes of Zion that were being organized we perceived the idea, possibly, of as many temples."

Elder Snow considered it a near "certainty" that before long the Saints would be "scattered over the American continent, building temples in a hundred other places."[2]

Other apostles and prophets looked even farther afield. In 1861 Brigham Young remarked that although the gathering to the mountains would continue for some time, "Zion will extend, eventually, all over this earth." On other occasions he spoke of "hundreds" of temples on the earth, sometimes placing his vision in a millennial context, sometimes leaving the timeframe unspoken.[3] When he said that Parley P. Pratt would yet build temples in Scotland, President Young acknowledged that he did not know whether it would happen before or after "the earth is glorified."[4]

When Brigham Young died, only one of the temples he had planned was finished—St. George. John Taylor and other successors shared Brigham's belief that the Saints would yet build "hundreds"of temples. These prophets encouraged the Saints to exhibit faith and to pay tithes to make it possible. In 1877 President Taylor remarked that "the spirit of Temple-building comes in the very same way as that of gathering together," that God had revealed the principle and "put it [into the hearts of the Saints], and we cannot get rid of it." Six months later, reviewing the labor on Utah's temples, President Taylor observed that the Saints seemed to have done about "the best they could," but he worried about negligence in the payment of tithing. "As a rule," he noted, "it is those who take delight in observing the law of Tithing that subscribe" their labor for temple building. Without wanting to "crowd or press upon the people," he added the following comment and exhortation: "Some people have an idea that these Temples ought to be built from the proceeds of the Tithing [alone–without voluntary labor from local members]; I do not object to it in the least, providing you will only pay your Tithing. But we cannot build Temples with something that exists only in name. You deal honestly with the Lord, handing over in due season that which belongs to his storehouse, and then we will show you whether we can not build Temples, as well as do everything else that may be required with it. In the mean time, we have got to do the best we can in these matters."[5]

NEW REVELATIONS FOR A NEW CENTURY

President Lorenzo Snow, whose administration bridged the nineteenth and twentieth centuries, made tithing a major theme of his ministry. When he asked a St. George congregation to teach their children to pay their "tithing in full," he explained that by so doing they would prepare a people to build Zion. He foresaw Zion encompassing "this entire continent" and promised that in time "there will be Temples established over every portion of the land." As the Saints prepared themselves, he added, Zion would spread "over the whole earth."[6] As a result of President Snow's vision, by 1907 his successor, Joseph F. Smith, could declare that, "At last we are in a position that we can pay as we go."[7] Like his predecessor, President Smith had a keen sense of *where* the Church should go, and he led out among the apostles in ministering to Latter-day Saints throughout the world, encouraging them to live the gospel in their homelands rather than gathering to Utah, even if it meant waiting for temple blessings.

In 1906 President Smith became the first president of the Church to visit the Saints in Europe. In Bern, Switzerland, during a tour of European missions, he felt inspired to promise members that "temples would be built in divers countries of the world."[8] Serge Balliff remembered an even more pointed promise: "The time will come when this land will be dotted with temples, where you can go and redeem your dead."⁹

The impressions of 1906 prompted other First Presidency statements in the next few years. A 1907 letter to the Netherlands Mission advised that Church policy was "not to entice or encourage people to leave their native lands," but to be "good citizens" and faithful Saints at home.¹⁰ In 1910 President Smith urged Swedish Saints not to emigrate, saying, "Be not troubled about the Temple ordinances, but live in faith and confidence in the truths, and wait patiently" at home.¹¹ Again in 1911 a First Presidency letter to a British newspaper explained that although "the establishment of the latter-day Zion on the American continent occasions the gathering of the Saints from all nations," this was neither "compulsory" nor currently even desired. Instead, Church leaders encouraged "our people [to] remain in their native lands and form congregations of a permanent character to aid in the work of proselyting."¹² Still, the hope for temple blessings drew some European Saints across the Atlantic, a fact that even non-Mormon immigration officials could recognize.¹³

President Smith saw that permanent congregations far from Church headquarters would require temples closer to them. As he toured Alberta in 1913, he dedicated a temple site at Cardston. Then in 1915, while visiting his old mission field of Hawaii, he felt impressed to dedicate a spot for a temple there. In general conference that year, President Smith shared his feelings about such temples.

Speaking first of the Alberta Temple, he cited the case of a faithful returned missionary, living in northern British Columbia, without the means to travel to a temple in Utah to be married. "Well, what can you do under circumstances of that kind?" the president asked. Answering his own question, he explained that the young man was given permission to be married by a bishop and sealed later. "What else could we say to him? Nothing else, so we said it; but by and by we will have a temple up there, and those who are in these circumstances will not be compelled to waste all their substance in travel . . . to a temple here."

Continuing his address, the president turned his thoughts to the people of the Pacific. "They need the same privileges that we do, and that we enjoy, but these are out of their power. . . . What shall we do with them?" At this point he announced the decision to build a temple in Hawaii for the use of Saints from those islands and others, such as New Zealand, "where they can get their blessings and return home and live in peace." Having announced his decision, President Smith asked for and received a vote sustaining the decision from the assembled Saints.[14]

The Hawaii Temple was dedicated in 1919, the first temple to be completed in the twentieth century. World War I delayed completion of the Alberta Temple until 1923. It was the first temple on truly foreign soil, although many of the Canadian citizens it served had settled there as colonists from Utah. The 1923 dedicatory services in Cardston were distinctive as the largest gathering yet of general authorities outside the United States. In his remarks at the services, President Heber J. Grant expressed satisfaction at the growing geographical dispersion of temples and he anticipated more to come, when conditions allowed.

"I believe the Lord is pleased—in fact I do not believe it, but know it—with our arranging, as far as possible, to accommodate the people that they will not have to take long trips in order to reach the Temples. I have no doubt in my mind that Temples of the Lord will be erected in Europe, none whatever. How soon that will come I do not know. It will not come until the spirit of peace has increased among the people of Europe, not until the spirit of selfishness that exists today among nations has disappeared to a very great extent."[15]

In some ways, of course, the erection of temples further from headquarters actually inspired *more* members to take long trips in search of blessings not yet received. Maori members in New Zealand, disappointed when they found that they had missed the Hawaii Temple dedication, sent six couples and two single men there by boat in May 1920. For the next two decades, the *Hui Tau* (the annual conference) usually culminated in a temple excursion, despite the relative poverty of the people. Other Polynesians either visited or migrated to Oahu to get to the temple.[16]

In 1924 a Utah Saint, reading the *Handbook of Genealogy and Temple Work* for ideas on a stake temple excursion, could learn of New Zealanders traveling "all the way" to Hawaii "to participate in the work of salvation for the dead."[17]

Long-distance "caravans" began in 1927 in the Northwestern States Mission, with members and missionaries driving from British

Columbia, Washington, Oregon, Idaho, and Montana to the temple in Cardston. William R. Sloan, president of the mission from 1927–34, organized the first caravans. During an initial tour of the mission, he found that fewer than one tenth of the married members had been endowed or sealed. In Tacoma, Washington, he received a clear impression of the Spirit: "What greater work could you do than to convert these good people to the importance of this most responsible duty?" Sloan received permission from the First Presidency to organize annual caravans, and during the next eight years, excursionists participated in more than thirty thousand ordinances in the temple,[18] paving the way for caravans sponsored by other missions, and establishing the foundation for stakes and temples in the region.[19]

Temple Worship in New Languages

Despite the cultural diversity of the Hawaii Temple's far-flung patrons, temple ceremonies had been conducted there in English. The Arizona Temple was dedicated by President Heber J. Grant in 1927. This edifice, like the one in Hawaii, was seen as a gathering place for remnants of Book of Mormon peoples. In the dedication at Mesa, President Grant prayed that many "descendants of Lehi" would in time "have the privilege of entering this holy house."[20] Since the majority of Hispanic, Mexican, and Central American Saints spoke Spanish, it soon became evident that temple instruction and ordinances should be available in that language.

By 1943 the president of the Spanish-American mission could report that "within the near future sessions in Spanish will be conducted at intervals in the Mesa Temple."[21] Meticulous efforts to translate the temple ceremonies and train temple workers took time, but the promise was fulfilled in November 1945, in connection with a "General Conference of the Lamanite Members of the Church of Jesus Christ of Latter-day Saints."[22] Some two hundred Spanish-speaking Saints from Mexico and the southwestern United States gathered in Mesa on Sunday and Monday, 4–5 November. David O. McKay of the First Presidency presided and informed the participants that they were about to make history. On Tuesday, 6 November, 167 Latino Latter-day Saints received the temple endowment in Spanish, the first time it had been performed in a language other than English.

Temple president Harry Payne, who had spent the preceding weeks teaching his workers their parts in Spanish, called the event "an epoch making day for temple work."[23]

The "Lamanite excursion" became a regular and memorable event at the Arizona Temple. During the 1940s and 1950s, one excursion took place each year. Thereafter the number of excursions grew with the number of participants. For example, in 1964, 688 Saints attended the temple in two waves; in 1973, 2,345 members participated in nine different excursions during the year. Wards and stakes in and around Mesa mobilized to help organize transportation, room and board, and other care for the travelers. Eventually a 266-bed dormitory was built to house excursionists.[24]

During the 1964 temple trips, members participated in over four thousand ordinances while local volunteers staffed a nursery and provided other services. While at the temple, 119 members received patriarchal blessings. The longest trek that year was a four-thousand-mile round-trip from Guatemala. After observing the Lamanite excursion, Elder William Critchlow, Assistant to the Quorum of the Twelve, remarked that "the sacrifices these people make to get to the temple should shame some 'saints' who live near a temple but seldom, if ever, go into [it]."[25]

DESIGNING A TEMPLE FOR MANY NATIONS

The "faithfulness and diligence" of Spanish-speaking Saints at the Arizona Temple demonstrated to Church leaders the wisdom of translating temple ordinances into new languages to serve members abroad.[26] The next major step in this direction came in April 1952, when the First Presidency and Quorum of the Twelve Apostles agreed that President McKay should identify a site for a temple in Switzerland. He did so and announced construction to the Church in July 1952 during a six-week tour of Europe. The temple, considered to be relatively inexpensive, would be "the first of a new style of temple building." The idea, President McKay explained, was for the Church to "bring temples to these people by building smaller edifices . . . and more of them."[27]

"When the revelation came" to build temples "on the outskirts of Zion and beyond," President McKay testified, "there came information also as to how the same covenants . . . the same direction and

spirit should be presented to the Saints." The challenge was to present temple rites in many languages with a modest contingent of volunteer temple workers on site. The answer was to redesign the
temple's architecture and make use of new audiovisual technologies
for instruction. As he dedicated the New Zealand Temple in 1958,
President McKay stated that "Brother [Gordon B.] Hinckley has done
more in assisting to bring about this work than any other person."[28]

In the fall of 1953 President McKay had asked Brother Hinckley to
"find a way to present the temple instruction in the various
languages of Europe while using a minimum number of temple
workers." A committee including Elders Joseph Fielding Smith,
Harold B. Lee, and Richard L. Evans was charged with oversight of
the work, but Brother Hinckley soon found himself working one on
one with the president on the fifth floor of the Salt Lake Temple.
Once they agreed that a film should be used, Brother Hinckley set
about assembling the necessary team of artistic, technical, and linguistic specialists required for the project. It was necessary to produce
a different film for each language. After the English version was complete and passed inspection, productions in French, German, Dutch,
Finnish, Danish, Swedish, and Norwegian followed. Filming took
place in a large room in the temple and each phase of production
was done in a way to safeguard the sacred content of the presentation.[29]

The translation and production teams faced a deadline imposed
by the dedication of the Swiss Temple in September 1955. At least
some of the productions were ready months earlier, however. In
remarks at general conference on 2 April 1955, President McKay told
bishops not to send recent immigrants to the temple too soon,
because "arrangements are being made, and have been made for
them to hear [the temple] ceremony in their native tongue." In addition to the existing Spanish translation, production of a German version was complete, and the rites were nearly finished in Norwegian,
Danish, French, and Dutch. Indeed, President McKay reported that
"we have already had a ceremony in the temple in the Swedish
language."[30]

Gordon Hinckley carried the film and audiotape to Switzerland for
the new temple. After a delicate encounter with Swiss customs officials over the materials in his possession, he helped the local staff set

up and operate the audiovisual equipment. Dedicatory services at Zollikofen were held in seven languages over five days, from 11 through 15 September. Before leaving Utah, President McKay had declared that the coming events would "bring the people of Europe all the blessings of the Gospel they can receive in Utah."[31] Those blessings began to be administered almost immediately after the dedication.

Apparently, some provision had been made to hold an endowment session for Saints from East and West Germany right after the dedication, on Friday, 16 September, and then to begin other temple work on the following Monday. At some point, however, leaders and members from other missions asked if similar arrangements could be made to accommodate them. Thus, during forty consecutive hours, as many as 280 Saints received the endowment in six different languages,[32] thanks to a few sturdy temple workers and the "indefatigable efforts of Elder Gordon Hinckley."[33]

According to his biography, because the temple engineer had not yet been endowed, Brother Hinckley actually operated the audiovisual machinery for the first sessions on Friday, even though he had stayed up until four o'clock that morning making sure that everything was properly set up. He remained in the temple until each of the first groups had completed their session. The week's events left him physically exhausted. Still, he wrote President Stephen L Richards, "I am satisfied that it would have been extremely difficult to present the service in the six languages, and to do so effectively, without something of the program we are using."[34]

A "World Church" with Worldwide Gatherings at Temples

After the initiatives of the 1950s, only one temple was completed in the 1960s—the temple in Oakland, California. But after this brief lull, temple building advanced on a whole new scale in the 1970s and especially in the 1980–90s. The acceleration employed new technologies for presenting the temple ceremonies, as well as new plans and techniques in the construction of the sacred edifices. As a result, most temples were smaller but used space more efficiently.[35] Just as important as the material breakthroughs was prophetic guidance that affirmed the Church's worldwide reach, the need to build Zion in many lands, and the urgency of temple work for the living and the dead.

President Joseph Fielding Smith instituted a practice of holding area conferences around the world. At the first such conference, in Manchester, England, in 1971, he stated that although the temple had drawn people "from many nations" to Utah in the past, "we are coming of age as a church and as a people." As such, he affirmed, "we are and shall be a world church."[36] A year later, in Mexico City, Elder Bruce R. McConkie gave a plain definition of the "law of gathering," which stated that "the gathering of Israel consists of joining the true Church, of [accepting] . . . saving truths, and of worshiping . . . in the congregations of the Saints in all nations." He added that "every nation is the gathering place for its own people."[37]

President Spencer W. Kimball strengthened and extended this message, and his expansion of international temple building symbolized the Church's commitment to this new phase of the gathering. In 1975 he opened area conferences in Brazil and Japan with surprise announcements of temples in those lands. In August that year, he told assembled Saints in South Korea that converts had gathered to Utah in the nineteenth century "largely because that was the only place in the whole world where there was a temple." He promised the members that if they would stay at home, teach their families, and strengthen their stakes, a temple must eventually come to them.[38]

Early in 1977 President Kimball told conference-goers in Lima, Peru, of his hopes that they would soon have a temple, citing past prophecies of "hundreds of temples." Such a day would require diligent Saints, "because it takes hundreds of people to operate a temple and millions, millions of ordinances ready to be performed."[39] At this same conference, Elder McConkie articulated an overview of the historical phases involved in building Zion, similar to the message he had preached in Mexico in 1972. He taught that Saints gathered for two reasons: first, "to strengthen each other"; and second, "to be where they can receive the blessings of the house of the Lord."[40] In the current era, in preparation for Christ's second coming, both goals would be accomplished in stakes throughout the nations. As President Kimball later summarized, any convert in any nation "has complied with the law of the gathering of Israel and is heir to all of the blessings promised the Saints in these last days."[41]

The emphasis on temple blessings for the living complemented new measures to teach the significance of the redemption of the dead. In 1976 two revelations on the subject were added to the standard works by proposal of the First Presidency and a vote at general conference. The 1978 revelation on the priesthood also opened temple privileges and responsibilities to all the people of the earth, living and deceased. In addition to canonizing the visions of the past and the revelations of the present, the living prophet spoke plainly about his expectations for the Saints.

In 1977 President Kimball stated that he felt the "same sense of urgency about temple work for the dead" as he did about extending gospel blessings to the living.[42] As more temples were built, he taught, more Saints must "accept their responsibility of performing temple ordinances" and identify their kindred dead through family history research.[43]

The most concrete expressions of this urgency came just before April general conference in 1980. President Kimball announced "an expanded worldwide temple-building effort," to begin with seven new "smaller" temples patterned on "three basic designs," ranging from 8,500 to 26,000 square feet in size.[44]

A year later the First Presidency unveiled plans to build nine more temples on five continents, including the promised temples in Lima, Peru, and Seoul, South Korea. The 1981 announcement meant that there would be at least one temple on each continent of the globe. "But these temples are only the beginning," President Kimball testified; "scores" would be built worldwide "as the work progresses" with more expected to follow.[45] President Kimball said, "We hope that temple building may be continuous . . . so that Latter-day Saints in every nation can have the blessings of the temples for their families."[46]

TEMPLE BLESSINGS: THE CAPSTONE OF GORDON B. HINCKLEY'S MINISTRY

That Gordon B. Hinckley should begin his service in the First Presidency in 1981 seems appropriate, considering all he had done—and would yet do—to aid the expansion of temple work. In the spring of 1973, while serving as chairman of the Temple Committee, Elder Hinckley had written the following words in his journal: "The church could build [many smaller] temples for the cost of the Washington Temple. . . . It would take the temples to the people instead of having the people travel great distances to get to them." One reason for the Washington Temple's size was its huge temple district—the entire eastern half of the United States, plus eastern Canada, the Caribbean, and South America. A month after writing the journal entry, Elder Hinckley was scouting sites for a temple in Sao Paulo, Brazil.[47]

Because he was called into the First Presidency just as the health of its other members was failing, President Hinckley dedicated fourteen of the sixteen temples announced in spring of 1980 and 1981. In 1985, thirty years after his unobtrusive mission to the Swiss Temple, he returned to Europe to dedicate temples on both sides of the Iron Curtain; that year he also dedicated the first temple in Africa.[48] During the same year, he reflected on lessons he had learned during his recent temple-related travels:

"This great impetus in temple building was given by President Kimball under revelation from the Lord. . . . The sacred and important work that goes on in temples must be accelerated, and for this to happen, it is necessary that temples be taken closer to the people rather than having the people travel so far to temples.

"I wish that anyone who has any doubt concerning the strength and power of this cause could have had the experiences I have had in recent months in these dedicatory services in the United States, in Asia and Australia, in Mexico, Central America, and South America, in Europe and Africa. I have looked into the faces of tens of thousands of Latter-day Saints. Their skins are of varying colors and hues. But their hearts beat as one with testimony and conviction concerning the truth of this great restored work of God."

Noting that "a surge of opposition" had accompanied the surge in temple dedications, President Hinckley concluded by saying that "those few who mock our temple work . . . cannot mock the Spirit, nor can they mock the truth."[49]

As a counselor to presidents Kimball, Benson, and Hunter, Gordon B. Hinckley continued to play a pivotal role in the planning and dedication of temples and the teaching of doctrines relating to their use.[50] Howard W. Hunter, his immediate predecessor as prophet, made the temple one of the two central themes in his brief term as president. In June 1994 he invited Church members to "look to the temple of the Lord as the great symbol of your membership." President Hunter reiterated the invitation at general conference, adding that "we desire to bring the temples closer to our people."[51] His words paved the way for the century's last and largest temple-building wave—what might be seen as the symbol of President Hinckley's ministry.

In his second general conference as the prophet, seer, and revelator, President Gordon B. Hinckley affirmed his "burning desire that a temple be located within reasonable access to Latter-day Saints throughout the world."[52] When the fiftieth temple of the Church was dedicated in St. Louis, Missouri, in June 1997, it was the twenty-fifth sacred edifice to be dedicated by President Hinckley. He had dedicated one half of the operating temples and it seemed to fuel his desire to extend the work.

That fall, as he reviewed temple construction plans with priesthood holders in conference, he turned his attention to Saints in relatively small bodies and in relatively remote areas. Would such members "be denied forever the blessings of the temple ordinances?" While pondering that question on a visit to just such an area, a solution "came bright and clear" to his mind. The answer was "to take the temples to the people," building smaller edifices staffed and maintained entirely by local Saints, located where possible adjacent to existing stake centers. Though President Hinckley said little at the time about the circumstances under which the "answer" came, later comments showed that he had received a revelation on the subject while in Colonia Juarez, Mexico, in June 1997.[53]

Six months after introducing his concept of "small temples," President Hinckley astonished members with the news of plans to build thirty-two more small temples, bringing the total number of operating temples to one hundred by the end of the century. "In this program we are moving on a scale the like of which we have never seen before," so as to provide far-flung members with access to "the crowning blessings" of the Church. President Hinckley followed the announcement by urging Saints to be "honest, and even generous" tithe payers so as to sustain the work. "When these 30 or 32 are built," he assured, "there will be more yet to come," a promise borne out in the century's closing months.[54]

CONCLUSION

In the course of the twentieth century, prophets directed an unprecedented acceleration of temple building on the earth. Drawing faith from the promises of past prophets, they sought additional light to expand their own vision as well as the vision of the general membership. They taught, first, that honest tithes would give the Church freedom to act. Then they affirmed that Saints who built stable families and congregations abroad would eventually merit temples in their midst.

As congregations matured among foreign nations and peoples, prophets drew on revelation and reason to design temples that could cater to a diverse membership. After these initial breakthroughs, prophets reinforced the members' understanding of the doctrinal foundations of temple work as they accelerated and refined temple building with divine guidance. The result was a beautiful work in progress.

NOTES

1. Gordon B. Hinckley, "Welcome to Conference," *Ensign*, November 1999, 5–6. For an example of ancient prophecy relevant to the spread of temples, see 1 Nephi 14:12–14.

2. Erastus Snow, in *Journal of Discourses*, 26 vols. (London: Latter-day Saints' Book Depot, 1854–86), 25:30–31. Elder Snow's thoughts about a pan-American Zion were consistent with Joseph Smith's statement in April 1844 (see *History of The Church of Jesus Christ of Latter-day Saints*, ed. B. H. Roberts, 7 vols. 2d ed. rev. [Salt Lake City: The Church of Jesus Christ of Latter-day Saints, 1932–51], 6:318–19).

3. Brigham Young, in *Journal of Discourses*, 9:138; see also 9:273; 10:254; 13:329–31.

4. Young, in *Journal of Discourses*, 1:77.

5. John Taylor, in *Journal of Discourses*, 19:240, 309. Compare Wilford Woodruff's 1877 statement: "When we shall have built the Temples now contemplated [in Utah], we will then begin to see the necessity of building others, for in proportion to the diligence of our labors in this direction, will we comprehend the extent of the work to be done, and the present is only a beginning." The millennium, he prophesied, would be "devoted to this work of redemption; and Temples will

appear all over this land of Joseph—North and South America—and also in Europe and elsewhere" (in *Journal of Discourses,* 19:229–30).

6. James R. Clark, comp., *Messages of the First Presidency of The Church of Jesus Christ of Latter-day Saints,* 6 vols. (Salt Lake City: Bookcraft, 1965–75), 3:313. For an overview of President Snow's tithing emphasis and the resulting relief from debt, see James B. Allen and Glen M. Leonard, *The Story of the Latter-day Saints,* 2d ed. rev. and enl. (Salt Lake City: Deseret Book, 1992), 454–55. For a summary of President Snow's feelings on the need to expand the Church's international reach, see Joseph F. Smith's editorial, "The Last Days of President Snow," *Juvenile Instructor,* 15 November 1901, 688–91.

7. Joseph F. Smith, in Conference Report, April 1907, 7.

8. Joseph F. Smith, as cited in Richard N. Holzapfel, "Establishing Zion in Preparation for the Second Coming," in Kent P. Jackson, ed., *Watch and Be Ready: Preparing for the Second Coming of the Lord* (Salt Lake City: Deseret Book, 1994), 128.

9. Serge Balliff, in Conference Report, October 1920, 90.

10. Clark, *Messages of the First Presidency,* 4:165.

11. Journal History of The Church of Jesus Christ of Latter-day Saints, 31 August 1910; see also Douglas D. Alder, "German-Speaking Immigration to Utah, 1850–1950," Master's thesis, University of Utah, 1959, 69.

12. Clark, *Messages of the First Presidency,* 4:222.

13. In 1923 a federal immigrant inspector asked a Church official if "the desire to have [temple] rites performed" would not exert "a strong influence upon sincere and fervid converts to come to the United States?" "Yes, in some instances," was the wary reply (transcript of an interview between D. A. Plumly, immigrant inspector, and Harold G. Reynolds, mission secretary, no. 707–11, 2 November 1923, 2–3, in Reed Smoot Papers, box 48, folder 11, Special Collections, Harold B. Lee Library, BYU).

14. Joseph F. Smith, in Conference Report, October 1915, 8. He also spoke of former hopes "to build another temple near the borders of the United States, in Mexico." It is hard not to recognize similarities between Joseph F. Smith's statements in 1915 and those of Gordon B. Hinckley in 1997–98, when the latter announced plans to build smaller temples to reach more members of the Church. Further, both prophets seem to have received pointed impressions regarding temple building while visiting Saints abroad.

15. Alberta Temple dedication proceedings, 26–29 August 1923, as cited in "Temple Building Principles as Historically Established in the Restored Church," typescript, 27 December 1974, section I, 2–3, Special Collections, Harold B. Lee Library, BYU.

16. R. Lanier Britsch, *Unto the Islands of the Sea: A History of the Latter-day Saints in the Pacific* (Salt Lake City: Deseret Book, 1986), 166, 303.

17. *Handbook of Genealogy and Temple Work* (Salt Lake City: Genealogical Society of Utah, 1924), 259.

18. V. A. Wood, *The Alberta Temple: Centre and Symbol of Faith* (Calgary: Detselig Enterprises, 1989), 121–22.

19. William R. Sloan, "Northwestern States Temple Caravan to Cardston, Alberta, Canada, July 1930," *Utah Genealogical and Historical Magazine,* January 1931, 8; John C. Thomas, "'A Mighty Linked Chain': The Temple Caravans of the Northwestern States Mission," in Dennis A. Wright and others, eds., *Regional Studies in Church History: Western Canada* (Provo: Brigham Young University, 2000), 251–75.

20. In N. B. Lundwall, *Temples of the Most High* (Salt Lake City: Bookcraft, 1966), 173.

21. "The Forgotten People," *Liahona: The Elders' Journal,* 23 May 1944, 560.

22. Henry A. Smith, "200 Lamanites Gather in History-Making Conference, Temple Sessions," *Church News,* 10 November 1945, 1.

23. Harry L. Payne Journal, 6 November 1945, Historical Department Archives, The Church of Jesus Christ of Latter-day Saints.

24. Lucius M. Mecham, "Lamanite Excursions and Microfilming of the Mexican Missions," microfilm, ca. 1950–68, Historical Department Archives.

25. Critchlow, "Report on Assignment to Temple Excursions, 19–24 September, 10–15 October 1964," letter dated 26 October 1964 in Mecham, "Lamanite Excursions," Historical Department Archives.

26. David O. McKay in "Pres. McKay Speaks about Temple Work," *Church News,* 29 October 1955, 2.

27. Doyle L. Green and Albert L. Zobell Jr. "President David O. McKay Visits Europe," *Improvement Era,* September 1952, 634; Richard O. Cowan, *Temples to Dot the Earth* (Salt Lake City: Bookcraft, 1989), 158.

28. David O. McKay, Dedicatory proceedings of New Zealand Temple, 20–23 April 1958, "Temple Building Principles" typescript, section I, 3, Special Collections, Harold B. Lee Library, BYU.

29. Sheri L. Dew, *Go Forward with Faith: The Biography of Gordon B. Hinckley* (Salt Lake City: Deseret Book, 1996), 176.

30. David O. McKay, in Conference Report, April 1955, 14. I assume that President McKay referred to the filmed and taped version of the ceremony presented in the same room where filming took place. Another possibility exists, however: Reid Johnson, who had recently returned from a mission in Sweden, was called with others to present a Scandinavian endowment in the Salt Lake Temple in 1952 or 1953; these sessions took place in the usual instructional format, with

participants using Danish, Norwegian, and Swedish in the same session (author's interview of Reid Johnson, 23 October 1997, Holladay, Utah).

31. "Pres. McKay to Attend Choir Concert Saturday at Glasgow," *Church News*, 20 August 1955, 2.

32. S. Perry Lee, "Pres. McKay Home, Pleased with Temple, Choir," *Church News*, 24 September 1955, 2.

33. "President McKay Reminds Church Members of Abundant Blessings," *Church News*, 8 October 1955, 2–3.

34. Dew, *Go Forward with Faith*, 184. Brother Hinckley also supervised the production of temple instruction materials in Spanish, Tongan, Tahitian, Samoan, and Maori (see Wendell J. Ashton, "Gordon B. Hinckley of the Quorum of the Twelve," *Improvement Era*, December 1961, 978).

35. For examples of these refinements, see Richard O. Cowan, *Temples to Dot the Earth* (Salt Lake City: Bookcraft, 1989), 178–79, 189.

36. Joseph Fielding Smith, in Conference Report, 27–29 August 1971, 5–6.

37. Bruce R. McConkie, in Conference Report, Mexico and Central America Area General Conference, 25–27 August 1972, 45. The substance of Elder McConkie's message was subsequently quoted and endorsed by President Harold B. Lee, in Conference Report, April 1973, 6.

38. Edward L. Kimball, ed., *The Teachings of Spencer W. Kimball* (Salt Lake City: Bookcraft, 1982), 439–40.

39. Spencer W. Kimball, in Conference Report, Lima Peru Area Conference, 25–27 February 1977, 2. When Elder McConkie finished talking, the prophet endorsed his address as "a masterpiece" and urged the group to "watch for this article when it is published" (34).

40. Bruce R. McConkie, "Come: Let Israel Build Zion," *Ensign*, May 1977, 117.

41. Kimball, *Teachings of Spencer W. Kimball*, 439. This statement was made in Honolulu in June 1978, ten days after the priesthood revelation was announced.

42. Spencer W. Kimball, "The True Way of Life and Salvation," *Ensign*, May 1978, 4.

43. "'We Feel an Urgency,'" *Ensign*, August 1980, 2.

44. "Church Launches Worldwide Temple-Building Emphasis with Announcement of Seven New Temples," *Ensign*, May 1980, 102.

45. "We Are on the Lord's Errand," *Ensign*, May 1981, 78.

46. "Nine New Temples Announced," *Ensign*, May 1981, 98.

47. Dew, *Go Forward with Faith*, 325.

48. For dated information on temple dedications, see *1999–2000*

Church Almanac (Salt Lake City: Deseret News, 1998), 441–42. The stirring story of a temple in what was then East Germany is told from the pages of Thomas S. Monson's journal in *Faith Rewarded: A Personal Account of Prophetic Promises to the East German Saints* (Salt Lake City: Deseret Book, 1996).

49. Gordon B. Hinckley, "Rejoice in This Great Era of Temple Building," *Ensign*, November 1985, 54, 60.

50. Jay M. Todd, "President Howard W. Hunter: Fourteenth President of the Church," *Ensign*, July 1994, 4–5.

51. Howard W. Hunter, "'Exceeding Great and Precious Promises,'" *Ensign*, November 1994, 8.

52. Gordon B. Hinckley, "Of Missions, Temples, and Stewardship," *Ensign*, November 1995, 52.

53. Gordon B. Hinckley, "Some Thoughts on Temples, Retention of Converts, and Missionary Service," *Ensign*, November 1997, 49–50. For insight into the revelation's setting, see excerpts from the dedicatory prayer of the Colonia Juarez Temple in "Temples Dedicated in Colonia Juarez and Madrid," *Ensign*, May 1999, 115.

54. Gordon B. Hinckley, "New Temples to Provide 'Crowning Blessings' of the Gospel," *Ensign*, May 1998, 88.

CHAPTER TWENTY-FOUR

EARLY MISSIONS TO OTTOMAN TURKEY, SYRIA, AND PALESTINE

JAMES A. TORONTO

On the northwestern outskirts of Aleppo, Syria, an ancient trading city near the Turkish border, lie the cemeteries of religious communities traditionally found in the Middle East: Muslim, Catholic, Armenian, Eastern Orthodox, Protestant, and Jewish. Under a small grove of trees in the northeastern corner of the Armenian Evangelical cemetery (adjacent to the Syrian Orthodox and Jewish), two grave markers of distinctive design stand side by side, commemorating the lives and service of two LDS missionaries.

On one marker, shaped like an obelisk and cut from local sandstone, is inscribed the name and testimony of Emil J. Huber, a convert from Switzerland who died in 1908. On the other marker, of granite quarried in England and shipped to Syria, is engraved the name and epitaph of Joseph Wilford Booth, a native of Alpine, Utah, who had served as a missionary and mission president for nearly seventeen years at the time of his death in 1928. These two monuments in a far-off, exotic land bear mute witness to the fascinating but little-known story of LDS efforts to establish a presence in the Middle East beginning in the mid-nineteenth century. This article provides a brief overview of those efforts and, drawing heavily on the extensive journals of President Booth, examines some of the major

James A. Toronto is an associate professor of Arabic and Islamic studies at Brigham Young University.

events and challenges of sharing the gospel among turn-of-the-century Middle Eastern cultures and peoples.

OVERVIEW OF LDS MISSIONARY WORK IN THE MIDDLE EAST

Before World War I the map of the Middle East was much different from the one we know today. Lands that comprise the modern nations of Turkey, Syria, Lebanon, Israel, the West Bank/Gaza, and Jordan were geographic divisions of the powerful Ottoman Empire and referred to as Asia Minor, Syria, and Palestine. The Ottomans, an Islamic dynasty that reached the zenith of its power in the sixteenth century and made Constantinople its capital, had established an administrative system called *millet* that allowed religious minorities, such as Christians and Jews, a degree of autonomy so long as they did not threaten Ottoman political authority. This social, cultural, and educational autonomy, together with the relative ease of traveling between different regions of the sprawling empire, attracted the attention of foreign missionaries who were anxious to share the message of Christ in the heartlands of Islam and in the Holy Lands of Christianity.

Thus, during the nineteenth century, often referred to as the century of Christian missions, the Ottoman Middle East became a focus of intense missionary activity. As early as 1820, Protestant missionaries were toiling in the Holy Lands (those such as Palestine, Syria, Turkey, and Egypt that have significance in biblical history), and by the end of the century there were Protestant churches, schools, universities, and hospitals scattered throughout the region. Having a prominent role in Christian history, doctrine, and eschatology, the Middle East was also a focus of interest to Latter-day Saints from the earliest days of our history.[1]

The first missionary efforts of the Church in the modern Middle East were initiated in Turkey, the heartland of the Ottoman Empire. On 31 December 1884 Elder Jacob Spori, the first full-time LDS missionary in the Middle East, arrived in Constantinople to open the Turkish Mission. He had been sent from the European Mission in response to a letter written by an Armenian man, Hagop Vartooguian, who suggested that LDS missionaries would find a fertile field in Turkey. Less than a week later, on 4 January, Spori baptized Vartooguian and his family, the first converts in the new mission.

In subsequent years, finding little success among Turkish Muslims or European Christians in the capital city, the missionaries decided to move inland and began gradually to establish branches of the Church in Armenian areas of central Turkey and northern Syria: Zara, Sivas, Marash, Aintab, and Aleppo. One of the early stalwart missionaries was President Ferdinand F. Hintze, who worked for many years to preach the gospel and to solidify the Church's presence among the Armenian people, arguably the oldest Christian community in the Middle East. Aintab eventually became the largest branch in the mission and, until 1907 when the mission headquarters was moved to Aleppo, Syria, it was a center of Church activity and administration.

In February 1890 Elder Edgar D. Simmons died of smallpox and was buried in the Protestant cemetery in Aintab, the first of five LDS missionaries who passed away during missionary service and are buried in Middle Eastern soil.[2] The membership of the Turkish Mission, which never exceeded two hundred members, consisted mainly of Armenians from central Turkey and northern Syria as well as a few European and Arab converts in other parts of the mission, including Palestine, Greece, Egypt, and Lebanon.

The mission was closed in 1896 when political conflict in Turkey threatened the members and missionaries, but it was reopened in 1897. Hintze finally received permission from the Ottoman government in 1899 to publish the first LDS literature—twenty-seven thousand tracts and twenty-eight sections of the Doctrine and Covenants were printed in several languages. Another milestone was achieved in 1906 when Hintze succeeded in having the first Turkish language-Armenian script Book of Mormon published in Boston.[3] The mission was closed again in 1909 due to increasing political turmoil in Turkey, and the members remained without outside leadership and assistance for twelve years until after the end of World War I and the dissolution of the Ottoman Empire.

In 1921 the mission was reopened by Joseph Booth (serving a second time as president of the mission) and renamed the Armenian Mission, with headquarters in Aleppo, Syria. For the next seven years President Booth, joined by his wife, Reba, in 1924, sought primarily to deal with the aftermath of a devastating war. They helped alleviate the suffering of Church members and helped them rebuild their lives. In December 1928 Booth died of cardiac arrest and overexertion while working with the members in Aleppo. With Booth's death, the mission was closed and not reopened until August 1933 when Badwagan Piranian and his wife, Berta, arrived to preside over the newly named Palestine-Syrian Mission. It was closed again in 1939 with the outbreak of World War II, reopened by the Piranians in 1947 after the end of the war, and renamed the Near East Mission in 1950. The mission was discontinued in January 1951.

ORGANIZATION AND METHODS OF MISSIONARY WORK

As noted in the preceding historical sketch, the sixty-five years of mission history (1885–1950) were marked by constant interruptions and by the suffering of members and missionaries as the fledgling Church attempted to cope with the turbulence of the times. These years were among the most chaotic in modern Middle Eastern history, witnessing much warfare, economic deprivation, and political upheaval.

The various changes in the name of the mission reflected these shifting geopolitical realities. Fortunately, we have a rich historical record—correspondence, journals, newspaper articles, and personal histories written by Church leaders, converts, and missionaries—that provides a wealth of information about early LDS proselyting efforts among Middle Eastern cultures during this period in Church history. A fascinating picture of the conditions, methods, and organization of missionary work emerges from these firsthand accounts. They also provide a contrast with those of the missionary program of the Church in the late twentieth century.

The missionaries who served in the Middle East arrived in the mission field without the benefit of any formal missionary preparation, language training, or cultural orientation. Many of them left behind a wife and children when they accepted the call to serve and then traveled alone for weeks or months as they made the always adventurous and often perilous journey from the United States or Europe to far-off Turkey. They came by steamship, carriage, horse, and foot, braving ocean storms, sea sickness, treacherous mountain paths, and marauding bands of robbers. They typically arrived at their assigned destination penniless, surrounded by a bewildering array of alien languages and customs, and with no one to greet them, help them get settled in, or tell them how to begin their labors. Elder Edward Robinson provided this poignant description of his arrival in Aleppo, Syria, after an arduous journey:

"It was last October when I arrived in [Aleppo] alone, with no idea of where I should find a church member, and with only 15 cents in my pocket. For three days I had followed my drunken guide along the rocky mountain trails and over the grassy plains, both mute and sullen, for we knew not each other's language."[4]

Then there were the adjustments to strange Oriental foods and exotic customs, such as sitting on the floor and using one's fingers to eat from a common dish, going to the local Turkish *hammam* (bath house) to have a priesthood meeting or social with Church members, and the segregation of men and women—even among Christians. Most of the elders were not highly educated. Instead they came from humble working-class backgrounds. Their primary qualifications were a firm faith in God and a fervent desire to share the message of the restored gospel wherever they could. Elder Spori, a German-speaking convert from Switzerland, exemplifies this background and outlook in a letter written shortly after his arrival in Constantinople in 1885:

"If the Turks and Armenians must have a man that makes a big show, then I am not the kind for them. If you only want to find out who I am, I will tell you in a few words. During the summer I am a wood-chopper, and now a modest man sent to preach the Gospel. If you, as I suspect, are not a wealthy man, I may go and eat with you, and what I must spend here will feed us both, and I can sleep in a blanket in some corner. And further, when people are not satisfied with a humble man, let them get somebody else to preach what they like."[5]

Typically there were only a handful of missionaries working in the entire mission at one time, and they would therefore work alone in different cities far apart to maximize their coverage. Living in remote areas of the Turkish interior, working without a companion, and going long periods with little or no contact with family or Church members (the postal system was notoriously slow and unreliable), missionary work was a lonely enterprise in the years before the first congregations of native members were established. Elder Spori, for example, spent almost an entire year by himself in Turkey before another missionary arrived. Likewise, Elder Frederick Stauffer, also a native of Switzerland, labored for more than two years without the benefit of association with other missionaries.

During the first months after arrival, missionaries spent many hours each day in their rented rooms, studying Turkish, the main language of the Ottoman Empire, and trying to acquire some capacity in two of the other commonly used languages, Armenian and Arabic. Elder Don Musser expressed the frustration that many of the missionaries felt:

"Another drawback in the Syrian part of the mission is the language, which, extremely difficult of itself, is made still more so by the many other languages a missionary is continually coming in contact with. The length of time spent in this mission is scarcely enough in which to master the language under existing circumstances, and when an Elder is released he is succeeded by someone totally inexperienced regarding the tongue and customs of this ancient and peculiar people."[6]

Because open proselyting by non-Muslims was forbidden, and religious literature was often confiscated by the Ottoman authorities, missionaries used a variety of alternative methods to contact people and teach the gospel. Working in the political tinderbox of Ottoman Turkey, in an environment fraught with invisible cultural and religious sensitivities, missionaries labored constantly under threat of arrest and imprisonment.[7]

One of the most common means of generating interest was to write articles about LDS doctrine and history for the local newspapers and to include an invitation for "callers," or visitors, to come to the missionary's room for further discussion. The missionaries taught anyone they could engage in conversation, regardless of religion or nationality, and although most of the early members came from the Armenian Christian community, the cosmopolitan population of the Ottoman Empire yielded some German, Russian, Bulgarian, Arab, Greek, and Turkish converts as well.

It was common for the LDS missionaries in Turkey to adopt an itinerant style of ministry, traveling alone from city to city, staying a few days or weeks in a rented room and entertaining callers who came to discuss religion. Even though Middle Eastern customs and government restrictions prevented door-to-door contacting, Mormon missionaries were quite well known in the interior mountain regions of Asia Minor, where strangers always attracted notice and word of their arrival spread quickly.[8] While touring the mission, Elder Anthon H. Lund, a member of the Twelve, wrote a vivid account of the missionaries' approach to sharing the gospel in a new city:

"Our coming had been heralded from the pulpits. The people had been warned against us. This had the opposite effect to the one intended. The people filled our meeting house weeks before we came, and when we did come our room was filled from morning till evening by eager enquirers. . . . It was interesting to watch the crowd of people sitting on the floor listening to what was said. Sometimes they would all want to talk and then there would be a babel of voices. . . . Every evening there were gatherings in different parts of the city and we divided up the brethren and sent them to the different places to answer questions and explain the gospel."[9]

Even though this peripatetic approach to missionary work yielded a few converts, it was generally not highly effective in bringing people to baptism. The majority of native members lived in major cities where missionaries had served consistently and had gradually built up a branch of the Church. Furthermore, most converts were among the relatives or friends of these established members. The missionaries understood the drawbacks of this method, but as Elder J. Alma Holdaway explained, their goal was to make contacts and lay a foundation upon which others could build:

"With only stopping one or six weeks in a city, we hardly expect to convert and baptize any, as it takes some time to bring people up to the standard necessary, before taking them down into the water; but we hope to continue as we have been doing, in making friends to the Gospel of both Christians and Islams [Muslims], and perhaps sow seeds that those following after may reap."[10]

President Ferdinand F. Hintze acknowledged that missionary work in the Orient "required a great deal of patience" but warned missionaries against thinking that "we are of no use" or measuring success solely by numbers of baptisms: "We are sent out to warn the nations as well as to reap the souls of men, and in patiently performing this duty we shall have performed a great work, though we

may not baptize a soul. . . . Here [in Turkey] we must sow and cultivate and patiently await the fruits."[11]

RELATIONS WITH OTHER RELIGIOUS COMMUNITIES

Within the borders of the Ottoman Empire were located the Holy
Lands of three major world religions—Judaism, Christianity, and
Islam—and the historical records reflect the constant interaction of
LDS members and missionaries with each of these religious communities. The Church was not well known in the early years of the mission because newspapers did not circulate widely, and people in the
interior regions had limited access to information about life outside
of Turkey. But opposition gradually increased as LDS missionary
activity reached more and more inland cities. Most of the problems
encountered by the missionaries at the hands of the dominant
Islamic community took the form of government restrictions and
social taboos that prevented the public distribution of Christian literature, door-to-door proselyting, and the conversion of Muslims.

There were large, thriving Jewish communities scattered throughout the Ottoman Empire, and the elders were always eager to discuss
the gospel with Jewish investigators because of LDS teachings about
the gathering of Israel and the imminent return of the Jews to
Palestine. Even though they had many opportunities to engage in
lengthy religious discussions with both Muslims and Jews, only one
or two members of those groups were ever baptized. While most of
the elders visited Jerusalem and other areas of Palestine and enjoyed
generally cordial relations with Jews and Muslims, it became the
accepted practice throughout mission history to work primarily
among the Christian communities of Palestine, Syria, and Turkey.

Relations between the various Christian churches of the Ottoman
Empire were characterized by rivalry, jealousy, and strife. The LDS
missionaries soon realized that, ironically, fellow Christians were the
source of strongest opposition to their work. Most of the problems
occurred when Catholic priests or Protestant ministers circulated false
information about the Mormons in an effort to turn local government leaders against the elders and to encourage the community to
resist their teaching. In several instances, LDS children were told they
could not attend private Christian schools, a fact that effectively

denied them educational opportunity because there were no public schools for poor families in central Turkey at that time.

Malicious rumors that all Mormons had many wives, that the missionaries were guilty of immorality, and that they paid others to join their Church were widely circulated. As a result, it was common for the elders to be harassed in the streets and stores, to be arrested and jailed on flimsy charges, and to be physically threatened and stoned by mobs.

To round out the picture of the Church's relations with other Christian groups in Turkey, it should be noted that the written sources contain many examples of genuine friendship, kindness, and compassion on the part of Christians, Muslims, and Jews toward the missionaries. It is interesting to note that, unlike today, missionaries often attended Protestant and Catholic meetings and were given the opportunity to expound their religious views. Frequently they reciprocated, inviting priests and pastors as guest speakers in LDS sacrament meetings and other gatherings.

President Joseph Booth's extensive journals reveal that two of the most renowned Protestant missionaries in central Turkey, Dr. and Mrs. Fred Shepard, were good friends of President and Sister Booth in Aintab. The two couples spent many pleasant hours playing chess and conversing on subjects of mutual interest to fellow Americans living in an isolated corner of the globe. The Shepards nursed Elder Booth back to health when he was suffering the near-fatal ravages of smallpox. Protestant ministers played a prominent role in the funerals of two LDS missionaries, Elders Simmons in Aintab and Elder Huber in Aleppo, by volunteering to make burial arrangements and to give the main eulogy.[12]

Living Conditions of Members and Missionaries

For the vast majority of citizens in the Ottoman Empire at the dawn of the twentieth century, life was relentlessly harsh and unpredictable. Most families suffered much from poverty, malnutrition, illiteracy, lack of sanitary facilities and clean water, high infant mortality, and such natural disasters as famines and epidemics. Political corruption and instability created an atmosphere of apathy, fear, and mistrust among the populace, who were arbitrarily subjected to exorbitant taxes, confiscation of property for military use, forced conscription into the Ottoman army, and the prospect of long prison terms if they did not cooperate.

To make matters worse, the Ottoman government viewed Christians and other religious minorities with suspicion, often accusing them of supporting Turkey's adversaries in the Christian West and of being therefore disloyal, untrustworthy subjects. Elder Hintze summed up the plight of the Armenians: "Having been driven to the wall by oppression and despotism, they are almost hopeless in the world. They see no relief in the future, but feel as a nation that they have no friends in the world."[13]

Journals and letters reflect the ambivalence that many missionaries felt as they enjoyed picturesque landscapes and historical sites, met fascinating people, and experienced the dust, heat, flies, foul water, and grim living conditions found in nearly every town and village. Elder Frederick A. Huish, after observing that Aleppo is a beautiful city when seen from afar, commented on the reality at street level:

"There are only a few streets in the city, and each one of them runs in almost every direction and is so narrow that a camel with a couple of sacks on his back crowds the pedestrians against the walls. A great deal of rubbish and slops are thrown into the streets, and you must keep your eyes open or you will catch some of it on your head, and, notwithstanding the efforts of the street sweepers who haul the trash away on the backs of little donkeys, they are very dirty and filthy, good nurseries for cholera and other diseases."[14]

The missionaries' journals also record that these "nurseries" did in fact create many serious health problems for those living in these impoverished, underdeveloped areas, including cholera epidemics and outbreaks of malaria, typhoid, and smallpox.

As mentioned earlier, most of the missionaries were constantly on the move and frequently stayed in the homes of villagers or in small inns (Turkish, *khan*) because they were cheap. The best-known travel guide of the time, however, contained a graphic description of these places and a warning to travelers to avoid using them: "The khan, or caravanserai, and the huts of the peasants, which are generally built of mud, should never be resorted to, except in case of absolute necessity, as they swarm with fleas and other vermin. . . . The tents of the Beduins are free from these insects, but, on the other hand, are terribly infested with lice. Scorpions abound in Syria, but they seldom sting unless irritated."[15]

The greatest challenge for missionaries and members in their efforts to establish the Church was poverty. A stagnant economy and lack of education pushed many people to live at a subsistence level, and this reality influenced every facet of missionary activity: proselyting, teaching, retaining members, and efforts to emigrate to Zion. Members were often forced to migrate in search of work to cities with no LDS presence, and many of them never returned to the Church. Thus, poverty and economic migration eroded the leadership and membership base in the existing branches and in the mission as a whole. President Joseph Booth wrote frequently and poignantly about the indigence of the Saints and their constant struggle to eke out a living while maintaining their faith and dignity:

"Very frequently we find our own brethren without food or fuel, and no work whatever to do. Only yesterday one of them came in for assistance, sat for an hour or so, got up and bid us good-bye and then stood at the door, too modest to make his wants known, until he was asked to come in again and say what he wanted. He had nothing to eat for his family, and had been walking the streets nearly all day in a rain storm trying to sell his only coat, offering it for less than a shilling but could find no buyer."[16]

On another occasion, while teaching at a school for LDS children in Aintab, he recorded this touching episode that reveals much about both the poor conditions of members and Booth's compassion for them:

"My class in school comes immediately before the noon recess and I remained a few moments to watch the children eat their lunch. There was a variety of the plain food peculiar to Turkish diet— unleavened bread, cheese, rice rolled in grape leaves, cucumbers, etc. As they seated themselves in little groups on the floor in different parts of the room and began eating their scanty meals, I noticed one little girl with downcast features slyly move away to an unoccupied part of the room as if to hide the secret of her exceptional condition. On inquiry I learned that she had no dinner, her parents being poor and the little sufferer had come to school to mingle with her more fortunate classmates in all their exercises. . . . I asked some of the children to divide up with their hungry sister but they either misunderstood me or were unable to conquer their own selfishness and I left the room with a heart half aching for my ill fated pupil. . . . I had concluded to return and take the young child a lunch from our own cupboard. With a small loaf of bread, some meat, and vegetables, I soon reached the school room again but was made glad by the news that one of her school mates had shared dinner with her and I then gave the lunch I had taken, to the two who had eaten but were still hungry."[17]

Because of these difficult conditions, the missionaries struggled continually with the problem of "rice Christians": people who desired to join a church primarily to satisfy material rather than spiritual needs. Elder Hintze commented that there were many good people in the mission, "bright and inquisitive . . . kind and apt and willing to learn," but because of poverty and persecution were often more interested in pragmatic concerns: "Are you recognized by the government? Can you tell how we may be protected from the ravishes of wicked men? Where shall we bury our dead?"[18]

Though the missionaries sometimes aggravated the problem by openly encouraging emigration to Zion (Utah), few members were able to make the trip because U.S. government sanctions against the Church had depleted its financial resources, including the Perpetual Emigrating Fund. Therefore, Elder Hintze observed, the Church was unable to help them emigrate, and even if the members managed to find their own means, the members had to "steal out of the country" because emigration to America was strictly prohibited by the Turkish government. For these and similar reasons, Hintze concluded, the numbers of converts in Turkey would remain relatively low because "the strain is very heavy."[19] A fascinating proposal for alleviating the "strain" on members, one that was supported by the missionaries in Turkey but never approved by Church leaders in Salt Lake City, was to purchase land and establish an LDS colony in the Middle East to provide an economic and spiritual refuge for the Saints.[20]

Despite the obstacles and problems, the message of the Restoration attracted many committed, faithful, spiritually converted members who were valiant in building the Church and sharing their testimony of the truth. Elder Booth recognized that, in spite of their destitute circumstances, the Saints in Aintab exhibited great faith in the principle of tithing: "Even with this meager wage, the poor pay a more honest tithe than do some of those who are abundantly provided with this world's goods, and they naturally receive spiritual blessings in proportion to their faithfulness."[21]

In the Turkish Mission, tithing funds were used locally to help support the poor and to pay Church expenses. Elder Andrew Larson gave this glowing report on the thriving branch of Saints in Zara:

"I continued my journey to Zara . . . where I found a very loving set of Saints. . . . I stayed with Nishan Sherinian, the presiding Elder. He appears to be a real Latter-day Saint. He is real well liked among the Saints, and is well thought of both among Islam and Christian as far as honesty and integrity are concerned. But as for Mormonism it is the same wherever we go, it has not many real friends in the world. . . . The Saints in Zara are very poor and have a great deal to fight against, but are quite strong in the faith. None of them use tobacco, coffee or tea. They live in the fear of God and are not afraid of men. They all live in hope of going to Zion some day. They are very much disgusted with the present [Ottoman] administration, and the people in general. I found them very obedient to the commandments of God and willing to listen to all truth."[22]

The Challenges and Adventures of Missionary Travel

Travel from place to place in the early period of the mission was risky and painstaking. Because of the remoteness and ruggedness of the mountain terrain in central Turkey, railways and carriage roads had not yet been constructed. Caravans of donkeys, mules, horses, or camels were still the most common means of transportation for the missionaries and members. President Hintze described a journey from Sivas to Marash as "perfect donkey speed, slow and tedious" and then observed:

"The roads which connect these principal cities of the interior of Asia Minor are no more than trails located in the nearest possible mountain passes. . . . When, therefore, two caravans meet on a dugway winding for miles around on the tops of high mountains, where the trail only admits of a single file, our mule drivers have a hard time in passing; not only because of the narrow road, but also because they seem to have imbibed somewhat of the mule nature. No one will move to accommodate a passage; thus by force of much quarreling a passage is made, often resulting in one or more of the animals moving off the dugway, and animal and burden going to the bottom of the ravine."[23]

Because lawlessness and brigandage were common in outlying areas of Turkey, the government required that an armed soldier escort all foreign travelers. Despite this provision, which was often ignored in practice, several of the missionaries reported being robbed of their money and personal belongings as they made their way along isolated trails in the mountains and deserts of the Ottoman Empire.

For a while at the turn of the century, the missionaries experimented with a form of transportation unknown in rural Turkey at that time: bicycles, or "wheels" as they called them. Elder Joseph Booth reported that the introduction of the wheel created some problems among the local people, even though it was a boon to the missionaries:

"Our bicycles, sent for last April, arrived early in the morning, and we took a ride out toward the college. The people were greatly astonished to see men going over the road at such speed on lifeless horses. They stared, yelled, and followed us as if we were from another world. . . . In a little ride alone out on the main highway, I suddenly rode up to a crowd of villagers coming into town with their animals laden with produce for the market. One of the donkeys frightened and in his attempt to escape from the approach of the bicycle, stumbled, fell, and the load went rolling in the dirt. It was melons and eggs and the sight was a mixture of unsavory proportions."[24]

Booth and two other missionaries, President Albert Herman and Elder Thomas Page, later embarked on a two-month bicycle tour of the mission that began in Aintab, Turkey, and continued through Aleppo, Damascus, Beirut, Caesarea Philippi, the Sea of Galilee, Nazareth, Haifa, and back to Aintab. This turned out to be a wild and memorable adventure that included another collision with a terrified donkey; a crash on a precipitous mountain trail that left clothes torn and limbs bleeding; mobs of angry rock-throwing villagers; eating exotic foods, like sheepshead soup and buffalo milk; suffering from inclement weather, malarial fever, and poor sleeping accommodations; and most of all, the sheer exhilaration of wheeling around the Holy Land.

Elder Booth's sense of humor is evident in his comment after falling and wrecking his bicycle near Damascus: "As I neared

Damascus I thought Paul was not the only one who had been called to a sudden halt in the vicinity." Booth's journal entry on New Year's Eve, 1900, a few days before arriving back in Aintab, captures the bittersweet nature of this unforgettable trip and life in general for LDS missionaries in Turkey: "Wet bedding and fever but still surrounded by the mercies of God brought me to 1901."[25]

President and Sister Booth's Missions and Humanitarian Work among the Armenian Saints

President Joseph Wilford Booth and his wife, Mary Rebecca (Reba) Moyle Booth, deserve special mention in this historical sketch because of the length and unique quality of their service to the Church in the Middle East. President Booth served for seventeen years during three missions to the Middle East: from 1898 to 1902 as a proselyting elder and from 1903 to 1909 and 1921 to 1928 as president. Sister Booth served for ten years (1903 to 1909 and 1924 to 1928) with her husband while he was presiding over the mission. The Booths' mission experiences following World War I are particularly noteworthy because of the exceptionally adverse conditions they encountered and their valiant efforts to preserve the lives of the members and to reestablish the Church.

In 1921, three years after the end of the war, Booth approached the First Presidency about providing help for the members in Turkey who had been sending letters pleading for assistance. In response, President Heber J. Grant called Booth as president of the newly named Armenian Mission and gave him the charge "to go to Turkey to carry help to the Saints there."[26] He and Sister Booth subsequently initiated clothing drives and fund-raising efforts to help Church members in the Middle East get back on their feet. One of the Church members living in Aintab at the time, a young man named Reuben Ouzounian, described the desperate circumstances under which the members of the Church and other Armenians had been living during and after the war:

"The First World War brought many horrors to the Armenian population. . . . In this terrible time, all the Aintab Branch presidency lost their lives, as did a great many of the members. At the end of the war, the surviving members returned to their country. . . . The time was 1918, and the more than fifty remaining members, all poor and hungry, used homes as their meeting places. . . . During this time, there was little food and clothing for the members, and they experienced a terrible time. At times, the people had to eat the leaves of trees."[27]

When President Booth arrived in the Middle East in November 1921, he found the mission in total disarray and ravaged by war. The number of Church members was depleted by death, emigration, and deportation, and those who remained were scattered, lonely, and suffering from disease and starvation. As a result, rather than pursuing normal ecclesiastical and missionary activities, Booth focused his efforts on dealing with humanitarian problems.

In December 1921, because of continued threats against Armenians and the dangers posed by the Turkish civil war, Booth petitioned General De Lamathe of France (France controlled Syria and parts of southern Turkey in the post-war mandate period) to evacuate LDS Church members from Aintab, Turkey, to Aleppo, Syria, where they could be given proper care and safekeeping. Booth reminded the general that the LDS Church had provided generous support to the relief fund for France and Belgium during the war. The general, though mindful of these contributions, was reluctant at first to approve Booth's request and thereby set a precedent that would "stir up strife" with other groups, but he finally relented. Booth noted in his journal:

"I have prayed almost night and day for the Lord to open the way for us to rescue the Saints, and they in Aintab have fasted for 8 days so they write, and I surely felt to thank God for his answer to my prayers when the General at last said, We will grant you permission to bring the 50. The general also expressed his gratitude for the friendship and sacrifice of the LDS Americans who had died in the Great War to help liberate France."

On 5 December President Booth joined a French army convoy consisting of 240 vehicles and several hundred drivers, infantry, and cavalry. Booth, age fifty-five, walked alongside the convoy and slept in a hay wagon at night. When he arrived two days later in Aintab, Turkey, the scene of many of his most memorable missionary experiences, he was inundated with requests for help and noted the irony: "There were many people now in this city who came pleading with me for assistance, but 22 years ago I was driven with Elder P. S. Maycock et al from the multitude by stones, etc."

Three days later, on Thursday, 8 December, the culminating moment arrived when Booth was scheduled to pick up the members' passports with the highly sought-after but hard-to-get visas for passage to Syria. He described the chaotic scene with dramatic flair:

"In the late afternoon I called at the passport office. The whole court below was filled with hundreds of people anxiously waiting to hear their names read out from the upstairs window. I sat and waited in an adjoining upper room and soon the window near me was opened. The roar and tumult of the crowd below was hushed at once on the harsh command of the man who appeared before the multitude to read the names. There was a thrill of joy for every one whose name was read out, but with it a corresponding sadness for all who were disappointed. About 150 names were read out in a clear ringing tone and then the words, 'Now come the Mormons' was followed by the reading of 51 names of my list—the remaining 7 were left for next list tomorrow—which ended the number of passports issued today. Within a few minutes the 51 papers were in the hands of Bro. Moses Hindoian who was with me to receive them. Though ours were the last to be read we were ushered into the room and received the first consideration. 'Mormons' were famous today in Aintab."

President Booth next turned his energies to the logistical challenges of transporting the members, including small children and women in poor health, and their household goods over sixty miles of wintry, muddy roads to Aleppo. He bargained for nine wagons and teams and settled reluctantly for a price he labeled "highway robbery." As preparations for departure neared completion, Booth began to have some second thoughts about the wisdom of this move, but these doubts quickly passed: "No persuasion could change the desire of the Saints to get out of the country in which they had seen so much suffering and bloodshed." After a stroll through the outdoor markets of Aintab, he was reassured that they should leave because "the very spirit of danger seemed to be in the air."

Booth then returned to Aleppo to prepare for the arrival of the Saints from Aintab, and to his great satisfaction was able to rent eight rooms with a communal kitchen and outdoor bathrooms in a building called Khan Jebria. On 16 December the train of ten wagons and fifty-seven people—including thirteen members, thirty-five non-members, and nine children—arrived in Aleppo after a grueling four-day journey from Aintab. Booth learned only then that "the Arabajas, wagon men, had been very mean, left several bundles and thrown out other articles on the way and had loaded several hundred lbs. of other goods and taken in other passengers—a violation of contract." Of the safe arrival of the little convoy, he later wrote with satisfaction and gratitude:

"All was confusion in mud and rain, but we finally settled down for the night. I am now thankful to the Lord for his mercy unto us. He has guided and controlled affairs for us in answer to our fastings and prayers in such a marvelous manner that I am truly anxious to manifest my gratitude and heartfelt thanks and praise unto Him who has led the little flock out of the danger of death and destruction which seems to be hanging over the city of once proud now almost ruined Aintab."

On the Sabbath two days later, the Saints enjoyed meeting and worshiping together for the first time in many years with their mission president: "With thankful hearts to the Lord for his manifold blessings we met in the morning about 10 A.M. and partook of the sacrament once more after this long period. We sang 'Artuk Zion Mesrur Alsun' (Let Zion Rejoice) . . . [and] 'Hershey Ne Guzel Lener,' my transliteration of Love at Home." This exodus from Aintab was subsequently viewed by the Armenian Saints as a miraculous event in Church history—a "manifestation of God's power and goodness" as Booth said—and was commemorated each year on 16 December in programs featuring original plays, poems, songs, essays, and stories written by the Armenian members.[28]

After gathering the members to Aleppo and establishing a communal home for them at Khan Jebria, President Booth sought tirelessly for the next seven years to alleviate the Saints' suffering and improve their lives: teaching them new skills like reading, writing, sewing, hat making, playing musical instruments, and carpentry; organizing cooperatives to produce rugs and other goods and market them overseas (primarily in Utah); regularly visiting and taking money, clothing, and food to member and nonmember families living in the squalid refugee camps in Aleppo; soliciting clothing and food donations from Church members in Utah; and dealing with the myriad complaints and quarrels that inevitably arose among the Saints as they experimented with their Oriental version of the United Order.

Sister Booth arrived in January 1924 to serve again with her husband, and her testimony and skills were a great strength to the mission. In particular, her presence helped the missionaries deal more effectively with one of their most complicated problems: how to help members overcome traditional Middle Eastern attitudes that severely limited women's status in public life. Contrary to accepted cultural practices of the time, the Booths insisted that the Armenian sisters participate fully and give speeches in Church meetings, establish active Relief Society and Young Women organizations to provide the sisters leadership and educational opportunities, and encouraged LDS families not to arrange marriages at a young age for their daughters but to send them to school.[29]

These years of communal life with the Armenian members were both extremely trying and deeply gratifying for the Booths. They were constantly confronted by relentless poverty, political tension, health problems, and the fickle behavior of some of the Church members. But there were also many reasons to rejoice and find satisfaction in the fruits of their labors. Booth's journal often records his pleasure in seeing the success and progress of the Saints, including this humorous example of the LDS branch's acting company that based a play on a familiar Book of Mormon story but with a clever cultural twist:

"All day the young people were busy with preparing for the drama tonight. . . . Attended the drama at night in the big Oriental Theater. We had about 400 present nearly half of which were complimentary including all the Saints who wished to go. There was a disturbance more or less by the rowdy populace, but the young amateurs did splendid. The name of the drama was changed from 'Nephi' to one they thought would be more suitable for the public here and the handbills read, 'The Death of a Drunkard and Five Marriages in One Night' and took up the events in the life of Lehi and Nephi to the joining of the family of the fleeing prophet with that of Ishmael at the tents in the wilderness."[30]

Another entry sums up Booth's feelings toward the Armenian members with whom he served so long and so well: "While [the

Saints] are generally of a poor and uneducated class yet many of them are dear, good, faithful souls and I love them as brethren and sisters in the Gospel."[31]

Over time, the Booths' patient tutelage and compassionate service paid rich dividends in terms of blessing the lives of the members. Elder David O. McKay, an apostle who toured the mission with President Booth in 1921, offered this assessment of the Booths' contributions and the progress of the Armenian Saints after a second visit to Syria in 1924:

"The greatest results of the past two years' devoted service are seen not in material things, but in the development of the members of the branch. To one who saw them in their discouragement and distress in 1921, the change wrought is wonderful. . . . In the joy of association in surroundings of safety, in the assurance of proper care and skill in times of sickness; in opportunity for mutual helpfulness, and for spiritual growth and enlightenment, the change is little short of a transformation. . . . Two years ago, very few of the Saints could muster courage to speak in meeting—very few could take part on the program. Today every member responds not only willingly, but intelligently. They sing, they pray, they bear testimony, give addresses, and participate in all appropriate exercises most enthusiastically. . . . Truly, a mighty work has been accomplished."[32]

Booth's final journal entry, dated 3 December 1928, reflects the energy, industry, and selflessness that had characterized his life of sixty-two years. It reads: "Was busy all day with checking, packing, and shipping the rugs." Just below that entry, written in Sister Booth's hand, is this touching note: "My dear husband, Joseph Wilford Booth, passed away Dec. 5, 1928, at Aleppo, Syria." President Booth was buried in Aleppo next to one of his own missionaries, Elder Emil Huber, whose funeral he had supervised twenty years earlier. Booth's own words, written in tribute to the four LDS missionaries who had died in the Middle East, apply now to him and make a fitting epitaph:

"We do not complain that they are here, neither do I think their loved ones at home feel that any slight has been intended. It seems more like the ruling of a wise Providence to allow their bodies to rest here under the dew and the sod, 'that their monuments might perpetuate their work in bearing witness of the truth.' . . . Each one has gained a good name, better than precious ointment. Each died in honor and in the harness of the priesthood, and surely the rest of each will be a glorious one."[33]

THE LEGACY OF THE MIDDLE EASTERN MISSIONS

What can be said, by way of conclusion, about LDS missionary efforts in the Middle East? What can we learn from the experience of these early members and missionaries? In October 1928, just two months before his death, President Joseph Booth cleverly summarized the mission's history: "Our past and present status may be briefly told by counting up to ten; thus: One lady missionary, two workers in the field today, three cities have served as our headquarters, four elders have died in the field, five nationalities have been baptized, six languages are needed to teach them, seven apostles have been here, eight cities now claim one or more of our members, and nine out of ten are in poverty."[34]

But numbers alone cannot tell the whole story. While there are some indications in the primary sources that Church leaders wanted to establish a mission in the Holy Land as a preparatory step for the gathering of the Jews and the return of the Savior, it appears that these motives were laid aside as the work progressed. Ironically, the missionaries did very little work in Palestine or among the Jews in general but focused their efforts on the Christians of Syria and Turkey.

Despite overwhelming odds against them—harsh living conditions and daunting cultural, political, and economic challenges that severely hampered their effectiveness—the missionaries accepted the call to serve in faraway lands and went forth with stunning vision, courage, humility, and love to preach the restored gospel of peace. Their goal was not merely to baptize, but to testify and warn and plant seeds, and they had a conviction that someday the seeds they planted would yield a harvest of souls and the foundation they laid would support a growing Church.

Though only about sixty missionaries served in the mission—and there were never more than two hundred members on the Church records at one time—the faith, efforts, and sacrifices of the members and missionaries of the various Middle Eastern missions yielded important results and, over time, made significant contributions to the growth and development of the Church. The numerous descendants of the LDS converts who emigrated to the U.S. from Syria, Turkey, and Palestine—families such as Grau, Kezerian, Sherinian, Hagopian, Vizerian, Orullian, Hindoian, Piranian, and Ouzounian—have enriched the Church and the communities in which they settled, adding their skills and Oriental perspectives to the rich tapestry of LDS experience.

The presence of five LDS grave markers in present-day Turkey, Syria, and Israel will continue, according to "wise Providence" as President Booth said, to "perpetuate [the elders'] work in bearing witness of the truth," to commemorate the faithful lives of valiant members and missionaries of yesteryear, and to provide opportunities for the Church to build bridges in the modern Middle East.

NOTES

1. Soon after its establishment in 1830, the Church began exploring ways to carry the message of the restored gospel to Palestine. The Prophet Joseph Smith sent Orson Hyde, one of the Twelve Apostles, to Jerusalem to dedicate the land for the in-gathering of Abraham's children—especially the Jews—and for the commencement of missionary work. Elder Hyde offered his dedicatory prayer on the Mount of Olives in Jerusalem in 1841, but it was more than forty years later when missionary labors officially began.

2. The five missionaries were Edgar D. Simmons, from Salt Lake City, Utah, died in 1890 of smallpox, buried in Aintab, Turkey; Adolf Haag, born in Stuttgart, Germany, died in 1892 of typhus, buried in Haifa, Palestine (now Israel); John A. Clark, born in Farmington, Utah, died in 1895 of smallpox, buried in Haifa, Palestine (now Israel); Emil J. Huber, from Zurich, Switzerland, died in 1908 of typhoid, buried in Aleppo, Syria; Joseph W. Booth, from Alpine, Utah, died in 1928 of cardiac arrest, buried in Aleppo, Syria.

3. Since there was virtually no Church literature in Turkish except the Bible during the first twenty years of the mission and no standardized system of teaching the gospel, the elders had to translate sections of LDS material from English or German in order to teach investigators.

4. Robinson letter to *Church and Farm,* 5 July 1895, in "Manuscript History of the Turkish Mission," Historical Department Archives, The Church of Jesus Christ of Latter-day Saints; see also Rao Lindsay, "A History of the Missionary Activities of The Church of Jesus Christ of Latter-day Saints in the Near East, 1884–1929," Master's thesis, Brigham Young University, 1958, 60.

5. Jacob Spori, in "Abstract of Correspondence," *Millennial Star,* 12 January 1885, 28.

6. Don Musser, *Deseret Weekly,* 2 December 1893, 749. Often the elders would trade lessons in one of these languages with a local native speaker for lessons in English, French, or German, and walk about town striking up simple conversations with shopkeepers, artisans, rug weavers, and people in restaurants and government offices to practice speaking and to make friends.

7. For example, Elder Stauffer was arrested in Marash in 1890 on suspicion of inciting unrest among the Armenians, and Elder Albert Herman was banished from Damascus in 1893 for teaching Muslims.

8. Evidence of this is the fact that the mailing address for missionaries typically consisted of their name, followed only by the city and country. Apparently, everyone in town knew who the foreigners were and where they were staying.

9. Anthon H. Lund, "A Word from the Far East," *Improvement Era,* July 1898, 683.

10. J. Alma Holdaway, *Millennial Star,* 15 August 1901, 540. Note that the correct term today for a person who practices the Islamic faith is *Muslim.* The name of the religion is *Islam.*

11. Ferdinand F. Hintze, in *Deseret Weekly,* 6 July 1889, 50.

12. Funeral and burial services were, in the eyes of the Turkish government, religious matters to be handled by duly authorized churches. Since the LDS Church was not recognized by the government, it did not have the authority to provide funeral services or cemetery plots. This unfortunate situation holds true today throughout the Islamic Middle East.

13. Ferdinand F. Hintze, *Millennial Star,* 1 February 1900, 74.

14. Frederick A. Huish, "Description of Aleppo," *Millennial Star,* 8 October 1894, 645.

15. Karl Baedeker, *Palestine and Syria, with Routes through Mesopotamia and Babylonia and the Island of Cyprus* (Leipzig: Karl Baedeker, 1912), xvii.

16. Joseph W. Booth, *Millennial Star,* 15 March 1900, 166.

17. Joseph W. Booth, "The Journals of Joseph Wilford Booth, 1886–1928," MSS 155, Special Collections and Manuscripts, Harold B. Lee Library, Brigham Young University, 16 June 1899.

18. Ferdinand F. Hintze, in *Deseret Weekly,* 7 December 1889, 763, note 12.

19. Ibid.

20. Rao H. Lindsay, "The Dream of a Mormon Colony in the Near East," *Dialogue: A Journal of Mormon Thought,* Winter 1966, 50–67.

21. Joseph W. Booth, in "Notes from the Mission Field," *Millennial Star,* 21 January 1904, 43.

22. Andrew Larson, in "Abstract of Correspondence," *Millennial Star,* 12 April 1900, 235.

23. Ferdinand F. Hintze, in *Deseret Weekly,* 12 January 1889, 75.

24. Booth, "Journals of Joseph Wilford Booth," 11, 25 October 1900.

25. Ibid., 19 November, 31 December 1900. See also David Charles's article on Mormon missionary travel in the Middle East (1884–1928) in *Mormon Historical Studies* 1 (Spring 2000).

26. Booth, "Journals of Joseph Wilford Booth," 19 August 1921. The name of the mission was changed from Turkish to Armenian out of respect for the feelings of the members, the vast majority of whom were Armenians who had suffered immensely at the hands of the Turkish government.

27. Reuben Ouzounian, "A Short History of The Church of Jesus Christ of Latter-day Saints in the Middle East," Historical Department Archives, 4–5.

28. Booth, "Journals of Joseph Wilford Booth," 2 December 1921–18 December 1921; see also Joseph Booth, "The Armenian Mission," *Improvement Era,* October 1928, 1050.

29. Booth's journals contain many references to the missionaries' efforts to elevate the status of women among the Armenian members. For more on Sister Booth's contributions to the missionary work during ten years of service, see Mary Rebecca Moyle Booth, "Papers 1904–1906; 1923–1933," Historical Department Archives.

30. Booth, "Journals of Joseph Wilford Booth," 1 August 1925; see also 14–16 April.

31. Booth, "Journals of Joseph Wilford Booth," 1 August 1922.

32. David O. McKay, "A Man Who Loves His Fellow-Men," *Millennial Star,* 28 February 1924, 137–38.

33. Joseph W. Booth, "Four Heroes Far Away," *Improvement Era,* September 1909, 900.

34. Booth, "Armenian Mission," 1048–49.

CHAPTER TWENTY-FIVE

A NATION IN A DAY: THE CHURCH IN GUATEMALA

KEITH J. WILSON

During the spring of 1917, the seventh of fourteen children was born to a poor Mormon family in La Madera, New Mexico. This family had previously been driven from Chihuahua, Mexico, because of the Mexican Revolution and was sequestered in a makeshift cabin while the father worked in a logging camp. This little boy's birth was inconspicuous at best, and his destiny, like his birth, seemed to be dictated by both poverty and isolation.

His religious community struggled with similar limitations. The Mormon Church in the year 1917 had half a million members, most of whom were centered in the state of Utah.[1] There were approximately fifteen hundred missionaries worldwide and seventy-five stakes. Joseph F. Smith, the son of Hyrum Smith, was the aging prophet of the Church. All this in a country of 103 million people and in the middle of the first world war. Considered collectively, this poor little boy belonged to an obscure church and could anticipate an uneventful life—that is unless his name was John Forres O'Donnal, a member of the Mormon Church in the year 1917. What follows is the phenomenal story of this man, his marriage to a native Guatemalan woman, and the beginnings of the Mormon Church in Guatemala.

John's father, John Christopher Franklin O'Donnal, was born in

---

Keith J. Wilson is assistant professor of ancient scripture at Brigham Young University.

Demotte, Indiana, in 1882. Frank (as he was known) and his family converted to the Church some ten years later and then heeded the call to gather to Zion. En route they were diverted to the Mormon colonies in Mexico, eventually settling in Colonia García. There Frank met his future wife, Sarah Ann Cluff, the third child of an established pioneer family. Frank and Sarah were married shortly before the Mexican Revolution and were then forced to flee in 1912.

During a ten-year span they moved four times and finally returned to Mexico in 1921. The twin forces of the Mexican Revolution and World War I economy made survival difficult. Yet they not only survived but found joy in the journey. John later described this period as "very happy times" from his childhood.[2]

These formative years stamped indelible impressions upon young John O'Donnal. This was a time when he first learned the nature of hard work. The family farmed, raised cattle, and even rented an apple orchard. Frank O'Donnal frequently had to leave his family and live at various job sites to support them. During high school John temporarily had to drop out and work at a cheese factory for a year. Once back in school, he continued to work part-time as a janitor. In addition to hard work, education became an important value. He attended grade school in Colonia Dublán and then he took his secondary education at Juárez Stake Academy. There he became a student leader, learned to speak Spanish, and prepared himself to serve a mission.

It was in November of his senior year that the Lord first allowed John to glimpse his larger mission in life. The Juárez patriarch promised him in his patriarchal blessing:

"You shall live to see great progress in the work of the Lord, in this land, among the people by whom we are surrounded and among all the natives in the nations south of us. . . . Our Heavenly Father will magnify you among them and make you the instrument in his hands of doing a great and glorious work."[3]

Even though John later admitted that this blessing outlined his future, as an eighteen-year-old boy he flippantly considered it a "peculiar blessing" and did not pay much attention to it during those years.[4] Much of his energy at the time was fixed on preparing to serve a mission and find an honorable profession. Yet his future was not destined to be so predictable.

After John graduated from the Juárez Academy, his bishop approached him about serving a mission. A subsequent physical examination revealed a possible heart murmur, and consequently his priesthood leaders withdrew their offer. Rather discouraged, John went from El Paso to Safford, Arizona, to work. While employed at a tire store, he heard talk of a job in Tucson for someone who wanted to work close to the university. Those words "penetrated my mind . . . and there arose in me a strong desire to go the university."[5] He began as an agriculture student in 1937 and finished in 1941. With the onset of World War II, he then applied to a military officer program but was again rejected, this time because of a double hernia. Once again his future seemed uncertain.

Yet the uncertainty dissipated within the month through a letter from a former professor who wrote the university seeking graduates with a knowledge of Spanish. John applied, and a cabled message confirmed his acceptance. He began in Washington, D.C., as a federal employee on 1 November 1941. Three months later he was sent to British Honduras to investigate the possibilities of rubber production in Central America. One of his first assignments was to determine whether or not Guatemala had a suitable climate for rubber production. When he submitted a very positive report, they assigned him to stay there and initiate a rubber program. John O'Donnal took those instructions quite literally. His eventual stay would cover almost fifty years, and his efforts would include both rubber and religion.

CARMEN GÁLVEZ

Meanwhile, a little Guatemalan girl named Carmen was growing up in a staunchly Catholic family. Her parents were descendants of Spanish royalty and had settled along the coastal plain of Guatemala. Since her mother wanted the best for her children, she often reminded them of their "blue blood" and worried about the time they spent playing with the native Indian children. The mother insisted that her children be active churchgoers even though she herself never went. As this young girl matured, she often questioned the validity of formal religion.

Then John and Carmen's paths crossed. Carmen was in a social club playing table tennis one afternoon when a young American man stopped by with some local friends. They met and within a short time fell in love. Stiff opposition mounted for both of them as Carmen's mother declared her dislike of "gringos," and John quietly considered marrying not only a foreigner but also a nonmember. As he later recalled, "There was a strong, unseen influence urging us on."[6] John finally convinced a Catholic priest to marry them in a civil ceremony. At the last moment, Carmen's mother acquiesced and attended the wedding. For John it was a bittersweet day. He had married his love, but she knew nothing about Mormonism, and John's family knew nothing of his decision.

Their marriage did little to quell the forces of opposition. Even though John had no doubts about her eventually joining the Church, teaching Carmen was fraught with difficulties. John had no Spanish Book of Mormon, nor any Church literature. In fact he was the only Mormon in the entire country. She remembers him telling her repeatedly of prophets, his patriarchal blessing, and bringing the gospel to these little villages. Eventually they did obtain a Spanish Book of Mormon, but these things meant nothing to Carmen. Exasperated, she asked John on one occasion, "Why in the world do I have to read this book? It doesn't mean anything to me."

John would not be deterred. As often as he could he took her with him on his travels. While going from one rubber farm to another, he would explain the First Vision and the plan of salvation. He sensed she was becoming converted, but because of opposition she struggled to admit it. When she could not accompany him, he would write to her, explaining doctrine and exhorting her to pray about it. Carmen recounts, however, that "it was a terrible experience for me to do that, because every time I tried to pray Satan was there. I could just feel this terrible spirit around me every time my husband wasn't there."[7]

Despite these pressures John and Carmen decided to begin their family. Because of the shortage of good medical facilities in Guatemala, they traveled to Mesa, Arizona, in August of 1945 to have their first daughter. There John introduced Carmen to the concept of temples and eternal families. He proudly proclaimed that some day they would be married there and sealed to their new little daughter. To Carmen it was nothing more than a beautiful building.

A year and a half later the O'Donnals again traveled to the United

States. By now John was beginning to worry because they had been married for three and a half years and still Carmen had not converted. He left Carmen at his sister's house in Albuquerque, New Mexico, and bought a bus ticket to Utah. He had never been to Salt Lake City before; he scarcely knew anyone there and had no appointment. Notwithstanding, on 31 December 1946, this twenty-nine-year-old man called on President George Albert Smith. President Smith received him warmly and in what John described as "one of the highlights of my life" showed great interest in his request that missionaries be sent to Guatemala.[8] President Smith asked for a detailed letter that he could take to the First Presidency.

Before departing from Salt Lake City, John submitted the letter. In it he fervently petitioned the brethren with his testimony: "I know that many people [in Guatemala] will accept the gospel . . . [and] my personal impressions are that there are thousands of the blood of Lehi who are anxious to hear the gospel message."[9] The First Presidency agreed with his request, and within a week they committed to send missionaries to Guatemala. For John the bus ride back to Albuquerque was not nearly as long as the ride to Salt Lake had been. The Church was coming to Guatemala.

Once back in the country the O'Donnals awaited the advent of missionaries. In July Guatemala and most of Central America were formally added to the Mexico Mission. On 4 September 1947 two elders arrived in Guatemala City and took up residence with the O'Donnals. At last the work had begun, but the years of darkness were not easily dispelled. By December one of the elders suffered from appendicitis and had to leave for surgery. The first district meeting was not held until almost one year had passed, and only sixty-six people attended the meeting, where John was set apart as the first district president. Yet no Guatemalans were ready for baptism.

Carmen was struggling as much as anyone. Even though she saw nothing in Catholicism, she could not be baptized just to please John. On one of his many business trips he felt a particular weight. The words from his own biography detailing his feelings recount an Enos-like experience. He located a tropical garden and a secluded spot under a tree where he poured out his soul to God. He pleaded for forgiveness of his own sins and begged the Lord to send Carmen a confirmation. Carmen had been laboring against so many odds:

her family, her friends, and her culture. John was unaware how long he had prayed, but he arose with a peaceful assurance that his prayer would be answered.

Meanwhile, Carmen's situation was nearing a breaking point. One evening while John was away she pleaded and cried for God to speak to her. A terrible feeling entered her room, and in an instant she sensed that thousands of faces were there wanting to kill her. Shaken, she left the room and sought refuge with the missionaries, who were living upstairs. They gave her a priesthood blessing, and she eventually was able to sleep. Following this experience she realized that Satan was trying to destroy her but that when the priesthood was present he was powerless. She had received her witness, and she committed to baptism. It had been more than fourteen months since proselyting in Guatemala had begun. On 13 November 1948 Carmen entered the waters of baptism as both the first Guatemalan and the first Central American to be baptized.[10]

EARLY CHURCH GROWTH IN GUATEMALA

On the same day that John baptized Carmen, three other converts joined the Church. It may have been an inauspicious beginning for a land of approximately a million people, but it was a start. Within a few weeks, Carmen was called as Relief Society president. In an interview she reminisced over the challenges of those days: "Besides working in the Relief Society I was working in every position in the Church. I was a teacher in Primary and also in the priesthood, because I was helping the missionaries teach the priesthood lessons to the people and helping them translate." Her Relief Society counselors consisted of a sister missionary and a supportive nonmember. On one occasion a female university professor who was investigating the Church ridiculed Carmen for being so young and inexperienced. The sister missionary deftly defused the criticism with the statement that Carmen had not sought these callings but had been selected by the Lord.[11]

Long before Carmen became a member, John had stressed the importance of the temple to her. During the summer of 1949, the O'Donnals visited Salt Lake City. While there, President McKay authorized John and Carmen to be sealed to their two little girls. It was, in John's words, "The happiest day of our lives."[12]

It took about four years for the Church in Guatemala to reach one hundred members. That year, 1952, also marked the time when the first apostle, Spencer W. Kimball, visited Guatemala. He came to split the Central American Mission and to dedicate the land. Speaking in Spanish he offered a most singular dedicatory prayer. This apostle to the Lamanites began his prayer with references to Guatemala as a promised land of Zion, made sacred by holy prophets and "especially sanctified by the repeated visits of Thy Beloved Son." He begged the Lord to relieve their sufferings and bring the people to a knowledge of their covenant status through the voice of the Book of Mormon. He concluded with the request that the Lord "let them be converted *'a nation in a day.'*"[13] To the one hundred or so members who heard this prayer it was both exciting and puzzling. Perhaps some of them sensed that they were standing on the threshold.

THE GATES BEGIN TO OPEN

Elder Kimball presided over another event while in Guatemala that year. He set apart Gordon Romney as a new mission president and charged him with the task of building the first chapel. President Romney, who was known for his practical skills, doubted the necessity of both the large size and the outlying location of the proposed structure. From President Romney's perspective it was absurd to build a building for fifteen hundred people when the current membership in Guatemala was one hundred. As first counselor, John O'Donnal was surprised by this skepticism, and he countered with a bold prediction about this first chapel: "Within ten years that chapel is going to be way too small."[14]

By 1955 the chapel was built and dedicated. The following year the first Indian area was opened for proselyting. Slowly the work began to progress, but it was still beset by difficult circumstances. Only eighty-five missionaries covered all of Central America in 1959. New converts often faced stiff opposition from their families and friends. Mormon children were routinely ostracized in the public schools. Carmen painfully remembered times when her two daughters would be sent outside during religious instruction at their school.[15] Up until 1958 the Church could not even own property in its name.

These were challenging times also for the O'Donnals. For fifteen years John had been employed in the rubber industry in Guatemala. During 1956 word came that he would have to leave Guatemala for another assignment or risk termination. He appealed but to no avail. His reassignment required him to be in Brazil by the middle of May. After much thought and prayer, John consigned himself to the change, and Carmen decided to take the children and temporarily relocate to the O'Donnal relatives in Arizona. As the separation approached, John was driving home one rainy evening when his car was broadsided by a freight train at a railroad crossing. Miraculously, he survived. While recuperating he realized that the Lord's hand was preserving and guiding him. He later recalled, "It took a pretty good sized freight train" to convince him that his place was in Guatemala.[16] His next move required deep faith. He notified the U.S. government that he would terminate his employment.

The Lord rewards the faithful. Goodyear Rubber Company offered John a job developing commercial rubber production in Guatemala. His production unit became the most profitable rubber operation for Goodyear and led the commercial rubber industry in Guatemala for the next nineteen years. He also helped Guatemala develop the only permanent rubber industry for all of Central America. In retrospect, however, John was hesitant to accept credit for the success of the industry, explaining, "My position with Goodyear was secondary, and it was there to sustain me while the other work was being carried on."[17]

And the other work was carried on. Elder Milton R. Hunter of the Seventy visited Guatemala twice during these years, making his first tour of Guatemala in 1956 and his second three years later. Following his second visit he described what he had witnessed as "the greatest transformation I have ever seen."[18] Specifically, he pointed to the incredible changes that he observed in the Guatemalans who were flocking to the Church. He noted the light in their eyes, the cleanliness of their appearance, and their emerging leadership qualities as they joined the Church. To demonstrate the phenomenal growth, he cited an Indian area which had been opened for proselyting after his first tour.

On Elder Hunter's second tour they held a meeting in this new area with more than 400 people in attendance and yet the members of record totaled only 141. In all he met with more than 3,000 people, a third of whom were investigators. His report was laced with superlatives as he described the work in Guatemala. The light was beginning to break forth.

The 1960s and early 1970s were times of continued service for the O'Donnals. Carmen continued to hold multiple callings, all the while supporting John in his assignments. John's callings were rather consistent. Beginning in 1952 and continuing though 1976, John served as mission counselor for twenty-four years to eight consecutive mission presidents. After John's employment change, Carmen took the girls with her to Arizona so they could attend a quality high school. Before she could unpack her bags, the bishop had called her to be a counselor in the Relief Society, where she served for three years. She described it as a terrible time.[19] First, there was the pain of discrimination, and second, she struggled with acquiring basic English. But she persevered, and in doing so prepared herself for significant future service as well.

An important Church milestone was achieved in 1967. Eleven years after the first chapel and a mere twenty years since the first missionaries arrived, Guatemala welcomed its first stake. Furthermore, it was organized by Elder Marion G. Romney, the same apostle who declared as early as 1940 that the "'day of the Lamanite' was here."[20] At the time, membership in Guatemala totaled approximately twelve thousand people. Considering the one hundred members of fifteen years before, the new stake heralded a new day in Guatemala.

This growth continued at an amazing pace during the late 1960s. Some months the Guatemala–El Salvador Mission led the entire Church in baptisms. Often the 170 missionaries would baptize three to four hundred new members per month. The seminary program was implemented, and other programs were put in place that helped strengthen the new converts. More and more native Guatemalans began to serve missions and assume leadership positions. By 1975 Church membership was around eighteen thousand.

At times it seemed as though a special spirit brooded over the land, pushing the work forward. Assistance came in both the public and the private spheres. The Church was granted legal status shortly after the first stake was organized, which facilitated the orderly development of the formal Church programs, such as buildings and real estate holdings. Another dimension also responded to this familiar voice. The Guatemalans frequently experienced dreams and manifestations that prefigured the arrival of the missionaries. In fact, John described this phenomenon by stating, "These people are great spiritual people. . . . They live on dreams. . . . They have a great many of them. Many of the people expressed the fact that they had seen the missionaries before they came, or they had seen the prophet, or they had had personal manifestations."[21] It was as if the missionaries were benefitting from unseen heavenly forces.

JOHN AND CARMEN PLACE ALL UPON THE ALTAR

By 1976 John had given over thirty-four years to the rubber industry in Guatemala. He and Carmen sensed it was time to lead in other ways. Taking early retirement from Goodyear, the O'Donnals eagerly accepted President N. Eldon Tanner's invitation to preside over the Guatemala City Mission beginning in July of 1976.

It is hard to imagine a mission president and his wife with the preparation of John and Carmen. Here was a couple who had been the first and second members of the Church in Guatemala and had served for decades in every possible calling. Both were fluent in Spanish and in English. They had been the consummate member missionaries, baptizing and fellowshipping their associates wherever they went. And, like their fellow converts, they too had dreamed dreams.

They set about to realize those dreams from the mission home in Guatemala City. They titled their opening remarks to their missionaries: "This is the beginning of a New Era."[22] Unlike the previous eight presidents, John was no foreigner to these people and knew most of them by name. This couple commenced their mission work, and even though they had been prepared in separate ways, their teamwork was invaluable. John recalled that they were accepted and could counsel, teach, and even scold the people without the fear of rejection.[23]

To this point, the bulk of Guatemalan converts had come from the Spanish-speaking areas of the country. Yet approximately two-thirds of the Guatemalans were native Indians, and most of them had never learned to speak Spanish. Missionary work had largely ignored this group of Guatemalans. Add to this the fact that John and Carmen had spent most of their time living in the western Indian areas of

Guatemala and it is apparent what they dreamed about. After a year in Guatemala City, the call finally came: organize a new mission in western Guatemala and take the gospel to the Indians.

FOR SUCH A TIME AS THIS

As John and Carmen embarked on their new assignment, they again sensed the Lord's hand upon them. It had now been two years since Elder Boyd K. Packer of the Quorum of the Twelve Apostles had toured western Guatemala and stated candidly to John, "You know, I have a feeling, a great strong feeling, that something should be done with these Lamanites [native Indians]." He later asked the question, "Don't you think that we should establish a mission for these people?"[24]

John and Carmen had nurtured the same feelings for years about these native Guatemalans. For John it had often come back to an indelible image impressed upon his mind. Whenever he traveled a certain route, he noticed a blind man by the road, and as he passed him his thoughts always lectured him with the same sermon. That blind man must have the gospel of Jesus Christ.[25] In an uncanny twist, this experience paralleled the New Testament account of the blind man at the temple gate whom Peter stopped to bless. For Carmen it was expressed best in her blessing as she was set apart for the mission. She remembers Elder William Bradford saying that they had been training for many years, preparing themselves to preside over this mission in Quetzaltenango. It was their time.[26]

There was no faltering for John and Carmen. They began a series of innovations that truly defined the course of their mission. High on their list of priorities was a statement by President Spencer W. Kimball that the gospel should be taught to each person in his own tongue. Native Guatemalans are divided into four Indian language groups: Cakchiquel, Quiché, Ke'Kchí, and Mam. The O'Donnals commenced an on-site language program for these four languages. This proved to be an enormous undertaking because these native languages were principally spoken rather than written languages. On one occasion John recalled conversing with a local Catholic priest who was astonished at the ability of the missionaries to speak with the natives in their own tongue. John simply smiled and attributed it to the "gift" of language.

A second innovation sprang from a small Church meeting in a mountainous area. After sacrament meeting John noticed a faithful member exiting the building rather than staying for the rest of the day's meetings. John invited him to stay, whereupon the Indian member politely declined. He explained that it required six hours of walking for him to get back to his house. John knew the Church could do better than that.

He submitted to Salt Lake a highly simplified, small chapel design that consisted of a single room with moveable partitions for dividing into classrooms. Money was eventually appropriated to build ten such chapels in Guatemala. Elder Packer dedicated these buildings, and the *Church News* reported the event by suggesting, "These chapels may provide a pattern for all developing countries, according to Church leaders."[27] For John it signified one of his proudest innovations.

Other contributions followed in a similar pattern. The need for a consolidated block of meetings became apparent as these Indians had to travel such demanding distances. These natives also lacked education. Rather than a forty-two-week Gospel Doctrine manual, they needed simple lessons about the basics of the gospel. A Church writer was brought in from Salt Lake and together with the O'Donnals outlined a basic instruction course. This eventually became the Gospel Essentials manual. Carmen characterized this simplified format as "the Ammon pattern" from the Book of Mormon. Finally, John suggested substantial changes in the finance policies for full-time missionaries.

As their mission drew to a close, Carmen wondered about their accomplishments. During the period of their mission alone, there had been about a thousand new converts and almost a 100 percent increase in Church units—from twenty-four to forty-six. The Church had surpassed twenty thousand members, yet the O'Donnals could see where so much remained to be done. In a tender farewell, John penned these words to the brethren in his final report: "[I am] thankful for the marvelous opportunity . . . of laboring with . . . the finest . . . missionaries in the Church, and among the best people on earth."[28]

THE CROWN JEWEL

The O'Donnals returned home following their mission and assumed they could enjoy retirement. For a few months they did, but somehow it did not fit their style. By November of 1979 ground had been broken for the Mexico City Temple. Looking forward to regular temple visits to the temple was a welcomed improvement. Then, to their surprise, they received a call. Elder William Grant Bangerter of the temple committee invited John to serve as a counselor in the new temple presidency. They graciously accepted as they had every calling. They trained for eighteen months and then supervised the construction processes. Finally, in December of 1983, the temple opened. It was truly a breath of fresh air after months of preparatory work. Yet, strangely enough the O'Donnals found themselves thinking increasingly about Guatemala.

Midway into their Mexico City call, President Kimball announced a temple for Guatemala City. Most Church members marveled at the placement of this holy building, but the O'Donnals were not among them. Their reason traced itself back to 1956 and John's brush with death in the train collision. While recuperating in his hospital room, he received a very singular vision, which he had Carmen record. He had kept the contents of that experience secret owing to the sacred nature of the temple. The following excerpts capture some of what Carmen recorded that day in 1956:

"This is a vision. . . . There will be a temple built here in Guatemala, a beautiful temple, so that the promises of the prophets will be fulfilled. Many poor . . . dark-skinned will enter the temple; and as they come forth from the temple they will appear white and pure. . . . I feel my life has been spared . . . for my life is not my own. My mission here is not finished; there is much left to do."[29]

The O'Donnals were not as surprised as they were excited by President Kimball's announcement. Their dreams were materializing.

The temple committee approached some of the Mexico City Temple workers about possibly serving in Guatemala, but they never asked John and Carmen. This was hardest on Carmen, especially as the time drew closer for the date of dedication. How she longed to work in her own people's temple. One day, after she had long given up hoping, John sent for her. As she entered his office he told her only that President Gordon B. Hinckley had called. In an instant she threw her arms around him and cried, "You told them 'Yes!'"[30]

That night the O'Donnals knew they were going home. For John and Carmen, their temple calling as temple president and matron was the zenith of their Church service. While it was often long and arduous, it was also sweet and invigorating. Among their deepest joys were those experiences with the Indians as they came to the Lord's house. As if scripted to the words of John's temple dream, when these humble people entered the temple, almost immediately the Spirit would fill the edifice. Even President Hinckley noticed something unusual about the temple during the dedication. He observed that he could not remember a time when he had felt the Spirit as strongly as he had at the Guatemalan temple dedication.[31] John and Carmen's three-year assignment passed all too quickly, and in 1987 President Hinckley released them.

One final calling still awaited this amazing couple. After working through some difficult health challenges, the O'Donnals received a call in 1990 to preside over the Missionary Training Center in Lima, Peru. There they served for about one year in a facility that badly needed their leadership and touch. Their service ended abruptly as terrorists threatened all foreigners who chose to remain. John and Carmen were forced to leave without even a good-bye.

CONCLUSION

John Forres O'Donnal's life is the account of a young, single man who felt impressed to accept a job in a country that he had never visited. He took with him a peculiar priesthood blessing that spoke of him as an instrument in the Lord's hand to bring forth a marvelous work. In Guatemala he met an unusual young Catholic woman. Neither imagined that they would marry, become united in their faith, and facilitate the establishment of The Church of Jesus Christ of Latter-day Saints in the land of Guatemala.

What started with one couple forty-eight years ago now stands as a church with over two hundred thousand members. There are currently thirty-five stakes in a country of twelve million people. The Church enjoys an annual growth rate there of 8 percent, and 1.3 percent of the population is LDS.[32]

Guatemala is home to a magnificent temple, a Missionary

Training Center, and the regional administrative offices of the Church. All this began through the impressions of one brave young man and one equally courageous young lady. President Hinckley paid tribute to John O'Donnal in a leadership meeting when he referred to him as "the father, the grandfather, and the great-grandfather of the Church in Guatemala."[33] A brief glance at his story confirms the accuracy of President Hinckley's accolade.

NOTES

1. *Church Almanac 1999–2000* (Salt Lake City: Deseret News, 1998), 551.

2. "Oral History of John F. and Carmen G. O'Donnal," James Moyle Oral History Program, interviewed by Gordon Irving, of The Church of Jesus Christ of Latter-day Saints, Salt Lake City, 1979, 3.

3. John Forres O'Donnal, *Pioneer in Guatemala: The Personal History of John Forres O'Donnal* (Yorba Linda: Shumway Family History Services, 1997), 6.

4. Author's interview of John Forres O'Donnal, Mesa, Arizona, 21 2000, 5.

5. O'Donnal, *Pioneer in Guatemala,* 8.

6. Ibid., 32.

7. "Oral History of John F. and Carmen G. O'Donnal," 12.

8. O'Donnal, *Pioneer in Guatemala,* 56.

9. Ibid., 56–57.

10. Ibid., 60–61.

11. "Oral History of John F. and Carmen G. O'Donnal," 13, 30.

12. O'Donnal, *Pioneer in Guatemala,* 62.

13. "Elder Spencer W. Kimball Dedicates Land of Central America as a Mission," *Church News,* 13 December 1952, 5, 13; emphasis added.

14. "Oral History of John F. and Carmen G. O'Donnal," 25.

15. Ibid., 37.

16. O'Donnal interview, 61; see also O'Donnal, *Pioneer in Guatemala,* 6.

17. "Oral History of John F. and Carmen G. O'Donnal," 35.

18. "Elder Hunter Notes Changes in Lives of Indian Converts," *Church News,* 14 February 1959, 6.

19. "Oral History of John F. and Carmen G. O'Donnal," 38.

20. O'Donnal, *Pioneer in Guatemala,* 80.

21. "Oral History of John F. and Carmen G. O'Donnal," 45; see also

"Coming of Elders to Central America Seen in Vision," *Church News*, 6 June 1959, 19.

22. O'Donnal, *Pioneer in Guatemala*, 115.

23. "Oral History of John F. and Carmen G. O'Donnal," 44.

24. Ibid., 58.

25. O'Donnal interview, 38.

26. "Oral History of John F. and Carmen G. O'Donnal," 126.

27. "Converts Fill 10 New Chapels," *Church News*, 23 June 1979, 3.

28. "Oral History of John F. and Carmen G. O'Donnal," 3, appendix.

29. O'Donnal, *Pioneer in Guatemala*, 95.

30. Ibid., 303.

31. O'Donnal interview, 27.

32. Grant Anderson, Church Historical Department, telephone interview, 25 February 2000.

33. O'Donnal, *Pioneer in Guatemala*, 353.

CHAPTER TWENTY-SIX

DAVID O. MCKAY, FATHER OF THE CHURCH EDUCATIONAL SYSTEM

MARY JANE WOODGER

Henry David Thoreau explained, "To be a philosopher is not merely to have subtle thoughts, nor even to found a school, but so to love wisdom as to live according to its dictates, a life of simplicity, independence, magnanimity, and trust. It is to solve some of the problems of life, not only theoretically, but practically."[1] If one uses Thoreau's ideas to define what a philosopher is, then President David O. McKay certainly was one: he lived according to his own brand of wisdom; his ideas consisted of simple independent thoughts that had an underlying trust in his religion; and he solved the educational problems of The Church of Jesus Christ of Latter-day Saints during the twentieth century in practical ways.

David O. McKay felt the most important entity was the individual. Individual worth directed his educational practices and was at the heart of his overall philosophy of life. President Boyd K. Packer, a well-known educator who is now acting president of the Quorum of the Twelve Apostles, observed that President McKay often "made statements about individual differences and accommodating the needs of individuals."[2] He valued all people and wanted to provide the same educational opportunities for all young members of the Church.

The ultimate goal of every Church education program is to develop students who possess the brand of integrity that President

Mary Jane Woodger is an assistant professor of Church history and doctrine at Brigham Young University.

379

McKay espoused. He saw The Church of Jesus Christ of Latter-day Saints as an educational institution, therefore, the purpose of the Church was synonymous with the purpose of education in general. President McKay stated:

"The . . . great purpose of the Church is to translate truth into a better social order, or in other words, to make our religion effective in the individual lives of men, and in improving social conditions. . . . Integrity [is] the first principle of success. . . . To maintain it in high places costs self-denial. . . . 'A man of integrity will never listen to any plea against conscience.' . . . Integrity requires the seeking after, as well as the dispensing of, the truth. . . . We translate our religion into better social conditions and bring salvation and peace to men here and now."[3]

Only through proper education can fundamental principles become fixed into the character of Latter-day Saint youth. President McKay's educational aims and purposes influenced Church education as his ideas were applied in countless ways by numerous educators. His basic concepts about education remained consistent throughout his life and were built around the principles of the gospel of Jesus Christ.[4] His educational aims and purposes influenced his generation and continue to influence our age.

Influence on Church Education

When David O. McKay became an apostle in 1908, his views took precedence in Church education decisions and have continued to do so during much of the twentieth century. Elder McKay's views may have become dominant in part because he was the first member of the Quorum of the Twelve Apostles to have completed a college program and receive a teaching certificate. Among LDS educators of the 1900s, David O. McKay was the key person to influence the educational policies of the LDS Church.

Two important facts allow us to conclude that he was the most influential apostle pertaining to Church educational ideas, policies, and practices. First, he served sixty-four years in the capacity of a general authority, longer than any previous man. Second, the very nature of Elder McKay's unique educational assignments in the Quorum of the Twelve Apostles suggests the scope of his influence on Church education policy. For instance, as general superintendent of the Sunday School from 1918 to 1934 David O. McKay exercised both direct and indirect influence on the education of Church members. He wrote *Ancient Apostles,* which originally was prepared as one of the first Sunday School lesson manuals for the Church. He became the first general authority directly in charge of the entire education program of the Church. No other apostle has served this long, had as many educational appointments, or left his distinctive mark on Church education in the same way.

APOSTLE EDUCATOR

In 1908 educational reforms began to seep into the Church. Educator Jack Monnett observed that the "sharp rise in educational innovations [in the LDS Church] is partially due to the inclusion of David O. McKay into the ranks of the LDS General Authorities."[5] He was trained during the 1890s, when progressive education was beginning to be developed by educators. At Weber Academy located in Ogden, Utah, he served as a teacher, principal, and board member.

Examples of his strong influence on Church education are found in his journal entries. For instance, on 20 June 1907 he recorded, "Met with the committee appointed to define the policy of church schools. We agreed unanimously that the general policy should be for high school work, that only one 'Training School,' and only one college should be maintained." A month later he recorded a meeting with the Church Board of Education in which a million dollars was appropriated for education. In 1908 he met with Dr. Milton Bennion to discuss possible institute courses.[6] In the beginning of 1909, Elder McKay was appointed as the chairman of the General Priesthood Committee, which gave him considerable latitude in policy making. Acting in his new position, he implemented a plan that gave special attention to weekly priesthood meetings with highly "educative features."[7]

In 1911 the main topic of discussion for the Church Board of Education was the expenditure of money. A special committee that was formed to curtail spending considered abandoning the teachers' college at Brigham Young University.[8] As a member of the executive committee of the Church Board of Education, Elder McKay literally saved BYU when the rest of the board's discussion centered on discontinuing the institution. He insisted that the Provo school remain open and even envisioned that it would one day become a full-scale university.[9] After his plea, the First Presidency not only decided to keep BYU but also encouraged its expansion.[10]

In 1915 David O. McKay was chosen as a member of the General Church Board of Education, a position that gave him even greater opportunities to change policy in the Church Educational System.[11] Three years later, on 23 November 1918, President Heber J. Grant became the new president of the Church and "quickly instituted changes he considered necessary in the Church school system."[12]

CHURCH COMMISSIONER OF EDUCATION, 1919–22

In 1919 under President Grant's leadership, the Church created a new Commission of Education, to which Elder McKay was appointed as first commissioner.[13] The commission immediately began to formulate new policy that was quickly approved by President Grant and the entire Board of Education.

Seven months after his appointment, Commissioner McKay reported to the First Presidency that the Church's current policy regarding the academics "is a policy that will inevitably bankrupt the Church." Commissioner McKay proposed that "all small schools in communities where LDS influence predominates be eliminated" and that the Church only "maintain four or five schools with the aim of giving first-class training to teachers."[14] On that occasion he declared, "Now is the time to step right in and get teachers into these public high schools and eliminate the spirit which dominates the schools now."[15] Two days later, at a meeting of the Board of Education on 15 March 1920, Commissioner McKay proposed a three-part solution to the problems facing Church education: "1) Most of the academies should be closed. . . . 2) A few of the academies, where college-level courses had already been incorporated . . . become Church junior colleges stressing . . . teacher-education programs. 3) Courses leading to a four-year degree be concentrated at Brigham Young University."[16]

Commissioner McKay also pointed out that this "psychological moment" was the right one for the Church to advance into the field of teacher education. The timing was perfect, because at that time Utah faced an extreme shortage of trained teachers. He believed that if the LDS normal programs could be expanded, by 1925 there would be enough LDS teachers to dominate teaching in Utah's public schools.[17]

TEACHER TRAINING

Commissioner McKay's goal was to establish Church colleges that would become, as he himself was, "very adept at training teachers" to teach the youth of the Church.[18] Elder David B. Haight, of the Quorum of the Twelve Apostles, explained that McKay had "a serious influence on the teachers at that time because of his background." He improved teacher training in the Church Educational System by bringing professional educators to assist in training teachers.[19] By drawing college professors into the training programs of the Church, he was able to pioneer ideas not only into the curriculum of Church-owned schools but also indirectly into state-owned institutions of higher learning.

Though Commissioner McKay had terminated the academy system, the education budget did not decline. President Grant reported at the next April conference that expenditures for 1921 were "more than 100 percent" above what they had been the previous year.[20] He also said his greatest concern was limiting "expansion of the appropriation for the Church school system."[21] His worries were well founded. Statistics show that 1912 expenditures for Church education were approximately $350,000; ten years later in 1922, under Commissioner McKay's administration they had risen to $850,000.[22] Much of this cost was due to the teacher training programs.[23] Commissioner McKay also fully supported the largest educational expenditure, which was running BYU. His support did not, however, relieve the university's financial distress. BYU ended its 1920 school year with a deficit of $34,154.[24]

Even amid the worry of financial burdens, Commissioner McKay's support of Brigham Young University was consistent. For instance, on 28 April 1920 he directed a commission meeting in which the discussion centered on strengthening BYU's faculty. The commissioner "stressed the need to keep 'strong men' in the faculty who could mold character." He also wanted to improve faculty caliber by proposing ways for teachers to further their own education and recommended that BYU professors be granted sabbaticals at half salary to "keep up the scholarship of the school."[25]

Other Church programs, such as seminary work, also implemented Commissioner McKay's instruction and advice. With the
many responsibilities placed on him, his name became "synonymous
with momentous growth and change" within the Church.
Biographer Dee Halverson claims that David O. McKay was the person responsible for "important steps . . . to enlarge the Church's role
as a major force throughout the world."[26] One of the first of these
important steps took place in 1921.

EDUCATIONAL AMBASSADOR ON WORLD TOUR, 1921–22

In 1921 President Grant asked Elder McKay to conduct a worldwide tour of the Church missions and schools. President Grant's
objective for the tour was to obtain firsthand information regarding
members of the Church throughout the world.[27] Traveling more than
sixty-two thousand miles, Commissioner McKay visited all the LDS
schools and missions except one in South Africa.[28]

While among the people of Hawaii, Commissioner McKay made
a profound educational commitment to Latter-day Saints living in
the Pacific. Much of the force behind this commitment stemmed
from an experience he had on the island of Oahu at a Church-owned
elementary school in the small town of Laie. While there, he participated in a flag-raising ceremony and was impressed with the many
nationalities of children, all pledging allegiance to the same country.
He envisioned the same scene duplicated on a large scale, picturing
the community of Laie as the intellectual center of the Pacific.[29]
Commissioner McKay's vision of Church education expanded as he
visited New Zealand, Israel, the Far East, Australia, Singapore, India,
Egypt, Palestine, Italy, Scotland, and several other countries.

FATHER OF CHURCH SCHOOLS IN THE PACIFIC

When Commissioner McKay returned home, the idea of providing schools for the youth of the Pacific area seemed to be constantly
on his mind, although he did not feel he could push it too vigorously. Edward L. Clissold, former Chairman of the Church Pacific
Board of Education, said that Commissioner McKay felt a great obligation to build schools in this area of the world.[30] That dream of
Pacific schools stayed with him for the next thirty-four years, and
one of his first official acts as the president of the Church was to

establish a college in Laie. When the Church College of Hawaii was dedicated, President McKay expressed his view that it would not only educate young Latter-day Saints but would have a significant impact on the world at large. He prophesied:

"From this school, I'll tell you, will go men and women whose influence will be felt for good towards the establishment of peace internationally. Four hundred and fifty million people waiting to hear the message over in China, a noble race. . . . I don't know how many million over in Japan. You prepare to go and carry that message. Three hundred and fifty million down in India. We have scarcely touched these great nations, and they're calling today."[31]

The Church College of Hawaii officially started classwork in September of 1955. Under President McKay's administration, other smaller schools were also established outside the United States.[32]

RELIGIOUS EDUCATION FOR LDS YOUTH WORLDWIDE

David O. McKay was not only concerned with the youth of the Pacific, he was also determined to make sure that all Latter-day Saints received the religious education necessary for a successful life. He felt a need to counteract the secular education the young members were receiving in public high schools. Several programs spearheaded by Commissioner McKay were devised for this purpose.

One strategy to educate LDS youth was the opening of a mission home in Salt Lake City during February 1925, where instruction included manners, punctuality, and missionary methods.[33] This was the beginning of the current missionary training centers. Another thrust was the introduction of seminaries on a large scale. Commissioner McKay devised a similar plan for college students, and on 17 April 1928 it was decided that the collegiate religious classes of the Church would be designated as "LDS institutes of religion." These programs expanded, and the Church began to construct buildings next to high schools and colleges.

In addition, an adult education program began with the first adult Education Week organized on the BYU campus. Originally this program was designed to train ward and stake leaders, but soon the general public was also invited to attend classes.[34] Commissioner McKay himself taught at the adult-oriented education weeks. Goals were set for teachers in these programs to offer the "finest religious education program in America."[35]

Throughout this period, David O. McKay was also constant in maintaining support for the few remaining Church schools. He exerted a powerful influence over education programs as the reorganization of the Board of Education took place on 2 February 1939. Up to that point BYU, Ricks College, and the LDS Business College had operated under separate boards of trustees. With the reorganization, local boards of trustees were released, and these institutions came under the centralized control of the General Church Board of Education, with David O. McKay as a lead board member and educational trailblazer.[36]

VIEW OF TRUTH

During David O. McKay's tenure as a member of the First Presidency, some considered him a liberal because of his generosity with Church funds, especially in the area of education. He was the unflappable optimist, always faithful that things would improve and that human nature basically wanted that which was good. According to Elder Robert L. Simpson, who served as a general authority, David O. McKay was a dreamer, always looking "toward the future and what is coming over the next rise," and yet at the same time he did not need to answer every question, though he "knew that the answer was out there someplace."[37] McKay biographer Lavina Fielding Anderson related that President McKay viewed "education as a form of spiritual and temporal salvation, [and] had a kind of love for the liberal educational tradition. . . . [McKay] would have fit in well at Cambridge or Oxford."[38]

As part of the liberal education tradition, David O. McKay was well read. At the heart of his extensive reading of literature was a search for the duplication of Mormon fundamentals. His confidence in his religious beliefs was secure; therefore, he was willing to find truth in any discipline without worrying that the new knowledge might deter him from his religious beliefs. Overriding everything that President McKay did and said was an overall openness to knowledge, learning, and information from any source.

David O. McKay's view of truth was extensive not exclusive, and he was willing to search any discipline to find it. He believed veracity can come from anyone and from any source. This philosophical stance can be found in a pamphlet he wrote called *The Search for Truth in Science and Religion,* insisting that they could simultaneously be viewed as truth.[39] Some theories that were widely accepted during this period, however, were not accepted by David O. McKay. He denounced "the law of pure nature, survival of the fittest, and self-preservation at the sacrifice of all else," as falsehoods perpetuated by men who lack the knowledge of the true purpose of life. Even with such sophistry passed off as truth, President McKay continued to search sources outside official Church publications for those who viewed mortality through a similar lens.

President McKay's children remember their father finding truths in many sources. In his addresses as a counselor in the First Presidency he cited scripture, often quoting Paul and other New Testament writers, along with quoting prominent poets and authors, such as Shakespeare, Burns, Milton, Tennyson, and Keats.[40] Nevertheless, President McKay felt all truth is not to be valued equally; there are some truths everyone needs to know that are absolutely essential for man to understand in order to progress.

For David O. McKay, truth was truth, but some truths were valued more than others and needed to be passed on to the next generation. He believed it is a fundamental truth that each individual is of great worth and is of the greatest value. Character, education, high ideals, and spirituality were also truths to be valued and taught throughout the Church.

PROPHET EDUCATOR

David O. McKay's more moderate view of truth came to the forefront in 1951, when he became president of the Church. With a more expansive view of the sources of truth, he was less inclined to be leery of the intellectual world in his assessment of education and favored a problem-oriented approach. President McKay established a Church education system more open to new ideas, less rigid in position, and more moderate in propensity. These attitudes can be seen in decisions that President McKay made as the prophet. For instance, he commissioned Obert C. Tanner, a rather liberal intellectual, to write a volume on ideals to be used in Church classrooms.[41]

Along with President McKay's coming into the First Presidency, another appointment greatly influenced the Church Educational System. Though David O. McKay had initially preferred Henry Aldous Dixon for the presidency of BYU, after meeting with Ernest L. Wilkinson he changed his mind. McKay wrote in his journal, "Wilkinson had the right viewpoint of the mission of BYU." That viewpoint was that "every department in the school should . . . be 'impregnated' with the spirit of the gospel, and that the teaching of the principles of the gospel should not be confined to a Theological Department."[42] Two days later Wilkinson was offered the job.[43] The relationship between these two men forged the direction of the Church in higher education for the next century.

Wilkinson was especially concerned with gaining approval from the president of the Board of Trustees, as was evident in minute details that Wilkinson oversaw, such as sending football tickets and other gifts to President McKay,[44] or a written apology for not using correct grammar.[45] In the correspondence between these two men, however, it becomes obvious that President McKay thought Wilkinson overstepped his authority at times. For instance, a lay member of the Church would find it quite inappropriate for the BYU president to suggest the following to a prophet:

"In your own interests and protection, [I'd] like to again suggest that when faculty members come to see you for discussion of matters of this kind that you refer them first to me as President of the Brigham Young University. If I cannot satisfy them, and there is any substantial reason for them seeing you, I will so inform them and you. In that way I think I could save you time and possible embarrassment."

On several occasions, Wilkinson seems to have tried to direct the prophet, but President McKay kept a tight rein on him. For instance, when a committee of Utah educators involved in higher education were discussing the weaknesses of private universities, Wilkinson reported to President McKay, "In view of your instructions, I remained completely silent and said nothing." Wilkinson and President McKay settled into a relationship that produced precedent-setting decisions for Church educators and Church higher education. The most salient decisions involved the advancement of Brigham Young University, federal aid to Church-owned schools, the unifying of Church-owned schools, and the decision on whether to build junior colleges or institutes of religion.[46]

BRIGHAM YOUNG UNIVERSITY POLICY

President McKay gave BYU his full support and was willing to expand the campus and the size of the student body. A year after he became prophet, he appropriated money for a new family living center.[47] He kept a close watch on all of BYU's activities. He was a constant drive in improving the College of Education so there would be enough LDS public school teachers to make a difference in the lives of LDS youth. Along with his formal policy, many of President McKay's behind-the-scenes activities planted the seeds of future trends. Under his presidency, student wards and stakes were established, fund-raising campaigns began, an educational television station was formed, and students began studying abroad.[48]

We can also see the germination of the current academic freedom policy at BYU from the following incident. In 1954 a member of the Quorum of the Twelve Apostles visited with an institute teacher and informed him that he was to teach doctrine pertaining to evolution according to that general authority's particular views. When President McKay caught wind of the situation, he called the teacher into his office and informed him, "Unless the First Presidency made announcements in fields pertaining to the age of the earth and the origin of death upon it, . . . the Brethren were under no obligation to teach the particular views of one individual."[49]

FEDERAL AID

One view that all members of the Board of Trustees consistently maintained was the philosophy of refusing to accept outright federal subsidies to Church schools. Wilkinson felt that President McKay's position on the subject of federal aid was in line with his own. He wrote to President McKay:

"I am happy that you believe there is no need for federal aid to education. I am completely convinced not only that there is no need but that the moment we have federal aid to education we inevitably have federal control and that this would be just one step further from the establishment of a socialistic state. Now that I have your opinion, I shall not hesitate to strike out against federal aid to education."[50]

The stance on federal aid during President McKay's administration established policy that led the Church Educational System into the twenty-first century.

UNIFIED CHURCH SCHOOL SYSTEM

President McKay wanted to keep the same kind of hands-on control he had at BYU over the entire Church Educational System, with all Church schools under one umbrella. Two years after he was ordained, President McKay created the Unified Church School System with Ernest L. Wilkinson as administrator; and in 1960 President McKay changed Wilkinson's title from administrator to chancellor with the implication that a chancellor was over several schools.[51]

President McKay was always clear that the purpose of all Church schools was to develop character, even when other scholars disagreed. For example, Sterling McMurrin published the following in a local paper:

"Certainly, the primary purpose of a university is not to create character. The primary purpose of education is the achievement and dissemination of knowledge and the cultivation of the intellect. The moment we give first place to the development of character, we will note a great decline in American education."[52]

In juxtaposition, President McKay made his mission for BYU plain in a faculty workshop:

"I think that the noblest aim is character, notwithstanding what some leading professors say about the special work of a university. What other conceivable purpose is there in making discoveries in science, in delving into marvelous powers hitherto hidden by nature, except for the development of the human soul?"[53]

President McKay often addressed the students and faculty of BYU. He was also involved in the hiring of professors and made intercession when necessary, such as when he intervened in having Dr. Virginia Cutler come from the University of Utah to head the Department of Home Economics.[54] Other problems President McKay dealt with were much larger and received public scrutiny. One such problem involved Church ownership of junior colleges.

JUNIOR COLLEGES

On 15 February 1954, as part of a program to relieve the state of undue financial burdens, Utah's governor J. Bracken Lee caused a bill to be introduced in the Utah State Senate that would turn the state-owned Weber, Snow, and Dixie colleges back to the Church.[55] Immediately after the introduction of the bill, there was heated opposition. Many factors contributed to the defeat of the proposal.

Utah's non-LDS population generally opposed replacement of state schools with Church institutions that would emphasize Latter-day Saint theology and standards. People in Ephraim and St. George favored returning Snow and Dixie to Church ownership, but most residents of Ogden did not want Weber to change hands. Debate was so heated that Governor Lee took Weber off the list. President McKay insisted that if the other schools were to be returned, Weber must be part of the package.[56]

Another objection to the transfer arose from the widespread allegation that for a number of years Church support of the junior colleges had been so meager that they could barely function. Many believed that the schools were better financed through taxes than tithing. The *Ogden Standard-Examiner* and the *Salt Lake Tribune* vehemently opposed the transfer.[57] Many people thought President McKay contributed to the defeat of the bill when he was quoted as saying:

"The Church is not campaigning for the colleges. Every voter is free to cast his vote for state retention of the colleges. This election is to determine whether the people of the state of Utah desire the state to continue to support the junior colleges. Only if they determine not to will the Church be willing to take over and continue the colleges."[58]

The three colleges were not returned to the Church. This decision precipitated a great change in direction for Church involvement in higher education. During this controversy, the Church was buying land to establish its own junior college system. President McKay did not feel institutes could have the same effect on young minds as a junior college experience. As early as 1953 the Church was looking at a site in Los Angeles for a Church-owned junior college. Land was also purchased in other areas for this same purpose. President McKay was, however, forced to abandon his dream of a Church-owned junior college system. In 1963 the decision was made that the Church could not finance new schools, and the current institute of religion program was born out of necessity.

When Ernest L. Wilkinson resigned as head of BYU to enter the political arena, two men were appointed to take his place, and the unification of all Church schools began to dissolve. This eventually resulted in a separation of BYU from the institutes of religion and the seminaries, which became permanent early in 1965.[59]

CONCLUSION

President McKay's educational aims and purposes were applied in countless ways in the development of all Church schools and institutions. Many have paid tribute to the accomplishments of this remarkable pioneer in education. Leon Hartshorn, former Department Chair of Church History and Doctrine at BYU, believes President McKay was "responsible more than any other one man in the Church for the great growth of the educational program."[60] Joseph T. Bentley, who was deeply involved with LDS education, said, President McKay "dignified [Church] education."[61] LDS administrator Adam S. Bennion called him "the inspiring teacher of our generation."[62]

The current Church Commissioner of Education, Elder Henry B. Eyring, says that President McKay left the "legacy of the tremendous importance of education" and the belief "that education could be important in the life of young people, [teaching] that the spirit of the work mattered." Elder Eyring believes that this conviction "still lifts the people who teach seminary and institute and . . . the people at BYU and other places."[63]

Truly, President McKay can rightfully be called the "father of the Church Educational System," bringing the education of LDS youth out of obscurity.

NOTES

1. Henry David Thoreau, *Walden* (Philadelphia: Running Press, 1854), 13.

2. Author's interview of Boyd K. Packer, McKay Research Project, Salt Lake City, Utah, 1996.

3. David O. McKay, in Conference Report, October 1927, 11, 13–14.

4. Author's letter from Alan C. Ashton, 1996.

5. Jack Monnett, "David O. McKay: Influential Mormon Educator?" in Frederick S. Buchanan Papers, University of Utah Special Collections, 1977, 7.

6. David O. McKay, "David O. McKay Microfilm, 1897–1956," University of Utah Special Collections, reel 4:445.

7. Richard O. Cowan, *The Church in the Twentieth Century* (Salt Lake City: Bookcraft, 1985), 76.

8. Thomas G. Alexander, *Mormons in Transition: A History of the Latter-day Saints 1890–1930* (Urbana: University of Illinois Press, 1986), 167–68.

9. Author's telephone interview of Francis M. Gibbons, McKay Research Project; see also Francis M. Gibbons, *David O. McKay: Apostle to the World, Prophet of God* (Salt Lake City: Deseret Book, 1986).

10. Alexander, *Mormons in Transition,* 168.

11. "David O. McKay Microfilm," 16 July 1915, reel 4:431.

12. Ernest L. Wilkinson and Leonard Arrington, eds., *Brigham Young University: The First Hundred Years,* 4 vols. (Provo: Brigham Young University Press, 1975), 1:454.

13. Richard C. Roberts and Richard W. Sadler, *History of the Weber State College* (Salt Lake City: Publishers Press, 1988), 47.

14. Church Commission of Education minutes, 24 February 1920, 3 March 1920, as cited in John D. Monnett, "The Mormon Church and Its Private School System in Utah: The Emergence of the Academies," Ph.D. diss., University of Utah, 1984, 211, 214.

15. James R. Clark, "Church and State Relationships in Education in Utah," Ed.D. diss., Utah State University, 1958, 269.

16. Cowan, *Church in the Twentieth Century,* 108.

17. Clark, "Church and State Relationships," 28.

18. Gibbons interview.

19. Author's interview of David B. Haight, McKay Research Project, Salt Lake City, 1996.

20. Alexander, *Mormons in Transition,* 159.

21. Cowan, *Church in the Twentieth Century,* 108.

22. Wilkinson and Arrington, *Brigham Young University,* 2:15.

23. Church Board of Education minutes, 31 March 1920, as cited in Alexander, *Mormons in Transition,* 159.

24. Executive Committee of BYU Board of Trustees to Church Commission of Education, 10 December 1920, as cited in Wilkinson and Arrington, *Brigham Young University,* 2:16.

25. Church Commission of Education minutes, 28 April 1920, 4 May 1920, as cited in Wilkinson and Arrington, *Brigham Young University,* 2:15.

26. Dee Halverson, *Stephen L Richards, 1879–1959* (Salt Lake City: Heritage Press, 1994), 145.

27. Owen J. Cook, KE AIAKA'I, 20 February 1970. LDS schools were built as follows: Church College of New Zealand, a high school, 1958; Liahona High School in Tonga, 1951; Church College of Western Samoa, a high school, 1960; Mapusaga High School in American Samoa, 1962; Church Elementary School in Tahiti, 1969; and several elementary schools attached to the high schools in Tonga and Samoa.

28. *David O. McKay* (Salt Lake City: International Society of Daughters of the Utah Pioneers, 19–.

29. Cowan, *Church in the Twentieth Century*, 235–36.

30. "Interview of Edward L. Clissold," James Moyle Oral History Program, interviewed by R. Lanier Britsch, Historical Department Archives, The Church of Jesus Christ of Latter-day Saints, Salt Lake City, 1976, 18–21.

31. David O. McKay, "Address of President David O. McKay at the Dedicatory Services at the Church College of Hawaii—Groundbreaking" (Laie, Hawaii: The Church of Jesus Christ of Latter-day Saints, 1955).

32. Cowan, *Church in the Twentieth Century*, 252–53.

33. *Church History in the Fulness of Times*, rev. ed. (Religion 341–43 student manual, 1993), 503.

34. Ibid., 506.

35. Lynn M. Bennion, *Recollections of a School of Man: The Autobiography of M. Lynn Bennion* (Salt Lake City: Western Epics, 1987), 87.

36. Wilkinson and Arrington, *Brigham Young University*, 2:360.

37. Author's interview of Robert L. Simpson, McKay Research Project, St. George, Utah, 1995.

38. Author's interview of Lavina Fielding Anderson, McKay Research Project, Salt Lake City, 1996.

39. David O. McKay, *The Search for Truth in Science and Religion* (Salt Lake City: The Church of Jesus Christ of Latter-day Saints, 1961).

40. Ashton letter; author's interview of Dr. Edward and Lottie McKay, McKay Research Project, Salt Lake City, Utah, 1996.

41. Tanner, *Christ's Ideals for Living* (Salt Lake City: Deseret Sunday School Union, 1955).

42. Diary of David O. McKay, 25 July 1950, Church Historical Department, as cited in Wilkinson and Arrington, *Brigham Young University*, 2:502.

43. Diary of George Albert Smith, 27 July 1950; Ernest L. Wilkinson to the First Presidency, 29 August 1950, Wilkinson Presidential Papers, as cited in Wilkinson and Arrington, *Brigham Young University*, 2:502.

44. Letter from David O. McKay to Ernest L. Wilkinson, 28 September 1956, Ernest L. Wilkinson Papers, Brigham Young University Special Collections.

45. Letter from Wilkinson to McKay, 7 August 1956, Ernest L. Wilkinson Papers, Special Collections, Harold B. Lee Library, Brigham Young University, Provo, Utah.

46. Letter from Wilkinson to McKay, 14 June 1955, Ernest L. Wilkinson Papers, Special Collections, Harold B. Lee Library, Brigham Young University, Provo, Utah.

47. Letter from Wilkinson to McKay, 21 September 1954, Ernest L. Wilkinson Papers, Special Collections, Harold B. Lee Library, Brigham Young University, Provo, Utah.

48. Wilkinson and Arrington, *Brigham Young University,* 2:713.

49. Ernest L. Wilkinson, memorandum of David O. McKay's visit with institute teachers, 17 November 1954, Ernest L. Wilkinson Papers, Special Collections, Harold B. Lee Library, Brigham Young University, Provo, Utah.

50. Letter from Wilkinson to McKay, 31 October 1955, Ernest L. Wilkinson Papers, Special Collections, Harold B. Lee Library, Brigham Young University, Provo, Utah.

51. Wilkinson and Arrington, *Brigham Young University,* 3:143.

52. In letter from Wilkinson to McKay, 21 September 1954, Ernest L. Wilkinson Papers, Special Collections, Harold B. Lee Library, Brigham Young University, Provo, Utah.

53. Wilkinson and Arrington, *Brigham Young University,* 2:565.

54. Letter from Wilkinson to McKay, 7 March 1953, Ernest L. Wilkinson Papers, Special Collections, Harold B. Lee Library, Brigham Young University, Provo, Utah.

55. "Governor Lee Proposes Return of Three Colleges to Church," *BYU Daily Universe,* 20 February 1951, as cited in Wilkinson and Arrington, *Brigham Young University,* 2:578.

56. Wilkinson and Arrington, *Brigham Young University,* 2:579.

57. "Utah's Educational Crisis: Are We Losing the American Way of Life?" *Ogden Standard-Examiner,* 13 October 1954; "McKay Denies LDS Drive for Colleges," *Salt Lake Tribune,* 29 October 1954.

58. "McKay Denies LDS Drive for Colleges"; see also Wilkinson and Arrington, *Brigham Young University,* 2:582.

59. Wilkinson and Arrington, *Brigham Young University,* 2:607; 3:150, 192, 583.

60. *Deseret News,* 7 September 1963; see also Leon Roundy Hartshorn, "Mormon Education in the Bold Years," Ph.D. diss., Stanford University, 1965, 38.

61. As cited in Hartshorn, "Mormon Education in the Bold Years," 38.

62. Adam S. Bennion, *The Candle of the Lord* (Salt Lake City: Deseret Book, 1962), 149.

63. Author's interview of Henry B. Eyring, McKay Research Project, Salt Lake City, 1996.

INDEX